An Active Learning Approach

Business Law

THE
OPEN
LEARNING
FOUNDATION

An Active Learning Approach

BUSINESS LAW

Peter Handley, Jim Clevenger,
John Vaughan, Tim Birtwistle,
Tony O'Neill and Sue Wall

Copyright © Open Learning Foundation Enterprises Ltd, 1996

First published 1996
Reprinted 1999, 2000

Blackwell Publishers Ltd
108 Cowley Road
Oxford OX4 1JF
UK

Blackwell Publishers Inc.
350 Main Street
Malden, Massachusetts 02148
USA

British Library Cataloguing in Publication Data

A CIP catalogue record for this book is available from
the British Library.

Library of Congress Cataloging-in-Publication Data

A CIP catalogue record for this book is available from
The Library of Congress

ISBN 0–631–201831

Typeset in 10 on 12pt Times New Roman

Printed in Great Britain by Athenaeum Press Ltd, Gateshead, Tyne & Wear

This book is printed on acid-free paper

Contents

Unit 1   The English Legal System

Unit 2   Legal Relationships

Unit 3   Business Contracts

Unit 4   Non-Contractual Obligations of the Seller/Producer

Unit 5   European Community Law

GUIDE FOR STUDENTS

Please read the course introduction section at the very beginning of your business law studies.

Each unit guide should be read at the appropriate point in your studies.

Course introduction

Welcome to your business law studies. The objectives of this introduction are:

- to give you an outline of the subject of law applied to business
- to explain why it is necessary for you to study law as part of your degree
- to describe the nature of the material on which this module is based
- to outline the programme which you will be following
- to offer some practical hints and advice on how to study business law using the open learning approach; and
- to point out some of the advantages to you of studying law by the method used in this course.

What is business law?

Business law is concerned with providing financial information about a particular organisation to managers to help them to manage. Management can be seen as a series of activities which involve:

- decision-making
- planning
- control.

Regardless of what the nature of your involvement in business is – and whether you are working in the private or public sector – as a business man or woman you will face an array of legal controls and obligations of an unprecedented scope and complexity.

This module consists of five units which are designed to introduce students who are preparing for a career in business to some of the legal rules and issues which you will encounter once you enter the world of commerce. You will not become an expert in any area of the law as a result of studying the module, however at the end of your study of this module it is hoped that you will not only have increased your knowledge about the law as it applies to the business world; but that you would have developed some competence at:

identifying legal issues

applying legal rules to factual situations

having a European perspective

The material in this module is broken down in the following way.

In Unit 1 we introduce you to the English legal system by examining the nature and sources of law, followed by an introduction to the courts and tribunals.

In Unit 2 you will be introduced to a range of legal relationships encountered in business law, including, liability, partnerships, forming a company and managing a company.

In Unit 3 you will be introduced to the law of contracts. The unit will examine making a contract, what can go wrong during the making of a contract, contractual terms and discharging a contract.

In Unit 4 you will consider some of the legal obligations which are imposed on those who sell or produce goods and services. The unit will examine the duty of care in negligence, aspects of tort and liability in respect of employees.

Unit 5 provides study of European Community law. The unit examines the development of the EC, functions of the institutions, the sources and integration of Community law at a national level and the enforcement of European Community law at a European level.

In this module you will therefore be dealing with the following general aspects of business law:

- the English legal system
- legal relationships
- business contracts
- obligations of the seller/producer
- European Community law.

Why do I need to know anything about law?

From the brief statement of what business law involves (given above) it should be clear that the legal function of the organisation is a central part of its system. It is important, therefore, that all business students should have a fairly clear idea of various aspects of business law.

Many, perhaps most, business students have a career goal of being a manager within some organisation, perhaps a personnel manager or a marketing manager. If you are one of these students, an understanding of a business legal framework is very important. When you become a manager, even a junior one, it is almost certain that you will need to consider legal aspects of your function to help you to carry out your management tasks.

If you do not understand what the legal position really means and to what extent therefore any actions are liable, you will find yourself at a distinct disadvantage to others who know their way round the system. This is not to say that you cannot be an effective and successful personnel or marketing manager unless you are a qualified lawyer as well. But it does mean that you need to acquire a bit of 'street wisdom' in business legal matters, in order to succeed. This business law module, is aimed at giving you that attribute.

What are the module materials?

These comprise:

THE MODULE STUDY UNITS

The core of the course materials are five study units. These were written by authors specifically for undergraduate business students. The material contained in the units is used on the first year business law courses of the BA (Hons) business studies at the University of Wolverhampton, Leeds Metropolitan University and the University of Derby. This material has been tried and tested over a couple of years on these courses. It has been revised to accommodate students' comments on it and to keep it up to date. The material has been very well received by nearly all students.

The units are specifically intended for students, like you, who are following a module where an open learning approach is being adopted. This reflects the style of learning which is used in the first year business law studies at the universities of authors. The features which make it particularly suitable for open learning include the:

- very careful sequencing of the material so that there is a clear and logical progression
- a step by step approach so that you will be able to understand each new point thoroughly before the units proceeds to the next one
- a very clear layout with relatively short headed sections and paragraphs
- many worked examples, particularly in the case areas and an emphasis on understanding
- lots of opportunities for you to check that you understand what you have just read through the large number of 'activities' and 'self-check questions' which are interspersed through the units, to which solutions are provided at the back of the relevant unit
- plenty of opportunities for you to test your progress through 'additional questions' to which solutions are provided.

How is the module organised?

Your lecturer will provide you with precise details of how the module is to be organised. However, there are certain general points concerning organisation which are set out below.

The module is divided into a number of study periods. During each of these study periods you will be given the task of working through a particular unit with the aid of the study guide (see above). There will be a number of 'surgeries' where you can go to get help with any points of difficulty. At the end of each of the study periods you may be tested on the work which you will have covered. Each of the study periods will start with a lecture which will introduce the topics which form the basis of your work. Following the test, or other form of assessment, for a particular study period there will be a lecture to review the assessed work. In addition to this, you may be involved with case study sessions in small groups at certain stages in the year.

Some expansion on some of these points may be useful.

SURGERIES

A room has been set aside during certain hours of the week. During all of those hours this room will be staffed by one or more of your law lecturers. The lecturers are there exclusively to give you as much help as you need. A quiet atmosphere will be maintained in the surgery room.

LECTURES

At the start of each of the study periods there will be a lecture. This lecture will set out the main principles of the material which is to be the subject of that study period. It will try to put the particular topics of that study period into context –both into context as regards the law module and as regards other modules on your course.

When you have completed your assessment for the study period and it has been marked there will be a lecture to review it.

ASSESSMENTS AND ASSIGNMENTS

At the end of certain study periods you will be required to complete a piece of work. These assessments/assignments will take various forms. These may include multiple-choice tests, case studies (which may include the use of law reports) and essays. The set work will seek to achieve three things:

1) To allow you and the lecturers to see how well you have mastered the material contained in each individual study period.

2) To give you an experience, for example preparing and presenting a case study, from which will actually learn something.

3) To provide a mark which can be aggregated to give your course work score for the period of the law module.

The timetable of study periods, surgeries, assessments and lectures will be provided by your lecturer in a separate schedule.

The open learning approach

The open learning approach which is being adopted brings it own specific challenges. Perhaps the major challenge is to see yourself as the 'owner' of your learning. This means you must recognise the demands that this approach places on the way in which you allocate your time and the need for you to be active in your learning by completing activities, self-check questions and additional exercises.

How shall I study?

SOME PRACTICAL HINTS

You now have all of the material you need to enable you to start on the first study period. The question now is, how should you set about mastering it?

The answer to this question is that you should study this module in whichever way you find most effective. Your lecturers will not mind how you work provided that you do work, that you achieve good standards and have a satisfying learning experience. The number of occasions when you will be required to be in a specific place at a set time is limited. Provided that you fulfil these obligations, you have considerable freedom as to how you organise your time.

Though you have a considerable amount of freedom as to how you study this module, you might find the following hints useful.

MAKE USE OF THE MATERIAL PROVIDED

The units and the supporting material have been developed specifically for the law module for business students which is being handled in a tutorially-supported self-study mode. It seems sensible therefore to use it in the manner in which it was intended to be used.

At the start of each study period you should read through the relevant part of the study guide. This will put the contents of each unit into context and guide you through it. Only after having done this should you start work on the units.

You should work through the units in the order in which your lecturer recommends. You should note the points which the study guide has identified as the more crucial aspects of the material.

Each unit is interspersed with a number of activities and self-check question. There are additional questions at the end of each unit. All of these are intended to be attempted by you as they arise and completed before you move on. The suggested solutions to each activity is given immediately following the relevant activity. The solutions to the self-check questions and additional questions are given at the end of the relevant unit.

The activities are intended to be a combination of a check that you are following the unit and understanding it on the one hand, and a way of making your learning a more active experience for you, on the other. By working through the activities you can effectively divide your study time between that necessary to taking on new ideas and that which is necessary to reinforce those ideas.

The self-check questions are intended to give you the opportunity to see whether you have really grasped the content of the unit. The additional questions are intended to give you further practice and the opportunity to reinforce your knowledge and understanding.

Typically, the activities will only take you a few minutes to deal with. By contrast, the self-check questions and additional questions may quite easily take 20 minutes or more to complete. It is important that you discipline yourself to complete each activity, self-check question or additional questions before you refer to the solution provided. If you get stuck part way through a question you should try to get help from the solution only on the point causing you difficulty and then continue to complete the question before referring to the solution again. Obviously if you get stuck for long, seek help at a surgery.

AVOID ROTE LEARNING

In respect of each topic in the module, it is important that you thoroughly understand what you are doing and why you are doing it. If you are clear on the underlying logic you will find it unnecessary to learn up a list of rules to be followed. This will mean that preparation for in-course tests and for the final examination will be easier for you. It will also mean that you will be fairly comfortable in dealing with unfamiliar problems. This is an important point since dealing with problems which require the application of principles and techniques which you have learned, but which are of a type which you have not specifically encountered before, will be a feature of assessments in this module.

Use the surgeries

You can use the surgeries in one of two ways:

● You can come to the surgery room and do your work there. You will be guaranteed a quiet, study-conducive atmosphere. If you encounter a problem with your law work you can get immediate help from the lecturer. This is obviously an efficient approach because you can get your problem solved immediately. You may also find that going into a quiet room puts you in the right frame of mind for study. Also, getting into a routine of going for regular hours during the week helps you to establish study discipline.

● You can study anywhere at any time during the week – in your digs, in the library, late at night, at weekends – and have almost complete flexibility. When you encounter a problem you know precisely where and when to go to find a lecturer who is there expressly to help you.

Probably the first approach is the better one, though it will not give you quite as much flexibility. Whichever way you use the surgeries, make sure that you get all of the help which you need. The system has been set up for you to get a very great deal of individual help: make sure that you exploit this fact to the full extent necessary.

SET ASIDE TIME FOR YOUR LAW STUDIES

It is necessary for you to spend an amount of time during each study period in mastering the material concerned. The flexibility which this system of study allows should not lead you to overlook this fact. Clearly at the start of the study period you will not know how long it will take to do the necessary work. It is sensible therefore, to make a start on the work at an early stage in the study period. Try to discipline yourself to set aside particular times in the week to study business law, though not necessarily the same times each week. You may well find it easier to work in a purposeful way if you commit yourself to going to surgeries for a particular number of hours each week and working there. Almost certainly, you will not be very successful if you leave starting your law studies until the last day of the study period.

The mode of study which you will be using on this module is particularly suitable for helping to avoid wasting time. For example if you have an hour between two classes, you may find using that hour to go to a law surgery an effective means of avoiding the hour from slipping through your hands, as such hours so easily do.

Why the open learning approach?

PERCEIVED WEAKNESSES OF THE TRADITIONAL APPROACH

The traditional method of teaching business law often involves a one hour lecture followed by a one hour tutorial. The lecture is basically a one-way communication exercise where the lecturer stands in front of the entire course (possibly well over 100 students) while students take notes. The tutorial tends to involve students working various practical examples of the subject matter of the lecture, obtaining individual help from the lecturer where necessary. The tutorial also tends to involve some reiteration of the lecture.

There is scepticism of the value of the traditional approach for several reasons. These include:

- the belief that lectures are generally an ineffective way of communicating information. In our experience, students tend to gain little from the lecture and make scant and unreliable notes. This point is supported by research findings.

- the fact that students work at different speeds. This difference between students is difficult to deal with in the traditional approach. Lecturers tend to try to judge the speed of the 'average' student and to progress at that rate. This can be very unsatisfactory to those students, probably the majority, who are faster or slower than average.

- the belief that the routine of lectures and tutorials can create in the student's mind a false impression of having made an effort and achieved. Students may be lulled into a feeling that this fairly passive involvement is sufficient.

The increase in student numbers and the deterioration of staff-student ratios of recent years has added to the problems of the traditional approach. The lecture has necessarily become more rigidly a one-way process of communication and the size of tutorial groups has reduced the opportunity for individual attention or a useful dialogue with students.

Perceived benefits of the open learning approach

We believe the approach used has a number of potential benefits for you, the student. These include:

- Good quality, reliable 'notes' are available in the form of the units. Research evidence shows that students (and no doubt other people as well) are very unreliable note-takers. Students frequently leave a lecture with an incomplete and incorrect version of what the lecturer has said. If you feel that you would find it useful to make your own notes from the units you can, of course, do this at your own pace rather than at the pace dictated by the lecturer. It is not particularly recommended that you do, in fact, make your own notes, but if you wish to do so, you have a permanent version of the 'lecture' to do it from.

- Something which is capable of being said is also capable of being written down and made available for students to read. Thus, the contents of a lecture can be incorporated into a text form which provides each student with a reliable set of notes.

- Most students find that they can work though the material without much help. Thus a form of 'management by exception' can usefully be introduced so that those students who find the subject relatively easy can work almost without help leaving those students who experience difficulties the lion's share of the lecturer's time. The more traditional approach tends to result in each student receiving a roughly equal amount of the lecturer's time, irrespective of individual need.

- Students work at different speeds and they may prefer to work at different times and locations. Open learning gives the opportunity for a great deal of flexibility.

- By placing the onus on you to manage your studies, you are likely to develop good study habits and greater self reliance. Ultimately, it is you who has to pass each module on the course. Though lecturers can be of great help to you in achieving this, they cannot do it for you. The open learning approach is likely to heighten your awareness of this fact.

● The fact that material is presented to students in written rather than in verbal form can promote greater quality. Written material tends to be more public which encourages the writer to be more scrupulous in preparing and refining material than may be the case with material presented verbally. Written material is more consistent in quality than a verbal presentation. Written material does not have 'off-days'.

We hope that you will find the open learning approach an enjoyable, as well as an effective, means of studying business law, and wish you every success in your studies.

GUIDE FOR LECTURERS

Introduction

This guide is written for lecturers who intend to adopt an open learning approach to the business law module for undergraduate business students. It forms part of a range of teaching/learning material which has been written and designed specifically for the purpose.

The objectives of this introduction are:

- to provide a rationale for open learning in the study of business law;

- to provide a rationale for the particular approach which has been taken to the subject of the module;

- to describe the material which is provided for a law course by open learning;

- to provide a suggested method of organising the course;

- to provide a detailed course programme which may be used.

Rationale for, and experiences of, an open learning approach to business law

It seems appropriate to begin this lecturers' guide with a justification for using the open learning approach with undergraduate business students studying law. Lecturers may also find it helpful to be aware of our experiences in applying this teaching/learning strategy generally to business studies degree first year business law module at the University of Wolverhampton, Leeds Metropolitan University and the University of Derby, using this open learning material and approach over several years.

PERCEIVED WEAKNESSES OF THE TRADITIONAL APPROACH

The traditional method of teaching business law uses a one hour lecture followed by a one hour tutorial. The lecture was basically a one-way communication exercise where the lecturer stood in front of the entire course (possibly well over 100 students) while students took notes. The tutorial tended to involve students working various practical examples of the subject matter of the lecture, obtaining individual help from the lecturer where necessary. The tutorial also tended to involve some re-iteration of the lecture.

Nationally, there has been scepticism about the value of the traditional approach for some time, for several reasons. These include:

- The belief that lectures are generally an ineffective way of communicating information. In our experience, students tend to gain little from the lecture and make scant and unreliable notes. This point is supported by research findings (see for example Hartley and Cameron, 1967).

- The fact that students work at different speeds. This difference between students is difficult to deal with in the traditional approach. Lecturers tend to try to judge the speed of the 'average' student and to progress at that rate. This can be very unsatisfactory to those students, probably the majority, who are faster or slower than average.

- The belief that the routine of lectures and tutorials can create in the student's mind a false impression of having made an effort and achieved. Students may be lulled into a feeling that this fairly passive involvement is sufficient.

The increase in student numbers and the deterioration of staff-student ratios of recent years has added to the problems of the traditional approach. The lecture has necessarily become more rigidly a one-way process of communication and the size of tutorial groups has reduced the opportunity for individual attention or a useful dialogue with students.

In practice, individual lecturers could repeat the same tutorial as many as eight or nine times and this inevitably leads to staleness and lack of effectiveness. Although multiple tutorials by an individual lecturer are not an inevitable consequence of large student numbers there has been, nevertheless, an understandable tendency for this to occur.

RATIONALE FOR USING OPEN LEARNING

Disaffection with the traditional approach has resulted in national and local university initiatives to seek an an alternative. Open learning commends itself, as it is believed that :

- Something which capable of being said is also capable of being written down and distributed to students in written form for them to read. Thus, the contents of a lecture can be incorporated into a text form which provides each student with a reliable set of notes.

- For most students, the working through of tutorial exercises can be done without lecturer supervision, provided that illustrative material and well explained solutions are made available.

- A form of 'management by exception' can usefully be introduced, so that those students who find the subject relatively easy can work almost without help, leaving those students who experience difficulties the lion's share of the lecturer's time. The traditional approach tended to result in each student receiving a roughly equal amount of the lecturer's time irrespective of individual need.

- Students work at different speeds and they may prefer to work at different times and locations. This makes open learning more appropriate than the traditional approach.

- By placing the onus on the student to manage his/her studies, good study habits and greater self reliance are likely to be developed.

The business law module at undergraduate level, lends itself to a structured approach which is particularly conducive to open learning.

An assessment of the open learning approach

The effectiveness of the open learning approach may be assessed in two ways:

- the acceptability to the students of this form of study
- the performance of the students in assessed work.

The acceptability to the students has been assessed through questionnaires completed by BA business studies students.

The questionnaires contained a number of questions, many of which were concerned with monitoring the quality of the written material provided to students. However, students were also asked to give their opinion of aspects of open learning in law. The results of these surveys have shown a consistently high level of student satisfaction with the open learning approach.

The effectiveness of open learning as measured by year-end examination performance has also been investigated, in other areas of business studies. The result of comparing the performance of students using the open learning approach with those of previous cohorts who were taught in the traditional way revealed a significant improvement in performance. Qualitative evidence from reports of external examiners also suggests that standards have been consistently higher since the introduction of open learning. Clearly, there are too many variables involved for us firmly to conclude that the improvement resulted from the change in the teaching/learning strategy, but the least we can say is that the change in the strategy seems not to have caused a deterioration in standards, despite a concurrent vast increase in student numbers.

What has been learned from experience to date

Experience has led to the conclusion that the open learning approach has benefits other than those identified above. These are:

- Written material is more consistent in quality than a verbal presentation: it does not have 'off-days'.

- Well-structured, well-documented courses make covering for absent colleagues much more straightforward than does the traditional approach. The covering lecturer knows exactly what material has already been dealt with and the subsequent programme is also clearly defined and material prepared. By the same token, colleagues taking a concurrent or consecutive course with the same students can establish precisely what material those students will cover and when it will be covered.

● Lecturers' time, freed from dealing with routine technical issues by structured open learning material, can be used to reinforce knowledge and understanding through case studies and other support activities.

● The task of teaching large groups, and perhaps small ones as well, is made much more stimulating and satisfying than the traditional approach. This is because the lecturers' time is devoted to helping individual students on an individual basis.

A criticism made of the open learning approach is a tendency for it to promote a mechanistic, inflexible and impersonal style of teaching. This is not by any means a necessary feature of the approach. It can be argued that, relieved of much of the drudgery of large lectures and repeating tutorials, lecturers have more enthusiasm and time for innovation and the introduction of non-routine activities.

The general principles underlying the open learning approach are not new. Keller (1968) outlined a system of instruction which involved the use of written material, self-paced learning and self-testing, but you should note that Keller did not use open learning in business law.

Rationale for the approach to the subject matter

The syllabus has been covered in an order which is not found in some texts. It seems appropriate, therefore, to explain why we have taken our particular approach to sequencing.

Regardless of what the nature of the student involvement in business is – and whether they are full time undergraduates or students working in the private or public sector – as a business man or woman they will face an array of legal controls and obligations of an unprecedented scope and complexity.

This module consists of five units which are designed to introduce students who are developing or preparing for a career in business, to some of the legal rules and issues which they will encounter once they enter the world of commerce. They will not become an expert in any area of the law as a result of studying the module; however at the end of your study of this module it is hoped that they will not only have increased their knowledge about the law as it applies to the business world, but that they would have developed some competence at:

identifying legal issues

applying legal rules to factual situations

having a European perspective

The material in this module is broken down into units in the following way.

In Unit 1 we introduce the English legal system by examining the nature and sources of law, followed by an introduction to the courts and tribunals.

In Unit 2 we introduce to a range of legal relationships encountered in business law, including, liability, partnerships, forming a company and managing a company.

In Unit 3 we introduce the law of contracts. The unit will examine making a contract, what can go wrong during the making of a contract, contractual terms and discharging a contract.

In Unit 4 we consider some of the legal obligations which are imposed on those who sell or produce goods and services. The unit will examine the duty of care in negligence, aspects of tort and liability in respect of employees.

Unit 5 provides study of European Community law. The unit examines the development of the EC, functions of the institutions, the sources and integration of Community law at a national level and the enforcement of European Community law at a European level.

The course materials

THESE COMPRISE:

The course units

The core of the course is a set of five units written by authors from three universities. These units were written specifically for undergraduate business students who are taking their business law module on an open learning basis. As has already been mentioned, it has been extensively class-tested on an open learning style of module. It has been revised to accommodate students' comments on it and to keep it up to date. It was observed that the material was very well received by all students.

The features which make it particularly suitable for open learning include:

- very careful sequencing of the material so that there is a clear and logical progression
- a step by step approach, so that students will be able to understand each new point thoroughly before being taken on to the next one
- a very clear layout with relatively short, headed sections and paragraphs.
- many worked examples
- an emphasis on understanding
- lots of opportunities for students to check that they understand what they have just read, through the large number of 'activities' and 'self-check questions' interspersed through the units, to which solutions are provided in the relevant unit

- plenty of opportunities for students to test their progress through 'additional questions' at the end the units, to which solutions are provided.

THE STUDENTS' GUIDE

Each student will have a general guide to the module. The objectives of this guide are:

- to give an outline of the subject of business law
- to explain why it is necessary for a business student to study law as part of the degree
- to describe the nature of the material on which the course is based
- to outline the programme which will be followed
- to offer some practical hints and advice on how to extend study of law following the recommended open learning programme
- to point out some of the advantages of studying law by the open learning approach; and
- to provide a unit-by-unit study guide(see below).

Despite the 'user-friendliness' of the units, a study guide has been written for each unit. The contents of the study guide include:

- highlighting key areas in each unit to which students must pay particular attention
- identifying areas of less importance where only a broad appreciation may be necessary
- going beyond the scope of the units, for example, to identify the key features of cases, which may be useful in the context of certain of the units; and
- providing references to further reading which students could usefully take up.

ASSESSMENT MATERIALS

This comprises all the material which will be necessary in order to assess the students' progress on the module. This can be used, in whole or in part, to provide the continuous assessment element which is a feature of most undergraduate business modules. The material is as follows:

- Case studies. These are intended to provide the student with the opportunity to demonstrate higher skills as well as technical competence. These cases could be used as individual assignments, perhaps under test conditions. Alternatively, they could be used as a small group exercise, perhaps culminating in a presentation to a tutorial group.

- Essay-type/response type self-check questions dealing with an important issue relating to law. Appropriate reference sources are provided for the student. This is designed to take the student beyond the course.

- An outline solution is provided for the lecturer.

Organisation of the module

I have set out below a suggested approach. This has been successfully operated at Wolverhampton, Leeds and Derby. However, there is an opportunity to organise the module in a number of different ways. Some suggestions for variations on the approach adopted generally at these universities are dealt with at the end of this section.

SURGERIES

A room needs to be set aside during certain hours of the week. During all of those hours this room needs to be staffed by one or more of the law lecturers. The lecturers will be there exclusively to respond to requests for help from individual students. A quiet atmosphere should be maintained in the surgery room.

Previous experience has shown that students tend to use the surgeries in one of two ways:

(i)   They come to the surgery room to work there. They will be guaranteed a quiet, study-conducive atmosphere. If they encounter a problem with the law work, immediate help is available from the lecturer. This is obviously an efficient approach because students can get the problem solved immediately. They may also find that going into a quiet room puts them in the right frame of mind for study. Also getting into a routine of going for regular hours during the week helps to establish a study discipline.

(ii) They can study anywhere, at any time, during the week and have almost complete flexibility. When they encounter a problem they know precisely where and when to go to find a lecturer who is there expressly to help.

Probably the first approach is the better one and students might be encouraged to adopt it, though it will not give them quite as much flexibility.

SELF-HELP STUDY GROUPS

In addition to the surgeries it would be useful to organise students into teams of four. Each team would be expected to meet on a regular basis (at least once per study period) outside of timetabled commitments in order to discuss the material relating to the study period and the problems which are raised. The teams would operate on a self-help basis. This should improve the opportunity for student interaction and prevent the feeling that learning is an isolated experience. Although some supervision of groups may be required at the beginning to ensure that they are working properly, this should become unnecessary as the students become more experienced in managing their own learning.

LECTURES AND REVIEWS

At the start of each of the study periods there should be a lecture. This lecture can 'set the scene' for the work which is the subject of the study period. It will set out the main principles to be dealt with and should try to put the particular topics of that study period into context, both as regards the law course and as regards other subjects on the course.

When the assessment for the study period has been marked there should be a lecture to review it. The assessment review and the introduction to the next study area could be combined in the one lecture, held shortly after the start of the new study period.

ASSESSMENTS AND ASSIGNMENTS

At the end of each of the study periods students should be required to complete a piece of work. These assessments/assignments will take various forms. There will be short tests (which could include some multiple-choice tests), case studies and essays. Details of the assessment material provided are given above. Other assignment material will be required to deal with the few study periods which the assessment material provided does not cover.

POSSIBLE VARIATIONS ON THE ORGANISATION OF THE MODULE

The surgery system could be operated in a number of ways. Generally at universities adopting open learning the surgeries are not mandatory and are 'open' to several groups of students following different modules and using different open learning material. However, the surgeries could be mandatory and could also be module specific, ie. only students following particular modules may be permitted to use the surgery at particular times. In the surgeries, students could be given additional exercises if required.

Some lecturers may feel that organised surgeries are too formal (particularly if student numbers are low). In which case, students may be invited to see the lecturer at agreed hours or on an open access basis.

Scene-setting lectures need not be given. General experiences suggest that students feel less need for such lectures as the module progresses and as they feel more confident in managing their own learning.

Greater or fewer assessments could be given to students. Some lecturers may feel that this new approach requires careful monitoring and, as a result, more assessments could be given. However, others may feel there is a danger of over-assessing students.

Self-help groups could be mandatory or optional. The lecturer may or may not decide to select the groupings.

In the students' guide, the operation of the module outlining the use of surgeries etc. Which is based on a nationally accepted model employed at several universities, is mentioned. You may wish to amend this information in the light of any changes to the basic model you decide to make.

An overview of the open learning programme

The law module represents approximately 100 hours of study. Below we outline a suggested open learning programme for the module. This programme assumes the module will be delivered over one academic semester/year to full-time students. We recognise that this is only one of several ways in which it may be delivered. However, it is likely that most students will study the module in this way.

The module is divided into five study periods each of one, two or three weeks' duration. During each period the students are directed to study a particular unit or units.

It is felt to be important to monitor student progress. There is a danger that some students will find it difficult, at first, to manage their own learning. They may not attend the open learning surgeries and lectures and may not do the set work. Weak students must be identified as early as possible and given appropriate counselling. It is also believed that frequent feedback to students on their progress is important, (see Beard, 1970). Thus, at the end of each study period the students should be given a piece of work on the contents of the relevant material which is marked by the lecturer. These could include objective (multiple choice) tests, the case study and a self-check.

A suggested course programme is provided below.

A detailed programme

COURSE PROGRAMME

A suggested course programme is as follows:

Week numbers (inclusive)	Unit numbers	Topic
1, 2 and 3	1	English Legal System
4, 5 and 6	2	Legal Relationships
7	Reading Week	
8 and 9	3	Business Contracts
10 and 11	4	Non-contractual Obligations of Seller/Producer
12 and 13	5	European Community Law
14	Revision	

As you can see this programme could easily be adapted to fit a 'semester' structure. This probably would involve covering Units 1 to 5 in the first or second semester. However it could be facilitated over a one academic year period.

ASSESSMENTS

A suggested timetable for assessments is set out below. This again assumes that the module will be delivered over one semester on a full-time basis. The timetable is as follows:

Week to be submitted /test taken	Objective test
4	Assessment
8	Case study
10	Essay
15	Examination

The module programme and suggested timetable for assignments have not been included in the students' guide as you may wish to deviate from the suggestions made. The students are informed in the study guide that a course programme and timetable for assignments will be provided separately.

Information technology

We recognise that student access to computers and staff attitudes to the place of IT in law, will vary significantly between institutions. Tasks involving the use of computers in this module are not supplied. Individual lecturers may, however, wish to expand on this area as they see fit.

Some remaining questions

There are a number of questions that may have occurred to you when considering the operation of the open learning approach. Below we have tried to anticipate some of these and to answer them on the basis of our experiences, in general.

What sort of staffing level is necessary in the surgeries?
Open surgeries are offered to about 250 students studying business law in group sizes varing between 30-80 at the basic level. These surgeries operate each afternoon from 14.00 to 17.00. Students may use the surgeries at any time during these hours. One member of staff is assigned to stay in the surgery during each afternoon and a second member of staff is assigned to act as a cover. This latter role will entail helping out when there is heavy demand and providing relief for coffee etc.

It has been observed that this level of staffing has been perfectly adequate. The level of student demand should vary significantly. Not surprisingly, demand will be high when a test is imminent!

What preparation do I need to do?
Students will need a work programme and a schedule of assignments at the beginning of the module. It will be necessary for you to read and be totally familiar with all of the material which the students will use. Self-help groups and surgery hours need to be organised at the beginning of the module.

How do I feed the material to students?

You should provide nearly all of the material at the very beginning of the module. The assignments, however, are issued in accordance with the schedule above.

Do students need to do all the assignments?

No. As mentioned earlier, it is a matter of choice how many assignments students are given. However, the assignments provided are designed to test different aspects of the business law module and to develop different cognitive skills.

How much additional time do you allow for marking?

None. Where student numbers are high, the number of assignments provided can place a burden on lecturers. However, as the surgeries are operated on a team basis in universities adopting this approach, you should expect the marking of assignments to be undertaken on a similar basis. Research students can help with invigilation of tests and with subsequent marking. In addition, staff operating the surgeries and marking assignments find this less demanding than the conventional lecture/tutorial system as the learning/assignment material has already been prepared.

How flexible is the sequencing of the material?

The sequencing of the material has been designed to be logical and does not lend itself to any significant deviation. However, you may wish to omit certain topics or expand on certain topics already covered.

REFERENCES

Beard R., 1970, *Teaching and Learning in Higher Education,* Penguin Books.
Hartley J., and Cameron A., 1967, 'Some observations on the
efficiency of lecturing,' *Educational Review,* Vol. 20, pp 30-37.
Keller F.S., 1968, 'Goodbye teacher,' *Journal of Applied Behavioural Analysis*
Vol. 1, pp 79-89.

UNIT 1

THE ENGLISH LEGAL SYSTEM

SECTION ONE

The Nature of Law

Introduction

This section provides an introduction to the law. When you have completed the section you will be able to:

- explain why we need law
- classify law in different ways
- describe and explain the difference between common law and equity
- describe the most important equitable rights and remedies
- outline what is meant by the maxims of equity
- contrast common law and equitable remedies.

We deal with the need for law in our society and explain something of the origins of our legal system. In particular there is material dealing with the difference between common law and equity but more importantly there is some discussion about the rights and remedies which each provides.

At a very early stage you will find that we use words and phrases with which you are unfamiliar or which you will realise have a different meaning in the context of the law from that which you know.

For example, what does the word 'consideration' mean to you?

It might mean something you will take into account or give thought to, for example, 'I'll take what you say into consideration.'

It might describe a thoughtful and caring attitude to another person, for example, 'Ever since I have known him, he has always treated me with the greatest consideration.'

You could add to this list, but in connection with the law of contract, 'consideration' has a special meaning. A contract is a legally enforceable agreement and one of its key elements is that it must be based upon a bargain, ie., each party must give something in return for the promise given by the other. What each party promises or undertakes to do in fulfilment of the contract is called 'consideration'.

Obviously this is an over-simplification but it serves to make the point. Look out for such words. Do not gloss over them: if you are in any doubt look them up in a legal dictionary or in a textbook. Finding out for yourself is an excellent way of learning! Compile your own glossary of legal words and expressions.

The section deals with some quite specific matters in connection with rights and remedies. This is necessary because it is what the law is all about: it does not exist in a vacuum. People go to law in search of some remedy or are taken to court because another seeks a remedy against them. You will become increasingly familiar with these matters when we deal with substantive areas of law such a contract and tort.

Some social functions of law

DISPUTE-SOLVING

On holiday you may wish to sit on the beach listening to loud music. Others may wish to enjoy the peace and quiet of the seaside. At home, you may throw frequent late-night parties, and play loud rock music until the early hours of the morning. Your neighbours, on the other hand, may well want to enjoy the comfort of their home without interference from your parties next door. In such situations as these, we have the potential for dispute. Clearly, you and your neighbours on the beach or at home may well be able to reach some kind of compromise, but in many cases, where no such compromise can be reached, the law can often be invoked to resolve the matter.

One of the functions of the law of contract, for example, is to provide a means of resolving disputes between parties who have entered into a contractual relationship in which something or other has gone wrong. And again in the law of torts, or 'civil wrongs', we find provision, through the law of private nuisance, for resolving the kind of 'bad neighbour' problem described above. In such cases, the law tries to balance competing interests in such a way as to make life bearable for all.

Another example of conflicting interests is the complaint by many people in public life such as politicians, media personalities or members of the royal family that their private lives are private and should not be subject to the intrusions of the press. The opposing view is that such 'private lives' are matters of legitimate public interest because of the possible impact which private conduct may have upon the performance of public duties. Here the tort of defamation, libel and slander, is often invoked, but many people feel that the law should go further and recognise a legally-protected right to privacy.

REGULATING BEHAVIOUR THROUGH RULES

One of the most basic functions of law is to set minimum standards of behaviour which everyone in society must observe. Often, through criminal law for example, the law simply sets out the kinds of conduct which we must not engage in: theft, violence against the person, drinking and driving, and so on. Such prohibitions can be justified because the activities in question would, if allowed, cause harm to others.

But what about conduct which affects only one's self and does not, it might seem, cause any harm to anyone else? Examples might be drug-taking, or homosexual activity. Even here, the law often intervenes. Until 1961 suicide, which would seem to be a most individual and private act, affecting no one else, was a crime. The use or even the possession of many drugs is a criminal offence. And there are many ways in which sexual activities, whether heterosexual or homosexual, may be criminal offences. You can probably think of several examples. Now, whilst everyone may not agree whether, and in what kind of situation, the law should regulate people's conduct, there is no doubt that the law is very much concerned with such regulation. This is not to suggest the law may never change. Every society needs provision for a mechanism to change the law. We can do so by, for example, lobbying MPs to press for new laws, or, more radically, changing those who make the laws by voting for a different government at a general election.

Of course, the law does not provide the only way in which disputes may be resolved. Morality, religion, cultural norms and even codes of etiquette or manners all play a part in regulating our behaviour quite apart from law. But what differentiates law from these other factors is that the law has what we might call the 'official stamp of authority'. We have specialised enforcement agencies, for example, the police, trading standards oficers, or the Health and Safety Executive, as well as specialised agencies, such as the courts or industrial tribunals, to adjudicate on disputes when they occur and to impose penalties or some remedy when a rule is breached.

Whereas moral codes or cultural norms may differ between social groups, law applies equally to and is binding on all members of society, whether they agree with the law or not. As a consequence, the law provides a framework within which individuals and organisations can conduct their affairs with confidence and a high degree of certainty. It is possible to plan in the knowledge that others will fulfill their obligations to you and that you will be obliged to do what the law requires in relation to other people. A good example is provided by the law of contract. Parties to a contract enter into a legally enforceable agreement, and each party must honour the promise he or she has made in return for what the other party has undertaken. If people were able to escape such obligations it is difficult to see how business could function or how we could conduct our private lives. If a contract is broken, a sanction may be imposed. Typically the aggrieved party will be awarded damages, that is, financial compensation to be paid by the party who broke the contract.

But, you may say, many people do break the law and seem to get away with it. What implication does this have for our notion that the law applies equally to everyone? For example, it is widely thought that motorists are allowed to drive a few miles an hour faster than a speed limit strictly permits: does this mean that the legal speed limit in a 30 m.p.h. zone is really 33 m.p.h.? And for some time, many supermarkets which opened on Sundays were clearly in breach of what were then quite strict laws on Sunday trading: does this mean that a law which is not obeyed is not really a law?

The answer to both questions is that the extent to which a law may or may not be obeyed has nothing to do with its status as a valid law. You could be prosecuted and convicted for driving at 33 m.p.h. in a 30 m.p.h. zone and stores could have been, and some were, prosecuted for breaches of the Sunday trading laws. The police and other enforcement agencies do not possess the resources to ensure that every breach of the law is followed by prosecution, but legal rules passed by Act of Parliament must nonetheless be taken as an authoritative statement of what the law is, and those rules will remain valid unless and until Parliament changes them.

Criminal and civil law

Law may be classified in various ways but for our purposes at this stage we will think of law as being either criminal or civil. An analysis of these two categories illustrates the different purposes which law serves. Some conduct will be both a crime and a civil wrong, for example, a physical assault on a person might leave the attacker facing criminal proceedings and an action for damages or compensation by the person who was assaulted.

By means of the criminal law the state helps regulate the conduct of individuals. Where the conduct is such as to represent a threat to the well-being of the rest of society the criminal law imposes sanctions in an attempt to suppress it.

Such criminal, or penal, sanctions can take different forms, either:

● imprisonment
● fines, or some other form of sanction not involving custody such as community service.

Such sanctions may be imposed for a variety of reasons which might include:

● retribution or revenge
● the protection of society
● to provide a deterrent
● to reform the offender
● to recompense the victim or society.

An accused person is prosecuted. The State acts in the name of the Queen and so the case is cited as R v Smith, 'R' being the abbreviation for Regina which is the Latin word for the Queen.

Since people are presumed to be innocent until proven guilty, the prosecution has to prove beyond reasonable doubt that the accused is guilty. This is a high standard of proof, which goes beyond the court merely considering if it seems likely or probable that the accused is guilty. Objective proof of guilt is needed that is capable of eliminating doubt and if any doubt does remain then the benefit of such doubt must be given to the accused and he or she must be acquitted.

Don't forget that, if convicted, people might lose their liberty and that they are pitted against the Crown Prosecution Service while possibly being of limited means themselves. As there is this imbalance, if there is any reasonable doubt, the benefit of any such doubt should be given to the individual who should not suffer the consequences of a doubtful conviction.

The public may regard justice as having been done if the criminal is successfully prosecuted and sentenced but the victim of the crime may have suffered substantial loss. The courts have the power to order a convicted person to pay compensation. However, the real purpose of criminal law is arguably to deal with the criminal and not to aid the victim.

People are often left to seek compensation for themselves through the courts: this is the concern of civil law.

ACTIVITY 1

Without looking back in the text, write down the possible reasons why sanctions are imposed on those who break the criminal law.

Now go back to the text and see if what you wrote down included the most important reasons.

Civil law deals with the disputes between individuals or organisations. The State's role is simply to provide the means by which they can be resolved.

It is in everyone's interests that legal obligations be fulfilled or that compensation be paid to anyone who has suffered loss as a result of a breach of legal obligations.

The civil law is concerned with enforcing obligations, the resolution of disputes and the payment of compensation, not with punishment.

The civil law protects many interests and there are many remedies that may be sought. You are most likely to have heard of damages and injunctions.

Damages represent financial compensation aimed primarily at putting the injured party in the position he or she would have been in if no loss had been suffered. For example, a person who breaks a contract may be ordered to pay a sum to the other party equivalent to the financial benefit that would have naturally arisen from the contract had it been performed.

But financial compensation may not be what is wanted. If, for example, a person is creating a nuisance, you do not want money: you want the nuisance to cease. By means of an injunction the court can order the cessation of the activity causing the nuisance. So an injunction is an order of the court which requires a party to an action either to do or, more usually, to refrain from doing a particular thing.

The civil law will deal, for example, with alleged breaches of contract or with torts. Torts are civil wrongs which cause harm whether intentionally or not in circumstances in which the law determines that there shall be a remedy. They include:

- negligence where there has been a breach of a duty of care owed by the defendant to the plaintiff which has caused recoverable loss

- nuisance where a person's quiet enjoyment of his or her land is unlawfully disturbed

- trespass where there is direct interference with the person or property of another

- defamation where there is an unjustified imputation damaging to the reputation of another person.

The list of torts is quite long.

We have spoken of the plaintiff bringing an action against the defendant. He or she sues the defendant. The action will be cited as Green v Brown; the 'v' is expressed verbally as 'and' or 'against'.

Normally the person who makes an allegation must prove what is alleged on a balance of probabilities: some element of doubt may remain but the matter in question is more rather than less likely.

Different courts are provided to deal with civil and criminal cases.

SELF-CHECK 1

Conduct which results in a case being pursued in the courts will usually be clearly either of a criminal or a civil nature. Can you think of conduct which might give rise to both criminal and civil proceedings?

Remember that the criminal law applies to business just as much as to individuals. There is a whole range of legislation directed at the regulation of business and the breach of such regulations is often a criminal offence. Failure to comply with the very many provisions of the Companies Acts is often a criminal offence. Some legislation is aimed at employee welfare such as the Factories Acts or the Health & Safety at Work etc Act. Acts such as the Trade Description Act are designed to provide consumer protection. Criminal prosecutions for breach of such Acts can result in heavy fines as well as adverse and damaging publicity.

Having noted the point made in the previous paragraph, you will soon discover that the study of business law is primarily concerned with civil law.

Common law and equity

It is necessary to give more detailed thought to the various remedies which the civil law provides. These derive either from common law or from equity and so we must now examine what these terms mean.

The term 'common law' has several meanings:

- it can be law common to the whole country rather than being limited to a particular locality or trade
- it can be the rules of law found in decided cases
- it can be the law which was developed in the old Common Law courts

Common law, however defined, has its origins in the common customs of the country and all of these definitions are valid. The meaning depends very much upon the context in which the term is used.

For our present purposes we will rely upon the last of these meanings.

The origin of common law

After the Conquest in 1066, the Normans found a country which had no central legal system.

Each part of the country had its own courts which applied its own local customs. Today we would think this unfair but it was not so important when there was a largely immobile population and generally poor communications. Individuals would accept the local law as all that need concern them.

The Normans set in train the process by which both the contents of the law and its administration became common to the whole country.

The early judges took and adopted the best of the local customs they found in one place and applied them when they moved on elsewhere. They met when they returned from time to time to the King's court and exchanged information about the cases they had heard and the customs they had found and applied. When they went out again they took with them these customs and so over a period of time the law in the country became more uniform or common.

It was in this practice that we can discover the origins of the doctrine of precedent. The judges would consider what had been decided in cases in the past similar to the particular case they were hearing. They knew what other judges had done on other occasions and would take that into account in arriving at their decisions. The operation of any system of precedent is dependent upon those implementing the law having access to records of what has been previously decided.

By the thirteenth century there was already a kind of law reporting developing; the Year Books, which recorded some of the decisions of the courts. Today law reporting is well organised and reliably accurate which means that the courts and the practitioners can have access to the records of previously decided cases. In principle the needs then were the same as they are now.

A court system became established both locally and centrally in which this common law was administered.

ACTIVITY 2

Write down in you own words a definition of precedent and then see how far your definition corresponds with that given below.

It is a judgment or a decision of a court which can be cited as an authority for deciding a later case based upon a similar set of facts or circumstances.

(Precedent as a source of law is considered in detail in Section two.)

The origin of equity

By the thirteenth century defects in the common law were becoming obvious:

- The precedent system was rigid. Because courts were bound by previous decisions in which the essential facts were the same as those in the case currently before them, there was little scope for the exercise of discretion where common fairness in a particular case seemed to demand, it. This was the price paid for the certainty and predictability that the system provided.
- Procedures were rigid. A writ, a very formal document, was necessary to start an action. It stated the plaintiff's claim and was issued in the name

of the King and ordered the defendant to do what the writ specified. They were issued by the clerks in the Chancellor's office and were expensive, which was in itself often enough to deny justice to a poor person. 'No writ, no remedy': there was a remedy if the facts of a claim could be made to fit within the terms of an existing writ but the list of writs was closed, that is, at an early stage it became impossible to create new causes of action to deal with the new situations which inevitably arose as society developed.

For example, there was no law of contract as we now know it because there was no writ which covered breach of contract. Those who were the victims of breach of what we today might recognise as contractual obligations were simply left without remedy.

- Remedies were limited: damages (financial compensation) were the principal means of remedy but they did not answer every case and there was, for example, no injunction
- Trusts were not recognised and so nothing stopped people, to whom property had been given for them to look after for the benefit of another, from abusing their position. A trust is an arrangement whereby the ownership of property is transferred to another, the trustee, for that trustee to hold for the benefit of a beneficiary
- The system provided complicated and technical defences which inevitably protracted proceedings
- Witnesses were not compellable, that is, they could not be made to attend and give testimony.

So, if a litigant, a party to the court proceedings, thought he or she was being denied justice by such a legal system, what could be done about it?

The answer was to avoid the law entirely. The custom grew of petitioning the King as the 'Fount of Justice' in the hope that he would apply common sense and ordinary fairness to give whatever remedy seemed appropriate regardless of strict legal form. The hope was that he would deal with the case with equity. Scant regard was given to precedent and it depended upon the King's subjective view.

In time, the power to hear petitions was delegated by the King to his Lord Chancellor and eventually even he could not deal with all such matters personally and so a Court of Chancery came into being to hear these equitable cases. Initially its rulings, too, were based upon individual justice and not rigid law. Although this satisfied the needs of the individual seeking redress, it ran counter to the concept of certainty and equality of treatment.

By the sixteenth century, formalised rules of equity had come into being which were based upon precedent. They were different from the common law rules but the emerging court of equity soon came to display the defects that had been found in the common law courts, that is, it was slow and rigid.

The significance was that whereas the common law's only real remedy was financial compensation, equity continued to offer the same kind of remedies that the King had originally given when he had been petitioned. For example, it was possible to order a person to perform his or her contractual obligations or to order a person not to perform a particular act.

ACTIVITY 3

Write down in your own words a definition of equity and then see how far your definition corresponds with that given below.

Originally, equity meant fairness and justice but now refers to a body of rules providing different rights and remedies from those provided by the common law.

So we had two legal systems operating in the country offering different procedures and different remedies: common law courts offering common law remedies and courts of equity offering equitable remedies.

This could produce unfortunate results. For example, litigants might pursue a costly action but then discover the required remedy could only be awarded by another court and they would have to start over again in the correct court.

It was not until the Judicature Acts 1873-1875 that the common law courts and the Equity courts were fused into one High Court.

The courts were fused, not the legal systems, which means that the remedies of each are available in the same court: an injunction can be sought in the Queen's Bench Division or the Chancery Division but according to the rules of equity.

The relevance of equity to modern law is that it has given a range of rights and remedies which did not exist before but which originally could only be requested and not demanded.

Today they are still discretionary unlike common law remedies which in appropriate circumstances may be demanded as of right, for example, for breach of contract. Equity is still applied in accordance with certain principles embodying concepts of justice and expressed in a series of maxims some of which are set out on pages 15 and 16.

ACTIVITY 4

Write down the defects in the Common Law that helped bring about the development of equity and then see if what you have written corresponds with that given below.

The common law had rigid and complicated procedures which did not permit the law to develop. Obtaining a remedy was expensive and, in any case, the remedies available were limited in nature. The common law failed to recognise certain rights, for example, those of a beneficiary under a trust.

It will be useful to know in outline the principal equitable rights and remedies.

Equitable rights

The following are examples of some important equitable rights.

TRUSTS

A significant equitable right is that of a beneficiary under a trust.

At common law a person who is the legal owner of property is regarded as the absolute owner and so such a person is able to dispose of such property. This is true even if the legal owner has only been entrusted with the property for it to be held for another person who is to receive the benefit of it.

If, for example, you had a young child, left property to benefit that child in your will and then died, there would be a problem. The child, not being legally capable of holding the property, would have a person with legal capacity to hold it for him or her and that person would become the legal owner. The law only recognised the rights of this legal owner or trustee and so the child who was the beneficiary would have no legal rights if the trustee abused his or her trust. It would mean that the legal owner could keep the benefit for him or herself thus defeating the entire purpose of the trust.

Equity recognises the rights of beneficiaries which require that trustees must hold the trust property for the benefit of the beneficiaries: remedies like injunctions were developed to ensure they do.

The trustee must act in good faith and perform his or her duties in strict accordance with the terms of the trust.

The benefit the beneficiaries have is normally the income from the trust property. When the trust comes to an end the property is conveyed to the beneficiaries.

Trusts make it possible to create a succession of interests, for example, a testator may leave his property to his wife with the remainder to his children. To achieve this the testator passes the property to trustees for them to hold it for her benefit so that she can enjoy the income it generates but the property is not hers. She cannot dispose of the property since when she dies it will pass to the children. The testator will have preserved the property for the benefit of his children but will not have imposed hardship on his wife during her lifetime.

SELF-CHECK 2

Can you think of any major uses of trusts in the world of business and finance?

LIEN

An equitable lien is an equitable right whereby one party acquires a charge on the property of another until a certain claim has been met.

A simple example is the right of an unpaid seller of goods to retain them until payment is made. It could also arise where a repairer of goods may keep them until payment has been made for the repair. In some circumstances the right may be not just to retain the goods but to sell them to defray expenses. At common law the ownership should be with the purchaser or the owner who commissioned the repair.

EQUITABLE ESTOPPEL

This arises when one party indicates that he or she does not intend to enforce his or her strict legal rights. That party then may be prevented from going back on that undertaking at some later stage. For example, if a landlord indicates that a lesser rent will be asked from a tenant than the rent originally agreed because of particularly difficult circumstances and as a result the tenant stays in occupation rather than giving up the tenancy, the landlord will be stopped from going back on the promise and demanding the full past rent. This is simply because the landlord will have let the tenant act to his or her detriment in the belief that the promise will be honoured.

You will see how this operates when you deal with the doctrine of consideration in the law of contract in the contract module.

Equitable remedies

INJUNCTIONS

An injunction is a court order either compelling a person to act in a particular way or preventing a person from acting in a particular way.

An injunction can take many forms but at present consider the following two types:

- mandatory: an order to perform an act, for example, an order to a trespasser to leave the owner's land
- prohibitory: an order not to do something, for example, to stop picketing, to stay away from the matrimonial home, not to carry on an activity in breach of contract.

Here is an example of the use of an injunction.

Kennaway v Thompson [1980] 3 All ER 329
Mrs Kennaway lived by a lake which was used for power boat racing: an activity which became increasingly frequent and noisy as time went by and which created a nuisance. Damages were an insufficient remedy: Mrs Kennaway wanted to have the quiet enjoyment of her property. The Court of Appeal granted an injunction ordering the boat club to curtail its activities by restricting noisy meetings to a limited number of occasions.

Remember that an injunction is discretionary and equitable: it will not be granted if damages are an adequate remedy or where the interests of the public at large outweigh those of the private individual.

Consider, for example, the case of **Miller v Jackson [1977] QB 966**

Cricket had been played on a village green for over seventy years. This caused some nuisance to the householders whose properties bordered the green because cricket balls were frequently hit into their gardens. They sought an injunction to stop the activity. It was held by a majority of the court that an injunction should not be granted but instead an award of damages was made to cover past and future nuisance. The public interest served by allowing this recreational activity outweighed the private interests of the householders who wanted the cricket stopped.

SPECIFIC PERFORMANCE

This is an order compelling a party to perform an obligation arising under a contract or a trust. Once again it is discretionary and will not be awarded where damages would be a sufficient remedy or where the plaintiff has behaved inequitably, for example, giving inadequate consideration or paying too small a price for the benefit that he or she is seeking to enforce.

Specific performance is only available for certain contracts, for example, concerning land or rare or unusual chattels. This is because no amount of financial compensation will put the injured party into the position he would have been in if the contract had been performed: there can be no substitute or alternative source of supply for a unique item.

It will never be used to enforce a contract for personal services: a person will never be ordered to work against his will.

ACTIVITY 5

Write down the essential characteristics of an injunction and then check to see how far your definition corresponds with that given below.

An injunction is an order of the court which is discretionary and which compels the person to whom it is addressed to act in a particular way or to refain from acting in a particular way.

There are other equitable remedies such as rectification, rescission and specific restitution which you will come across later in the contract module.

Maxims of equity

There is quite a long list of the so-called maxims of equity to which we referred on page 12. It is worth looking at a few examples here because they indicate the approach the courts adopt when deciding whether or not to grant an equitable remedy.

Here are a few examples:

● 'Equity does not suffer a wrong to be without a remedy'. It provided new remedies where a remedy at common law was deficient. It was this principle that lay behind the creation of such remedies as injunctions to prevent wrongs being perpetrated and decrees of specific performance to enforce the fulfilment of contractual obligations. We have already discussed these remedies.

- 'Equity will not assist a volunteer'. Specific performance will not be granted to a person who has given no consideration in return for the obligation he or she wants to have enforced. For example, equity will not enforce a promise to create a trust in favour of a person who has provided no consideration. It seems reasonable that the courts should not protect the interests of a person who wants something for nothing.
- 'He who comes to equity must come with clean hands'. For example, there will be no remedy for someone who has behaved improperly such as a beneficiary who has been a party to a breach of trust
- 'Equity looks on that as done which ought to be done'. For example, equity will give effect to the parties' intentions notwithstanding the absence of some formality, thus an agreement to create a formal lease may be as effective as the lease itself.
- 'Delay defeats equity'. Where the plaintiff has been dilatory or negligent in pursuing a claim the remedy sought may be denied even though all other conditions have been met. Common law remedies have specific time limits: equity may allow less time.

All these measures are designed to provide a remedy or at least ameliorate the position of the successful party to a legal dispute.

Common law damages

Now we will consider the use of common law damages. The common law remedy of damages is used and is appropriate in a number of situations.

In contract, damages may be ordered to put the injured parties in the same financial position they would have been in if the contract had been performed in accordance with its terms.

The court tries to assess the damages that can be regarded as naturally resulting from the breach. These are damages that could have been anticipated by the party who broke the contract and so it is thought reasonable to impose financial liability on such party for the breach. If any other losses arise which are of a special nature and which could not be ordinarily anticipated as a result of the breach, the party in default will only be liable if he or she had been warned at the time of contracting of the possibility of such special loss.

In tort, damages attempt to provide financial compensation to put the injured parties in position they would have been if they had not been the victim of the tort. The court tries to put a monetary value on the loss suffered.

This is a difficult task. How do you work out the compensation due to somebody who, as a result of another person's negligence, is so injured as to need to use a wheelchair for the rest of his or her life? There is no easy answer. At best money can enable the victim to buy equipment and care to make life more bearable. Although damages are an imperfect means of compensating they are often all that is available.

On occasion the court will make an award that shows its real opinion of the conduct of one or other of the parties.

It is possible to award contemptuous damages. For example, in an action for defamation of character the plaintiff might win on a technicality but the court might think there is little merit in the case and that it should not have been brought. In such circumstances the award might be of the smallest denomination of currency available. If the court combines this with not making an award of costs in favour of the successful plaintiff you will see that the plaintiff, although having won, will be greatly out of pocket.

Sometimes nominal damages are awarded. They are appropriate where the plaintiff has suffered no quantifiable financial loss but the court wishes to indicate approval of the claim. There is no fixed sum but even nominal damages of, say, £5 might answer the purpose. The court can further assist the plaintiff and indicate support for his or her position by making an order as to costs in the plaintiff's favour.

Under special circumstances the court can award exemplary damages. These go beyond providing simple financial compensation and do have a punitive element. They are only available in three circumstances:

(i)   if authorised by statute, or

(ii) if there has been an oppressive, arbitary or unconstitutional act by a servant of the government such as a local authority or a police officer, or

(iii) if the defendant has proceeded to commit a tort having decided that the profits of doing so will exceed any financial loss to the plaintiff. For example, this could apply to an author who publishes an article knowing it to be libellous but expecting it in consequence to sell very well. Exemplary damages will deprive such a publisher of the profits arising from such sales.

So although damages do not meet the needs of every case they can be seen to be not quite the 'blunt instrument' they first appear to be.

ACTIVITY 6

Close the text and try to recall the purpose of an award of damages and the basis of their assessment in the case of both contract and tort.

Go back to the text to check how accurate your recall was.

Summary of section one

- In this section we have reviewed the need for law in our society and how common law and equity began and developed to meet such need. We have seen that at the very least law helps provide an ordered and safe society in which individuals and organisations can conduct their business.
- We have paid attention to the equitable rights and remedies and to the common law remedy of damages. A knowledge of these matters is essential for anyone studying business law since it helps a person to appreciate the probable consequences of particular courses of action.

Suggested answers to section one self-check questions

SELF-CHECK 1

Your list is likely to include motoring offences where injury has been caused: the offender may be prosecuted for dangerous driving and then sued by the victim to recover compensation for the injury suffered.

Breaches of the Health & Safety at Work regulations can result in prosecution and in a civil claim for compensation if there has been an accident causing injury.

A physical assault on a person is a crime since the State has an interest in maintaining a peaceful and orderly society in which people can go about their ordinary business without fear. It is also a trespass against the person and so the victim of an assault can bring a civil action for damages.

SELF-CHECK 2

Two examples come immediately to mind.

Possibly the most significant use is in connection with pension funds. Billions of pounds are invested in pension funds in this country. Since for obvious practical reasons the millions of people who are members cannot individually join in the ownership and management of the funds to which they have contributed, the funds must be held and managed by trustees. The stringent obligations imposed on trustees should ensure, in theory at least, that the fund is protected and only used for its proper purpose, ie., to provide pensions for retired members who are the beneficiaries.

Unit trusts enable individuals to participate in the benefits of the investment of large funds which can be placed in diverse holdings. The savings of the individuals who place their money in such trusts are made available to industry but are more secure because of the spread investments. The funds are under the control of managers or trustees who use their specialist skills to look after the best interests of the unit holders or beneficiaries.

SECTION TWO
Sources of Law

This section introduces you to the principal sources of law in Britain today. When you have completed the section you will be able to:

- explain what is meant by Parliamentary supremacy
- categorise Acts of Parliament
- outline the purpose of delegated legislation
- explain the need for the courts to interpret statutes
- describe and evaluate the main statutory and common law rules of statutory interpretation
- explain how the system of binding and persuasive precedent operates
- outline the contribution made by the European Union to United Kingdom law.

An elected Parliament passes laws which may be in fulfilment of the manifesto promises of the ruling party and which will almost certainly reflect the political attitude of the Government.

The courts too can make law. It might be argued that law is made or, at least, marginally adjusted every time a judge makes a decision.

Both are important, but whereas Parliament can by a single Act fundamentally alter the law governing a particular aspect of our lives, the courts' power is much more limited. They can only deal with issues which happen to be brought before them and, even then, as we will see, they have a limited discretion.

Finally, we will see that by becoming a member of the then European Economic Community, now the European Union, we have given power to the Union to make rules that, in some circumstances, have binding effect in this country without ever having to be legislated in our own Parliament.

Legislation

We have an elected Parliament which is responsible for the government of the country. The political party commanding a majority in the House of Commons forms the Government and inevitably the Government dominates Parliament. To give effect to its policies the Government will need to create new laws or at least to amend existing laws. It does this by means of Acts of Parliament.

You will find Acts of Parliament also referred to as statutes or, sometimes, as being primary legislation.

You must note that it is Parliament that legislates but it is normally the Government that decides the subject of the legislation and makes sure that it reaches the statute book, sometimes in the face of vociferous and determined opposition from the minority parties.

Parliament consists of two Houses: the House of Commons with 650 elected members and the House of Lords consisting of both hereditary members and life peers. The House of Commons is the dominant body while the House of Lords has, at the most, power to delay legislation, but it does useful work revising and reviewing proposed legislation.

Legislation is introduced into Parliament as a bill. To become law it has to be passed by both Houses and then receive the royal assent. The royal assent is a formality: should it be denied by the monarch there could well be a constitutional crisis. It would mean that the monarch was denying the supremacy of Parliament and it would be seen a political act preventing the party forming the Government from carrying through a particular piece of legislation. Such an action could threaten the continuing role of the monarchy and accordingly is very unlikely.

SELF-CHECK 1

Write down your explanation of the difference between 'Parliament' and 'the Government'.

PARLIAMENTARY SOVEREIGNTY

Parliament is sovereign, that is, it is the supreme law-making body: it can make, alter or repeal any law. There is no limit on its power. It does not matter if a law made by Parliament is extremely unpopular or seems to defy reason: it still has binding effect.

It is not possible for the courts to challenge the validity of an Act of Parliament except on the one ground that Parliament was not properly constituted; for example, that the Act was passed by the Commons and had received the royal assent but had not been passed by the Lords. Such a challenge would not really be aimed at the validity of the contents or purpose of the Act but would question whether it was an Act at all. There is no possibility, as there is in some countries, of the courts declaring an Act to be unconstitutional. We have no written constitution and so it seems that if an Act of Parliament has been properly passed then it must be, almost by definition, constitutional.

If there is a procedural defect in the course of the passage of a bill through Parliament then Parliament must remedy the matter: it is not the concern of the courts.

The task of the courts is to interpret and apply the Acts and thereby to give effect to the expressed will of Parliament.

British Railways Board v Picken [1974] AC 765
Lord Morris of Borthy-y-Gest in his judgement in this case said 'When an enactment is passed there is finality unless and until it is amended or repealed by Parliament. In the courts there may be argument as to the correct interpretation of the enactment: there must be none as to whether it should be on the statute-book at all.'

An Act of Parliament stands even if it conflicts with an international treaty.

Cheney v Conn [1968] 1 WLR 242
An income tax assessment was made under the Finance Act 1964. An appeal against it was made on a number of grounds one of which was that some of the tax

levied would be used to make nuclear weapons. The taxpayer argued that this was a breach of international law. He claimed that the illegal purpose to which the statute was being applied invalidated the assessment.

Ungoed-Thomas, J said 'What the statute itself enacts cannot be unlawful, because what the statute says and provides is itself the law, and the highest form of law that is known to this country. It is the law which prevails over every other form of law, and it is not for the court to say that a Parliamentary enactment, the highest law in this country, is illegal.'

The view expressed in this judgement may not still be tenable in the light of our membership of the European Union. The final part of this section discusses European Union law. If you refer to it briefly now you will see that European Union regulations have direct application in this country and so they are in effect law even though not passed by our Parliament. It also seems that European Union law takes precedence over the law of a member state if there is ambiguity or conflict between the two. The result is that although no challenge to the supremacy of Parliament can be made by any institution or person within the country, a challenge may be properly made by the European Court of Justice since by joining the Union we have given that Court such a power. When we joined the European Union it was the European Communities Act 1972 that established among other things that European Union law overrides an inconsistent English law. Presumably ultimate Parliamentary sovereignty could be regained by the simple expedient of repealing the 1972 Act and leaving the European Union! In practice this is very unlikely.

Parliament cannot pass an Act to bind its successors. It cannot say, for example, that any subsequent provision repealing the law in question shall be void. You might argue that if it is really supreme it could do whatever it wished including passing such a law. To do this would however be to deny the sovereignty of a subsequent Parliament.

The position is logically difficult and the view is taken that Parliament is not bound by the decisions of its predecessors. This is a sensible approach since circumstances and needs do change and our laws must be able to respond appropriately. The practical implication is that if the courts are faced with two incompatible statutory provisions then they must apply the most recent.

ACTIVITY 7

Write down the circumstances, if any, in which the authority of an Act of Parliament may be challenged. See how far what you have written corresponds with that below.

Basically, a challenge can only be made if an Act has not been through the proper Parliamentary procedure, for example, it has not been passed by the House of Lords. Such a defect is in reality extremely improbable. A challenge could come from the European Union. As a result of an aspect of a case being referred to the European Court of Justice for a decision, a provision of an Act of Parliament could be declared to be incompatible with European Union Law. Parliament would be under an obligation to address the matter.

CLASSIFICATION OF ACTS OF PARLIAMENT

Acts of Parliament may be classified as being Public Acts or Private Acts.

Public Acts deal with matters of public policy and are usually introduced by a Government minister. When a bill is introduced by a minister it is normally certain that it will reach the statute-book. It may implement a particular stated objective of Government or at least will reflect general Government policy. The Government which can dictate the Parliamentary timetable will find the necessary time for the measure to go through Parliament and will work to ensure that it receives support from the Government's own Members of Parliament.

Sometimes Public Acts are introduced as private members' bills which can succeed if the Government is prepared to make time available and to co-operate but this is exceptional. Private members bills can deal with matters of considerable importance, for example, The Abortion Act 1967 was introduced into the House of Commons as such a bill by David Steel. Even if private members' bills fail the mere fact that they have been introduced will have enabled the Member of Parliament to give publicity to whatever the subject matter of the bill was.

Private Acts usually deal with matters of private or local interest, for example, where local authorities, public undertakings or companies are seeking special powers, perhaps, to use land in a particular way. Private bills are checked to make sure that notice has been given to parties likely to be affected by them but once this has been done they pass through the rest of the procedure without significant debate.

Some Acts are designed to consolidate or to codify the law.

A Consolidating Act does not change the law but merely re-enacts in one statute the scattered statutory provisions dealing with a particular topic that may have been passed from time to time. This is convenient for the practitioner who only has to refer to one Act rather than having to search through many Acts with the risk of missing some important matter. Such Acts are used in company law. There is frequent legislation concerning the regulation of companies and so there is a need to bring it all together at appropriate intervals into a Consolidating Act.

A Codifying Act serves a different purpose. It brings together all the law on a particular topic from whatever source and re-enacts it in a single statute while at the same time altering and improving the law if necessary. In this respect codification differs from consolidation: a Consolidating Act does not change the law. The Theft Act 1968 was a Codifying Act.

ACTIVITY 8

Without looking back in the text, what are the differences between:

a) private bills and private members' bills, and

b) consolidation and codification?

Now go back in the text and see if what you wrote down included the most important points.

Delegated legislation

Sometimes Parliament does not legislate directly upon a particular matter but gives some other body the power to make the necessary laws. Such laws may be referred to as delegated or secondary legislation.

Examples include the by-laws of local authorities and statutory instruments made by Government departments and ministers, for example, the many safety regulations made under the Factories Acts and the Health and Safety at Work Act 1974. A statutory instrument is simply the document in which the delegated legislation is set out.

Unlike Acts of Parliament such legislation may be challenged in the courts, for instance, on the grounds that it is *ultra vires*. *'Ultra vires'* means 'beyond the powers' and so the courts may examine the delegated legislation to see if the enabling Act actually empowered the subordinate body to make such laws. In addition there are arrangements for some parliamentary control of delegated legislation often taking the form of providing for parliamentary scrutiny when it is first made.

Delegated legislation can save a lot of parliamentary time and is obviously appropriate if the subject matter is very detailed and highly technical or calls for local knowledge.

It can be altered relatively quickly without the need for parliamentary debate. This is helpful, for example, in times of national emergency or if a measure has been introduced as an experiment and is then found to need amendment.

Statutory interpretation

If Acts of Parliament were consistently unambiguous and clear there would be far less work for the lawyers and the courts would be far emptier! Unfortunately it is almost inevitable that difficulties will arise as to the meaning of statutes and the task of discovering the meaning falls to the judges.

THE NEED TO INTERPRET

Statutes often deal with highly complex issues and so the language used will necessarily be complex. In this country statutes are not broad expressions of policy stating in general terms what the legislature wishes to be achieved. Statutes are usually detailed, attempting to cover all eventualities and the words used frequently have a technical meaning. The result is that situations arise in which it is difficult to determine whether they are covered by the Act or not and, if so, in what way.

Consider, for example, **Fisher v Bell** [1961] 1 QB 394 in which a need arose to interpret the **Restriction of Offensive Weapons Act 1959.** The Act had made it an offence to offer for sale certain offensive weapons including flick knives. A shopkeeper was discovered displaying such knives in his shop window and he was prepared to sell one to anyone who came into the shop and asked for it.

Was he guilty of an offence under the Act? The layman would be tempted to say, 'Yes, of course, the Act was passed expressly to stop such an activity.'

In fact the judge decided that there was no offence. He had to determine what was meant by 'to offer for sale'. Although this was a criminal case he used the reasoning that is used in the civil law of contract: displaying goods in a shop window is not offering them for sale but it is an invitation to treat. It indicates that the shopkeeper is prepared to do business and will respond to offers made by potential customers. Perhaps the judge could have decided that the meaning of the words was different in the context of criminal law but he did not and so the shopkeeper was acquitted.

This is a simple illustration of the kind of problem that can arise. Was the clear intention of Parliament defeated? Possibly, but if the intention had been clear there would have been no difficulty and Parliament would have expressed the provision in such a way as to leave no doubt.

Parliament having created uncertainty was left with the task of eliminating it since the courts had not done so. An Act was passed in 1961 to close the loophole.

This was regarded by Parliament as being an important matter and so an amending Act was passed but this does not always happen. An interpretation of an Act is sometimes widely acknowledged to be incorrect but it stands and is subsequently followed simply because Parliament does not regard it as sufficiently important to find time to deal with it.

SELF-CHECK 2

Write down reasons you think might lead to a statute being drafted in such a way as to leave ambiguities and difficulties for the courts to resolve.

THE 'RULES' OF INTERPRETATION

There are certain statutory rules to help the judges:

- Many Acts have an interpretation section which explains the meaning of particular words in the context of the Act
- The Interpretation Act 1978 determines some basic rules that apply to all Acts. For example, 'words of the masculine gender import the feminine gender' and vice versa, 'singular includes the plural' and vice versa or the word 'month' means calendar month
- The Act itself may help. Headings, side notes and punctuation may be looked at if there is ambiguity.

There are certain other common law rules of interpretation to be considered:

- the literal rule
- the golden rule
- the mischief rule

Although these are called 'rules', the term is quite misleading. They are not rules but are rather labels that might be attached, after the event, to the approach which the judge appears to have adopted in a particular case. It is, however, possible to discern a pattern that makes analysis of these so-called rules a worthwhile activity.

THE LITERAL RULE

The words used in a statute are given their plain, ordinary or literal meaning. The words used in a statute are probably the most useful guide to Parliament's intention.

The rule is that if words are quite clear they must be applied even though the result is absurd. After all, what is 'absurd'? It is a subjective concept. If Parliament has used words which are capable of a clear meaning it is arguably not appropriate for the courts to question that meaning. To do so could be interpreted as a challenge to Parliament.

The rule does, at least, make for greater certainty and it is straightforward and not controversial.

There may not be a natural and ordinary meaning. If there were, many cases would not have been brought in the first place. In such a situation the judges will still be presented with the task of interpretation.

ACTIVITY 9

Without looking back in the text, write down a definition of the literal rule.

Now go back to the text and see if what you wrote down covered the main points.

THE GOLDEN RULE

An early formulation of this rule is to be found in the words of Lord Wensleydale in **Grey v Pearson** [1857]:

'....the grammatical and ordinary sense of the words is to be adhered to, unless that would lead to some absurdity, or some repugnance or inconsistency with the rest of the instrument, in which case the grammatical and ordinary sense of the words may be modified, so as to avoid that absurdity and inconsistency, but no farther.'

The rule may be used in two ways:

- first, if words are ambiguous then they should be interpreted so as to avoid an absurd outcome

- second, sometimes the words are clear and are capable of only one meaning but applying such a meaning gives an unacceptable outcome

This second application of the rule is difficult because it will once again involve a judge in taking a subjective decision as to what is an unacceptable outcome. A further difficulty arises because it cannot be anticipated whether or not the judge will use the rule: there is no compulsion or recognisable set of guidelines.

ACTIVITY 10

Without looking back in the text, write down the two applications of the golden rule. See how far your answer corresponds with that given below.

The first (or 'narrow') application is where there is an ambiguity to be resolved and the court chooses the meaning which avoids an absurd result or appears the most sensible in the context of the instrument as a whole.

The second (or 'broader') application is where there is not necessarily an ambiguity but the literal rule would produce a repugnant or unacceptable outcome.

THE MISCHIEF RULE

Essentially the 'mischief rule' requires the judge to know what the law was before the Act to be interpreted was passed. It also presupposes that the judge will know or be able to discover in what way the old law failed to deal adequately with the issue that was the subject of the Act. The court must then look at the Act to see just how the legislation proposed to put right that failing and then the courts must interpret the Act in such a way as to achieve the purpose which it thinks Parliament intends. In other words the courts will interpret the Act so as to remedy the mischief in the law which Parliament had identified and sought to remedy.

It was first voiced at a time when Acts of Parliament were not such a potent source of law as they are today. The Acts of the day were often couched in general terms and constitutional supremacy of Parliament had yet to be established. Today, perhaps, the mischief rule should only be used where there is ambiguity because otherwise the courts might appear to be trespassing on Parliament's territory.

It seems like the purposive approach that is advocated by some today which requires that the judge has some knowledge of the social, financial or political circumstances giving rise to legislation and so may better understand the purpose of the legislation. If the purpose is understood it can be argued that a judge, far from usurping Parliament's legislative function, will assist it in achieving what it wants.

There is the unified approach which Sir Rupert Cross describes in his book *Statutory Interpretation* (1976). It represents a considerable move from a straightforward application of the literal rule. The judge considers not just the literal meaning of words but puts them in the general context of the Act. Should a literal interpretation produce a result which is inconsistent with the purpose of the Act then the judge will apply a secondary meaning of which the words are capable. This of course presupposes that the judge has been free to give thought to the purpose of the Act. The judge also will add to, alter or ignore words in the Act which seem to run counter to the purpose of the Act.

Cross writes:

'1. The judge must give effect to the grammatical and ordinary or, where appropriate, the technical meaning of words in the general context of the statute; he must also determine the extent of general words with reference to that context.

2. If the judge considers that the application of the words in their grammatical and ordinary sense would produce a result which is contrary to the purpose of the statute, he may apply them in any secondary meaning which they are capable of bearing.

3. The judge may read in words which he considers to be necessarily implied by words which are already in the statute and he has a limited power to add to, alter or ignore statutory words in order to prevent a provision from being unintelligible or absurd or totally unreasonable, unworkable, or totally irreconcilable with the rest of the statute.

4. In applying the above rules the judge may resort to certain aids to construction and presumptions...'(Bailey and Gunn, 1991:325)

SELF-CHECK 3

Explain what problems, if any, arise from there being three 'rules' of interpretation?

There are other 'aids to construction and presumptions' to which Sir Rupert Cross referred, (see above), that can be used to assist in the task of interpretation. We will now explain what these terms mean.

PRESUMPTIONS

Certain presumptions apply if there are no clear words excluding them. If there are completely clear words then the presumptions have no place. There is quite a long list. You will find an interesting discussion of a number of the presumptions in *The English Legal Process* by Terence Ingman. By way of illustration we refer to two of them here.

The presumption against retrospective effect

This is especially important in criminal law. It would be most unfair if you had acted yesterday in a way that was perfectly legal only to find that an Act passed today made what you did yesterday a criminal offence for which you are liable.

Of course, because Parliament is sovereign it can act in this way if it wishes but there is a presumption against retrospective effect unless there is a clear statement to the contrary.

Parliament did this in **Burmah Oil Co Ltd v Lord Advocate** [1965] AC 75. The Company's oil installations in Burma, then a British colony, were destroyed by British forces acting under orders of the British Government in 1942 to prevent them falling into the hands of the advancing Japanese. The company sued the Crown for compensation. The Crown argued that no compensation was payable when property was destroyed under the Royal Prerogative.

The House of Lords held that compensation was payable and an inquiry was ordered to determine the level of damages. This was unpalatable to the Government of the day and so before the damages had been assessed the War Damages Act 1965 was passed specifically to overrule the House of Lords with retrospective effect!

The presumption that the Crown is not bound by an Act

BBC v Johns [1965] Ch 32
Per Lord Diplock, 'Since laws are made by rulers for subjects a general expression in a statute such as "any person", descriptive of those upon whom the statute imposes obligations or restraints is not to be read as including the ruler himself.'

SELF-CHECK 4

Explain who we mean by 'the ruler himself' in modern Britain. By the 'Crown', do you think we mean the Queen herself?

In **Lord Advocate v Dumbarton District Council** [1990] 1 AllER 1, it was held that the Crown was not bound by Scottish planning and roads legislation that called for local authority planning consent before a road could be closed. The Crown had caused a stretch of road to be closed so that it could be used for the storage of building materials during the building of a security fence at the Faslane submarine base.

Often as a matter of policy the Crown is expressly bound by the provisions of an Act, e.g., Occupiers Liability Acts 1957 & 1984 and Equal Pay Act 1970.

OTHER 'RULES'

● '*Noscitur a sociis*' - An Act is to be read as a whole and so words must be interpreted in their context from which their meaning may be gathered.

● '*Expressio unius est exclusio alterius*' - the expression of one thing implies the exclusion of another. If specific words are used and are not followed by general words then the Act will only apply to the specific matters mentioned.

● The '*ejusdem generis*' rule - where general words follow particular words, the general words are construed as being limited to persons, things or matters within the class indicated by the particular words.

Powell v Kempton Park Racecourse Co [1899] AC 143. The Betting Act 1853 had prohibited keeping a 'house, office, room or other place' for people to call to place bets. Tattersall's ring was an outdoor place at a racecourse. Was it an 'other place' falling within the Act? The House of Lords held not because the particular words all referred to indoor places and 'other place' had to be construed *ejusdem generis*.

So far in this section we have been concerned with Acts of Parliament which are arguably the most important source of new law. When a case comes before a court it will frequently involve the judge in interpreting a statutory provision. In this way decided cases help make clear just what the law is and, in some cases, extend and develop it. This useful process can in some situations amount to actual judicial law-making.

Not all cases that have to be decided involve statutory interpretation: new situations arise or, at least, new variations of old situations, and a judgement is required. Issues are discussed which have never been the subject of an Act of Parliament but which are nonetheless the subject of a large body of law. The law relating to both contract and tort is very important to every one of us whatever our role in life but it is largely unregulated by statute. Of course, there are many Acts of Parliament which are relevant, for example, the Sale of Goods Act 1979 or the Unfair Contract Terms Act 1977 but the laws are not expressed in comprehensive statutory enactments.

It is obvious that the courts have an important part to play in the constant process of change in the law. Sometimes change is gradual and sometimes quite dramatic when policy seems to have been completely reversed. We need to look at the workings of the doctrine of precedent to see just how all of this happens. It is legitimate to regard precedent as a source of law either in the limited sense of giving effect to statute or in the broader sense of determining issues that have not previously been before a court.

Precedent

When a case has been heard and the judge has arrived at a decision, he or she does not simply state who has won and who has lost. Instead a judgment is delivered which may be quite brief or very long and which is made up of three parts:

- a finding of the material facts, introduced as evidence or inferred from the circumstances
- a statement of the law as it applies to the legal problem raised by the facts, the *ratio decidendi*.
  Prof. Michael Zander in his book *The Law Making Process* writes '...(the *ratio decidendi* is) a proposition of law which decides the case in the light or in the context of the material facts.' It is the reason for a judicial decision.
- a judgement or decision in favour on one of the parties.

It is critically important to identify the *ratio decidendi* because that is the potential source of law. The problem is that the *ratio* might be quite hard to identify: the judge does not do it for us. A court when hearing a subsequent case must decide which facts were regarded as material and exactly what rule of law was being applied by analysing the speech which may have contained much else that was not of such direct relevance.

The court must also decide if the law that was stated is capable of having an application to circumstances other than those particularly identified as material in the case in question. A judge in a future case is unlikely to be presented with identical facts but they may well be similar: does the same principle of law apply in both cases? The judge will have to decide if it is a broad principle with application to many sets of facts or if it is narrowly limited to the circumstances of the particular case in which it was voiced.

These matters are of great importance because of the nature of binding precedent which depends upon two principles:

1. The first is *stare decisis* '. ..other things being equal, one court should follow the decision of another where the facts appear to be similar'(Zander, 1994).

    This seems reasonable: equality of treatment and certainty are two immediately obvious merits. It does mean that you must be able to find what earlier decisions were and so there must be good law reporting. There is a danger that the law becomes inflexible because a precedent must be followed even if changing social conditions or attitudes have made it inappropriate.

    A further difficulty is that there are so many decided cases all of which contribute to the law. The sheer volume of reported cases presents a problem for the practitioner. A case which might help can be overlooked and the difference between one case and another might be very subtle.

    If it seems to a judge that there is a material difference between the case before the court and a previously decided case cited as a precedent then that case can be distinguished. This means that the court does not have to follow that precedent.

    Law created by a court deciding a case has the advantage that it is based upon an event that has actually occurred. Over time cases will be heard dealing with most aspects of contentious human activity and so law based upon precedent will become comprehensive. The difference between one case and another may be small but significant. Acts of Parliament can only anticipate needs and so will be less complete: the courts by the operation of precedent will fill the gaps.

ACTIVITY 11

Without looking back in the text, using your own words write down what is meant by '*ratio decidendi*' and '*stare decisis*'.

Now go back to the text and see if what you wrote included the most important points.

2. The second principle is that there is a hierarchy of authority within our court structure. Broadly speaking courts bind other courts below them in the hierarchy but are not bound by those below them.

We are really only concerned with the House of Lords, the Court of Appeal and, to some extent, with the High Court.

BINDING PRECEDENT

A binding precedent must fulfil the following conditions:

- the precedent must be from an earlier decision of a court which binds the court considering the case in hand
- the binding proposition of law must have been part of the *ratio decidendi* of that earlier decision
- the facts of the present case must be essentially similar to those found in the precedent.

Not every previous decision will create a precedent. Note:

- those that are '*per incuriam*', that is, given by mistake because the court's attention was not drawn to some relevant statute or authority that would have affected the decision
- those that may be distinguished because the material facts of the case before the court are sufficiently different from those of the previous case
- those that have been overruled by statute or a later case: look back, for example, at what happened following the decision in **Fisher v Bell** [1961], which you will find above in the part of this section discussing the need to interpret statutes
- those made by a court which does not bind the present court.

THE HIERARCHY OF THE COURTS

In Section Three we will examine the structure of the English courts in some detail but for the present it is sufficient to know that the House of Lords (as a court, properly known as the Judicial Committee of the House of Lords, and not to be confused with the House of Lords in its capacity as a part of Parliament) is the highest court in the land. It stands above the Court of Appeal which in turn is superior to the High Court.

You will find diagrams illustrating both the civil courts and the criminal courts on the second and third pages of Section Three.

HOUSE OF LORDS DECISIONS BIND ALL OTHER COURTS.

Until 1966 the House of Lords held itself to be bound by its own previous decisions but in that year the Lord Chancellor issued a Practice Statement saying that the House would henceforward no longer consider itself bound by its own previous decisions when to do so might cause injustice. This discretion has been used sparingly but, nonetheless, does allow the House to change the law by departing from its own previous decisions when it appears right to do so.

Although the House of Lords is the final court of appeal it does not hear many cases a year. An appeal can only be brought if leave is given and this will only be given if a point of law of general public importance is involved. Further, many litigants are deterred by the high cost and the delays.

If a case raises a difficulty concerning the interpretation of European Union law the House of Lords, or indeed the Court of Appeal or the High Court, will refer the particular issue to the European Court of Justice for a ruling. The European Court's interpretation will be accepted by the domestic court and applied in deciding the case.

COURT OF APPEAL

The Court of Appeal sits in two divisions: civil and criminal.

Its decisions bind all lower courts, ie., all three divisions of the High Court and the County Court.

Although for most litigants the Court of Appeal is the final court of appeal it is nonetheless bound by its own precedents. The discretion that the House of Lords has to depart from its own precedents is not allowed to the Court of Appeal.

If the Court of Appeal regards one of its precedents as being in need of overruling then it must hope that either the House of Lords or Parliament will attend to the matter.

There are three technical situations, however, in which the Court of Appeal may depart from its precedents. They were voiced in **Young v Bristol Aeroplane Co Ltd** [1944] KB 718 and have been subsequently judicially confirmed. They are:

- when the previous Court of Appeal decision is *per incuriam* (see above)
- when the previous Court of Appeal decision cannot stand with a House of Lords decision
- when there are two conflicting Court of Appeal decisions.

The Court of Appeal is a busy court: it hears many cases each year. It is arguable that it should be allowed, on appropriate occasions, to depart from its precedents. Why should a law that has become out-dated in the light of social and political change be followed when the Court of Appeal could take the opportunity of a relevant case coming before it to change it? Surely the Court of Appeal can be trusted to be circumspect in handling such cases?

The answer seems to be that the House of Lords which can in effect control the Court of Appeal, regards certainty as being a great virtue in the law. They say that if an issue is sufficiently important it will come before them when they can remedy the defect and that they must reserve the power to change the law for themselves.

SELF-CHECK 5

Explain whether you think the rules of precedent which bind the Court of Appeal are satisfactory.

HIGH COURT

High Court decisions bind the County Court but not the High Court itself. Perhaps this is partly the result of the huge volume of cases dealt with by the High Court which makes it difficult to keep track of all the precedents. In practice although High Court judges are not strictly bound by the precedents of fellow judges they will normally follow them and they will regard them as highly persuasive.

COUNTY COURT

County Court decisions have no binding authority.

ACTIVITY 12

Write down the conditions that must be fulfilled for a precedent to become binding. See how far your answer corresponds with that given below.

There are three basic conditions. First, the precedent must have been established in a court which binds the court considering the present case. Second, the proposition of law, to be binding, must be found in the *ratio decidendi*. Third, the present case must have facts which are materially similiar to those found in the precedent.

THE WEIGHT OF AUTHORITY OF A PRECEDENT

The weight of authority (or importance) given to any precedent by judges in future cases will depend upon a number of factors:

- Which court in the hierarchy decided the case. The more senior the court, the more weight will be attached to what is said there.
- Which judge and how many judges were involved.
- If there was a dissenting opinion and who dissented. It may be that more than one judge sits to hear a case. In such cases the decision of the court is that of the majority of the judges. The precedent will be weakened if one or more judges of recognised high standing express a dissenting view.
- How the precedent fits in with surrounding law. It will carry more weight if it complements existing law on the matter concerned.
- How decisions based on the precedent have fared. It will help if, for example, they have been consistently upheld.
- Whether the precedent has been frequently distinguished. If it has it implies that it does not have general application.
- Whether the precedent has stood for long. If it has remained unchallenged for a long time that will add to its authority as a statement of law.
- If it was a reserved judgment, that is, one that was delivered at a later time when the judge had had time to deliberate as opposed to a judgment delivered as soon as the trial ended.

PERSUASIVE PRECEDENTS

So far we have been thinking primarily of binding precedents but some precedents are only persuasive in which case a judge is not obliged to follow them.

PERSUASIVE PRECEDENTS INCLUDE:

- '*Obiter dicta*', things said by the way, not forming a part of the *ratio*. Judges, for example, might outline what the law would have been if the facts in the case had been different or they might put forward a view of the general law on a topic whereas the case before him is concerned with a narrow and particular aspect.
- Decisions of the Judicial Committee of the Privy Council. This is a body made up of very senior judges, for example, the Lord Chancellor and the judges who sit in the House of Lords. Its jurisdiction includes hearing appeals from certain Commonwealth countries. Its decisions are not binding on other courts but because of the eminence of its members its jugements are treated with great respect as strongly persuasive precedents.

- Dissenting judgements (see above).
- Decisions of courts lower in the hierarchy than the court considering the case in hand.

Persuasive precedent can be an important source of law. For example, the *obiter dicta* or a dissenting judgement of an eminent and learned judge will command great respect. If, in a later case, an issue arises to which such *dicta* or the dissenting judgement has relevance then the judge may decide to adopt and apply the reasoning that had been used perhaps thereby creating a binding precedent. Much will depend upon the authority of the persuasive precedent: some of the factors will be the same as those discussed above. For example, from which court did the precedent come? If it was *obiter dicta* from the House of Lords voiced by a distinguished Law Lord it is likely to have great authority.

ACTIVITY 13

Close the text and try to recall the factors that help determine the weight given to a precedent.

Now go back to the text and check how accurate your recall was.

Always remember that a system of precedent can only work if there is good law reporting. You must have easy access to what decisions were taken and to the reasoning that was employed if you are to apply them in subsequent cases.

Finally, remember Parliament is sovereign and so if there is a conflict between statute and common law, then statute prevails.

European Union law

Many areas of United Kingdom law are not affected by our membership of the European Union, for example, it leaves criminal law, family law, contract and tort as the preserve of domestic law. One of the significant original reasons for the creation of the Union was economic: to create a common market across the member states. Accordingly it is unsurprising that European Union law primarily deals with matters such as competition, restrictive trade practices, employment law and consumer protection: all to do with trade and freedom of movement of capital and labour within the Union. The aim of such laws is, in general, to ensure that similar trading conditions prevail throughout the Union so that member states compete on equal terms.

The different institutions of the European Union play different roles in the law-making process.

The Council of Ministers is the primary legislative body of the European Union which can issue regulations and directives. It is the primary forum for the expression of national interest.

The Commission is the guardian of the treaty making sure treaty obligations are fulfilled by the Member States and is also a primary initiator of law.

The European Parliament has only an advisory and supervisory role.

The European Court of Justice is the interpreter of the meaning of the Treaty and the secondary legislation issued by the Council or the Commission.

European Union law derives from three sources:

1. European Union treaties
    The treaties, most notably the Treaty of Rome, are the primary sources of the law of the European Union. The provisions of the treaties are automatically incorporated into UK law without the need for an Act of Parliament.

2. Secondary legislation
    - regulations are binding in their entirety in the UK without any need of an Act of Parliament
    - directives are binding as to the result to be achieved but with the choice of method of implementation being left to the member state
    - decisions are binding in their entirety, i.e., directly applicable, but only on those parties to whom they are specifically addressed
    - recommendations and opinions made by either the Council of Ministers or the Commission of the European Union have no binding force in the United Kingdom unless and until they are given effect either by statute or by delegated legislation made under the European Communites Acts 1972.

3. Decisions of the European Court of Justice
    The European Court has consistently held that European Union law takes precedence over that of any Member State. Any ambiguity in United Kingdom law has been interpreted to run consistently with European law.

European Union law has been preferred to United Kingdom law. Rights and obligations not found in United Kingdom law but present in European Union law have been affirmed or imposed.

The European Court gives preliminary rulings on questions concerning European Union law. National courts of the last instance, eg., the House of Lords, must refer such questions unless the interpretation is clear.

Private parties may require a United Kingdom court to apply European Union law and the court may, of course, refer the case to the European Court for an interpretation.

THE STATUS OF EUROPEAN UNION LAW

There is a parallel between European Union law and domestic law. Just as an Act of Parliament cannot be challenged in our courts, it is not possible to challenge the validity of the European Union treaties which are the source of the Union's primary legislation. The role of the courts is to interpret the treaties.

The European Court of Justice can challenge the validity of secondary legislation, for example on the grounds that it is procedurally or substantively *ultra vires* or that it is in conflict with the treaties. Thus as with domestic delegated legislation the courts are not limited to the role of interpreters of meaning.

ACTIVITY 14

Write down the difference between a European Union regulation and a European Union directive. See how far your answer corresponds with that given below.

A regulation is binding in its entirety upon all Member States of the European Union without there being any need for the legislature of a Member State to pass a law to give it effect. By contrast, a directive is only given effect by the national legislatures of Member States passing appropriate laws which, however, they are obliged to do.

Summary of section two

● In this section we have considered the various sources of the many laws that exist and which govern the conduct of our lives.

- The most significant source must be legislation passed by our own Parliament, not necessarily because it is the most prolific source of new law, but because Parliament is supreme and can make or revoke any law at any time. To this extent all law from other sources only exists because Parliament allows them to continue unchallenged. Even European Union law could cease to have effect if Parliament so decreed although this would inevitably also signify the end of our membership of the Union.

- In practical terms the judiciary is both a determiner of what the law actually is through its role as an interpreter of statute and is also a maker of law through the operation of the doctrine of precedent. You will have observed how the law emerges from the interaction of the legislature and the judiciary. Often, although there has been legislation, the law remains uncertain until it has been the subject of a judicial decision.

- Finally, we looked briefly at the European Union. While we remain in the Union which seems most probable in the foreseeable future, this is likely to become an increasingly important source of law at least in connection with the regulation of trade and services. As with domestic law, European Union law requires the active involvement of the courts to help make it certain.

Suggested answers to section two self-check questions

SELF-CHECK 1

Parliament is the legislative body which has supreme law-making power in this country. It comprises both Houses of Parliament, the Commons and the Lords. Membership of the House of Commons which is the dominant House is made up of all the elected Members of Parliament each of whom will represent a particular constituency. It follows that Parliament is comprised of a membership made up of people owing allegiance to different political parties and having a wide range of different views. It has its own rules and procedures which must be followed quite regardless of the political complexion of the party which can command a majority in the House.

The Government of the day is made up of members of the party which has a majority in the House. Because of its majority it can largely determine what laws Parliament will pass. If the Government fails for whatever reason to win a particular vote then it has no choice but to accept the result since it reflects the will of Parliament.

The leader of the party which has a majority in the House of Commons is invited to form the Government. If no party has a majority then some form of coalition between groups who between them can obtain a majority may be necessary.

If the issue upon which a Government is defeated in the House is very important to Government policy then the Government may have to resign. If this happens, that particular Government goes but Parliament always continues.

SELF-CHECK 2

There may well be no single reason but elements of the following reasons may combine to create the problem:

- quite simply bad drafting and carelessness
- haste, leaving insufficient time for proper debate and consideration: debate may be deliberately curtailed
- simple failure to recognise the full implications of the measure in social terms or in the context of pre-existing related law
- where the measure is technically complex as in, for example, much taxation legislation, the legislators may not fully understand it themselves
- the attempt to make detailed provision will involve complex language and constructions which will need close scrutiny
- an acknowledgement that it is impossible to anticipate and cover every eventuality and that having established the general principle the courts should be left to apply it.

The difficulty that these shortcomings produce can present the courts with considerable difficulty. The judges must try to find the meaning of what Parliament has said but the meaning will often be far from clear and so inevitably a judge who responds positively may be said to be making law to a greater or lesser extent.

SELF-CHECK 3

Because there is no compulsion upon a judge to use a particular approach, there is no way of anticipating how an individual judge will respond. Perhaps this introduces an arbitrariness and degree of uncertainty into both the contents and application of law.

Think of the literal rule. What is absurd is subjective: Parliament should know what it intends and so why should a judge intervene? If Parliament has made a mistake surely Parliament and not the judges should correct it? At the least this 'rule' makes for greater certainty and it is easier for a judge to follow it.

The response could be that an application of this rule will defeat what everyone believes to be Parliament's intention and so the judges should respond and, anyway, if the words had an ordinary meaning there would never have been a case based on their interpretation in the first place!

In the case of the golden rule the courts endeavour to sort out whatever problems emerge and so save the need for subsequent Parliamentary intervention assuming, of course, that the courts get it right! But, once again, its use is based upon a subjective test of absurdity and it is impossible to tell in advance when the rule will be applied.

Judges tend to be conservative by nature and to act in a predictable and 'safe' manner. They usually adopt an approach that will not leave them open to criticism and so the literal rule will have a great deal to recommend it to most judges who will not enjoy having their decisions reversed or overruled.

Much will depend upon the character of the judge and the extent to which he or she acknowledges that there is a problem of interpretation and is then prepared to deal with it in a positive manner.

SELF-CHECK 4

The 'ruler' must be the person who makes the rules and, as we have seen, in this country rules are made by Parliament. It follows therefore that in the context of Lord Diplock's dictum the 'ruler himself' means Parliament and all the various departments and agencies deriving their authority from Parliament.

The 'Crown' has a very similar meaning although it can also mean the monarch in person. It refers to the titular Head of State, whoever he or she might be at any particular time, in whose name the agencies of the State often act. For example, prosecutions are brought in the name of the Crown by the Crown Prosecution Service.

SELF-CHECK 5

Certainty does have a lot to recommend it but the present system can mean that the law can become fossilised. Change depends upon:

- Parliament finding time to pass legislation, or
- the chance of a particular issue coming before the courts and the parties having the resources, time and enthusiasm to pursue the case to the House of Lords which might or might not then decide to use the Practice Statement.

It all seems a bit hit and miss and law is being made at the expense of individual litigants. Why not let the process be carried on at an early stage in the Court of Appeal? The Court of Appeal is comprised of very senior judges who could be trusted to exercise a greater flexibility with discretion. It is the final court of appeal for most people and allowing it to depart from its own precedents would therefore effect the rigidity inherent in any system relying upon precedent.

Just as the House of Lords is sparing in its use of the practice statement the Court of Appeal could be similarly cautious and apply the same criteria. There have been cases in which the Court of Appeal has been rebuked by the House of Lords for having attempted to depart from its own precedents only to be told that what it sought was correct and then implemented by the House itself.

Although the Court of Appeal should be restrained from departing from House of Lords precedents there is a good case to be made for it being able to depart from its own.

SECTION THREE

The Courts and Tribunals

This section deals with the courts and other bodies that have been established to resolve disputes. When you have completed the section you will be able to:

- describe the different roles of the civil and criminal courts
- describe the hierarchical structure of the courts
- explain in which court a particular case will be heard
- analyse the difference between a court and a tribunal in terms of function, powers, composition and procedure
- explain what is meant by arbitration and by mediation and what each involves
- discuss the factors which the parties take into account in deciding which forum to use where they have a choice.

In Sections One and Two we frequently referred to the courts and their role in the legal system of this country. We have seen that they play a significant part in the continuing development of the law. In this section we look at the courts in greater detail.

Sometimes a court is not considered appropriate for the resolution of a dispute. It may be dealt with by a tribunal or, perhaps, the parties might wish to use some entirely different means such as agreeing to submit to the findings of an arbitrator. Alternatively they may wish to avoid handing the determination of their dispute to a third party but may prefer instead to come to their own settlement with the help of a mediator.

The next two pages simply illustrate graphically the hierarchical structure of the courts. You will notice that although the civil and criminal courts are different from each other, they share the same final court of appeal.

Possible classifications

Some courts are courts of first instance only, another way of saying they are only trial courts and they do not hear appeals from other courts. Magistrates' courts are courts of first instance only.

Other courts only have appellate jurisdiction, that is, they only hear appeals. The House of Lords is such a court.

The High Court and the County Court provide examples of courts with dual jurisdiction.

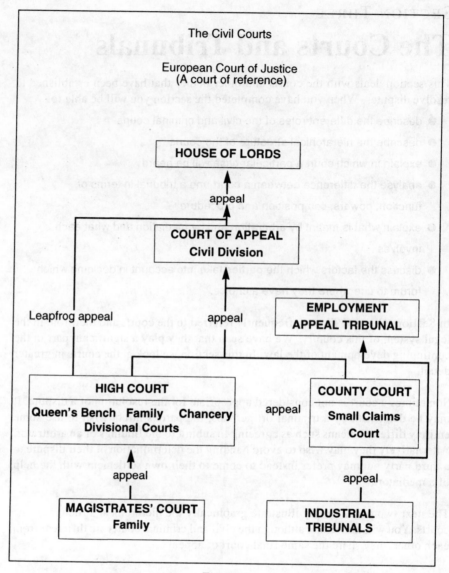

Figure 1

Courts may also be classified as being either superior courts or inferior courts.

Superior courts have unlimited jurisdiction and can make binding precedents, eg., the House of Lords, the Court of Appeal, the High Court and the crown court.

Inferior courts are subject to the supervisory jurisdiction of the High Court. This means the High Court has power to intervene in their proceedings if they are breaking their own rules or are acting in excess of their powers. Such courts include county courts and the magistrates' courts.

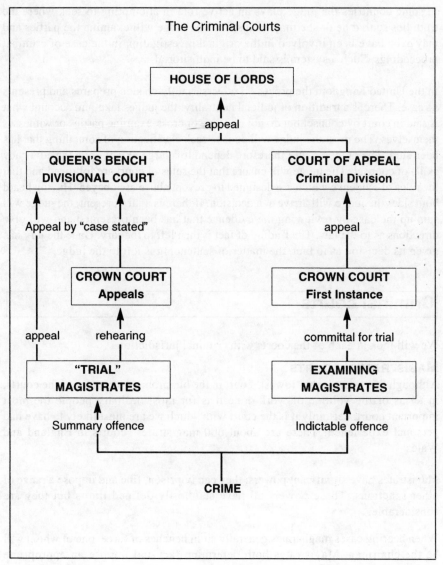

Figure 2

The legal process

We need to think about the purpose of the legal process:

● is it to discover the truth?
● is it a fair system with evidence being presented by each side which is open to challenge by the other?

In some countries the judge plays an active role in attempting to seek where the truth lies so that he or she may do justice. The judge will examine the parties and may even have been involved in the original investigation in the case of criminal proceedings. Such a system is said to be inquisitorial.

In the United Kingdom the process is adversarial. Each side prepares and presents its case. There is a tradition of judicial neutrality: the judges take into account what is said in court by counsel but do not examine or cross-examine parties or witnesses themselves. The most the judge will do is to seek clarification of something that has been said. The outcome will therefore depend to a large extent upon the advocacy skills of counsel. The judge will ensure that the rules of court are followed and that the rules of evidence which are designed to prevent abuse are obeyed. Having heard both sides the judge will arrive at a decision. If there is a jury present, the judge will sum up the case by reviewing the evidence that has been presented and will give directions as to the law. The finding of fact is then left to the jury. Once the jury has given its decision as to fact, the matter of sentencing is left to the judge.

Criminal courts

We will look at each of the courts with criminal jurisdiction.

MAGISTRATES' COURTS

Although this court is the 'lowest' court in the hierarchical structure of the courts, in terms of the volume of work done it is for most ordinary people the most important court: certainly it is the court with which we are most likely to have had personal experience! There are about 600 magistrates' courts in England and Wales.

Magistrates have significant powers: they can imprison, fine and impose a range of other sanctions. These powers all have statutorily defined limits but they are considerable.

When hearing cases magistrates generally sit in benches of three, one of whom will be the chairman. Magistrates both determine fact and impose an appropriate sanction. They are assisted by a clerk to the justices who will be a qualified lawyer to advise them as necessary in legal matters.

The two key functions are to conduct summary trials and to deal with committal proceedings.

TYPES OF OFFENCES

To understand what is meant by summary trial and committal proceedings we must look at the way crimes are categorised. Under the Criminal Justice Act 1977 all crimes are either:

- indictable, or
- summary, or
- triable either way

It is this categorisation that determines the mode of trial.

Indictable offences must be tried in a crown court by a judge and jury. The most serious offences fall into this category, eg., murder, manslaughter, rape, blackmail, etc. The indictment is the formal document which states the charge the defendant is to answer at the crown court.

Summary offences must be tried summarily by magistrates. These are offences which are regarded as being less serious, eg., some public order offences and many road traffic offences.

Offences triable either way can leave the accused with some choice. Not all offences in this category are viewed with the same seriousness. Theft is perhaps the most significant example of an offence in this category.

We will now look in more detail at how the courts deal with each type of offence.

Indictable offences

A person who has been charged with an indictable offence is brought before magistrates for committal proceedings to be held. It must be shown that there is a case to answer. If this is done then the magistrates will commit the defendant for trial at the Crown Court.

Normally committal proceedings are dealt with quickly. This is because the **Magistrates' Courts Act 1980 s.6(2)** provides for committals without consideration of the written evidence that will have been prepared in standard written form. The proceedings are formal but they serve a useful purpose since questions such as bail and legal aid can be determined. Committals of this kind can only be held when the defendant is legally represented and does not claim that there is 'no case to answer.' Not challenging the committal simply acknowledges that there is a prima facie case to answer: it is not an admission of guilt.

It is possible that a defendant will challenge the committal arguing that there is no case to answer. In this case there will be full committal proceedings under the **Magistrates' Courts Act 1980 s.6(1)**. At one time all committals had to take this form which is why today they are sometimes referred to as 'old style committals'. The prosecution must produce sufficient evidence to show that there is a case to answer. Its witnesses will be subject to cross-examination by the defence. What is said by each witness is taken down in writing and signed by the witness. These 'depositions' are sent to the Crown Court if the defendant is committed for trial. Committal proceedings are not a trial and do not establish innocence or guilt. They simply result in a person being either committed for trial or discharged if the magistrates have formed the view that the prosecution have not shown that there is a case to answer. Such proceedings are far more time consuming than those under s.6(2).

A person who has not been committed for trial after such proceedings has not been acquitted and so he or she could be charged with the same offence at some later date if more evidence were to be found. Trials of indictable offences can only be held at a Crown Court and, of course, acquittal there by a jury is final.

The **Criminal Justice and Public Order Act 1994** made provision for the abolition of committal proceedings and for their replacement by a procedure called 'transfer for trial'. This part of the Act has not been given effect and so committal proceedings continue to be held.

Summary offences

Magistrates have exclusive jurisdiction over such offences. They are all the creation of statute since at common law there was always a right to be tried by one's peers, ie., a right to trial by jury. Over the years this right has been removed in respect of 'lesser' offences because it is administratively easier and, certainly, quicker and cheaper to have cases heard by magistrates.

Briefly, at a trial the defendant is asked to plead 'guilty' or 'not guilty'. If the plea is 'not guilty', the trial will commence with the prosecution outlining its case. The prosecution will call its witnesses who will be subject to cross-examination by the defence.

At this stage the defendant may submit that there is no case to answer. If this is not done, or if the submission fails, the defence will then present its case and call its witnesses. These too will be subject to cross-examination by the prosecution.

If the defendant has given evidence and if any other witness has been called, the defence may address the court again. If this happens the prosecution may also speak again just before the defence. So the defence is allowed the last word.

If found guilty the court will have to decide on appropriate sentence. The court will be told of any previous convictions while the defence will introduce evidence of good character. The defence may also make a plea in mitigation.

Magistrates have the support of administrative staff and, in particular, of a clerk to the justices but it is the magistrates who actually make the important decisions.

Offences triable either way

These are offences which can be very serious or quite trivial. In this country we tend to argue by results: a theft of a large sum is regarded as being more serious than a theft of a few pence. Is this reasonable? Is the person who steals the large sum morally more culpable? Defendants who know themselves to be innocent will not regard the accusation of having committed a small theft as being a matter of little importance: their good names and even their livelihoods may be at stake. They will elect to be tried wherever they think they stand the best chance of being acquitted.

If the magistrates decide that the accused should be tried at the crown court then he or she has no choice and will be committed for trial there.

If, on the other hand, the magistrates decide that they will hear the case themselves the accused must be told that he or she may either agree to this or ask for committal to the crown court for trial by jury. Even if he or she agrees to the magistrates hearing the case, it is always possible that after the trial he or she may be committed to the crown court for sentence if the magistrates feel they have insufficient sentencing power to deal with the gravity of the case.

Over 100,000 cases per annum are committed to the crown court, of which 80 per cent are those in which defendants have exercised their right to such a trial.

SELF-CHECK 1

What factors do you think a defendant might take into account when deciding whether to seek trial by jury at the crown court?

APPEAL FROM THE MAGISTRATES' COURT

The first issue to be decided is what is being appealed against. Perhaps the defendant accepts the finding of guilt but considers the sentence imposed is too harsh and so wants to appeal against it.

On the other hand the appeal may be against the conviction itself, in other words, the defendant still claims to be innocent

The grounds of appeal may be that the magistrates were wrong in the determination of fact, were wrong in their application of the law or were wrong on both counts.

Generally appeal lies to the crown court where there can be a rehearing if the appeal is against conviction. The appeal will be heard by a judge sitting with between two and four lay magistrates. The crown court will also review sentence if that is the subject of the appeal although there is no need for a full rehearing.

If it seems that there has been an error of law or some other defect in the proceedings then either the defence or the prosecution can require the magistrates to state a case to the Queen's Bench Divisional Court. An appeal is normally only available to a defendant but this provides the one exception to the rule that the prosecution has no appeal against an acquittal. The magistrates will send a written statement explaining what they did which will be reviewed by the High Court. It is not a rehearing and is decided after scrutiny of the documents submitted and having heard the legal argument by each side. The High Court will then determine the issue and give a ruling. The outcome may be that the magistrates will be told to rehear the case applying the correct law.

ACTIVITY 15

Without looking back in the text, answer the following questions.

Does a failure to commit a person for trial after committal proceedings prevent that person being charged again with the same offence?

Can the prosecution ever appeal against an acquittal?

Now go back to the text to check that your answers are correct.

CROWN COURTS

The crown court is both a trial court and, as we have seen, a court of appeal. The crown court is held in about 90 of the major towns in England and Wales.

We will consider first its role as a trial court.

The crown court as a trial court

When it sits as a trial court there will be a judge and jury present. The judge will preside over the trial to ensure that it is properly conducted in accordance with the rules of the court. The judge will make sure that the rules concerning the admissibility of evidence are correctly followed.

The judge will also have to be mindful of the jury. He or she will advise them as to the law and as to what they should and should not take into account when coming to their decision. Although the actual determination of guilt or innocence is entirely a matter for the jury, before they retire to consider their verdict the judge will assist by summing up the case for them. A summing-up is clearly helpful and necessary after a long and complex trial: the problem is that the summing-up may itself be long and complex!

The crown court will try cases which are regarded as sufficiently serious to be classified as indictable. It also hears those cases which are triable either way which

have been committed to the crown court by the magistrates or at the request of the
defendant.

The crown court as an appeal court

As an appeal court it hears appeals from the magistrates' court. In such cases there
is the possibility of a further appeal to the Divisional Court of the Queen's Bench
Division but only on the grounds that the decision was wrong in law or in excess
of jurisdiction

Obviously a defendant can only appeal against conviction if the plea was 'not
guilty' in the magistrates' court. Whether the plea was guilty or not, appeal can be
made against sentence. There is a risk because the crown court can increase the
sentence that was imposed by the magistrates.

If the appeal is against conviction then the crown court will rehear the case but not
with a jury, instead there will be a judge sitting with between two and four lay
magistrates.

APPEAL FROM THE CROWN COURT

Appeal lies as of right against conviction to the Court of Appeal, Criminal Division,
on a question of law.

If the appeal concerns a question of fact or mixed fact and law then an appeal can
only be made with the leave of the Court of Appeal unless the trial judge has
granted a certificate that the case is fit for appeal.

An appeal against sentence can only be made with the leave of the Court of Appeal.
On such an appeal by the defendant the court cannot increase sentence.

ACTIVITY 16

Close the text and try to recall the composition of the crown court when
sitting a) as a trial court and b) as an appeal court.

Now go back to the text and check how accurate your recall was.

THE COURT OF APPEAL, CRIMINAL DIVISION

This court is presided over by the Lord Chief Justice. The appeal is heard by three
Lords Justices of Appeal. It is not a retrial in the sense that the case is not represented and, for example, witnesses are not called and re-examined. The decision

is reached after having read the papers in the case and listened to counsels' argument.

THE HOUSE OF LORDS

Appeals are usually heard by five Lords of Appeal in Ordinary, the Law Lords. Although this is regarded as the highest court in the land for most people the final court of appeal is the Court of Appeal itself.

Of the 53 cases determined by the House in 1990 only two were criminal cases from the Court of Appeal: hardly a significant number. Before an appeal can be taken to the House of Lords leave must be obtained. Such leave will only be granted if:

- the Court of Appeal certifies that a point of law of general public importance is involved in the decision; AND
- either the Court of Appeal or the House gives leave to appeal on the ground that the point is one which ought to be considered by the House.

The certificate is needed to prevent the House being innundated with hopeless cases.

Civil courts

We will now consider the civil courts beginning once again at the base of the hierarchy.

MAGISTRATES' COURTS

Although we have discussed this court in the context of the criminal law, it has a significant civil role.

The court deals with several administrative matters and, in particular, with licensing the sale of liquor.

Very importantly, there are family proceedings where family matters often involving children are considered. The court has powers over, for example, adoption, residence and contact orders as well as maintenance.

Appeals in family matters lie to the Family Division of the High Court but otherwise appeal generally lies to the crown court.

COUNTY COURTS

These courts were established to provide a forum for local, inexpensive and speedy resolution of disputes. To an extent that remains their function today although because they are so much used it is inevitable that they are no longer particularly cheap or speedy. There are approximately 270 such courts in England and Wales.

The county court and the High Court which have overlapping jurisdiction are the principal civil courts.

The allocation of business between the county court and the High Court is according to the criteria of substance, importance and complexity and judicial availability. In simple terms, for example, an action for a large sum of money which involves the application of complicated legal principles which when decided authoritatively will lead to a clarification of the relevant law is likely to be allocated to the High Court.

As a result of an order made in 1991 to give effect to certain provisions of the Courts and Legal Services Act 1990, the jurisdiction of the county courts has been much enlarged.

The main areas covered by the county courts are:

a) claims founded in contract or tort which will most probably be tried in the county court.

The present position is:

- actions which include a claim for damages for personal injury are commenced in the County Court unless the claim is for £50,000 or more
- actions of which the value is less than £25,000 are to be tried in the county court unless they are more suitable for trial in the High Court
- actions of which the value is £50,000 or more are to be tried in the High Court unless they are more suitable for trial in the county court
- actions of which the value is between £25,000 and £50,000 will be allocated by reference to the criteria.

The courts have power to transfer an action to a more suitable court. In determining whether to transfer an action to the county court from the High Court, the factors to be taken into account include:

- the financial substance of the action
- whether the action is otherwise important and, in particular, whether it raises questions of importance to persons who are not parties or questions of general public interest
- the complexity of the facts, legal issues, remedies or procedures involved, and
- whether transfer is likely to result in a more speedy trial of action.

Certain actions are considered not suitable for tranfer to a county court:

- professional negligence
- fatal accident
- allegations of fraud or undue influence

- defamation
- malicious prosecution or false imprisonment
- claims against the police.

The overall and deliberate effect of transfers is to relieve the High Court of many of the cases it would have heard before the Courts and Legal Services Act 1990 was passed by allocating them to the county court. The result is that the High Court is freed to deal with more important work and to expedite its proceedings.

ACTIVITY 17

Write down the financial criteria for helping determine whether an action based on contract or tort is heard in the county court or High Court. See how far your answer corresponds with that given below.

If the amount in question is less than £25,000 then the case will normally be heard in the county court. If the amount is over £50,000 it will normally be heard in the High Court. For amounts of between £25,000 and £50,000 the case may be heard in either court, regard being given to other specified criteria.

It is to be noted that an action for personal injury for a sum of less than £50,000 is to be commenced in the county court.

b) Actions for the recovery of land or involving title to land regardless of its value.

c) Equity matters such as trusts, mortgages and dissolution of partnerships provided the sum involved does not exceed £30,000.

In addition, some county courts hear insolvency cases and can deal with all company matters where the company concerned has a paid-up capital of less than £120,000.

Other courts are designated as divorce courts and can hear petitions for divorce, nullity of marriage or judicial separation.

SMALL CLAIMS COURTS

Within the county court there is a small claims arbitration service. If your claim is for less than £3,000 it is automatically referred to arbitration in the small claims court. In this event a district judge (formerly known as the county court registrar) who is rather like a deputy county court judge and who has an administrative role will hear the case.

Proceedings are less formal than in the county court proper and they are held in private. Parties are encouraged to represent themselves and the district judge will play a more active part than is usual in trying to discover the truth of the matter. Legal Aid is not available and generally losing parties do not have costs awarded against them, ie., the winners have to pay their own costs which in itself is an incentive not to be represented. All the loser has to pay is the out-of-pocket expenses of the winner, eg., witnesses' fees, loss of earnings.

The overall result is that such arbitration is cheap, speedy and far less daunting than a full trial. The district judge will however determine the case in accordance with the law and he or she can only take into account what has actually been said; in other words the judge's helpfulness and informality can only go so far.

There are many county courts up and down the country and they will be found in most large centres of population. A plaintiff can issue a default summons in any county court but otherwise proceedings must be commenced either in the county court for the district in which the defendant lives or carries on business or in the county court for the district where the cause of action arose.

A default action is one in which the claim is simply for the payment of money.

ACTIVITY 19

Without looking at the text you have just read, list the perceived advantages of arbitration in the small claims court.

Now go back to the text to check the accuracy of your list.

THE HIGH COURT

The High Court is both a trial court and a court of appeal. It sits both in London and in about 25 regional centres.

It comprises three divisions which are:

- Queen's Bench Division
- Family Division
- Chancery Division.

Each division has its own area of jurisdiction and particular expertise.

Each division can sit as a trial court when it has one judge sitting alone who will determine fact and law. Contrast this with the criminal cases in the crown court where there is a judge and jury. (Exceptionally there may be a jury in the Queen's Bench Division.)

Each division can sit as an appeal court when it is referred to as a divisional court. Normally three judges will sit in a divisional court, exceptionally there may be five.

High Court judges are also known as puisne judges (pronounced 'puny'). It means 'younger' and strictly speaking is a reference to any judge of the High Court of Justice who is neither the Lord Chancellor, the Lord Chief Justice nor the President of the Family Division.

Queen's Bench Division

This division is the biggest of the three having more than 60 puisne judges allocated to it. Its jurisdiction is over matters which are not specifically allocated elsewhere.

Its jurisdiction includes: actions based on contract and tort, commercial matters and admiralty cases (eg. salvage).

The most common action in the High Court is for personal injury arising from the tort of negligence.

The Commercial Court is part of the Queen's Bench Division: it is not really a separate court. The judges nominated for the court are specialists in commercial matters. Its jurisdiction includes: banking, insurance, construction of documents such as negotiable instruments and charterparties.

The Family Division

This division is presided over by the President of the Family Division and has less than 20 judges. Its jurisdiction includes: divorce, nullity, children (including wardship and adoption), maintenance & matrimonial property.

The Chancery Division

This division is presided over by the Vice-Chancellor who sits together with some 15 judges. Company business is assigned to a separate court within the Chancery Division called the Company Court.

Its jurisdiction includes: land, mortgages & trust matters, revenue law, partnership, rectification of deeds and documents, administration of estates and contentious probate, insolvency, intellectual property.

SELF-CHECK 2

Explain why you think the High Court sits in three divisions.

THE HIGH COURT AS AN APPEAL COURT

The Divisional Court of the Queen's Bench hears appeals 'case stated' on points of law from the magistrate's court and the county court. It also hears appeals from various tribunals.

It has a supervisory jurisdiction over inferior tribunals. It can conduct judicial review.

Application for judicial review can only be made with leave. The Court will literally review what the body has done and, if need be, issue an order to remedy the matter. Judicial review is only available against the Crown or public authorities, not against private persons or bodies. It is concerned with the way in which a decision was reached rather than with the decision itself.

There are three basic grounds:

● illegality: where there has been an error of law, eg., if a body purports to exercise a power which it does not possess

● irrationality: where an authority has acted so unreasonably that no reasonable authority would have made the decision, 'a decision which is so outrageous in its defiance of logic or of accepted moral standards that no sensible person who had applied his mind to the question to be decided could have arrived at it', per Lord Diplock, **CCSU v Minister for the Civil Service** [1984] 3 All ER 951

● procedural impropriety: where the authority has failed to act fairly, for example, by a violation of the rules of natural justice such as not hearing both parties to a dispute.

SELF-CHECK 3

Explain what you think the difference is between an appeal and judicial review.

The Divisional Court of the Family Division hears appeals from the magistrates court in matrimonial and family matters. The appeal is usually heard by a single judge.

The Divisional Court of the Chancery Division hears appeals from the county court in matters such as bankruptcy and land registration.

Appeals from the High Court on either fact or law may be taken as of right to the Court of Appeal, Civil Division. The sanction against frivolous appeals lies in costs.

The Administration of Justice Act 1969 Sections 12-15 introduced a 'leapfrog' procedure: with leave, the appeal can bypass the Court of Appeal and go directly to the House of Lords. The conditions are:

a) the agreement of the parties;

b) that it involves a point of law of general public interest concerning the construction of a statute or where the trial judge was bound by a precedent of the Court of Appeal or the House of Lords, certified as such by the trial judge. This certification is discretionary and no appeal is possible against its grant or refusal; and

c) the leave of the House of Lords is necessary.

It is appropriate where the House of Lords might overrule because the Court of Appeal cannot do so and, if a case is destined to go to the Lords for a decision, why waste time and money in the Court of Appeal? In practice the provision is little used.

THE COURT OF APPEAL, CIVIL DIVISION
The Master of the Rolls presides over the Civil Division.

The Civil Division is a busy court which usually sits in benches of three judges, sometimes five.

It hears appeals from all divisions of the High Court, the county court on points of fact or law, the Employment Appeal Tribunal, the Restrictive Practices Court, the Land Tribunal etc. In all it hears about 800 appeals each year.

It has power to:

- make any order that should have been made in the court below
- deal with points not raised in the trial
- order a re-trial
- substitute its own order as to liability, damages, etc., except where a jury has made the award.

THE HOUSE OF LORDS

It comprises the Lord Chancellor with between seven and twelve Lords of Appeal in Ordinary.

It hears appeals from the Court of Appeal and from the High Court under the 'leapfrog' procedure. It is also the final court of appeal for Scotland and Northern Ireland.

It hears appeals from the Divisional Courts of the High Court directly: they do not go via the Court of Appeal.

The Lords is not really a recourse of justice for the individual since there is no right of appeal. An appeal must be on a point of law and must be with leave: the point of law must be of general public importance

It is really the custodian of the common law.

Costs are very high and leave is by no means always granted: the Lords hear, say, 75 cases each year. Most cases going to the Lords involve large commercial organisations or the Inland Revenue where there is a need to establish just what the law really is on a particular point.

The hearing is not a re-trial: no oral evidence is given. The judges read all the documents in the case and listen to counsels' arguments. Since 1963 judgements have not been delivered orally but are handed to the parties and their counsel already printed.

ACTIVITY 19

Write down the routes of appeal from a decision of the High Court stating when an appeal may be made as of right. See how far your answer corresponds with that given below.

Normally appeal from the High Court lies to the Court of Appeal, Civil Division and appeal may be made as of right on a question of fact or of law. Exceptionally, by virtue of the Administration of Justice Act 1969 Sections 12–15, an appeal may be taken directly from the High Court to the House of Lords. For this to happen the parties must agree and the House of Lords must give leave, which it will only grant if there is a point of law of general public importance at issue.

THE JUDICIAL COMMITTEE OF THE PRIVY COUNCIL

The Judicial Committee of the Privy Council comprises of Law Lords together with senior judges from the country from which the appeal has been sent.

It hears appeals from certain Commonwealth countries who have for various reasons chosen to keep it as their final court of appeal, eg., Bermuda, Jamaica, Hong Kong, New Zealand, the Seychelles.

It also hears appeals from various disciplinary tribunals against the erasure of names from a professional register. Those with such a right of appeal include medical practitioners, dentists, opticians and veterinary surgeons.

Because of its composition, the Committee is strongly influential on English law.

THE EUROPEAN COURT OF JUSTICE

The court of the European Union was established under Article 164 of the Treaty of Rome. Its jurisdiction is in matters arising from the European Union, its treaties, directives, etc.

It is a court of reference, not appeal. Article 177 gives the terms of referral: a whole case is not referred but a particular point is referred for a ruling which the domestic court then applies. It is thus a part of our legal system but outside the mainstream.

There is one judge from each Member State and the president of the court is chosen by the judges from among their own number. The court is assisted by six advocates-general.

An advocate-general is assigned to each case and delivers an opinion as to the issues it raises and a reasoned conclusion. This opinion will not be binding on the court but it will be taken into account by the court in reaching its decision.

Its jurisdiction is quite wide. It hears complaints that a Member State has not fulfilled its obligations under the treaties, decides upon the legality of the actions of the Council of Ministers and the Commission and decides disputes between Members States about the subject matter of the treaties.

SELF-CHECK 4

Explain whether or not you think that the status given to the European Court represents a departure from anything known to the British constitution.

Article 177 makes two points:

- the highest court of a Member State must refer any point of European law about which it is in dispute before such national court where there is uncertainty as to the correct interpretation;
- a national court below the highest has a discretion to refer a point of European law in such circumstance.

Tribunals

Not all disputes are resolved in the courts of law. There is elaborate provision for certain disputes to be heard by tribunals while others may be decided by arbitration or mediation.

In the absence of a provision to the contrary all disputes are to be settled by the courts but increasingly such contrary provision has been made. There has been a great increase in their use since the Second World War. With the advent of the welfare state there has been a growing list of benefits to which an individual might be entitled. Clearly disputes arise as to whether there is a right to such benefits: many tribunals have been created especially to deal with such disputes.

Other tribunals have been charged with dealing with other areas of life in which problems arise, for example, rent tribunals, land tribunals and, very importantly, industrial tribunals.

Administrative tribunals are so described because they are not presided over by a judge but they are now often quasi-judicial in their practices. Each tribunal has its own composition, procedures and rights of appeal which are determined by statute but they do have features in common.

The usual common features of tribunals are:

- a three person panel with a legally qualified chairman
- no restrictions on rights of audience
- no legal aid available
- inquisitorial approach
- informality.

Legislation has helped make tribunal procedure and practice more uniform than was the case when they first came into existence. In particular:

- hearings are held in public unless there is a compelling reason for privacy such as national security
- reasoned decisions are given if requested
- appeal on points of law lies from most tribunals to the Divisional Court of the Queen's Bench. The tribunal remains the only decider of fact.

The main benefits of tribunals are:

- relative informality
- cheapness
- speed
- specialisation since each tribunal deals with a narrow band of cases
- the volume of work undertaken thereby relieving the courts.

There is a Council on Tribunals, a sort of watch-dog body with between 10 and 15 members appointed by the Lord Chancellor and the Secretary of State. It keeps all scheduled tribunals under review and reports on them from time to time. Its reports are laid before Parliament annually.

Tribunals are thus under the supervisory jurisdiction of the courts through judicial review and because there is often a right of appeal to the courts and they are subject to Parliamentary scrutiny.

Let us consider one of many tribunals: the industrial tribunal.

Originally established in 1964 to deal with disputes arising in connection with employers' liability to pay a levy to the Industrial Training Boards, the tribunals now deal with a variety of matters including redundancy payments, equality clauses under equal pay legislation, unfair dismissal and complaints of unlawful racial discrimination in employment.

More than 80 industrial tribunals sit every working day and this fact alone underlines their importance. More than two-thirds of cases involve claims of unfair dismissal.

Predictably there is a legally qualified chairman, a lawyer of at least seven years standing. The lay members on the tribunal are representatives of each 'side' of industry, perhaps a trade union official and a representative of an employers' organisation. There are panels made up of such people who are asked to sit as the occasion arises.

Legal aid is not available and costs are not usually awarded unless a party has acted frivolously.

Statute has given the tribunal a number of special powers. It can, for example, in the context of unfair dismissal order reinstatement, re-engagement and award compensation.

The compensation can build up to be quite a large sum. There will be a basic award calculated by reference to length of service in much the same way as redundancy pay is calculated. In addition there can be a compensatory award assessed as for breach of contract.

Then there may be a special award which arises where re-engagement or reinstatement has been ordered after unfair dismissal in connection with trade union activities or for not being in a union but the order has been disobeyed.

Finally there could be an additional award where an order to re-engage or reinstate has been disobeyed for reasons other than those giving rise to special awards

Industrial tribunals provide an example of a tribunal having its own appeal route. Appeal lies to the Employment Appeal Tribunal. Despite its name this is, in fact, a superior court of record. It consists of Court of Appeal and High Court judges nominated by the Lord Chancellor with lay members appointed by the Queen on the joint recommendation of the Lord Chancellor and the Secretary of State for Employment. An appeal is heard by a judge sitting with two or four lay members.

The procedure once again is relatively quick and cheap as well as informal. Strict rules of evidence do not apply and there are no restrictive rights of audience.

A decision of the Employment Appeal Tribunal on fact is final but appeal lies to the Court of Appeal on a question of law although leave to appeal is required.

ACTIVITY 20

Without looking back in the text write down the main benefits of tribunals and their usual features.

Now go back in the text and see if what you wrote down included the most important points.

Arbitration

This provides a useful way of resolving civil disputes without resorting to court action. An appropriately qualified person agreed upon by the parties to the dispute is appointed by them to decide the issue in contention.

The parties must agree to arbitration. Such an agreement can be inserted into the agreement when the contract is made. Arbitration clauses may be found in standard form contracts such as holiday contracts. In the commercial world they are common in certain contracts, for example, they are found in Royal Institute of British Architects contracts in the building industry. Alternatively the agreement to go to arbitration might be made when a dispute arises.

Arbitration is good when the parties genuinely agree to it and they are of equal power.

Arbitration offers:

- privacy
- speed
- cheapness
- expertise
- a great deal more convenience than a legal action.

It follows that there can only be very limited rights of appeal: after all, if following arbitration a party appeals to the courts much of the original merit in using arbitration in the first place is lost.

Legal aid is not available.

The Arbitration Act 1979 provides for the possibility of appeal on a point of law only to the Divisional Court of the Queen's Bench but only with the agreement of the parties or the leave of the court. Once an arbitration has commenced the parties can agree to exclude even this possibility of appeal.

Arbitration is subject to judicial review but this does not affect the finding of fact. An award could be set aside on a procedural ground such as delay, bias or misconduct.

The issues must be decided according to ordinary rules of English law unless agreed otherwise and normal judicial procedures apply but these too are often dispensed with by agreement. Proceedings are nearly always before a single arbitrator who decides fact and law. It is normal for the arbitration clause to refer the nomination of the arbitrator to an independent body such as the Royal Institute of British Architects or for it to be agreed between the parties. An arbitrator might typically be a barrister or a member of the Chartered Institute of Arbitrators and drawn from one of its specialist panels.

Mediation

It is becoming an increasingly common practice for industry and commerce to use the services of a mediator to resolve disputes.

Mediation has many of the advantages of arbitration in terms of privacy, speed, cheapness and convenience but it is fundamentally different. With arbitration, as with proceedings before a court or tribunal, the parties are placing the dispute before a third party and asking that third party to adjudicate and so determine the issue for them.

A mediator brings the parties together, hears statements from both sides to help clarify what the real issue is and then acts as a go-between.

The mediator will speak to each side separately and try to find areas of agreement and to discover what kind of compromise each is prepared to make. The aim will be to discover what settlement each is willing to accept. Proceedings can be conducted in a calm and non-confrontational atmosphere in which parties are not driven into entrenched positions.

The mediator does not impose a settlement but merely facilitates the parties coming to their own mutually agreed settlement.

It is quite possible that a commercial relationship will survive a dispute that has been settled by mediation but this is not likely to be the case where a case has been heard before a court.

Since much litigation is settled at the door of the court after a considerable expenditure of time, money and distraction, it seems sensible to save a great deal of trouble and to proceed straight to a mediated settlement.

Summary of section three

- In this section we have examined the various fora provided for the resolution of dispute. Each has its own special function, powers, composition and procedure. Most are provided by the state which recognises that we all have an interest in differences being settled in a proper and peaceful manner.

- It is important to remember that often the individual has no choice as to where a case is heard. Criminal cases are referred to the appropriate criminal court and choice is limited to a person charged with an offence 'triable either way' being able to elect trial by jury.

- If a civil action is to be heard in the courts then it will be allocated to either the High Court or the county court in accordance with known criteria. If a claim is commenced in the county court for a sum of less than £3,000 then it is automatically referred to the small claims court. Certain types of claims are allocated by statute to designated tribunals and claimants cannot elect to have the case heard by the courts instead. This might be taken to indicate that there is no choice available to the individual in civil actions but this is not entirely true.

- The real choice for parties to a civil dispute is whether to use the courts at all with all the consequent delay, expense and inconvenience. For many people arbitration seems an attractive alternative. It still involves giving to another person the task of deciding the issue but at least the parties have a say in the selection of that person.

● Finally the parties may decide to use a mediator. At the end of the day every dispute needs to be settled. Successful mediation allows the parties to resolve the dispute for themselves and since it is their own resolution it is far more likely to be accepted than anything that is imposed.

Suggested answers to section three self-check questions

SELF-CHECK 1

There is a general belief that there is a better chance of acquittal by a jury. There is no evidence to suggest that this is true.

Juries are made up of ordinary men and women who are perhaps not as case-hardened or prosecution-minded as many magistrates are thought to be. It is questionable whether this perception of magistrates is fair. The defendant might hope that the jury members will be lenient recognising that things that they have done could easily have put them in the dock in the past! Certainly on occasions juries do seem to give remarkably perverse decisions and so a defendant might hope to be a beneficiary of such a decision.

There is some attraction in the thought of being tried by one's peers chosen at random from the list of registered electors. If, however, the members of the jury are present unwillingly, are not really capable of following all that is said and are likely to be unduly swayed by a persuasive advocate then it cannot be predicted whether the prosecution or defence will benefit most from the presence of a jury.

For the guilty defendant the delay before a case comes to trial in the crown court may be useful since at the very least it puts off the day of reckoning.

An acquittal by a jury is final whereas there may be an appeal case stated by the prosecution against an acquittal by magistrates in some situations.

Summary trial is quicker, shorter and cheaper.

SELF-CHECK 2

The original reasons were historic and were a result of the merging of a number of specialist courts under the Judicature Acts 1873-1875 to form the High Court. For example, the work of the old Court of Chancery was taken over by the Chancery Division of the then new High Court. It is this specialism that remains the justification for there being three divisions.

It is very convenient to allocate business to a division where there will be a body of judges with particular expertise and knowledge of the law concerned. Law is such a vast subject that it is not reasonable to expect judges to have the same high level of expertise in all its aspects.

If there were not three divisions judges could still specialise and handle only cases of a particular nature but this would be less administratively convenient than the present arrangements.

SELF-CHECK 3

When there is a appeal the case itself is reconsidered. The evidence may be re-examined or the court may consider whether or not the law has been correctly interpreted and applied.

The appeal court may alter the decision of the court from which the appeal has been made. For example, the court may find that evidence upon which the lower court relied was unreliable and so the outcome is entirely different.

In judicial review the actual decision is not considered or reviewed. The court is concerned with how the inferior court or body has conducted itself. The court will examine whether the court acted properly within its jurisdiction. The outcome may be that the lower court is ordered to reconsider the case taking into account the findings of the judicial review. For example, a court might be ordered to rehear a case and to admit evidence that it had previously improperly excluded. The main concern is therefore with procedure.

As far as the litigant is concerned the result of the two processes may seem very similar.

SELF-CHECK 4

Not only does the European Union have constitutional documents, the treaties, but there is a court which can test the validity of the actions of the legislature in the context of the treaties.

In the United Kingdom there is no written constitution against which the validity of the acts of the legislature can be tested.

In addition the doctrine of the supremacy of Parliament means that even when a particular statute is enacted it cannot be challenged however fundamental a change it makes to what everybody previously believed the constitutional position to be.

It also grants authority to an outside body to take decisions which are binding on our courts.

SECTION FOUR
Legal Personnel and Legal Aid

This Section aims to acquaint you with some of the personnel who are to be found in the legal system and to provide a brief introduction to legal aid. When you have completed this section you will be able to:

- describe and assess the contribution lay people make to the legal system
- describe the different roles of solicitors and barristers and discuss the advantages and disadvantages of having a legal profession with two separate branches
- explain what is meant by the briefing system
- identify the judges at different levels of the judiciary
- describe the functions of judges and appraise the manner in which they discharge their duties
- discuss the problems of judicial selection
- outline the main sources of legal advice, assistance and aid for those who cannot afford it for themselves and comment upon the adequacy of such sources.

The processes of the law are elaborate and as the population has grown and society become more complex it is questionable whether or not the system is capable of dealing properly with the volume of work it is given. Do we need more lawyers, more judges and more courts? If justice is to be done, do we need freer access to the courts? Approaching a solicitor may be regarded as a rather daunting prospect by many ordinary people and yet their advice may be critically important. There seems to be a very large number of people involved in the administration of law making a variety of contributions. We need to look at just what these people do and to strip them of their 'mystique'.

Obtaining legal assistance and taking a case to court can be expensive. In itself this understandably deters many people from going to a solicitor. If a person cannot afford access to the law then the rights and remedies it offers are of little use. We will see how effectively this problem is addressed.

THE ROLE OF THE LAY PERSON
The English legal system appears to be dominated by the professional lawyers such as solicitors, barristers and the judges. Few would challenge this perception but we must not lose sight of the contribution made by lay people.

Lay people become magistrates, sit on juries and are to be found as members of many tribunal panels.

Magistrates

There are about 30,000 magistrates in England and Wales and they sit in about 600 magistrates courts. They are also known as Justices of the Peace.

THE APPOINTMENT OF MAGISTRATES

They are appointed in the name of the Queen by the Lord Chancellor in consultation with a local advisory committee.

Every county has such a committee normally chaired by the Lord-Lieutenant of the county. In addition there are a number of sub-committees within each area. The membership of the committee remains private so that it can take decisions without being subjected to lobbying or other pressure. The committee members are almost invariably existing magistrates. This makes the magistracy a self-perpetuating body.

Names are suggested by groups such as political parties, trade unions, the churches and chambers of commerce. It is possible for the committees to advertise inviting the members of the public to put forward either themselves or those they know. Magistrates tend to appoint others like themselves and so any change in the character of the magistracy will be slow.

Certain people will not be appointed for various reasons, some of which are self-evident including:

- those who have been convicted of a serious offence
- those who are undischarged bankrupts
- police officers or traffic wardens
- those over sixty years of age.

Magistrates will need to be recognised as 'respectable' members of the community.

They must live within 15 miles of the area for which they are commissioned.

SELF-CHECK 1

What do you think the 'self-evident' reasons are why the four categories of people mentioned above will not be appointed to the bench?

TRAINING

On appointment magistrates take part in a year-long training programme when they will attend lectures given by the clerk to the justices covering both general legal topics and those of special relevance to the magistracy. During the year they will visit prisons, detention centres and remand centres. Most importantly new magistrates sit in court as observers to learn what will be expected of them. None of this is expected to give a detailed knowledge of the law itself.

Refresher training is also required – up to twelve hours every three years.

FINANCIAL AND EMPLOYMENT CONSIDERATIONS

Magistrates are not paid. The result is that being a magistrate can impose a difficult financial burden which prevents many people from allowing their names to go forward. To overcome this problem, at least in part, magistrates are paid for loss of earnings, travel expenses and subsistence.

The Employment Protection (Consolidation) Act 1978 provides that employers must allow employees time off to perform their magisterial duties.

RETIREMENT

At the age of seventy they are placed on the 'supplemental list'. They retain the right to put JP after their names. Thereafter they may only perform a minor administrative role: they no longer sit in court.

THE ROLE OF THE MAGISTRATE

Magistrates exercise summary criminal jurisdiction, that is, hear summary offences and offences triable either way which are dealt with summarily.

They conduct the committal proceedings for those accused of indictable offences.

They exercise some civil jurisdiction and deal with certain administrative matters.

They sit with the crown court judge when the crown court is hearing an appeal or is dealing with a committal for sentence.

The magistracy makes a major contribution to the working of the legal system. There can be little doubt that most magistrates take their duties seriously but some criticisms may be made.

Criticisms of the magistracy include:
- magistrates are drawn from a too limited section of the community and may be characterised as white, middle-aged and middle class
- that their appointment is political in character in that their names are suggested by groups with particular vested interests
- that they are dominated by the clerks to the justices
- that they do not know substantive law
- that they become 'case hardened' and 'prosecution minded'.

The extent to which these criticisms are justified is the subject of much debate. It would be unfair to suggest that the vast majority have anything other than the best of motives or behave with anything other than complete integrity. Whether the system could be improved is another question.

ACTIVITY 21

Close the text and try to recall the principal functions of magistrates.

Now go back to the text and check how accurate your recall was.

Juries

There is a long tradition of using juries in this country although as we have seen, in practice, the vast majority of criminal trials are conducted by magistrates and not before a jury. The idea of being tried by one's peers, ordinary people with a fund of common sense, remains very appealing for most of us.

COMPOSITION OF JURIES

Anyone may be a juror who

- is between eighteen and seventy years of age (people over 65 are
  excusable as of right),
- has been ordinarily resident in the UK for any period of at least five years
  since the age of thirteen, and
- is registered as a parliamentary or local government elector.

Certain people are disqualified.

These include:

- those who have ever been sentenced to five years imprisonment or more
- those who have in the past ten years in the UK served any part of a
  prison sentence
- those who have in the past five years been placed on probation.

Certain people are ineligible.

These include:

- those who have certain occupations, mainly concerned with the administration of justice, such as judges, Justices of the Peace, chairmen of tribunals, members of the legal professions and police officers
- those who are mentally ill.

Certain people may be excused as of right.

These include:

- those whose jobs involve them in state duties or with the relief of pain and suffering, such as, Members of Parliament, members of the armed forces, practising doctors, dentists, nurses and vets.

ACTIVITY 22

Without looking back in the text, write down who can serve as a juror, who is disqualified and who is ineligible.

Now go back to the text and see if what you wrote down included the most important points.

There may also be a discretionary excusal if a person can show a 'good reason' on a particular occasion, such as, illness or holiday commitments.

A person who sits on a jury when disqualified may be fined up to £2,000 and a person who fails to turn up when summoned or who is unfit to serve due to drink or drugs may be fined up to £400.

SELF-CHECK 2

Explain whether you think this list of those who are disqualified, ineligible or who may be excused is reasonable.

CHALLENGES

Any or all jurors may be challenged for cause, that is, either side may claim that there is a good reason why a particular person should not serve on the jury. Any such challenge is tried as a preliminary matter by the trial judge.

The prosecution can require that a juror 'stand-by', that is, the person stands down and so does not serve on that particular jury. This is a considerable power because the inquiry into the reason for a juror being stood-by is postponed until a later date. If there are enough qualified people present to make up the jury the trial proceeds without the person stood-by and so the prosecution's cause is never investigated.

JURY VETTING

There are three basic principles concerning jury selection:

● the jury should be chosen at random

● only matters in the Juries Act 1974 should disqualify a person from jury service

● the correct way for the prosecution to exclude a prospective juror is to 'stand him by' or to challenge for cause.

Vetting does however take place. It takes the form of checking police criminal records and Special Branch records. The prosecution can stand-by a person without a reason being given in open court but this should not be done unless the check reveals a good basis to believe he or she might be a security risk or influenced in respect of the verdict. If the check shows the juror might be biased against the accused the defence should be warned. Such vetting does at least help eliminate the disqualified.

Vetting should not be used to discover and eliminate from a jury people of, say, particular political persuasions or religious beliefs.

MAJORITY VERDICTS

In crown courts a majority verdict is acceptable if:

● there are not less than eleven jurors and ten agree, or

● there are ten jurors and nine agree.

The judge must encourage the jury to make a unanimous finding and there must be at least two hours deliberation before the judge may direct them as to the possibility of a majority verdict.

ACTIVITY 23

Write down the single basic principle upon which jury selection is based. See how far your answer corresponds with that given below.

The basic principle is random selection. It is not open to either side to seek to influence the composition of a jury in the hope that it will thereby obtain one that will view its case with sympathy. Although there can be challenges for cause it is not possible to challenge a juror on the grounds of, say, gender, age, religious affiliation or ethnic origin.

THE JURY'S FUNCTION

Jurors are said to be essentially judges of fact but in reality the decision is on mixed fact and law. They listen to both sides, to the trial judge's summing up and to any directions he may give on the law.

Their proceedings are secret and their verdict is final.

It is a contempt of court to seek to find out how the jury arrived at its decision. There is no way of knowing whether an individual jury has behaved conscientiously or casually. Perhaps sometimes they are dominated by one strong-minded juror who leads the jury to a decision with which many of the jurors are uneasy. It cannot be said with certainty that the jury pays attention to what the judge says in the summing-up. Certainly on occasions juries have given apparently perverse decisions. The fear is that a juror who is reluctantly present will have an interest in the jury coming to a prompt decision just to be released to go home. Nothing is known about the intellectual capabilities of jurors who may have sat through the trial without really understanding the proceedings at all.

On the other hand juries may be very efficient and fair. It seems regrettable that the law prevents real research into this question. It would help decide whether jury trial should be kept.

JURIES IN CIVIL TRIALS

The use of juries in civil trials is now very rare.

Under the Supreme Court Act 1981 there is a right to trial by jury in four situations:

- fraud
- defamation
- malicious prosecution
- false imprisonment.

Even in these cases the court may order that the trial is to be before a judge alone, for example, if the case requires a lengthy examination of accounts and documents or a scientific or local investigation which would be complicated with a jury.

The most frequent use is in actions founded on defamation.

A jury is possible in other civil actions but there is no 'right' to have one. They should not be used in personal injury cases where the aim is to achieve uniformity, assessability and predictability of damages awarded: best achieved by a judge alone. They might be used in exceptional circumstances where, for example, there is substantial doubt about facts.

Members of tribunals

One of the merits of the present extensive use of tribunals is that they offer specialist skills and knowledge of the matters within their particular jurisdiction. This specialism is normally supplied by laymen who have been recruited to form panels from which tribunal members may be drawn. In this way legally qualified chairmen of tribunals will find thimselves sitting with experts, possibly surveyors, doctors, accountants, trade unionists, business people or whoever the occasion demands.

For example, an industrial tribunal will, for the sake of balance, have two lay people: one who is an employers' representative and one who is an employees' representative. The panels from which they are drawn are appointed by the Secretary of State after consultation with the organisations which represent the employers and the employees. An individual might be asked to sit perhaps twice a month.

ACTIVITY 24

Write down the essential difference between magistrates and tribunal members on one hand and jurors on the other. See how your answer corresponds with that given below.

Magistrates and tribunal members are carefully selected taking into account their various personal characteristics and attributes. Their appointment is of a permanent nature and they will be called upon to sit on a regular basis. Jurors however are chosen at random without any regard to their personal characteristics and so there may be jury members sitting in judgements who would never be considered for the magistracy. They only sit during the limited period of their jury service and will not sit again unless summoned for service as a result of the random selection procedure upon a quite separate, later, occasion.

THE ROLE OF THE PRACTITIONER

The legal profession is divided into two: solicitors and barristers. They perform different functions although you might question whether this division is strictly necessary.

The solicitor

The solicitor is the lawyer who the person in the street will most frequently encounter. The person who needs legal advice or assistance can directly approach a solicitor. There will be solicitors' offices situated in the High Street of almost every town.

THE SOLICITOR'S FUNCTION

A lot of their work is non-contentious, that is, it does not involve disputes and the possibility of consequent court proceedings. It includes the conveyancing of land and probate matters: major sources of work over which, until recently, solicitors enjoyed a monopoly.

The list of other work is long: contracts must be drawn up to regulate all sorts of activity from the purchase of a business to the letting of a flat. Advice has to be given about matters as diverse as the meaning of a holiday booking insurance form or the need for permission to fell a tree in a back garden.

The services of a solicitor are also required when a person is involved in court proceedings. Possibly a person will have been charged with a criminal offence and will need advice and, perhaps, representation in court. Sometimes a client will wish to either bring or defend a civil action, perhaps, in pursuit of a debt or seeking compensation for injury suffered. Until recently solicitors only had a right of audience in the county court and the magistrate's court together with certain limited rights in the the crown court. They could appear, defend and address the crown court in civil and criminal appeals, and in committals for sentence when either the solicitor or his or her partner or employee had appeared for the defendant in the magistrate's court.

Some solicitors specialise in such advocacy.

Under the provisions of the **Courts and Legal Services Act 1990** solicitors' rights of audience were extended in December 1993 so that suitably qualified solicitors will have unrestricted rights of audience in the crown court, the High Court, the Court of Appeal and the House of Lords. They will have to apply for a qualification to appear in the higher courts and will have to demonstrate appropriate advocacy experience, pass various tests and attend advocacy training courses. The majority of solicitors are unlikely to embark upon such a course of action.

If a client requires representation in a court in which his or her particular solicitor has no right of audience then the solicitor will brief a barrister or a qualified solicitor to represent the client. Barristers have a right of audience in all courts.

ACTIVITY 25

Write down the main types of service that a solicitor offers the public. See how your answer corresponds with that given below.

Your list could be long but it should certainly include two major activities – conveyancing of land and dealing with probate, that is, the estates of deceased persons.

There are all sorts of other matters upon which the advice of a solicitor is sought. These can be as varied as contracts, insurance, employer–employee disputes or personal injury.

If a person is contemplating bringing or defending a civil action in court, or is involved in criminal court proceedings, it is almost inevitable that advice will first be sought from a solicitor.

THE SOLICITOR'S TRAINING

First, there is an academic requirement. It is necessary to have a law degree or any degree followed by the Common Professional Examinations. Then there is a year-long legal practice course to be passed. Finally there is a two-year training contract to be undertaken. This is a period of professional practical training under the guidance of an established solicitor. At the end of the training contract the person will be entered on the Roll of Solicitors and will be qualified. The Roll is maintained by the Law Society, the professional body responsible for professional education, standards, conduct, etiquette and discipline.

While the Law Society is the body which represents the interests of the profession it should also protect the public by imposing stringent codes of conduct on its members.

There are more than 60,000 solicitors in practice.

The barrister

Subject to limited exceptions, a barrister may not be approached directly by the client but instead will be briefed by the client's solicitor.

Briefs are the instructions given to barristers to enable them to represent the client in court. Normally they set out the facts of the case and refer to the relevant law.

There will also be copies of material documents, the pleadings and of relevant correspondence. They are intended to put the barrister 'in the picture.'

The first contact the client will have with the barrister may well be at a conference also attended by the solicitor (or a trainee solicitor) just before the case comes to trial.

Unlike solicitors who operate from offices easily accessible to the public and who may form partnerships, barristers operate from chambers on an individual basis. They are actually prohibited by their own rules from entering into partnership with others.

THE BARRISTER'S FUNCTION

Primarily barristers are advocates: they represent their clients in court. Not only must they present their own prepared case but they must have the mental agility to respond to the points made by the opposing side. They must be able to absorb essential information quickly: they may only receive the brief a matter of hours before the case is due to come on. In that time they must familiarise themselves with the client's case and research the necessary areas of law.

Barristers may be involved with the drafting of pleadings, the documents produced by each side for the other side and the court which set out the nature of the claim, defence or counter-claim that each is making. They may also be employed in drafting other legal documents.

Once barristers have acquired an established reputation as experts in a particular aspect of law they may be asked to give opinions. An opinion as to the law concerning the problem confronting a client may cost hundreds or even thousands of pounds but it will indicate what the probable outcome would be if the matter were to be taken to court. This may save the time and cost of going to court needlessly to test the issue and so may be well worthwhile.

QUEEN'S COUNSEL

When barristers consider that they are well advanced in their profession and have a good reputation they can apply to 'take silk' or, in other words, to become Queen's Counsel. Because it is a mark of the recognition of seniority it will mean that they will be able to command higher fees when they appear in court. Queen's Counsel will not normally appear on their own but will have a junior with him or her in court to assist. The client will thus have to pay for two barristers not just one. A junior in this sense is simply a barrister who has not 'taken silk' but may in fact be a distinguished and able barrister of many years standing.

ACTIVITY 26

Without looking back in the text write down three of the services which a barrister might offer.

Now go back to the text and see if what you wrote down was correct.

THE BARRISTER'S TRAINING

After taking a law degree or any degree followed by the Common Professional Examinations, the candidate must take the Bar Finals. The course leading to Bar Finals is run in London where it is limited to about 1,000 candidates each year and in a limited number of regional centres. Next the would-be barrister must obtain 12 months pupillage in chambers. Pupillage is unpaid.

It is not easy to find a place in chambers which combines with the problem of being unpaid to make life at the Bar very difficult for young barristers.

Every barrister is a member of one of the four Inns of Court and as a part of their training candidates for the Bar are required to attend dinners at their Inn of Court. The idea is that it will introduce them to the customs and traditions of the Bar and enable them to meet senior members of the profession.

There are more than 7,500 practising barristers in England and Wales.

The judges

Judges are invariably drawn from the ranks of legal practitioners. It has always been the view of the establishment that experience as a solicitor or a barrister is essential for somebody who is later to adjudicate in a court. In other countries judges are trained from the beginning to be judges: the argument being that quite different skills are needed from those which are required in a good advocate.

All judges need a good knowledge of the law since one of their functions is to rule on points of law as they arise. Unless there is a jury present the judge also determines fact and even if a jury is present the judge must give it appropriate directions.

A judge presides over the court and ensures that justice is both done and is seen to be done. Trials in the United Kingdom are adversarial and so the court adjudicates upon the basis of the arguments put forward by each side. This means that the judge does not have to become involved personally in establishing the facts of a case. Some argue that the courts might be more efficient if the judges adopted an inquisitorial approach and were more interventionist in the course of a trial: a well-timed intervention or astute question from the bench might save a lot of time. A judge needs to be well-educated and wise and must combine courtesy with firmness of character and efficiency. Sadly because judges are human some of these characteristics are only too evidently lacking.

STIPENDIARY MAGISTRATES

In addition to the lay magistrates we have discussed earlier there are more than 60 stipendiary magistrates. They are found in London and in the larger centres of population. They sit alone and perform the same function as a bench of lay magistrates. They work full-time and are paid. A stipendiary is appointed by the Queen on the recommendation of the Lord Chancellor from the ranks of lawyers who have a seven-year general qualification (see below).

RECORDERS

These are part-time circuit judges (see below) appointed by the Queen on the advice of the Lord Chancellor. Unlike other judges their appointment is for a specified period which will however normally be extended from time to time.

CIRCUIT JUDGES

Circuit judges are full-time judges who will be allocated to sit in either the crown court or in the county court. The appointment is full-time and permanent. There are about 500 such judges.

To be considered, a person must have a ten-year crown court or a ten-year county court qualification, or may have been a recorder for three years. Appointment is once again by the Queen on the advice of the Lord Chancellor. Normally a circuit judge will retire at seventy-two but may be removed from office by the Lord Chancellor on the ground of incapacity or misconduct.

HIGH COURT OR PUISNE JUDGES

Justices of the High Court (at present the maximum number is 98) are chosen from among those who have a ten-year High Court qualification or who have been a circuit judge for at least two years.

Normally a High Court judge will be knighted upon appointment which will be made by the Queen on the advice of the Lord Chancellor. A judge will be assigned by the Lord Chancellor to a particular division of the High Court but may sit in any division. The retirement age is seventy-five but otherwise it is very difficult to remove a judge of the supreme court who 'shall hold that office during good behaviour, subject to power of removal by Her Majesty on an address presented to Her by both Houses of Parliament'.

LORD JUSTICES OF APPEAL

These are the Court of Appeal judges (at present the maximum number is 29) who must have a ten-year High Court qualification or must have been a High Court judge. It is possible for a person to be appointed directly to the Court of Appeal without having had previous experience as a judge.

LORDS OF APPEAL IN ORDINARY

The so-called Law Lords (at present the maximum number is 12) who sit in the Judicial Committee of the House of Lords. For practitioners to become Law Lords they must have had a general right of audience in the Supreme Court for fifteen years.

ACTIVITY 27

Write down the principal functions of a judge at a trial. See how your answer corresponds with that given below.

The judge presides at a trial and must see that justice is done and that each side is allowed to make proper representation in accordance with the rules of the court.

The judge must rule on points of law which is one reason why judges are chosen from the ranks of lawyers of proven ability.

Sometimes the judge is left to determine the facts, but where that task is given to a jury it will have the benefit of directions given by the judge.

The question of sentence in criminal cases is left to the judge and in civil cases it is normally the judge who decides what award will be made.

The rules concerning eligibility for appointment are to be found in the Courts and Legal Services Act 1990 Section 71.

The reference to 'qualification' is to the right of audience. Thus a 'crown court qualification' means the possessor has a right of audience in respect of all proceedings in the crown court. A 'general qualification' gives the possessor a right of audience in relation to any class of proceedings in any part of the supreme court, or all proceedings in county courts or magistrate's court.

Since barristers have, by virtue of being barristers, a general qualification they are eligible for appointment to any judicial office. Before the 1990 Act it was impossible for anyone other than a barrister to hold any office higher than that of Circuit Court judge. The Act opens the way for solicitors to be advanced:

a) since solicitors can become circuit judges and someone who has been circuit judge for two years may be appointed a High Court judge, and
b) the Act contemplates solicitors being given greater rights of audience beyond those they enjoy at present.

SELECTION OF JUDGES

We have discussed the eligibility for judicial appointment in purely technical terms but how are judges actually selected?

The entire process is shrouded in secrecy and the role of the Lord Chancellor's Department is pivotal. Don't forget that although the Lord Chancellor is head of the judiciary and the judiciary is meant to be independent, the Lord Chancellor is a member of the Cabinet and is appointed by the Prime Minister of the day.

It is possible to apply to be a recorder or a circuit judge but the names of High Court judges 'emerge': people are invited to say if they would consider accepting appointment. Private records are kept to which the individuals concerned have no access and which may contain inaccuracies which cannot therefore be corrected. Observations and comments are made by existing judges as to the suitability of those who have appeared in their courts for advancement. The consequence is that good barristers who have pressed their client's case forcibly and have irritated the judge may have reduced their chances of being made judges themselves.

The system tends to lead to the appointment of 'safe men' who will conform. The judiciary is made up of those who are predominantly white, male and who are not appointed until middle-age. They tend to have fairly predictably conservative attitudes and to favour the maintenace of the 'status quo'.

Judges have typically been educated at public school followed by Oxford or Cambridge. It would be wrong to suggest that such people are unable to adjudicate fairly but they are not representative of the population as a whole and the system ensures that they are the ones who come forward. Their whole training and experience at the Bar tends to make them conformist. Suggestions that there should be a 'fast-track' for women and members of ethnic minorities to make the judiciary more representative have been rejected.

It has been suggested that the process of selection should be more open. Why not have a selection board to which application could be made for appointment to all levels of the judiciary? Why shouldn't the whole process be carried on out in the open? These ideas too have found little favour. In 1994 a limited change was announced which will involve some lay participation in the selection procedure of judges below the rank of the High Court but the final decision will still rest with the Lord Chancellor's Department.

TRAINING OF JUDGES

Once appointed the training that judges are given is very limited. It is short and given by existing judges.

There is a course for novices – mainly newly appointed recorders – which lasts three days. There are lectures by experienced judges on duties that have to be carried out in court, how to conduct a trial and possible problems. The main focus is on sentencing.

There are some advanced courses for experienced judges to keep them up-to-date with case law and trends in sentencing policy and penology.

Senior judges are not obliged to undertake any refresher training.

SELF-CHECK 3

Given the power and security of tenure that judges enjoy is their selection process reasonable?

Although objectivity is a virtue there is a danger that the gulf between the life experience of the typical judge and of the typical person appearing before him is too great. In other words judges are perceived as being, and may in fact be, far too remote.

It is noteworthy that in early 1994, out of 487 circuit judges four came from the ethnic minorities and there were six recorders from the ethnic minorities out of 795.

Women were represented by one Lord Justice of Appeal, six High Court judges, twenty-eight Circuit judges and forty-two recorders.

Legal aid and other sources of legal assistance

Many of the people we have been discussing in this session will only be available to those who can afford to pay them. The services of solicitors and barristers cost a great deal. Quite possibly they are good value for money but in absolute terms a lot of people find the cost prohibitive. The consequence is that justice is denied to those without access to legal advice and the courts by reason of their relative poverty.

There is a statutory legal aid scheme which was originally designed to meet the needs of those requiring help which they cannot afford.

Unfortunately legal aid itself costs the country a great deal of money and in recent years Government has taken steps to reduce significantly the number of people eligible for legal aid in an attempt to stem the constantly rising cost.

A person seeking legal aid has to clear a number of hurdles.

First, there is an examination of the applicant's disposable income and disposable capital.

Although account is taken of the applicant's responsibilities such as dependent family members when assessing disposable income, the limit is very low and so only the poorest are eligible for full legal aid. Above this lower limit the applicant has to make a contribution on a sliding scale until all rights to aid have been exhausted.

Equally although disposable capitial is assessed after deducting, for example, the value of a person's home and tools of trade, an applicant with quite modest savings will have to make a contribution from them to the costs.

Secondly, the applicant has to pass a 'merits' test. The Legal Aid Board has to be persuaded that the applicant has a satisfactory reason to bring, defend or be a party to proceedings. Basically the Board must be of the view that if the applicant was paying for the legal assistance personally that the advice would still be to go ahead with the matter.

In the case of criminal legal aid there are quite severe tests. Just because a person has been summoned to appear before a court and has no choice in the matter does not mean that legal aid will be forthcoming. Application for legal aid in criminal cases is made in the first instance to the court. A major criticism is the lack of consistency: some courts are very unwilling to grant legal aid in circumstances in which other courts would make a grant.

The factors taken into account include:

- whether the charge is grave, for example, if proved, could it result in a loss of liberty, loss of employment or loss of reputation?
- whether a substantial question of law is raised
- whether the accused is unable to follow proceedings or to state his or her case because of, for example, lack of English or mental incapacity
- if the nature of the defence involves tracing or interviewing witnesses or the cross-examination of experts.

Legal aid is not free in the sense that if an aided litigant wins an action and recovers money or property then, subject to limited exceptions, the legal aid fund has to be repaid from what has been recovered.

Not only is it difficult to obtain legal aid for ordinary court actions but in some cases it is not available at all. legal aid cannot be obtained for an action in the small claims court nor for a claim before, subject to minor exceptions, tribunals.

The unavailablity of legal aid in industrial tribunal cases is particularly significant since unfair dismissal claims may be of critical importance to the individual concerned who stands in real need of effective representation.

There is in addition a means-tested so-called green form scheme under which a solicitor can give up to two hours legal advice and assistance on all sorts of legal matters. The scheme does not provide for representation. The idea is sound but to qualify an applicant's disposable income must not exceed the level at which income support is payable.

It seems that legal services are available to those who can afford to pay for them and, in some situations, they are available to the poorer members of society. A person does not have to be very well-off to fail to qualify for legal aid and so it is the people in the lower to middle income range who are above the poverty line who can find it hardest to obtain legal services.

ACTIVITY 28

What does an applicant have to show before he or she can obtain legal aid?

See how your answer corresponds with that given below.

The applicant must pass what is often referred to as the 'means test' as regards disposable income. The aim is to ensure that only those who are perceived as being unable to afford assistance for themselves, receive legal aid.

There is also a 'merits' test which has different criteria according to whether it is a civil or criminal case for which application is being made.

SELF-CHECK 4

Do you think there may be good reason for making it difficult to obtain legal aid?

OTHER SOURCES OF HELP

Legal assistance is available to certain categories of people.

Members of trade unions can usually obtain help from their union. This is especially helpful in claims before tribunals involving, say, unfair dismissal or redundancy.

For others, professional bodies can offer much the same kind of help.

Even organisations such as the RAC can provide help on a limited basis to its members.

It is becoming increasingly common to take out legal insurance so that help can be obtained should it be needed. Unfortunately not everyone can afford the premiums or is persuaded of the need until it is too late.

Textbooks refer to law centres and legal advice centres which do admirable work where they exist. The reality is that as a consequence of inadequate funding there are not many of them.

The only provider of advice which is to be found in most centres of population of any size is the Citizens Advice Bureau. The bureaux are staffed by volunteers who are given some training but who are not lawyers. Some bureaux have weekly sessions when the local solicitors attend on the basis of a voluntary rota which is clearly helpful.

Some bureaux volunteers are trained to represent clients in those places where they have a right of audience such as the industrial tribunals. This is invaluable for the small minority who are represented but there remains a large unmet need.

The best that most bureaux can do most of the time is to give good advice and then leave the client to follow it as best as he or she can.

One is forced to conclude that many of those who cannot afford legal advice and assistance for themselves must do without it.

Summary of section four

- In this section we have considered the role of both lay people and professionals in making the system work.
- In general, lay people are involved because of the ordinary common sense which they bring to deciding questions of fact: you do not need to be a lawyer to assess character and decide where the truth lies. The contribution of lawyers whether as practitioners or judges is to apply the law to the question which is being addressed. They must have expert knowledge of the contents and application of the law not only to cases before a court but also to the many non-contentious matters in which their help is sought. We have seen that there is not a single profession but rather a two-branch profession with each branch having its own role and career structure.

● We have looked briefly at the provision of legal aid: a scheme that in
theory makes help available to those who cannot afford it for themselves.
We have also seen that quite stringent financial means as well as merit
tests are applied to applications for legal aid. Clearly legal aid is not
generally and automatically available and so many people who are not
well off are expected to fund their own litigation. Whether this is
reasonable involves some social and political considerations outside the
scope of this module.

Suggested answers to section four self-check questions

SELF-CHECK 1

There is a feeling that people who are over 60 years of age will be out of touch with
contemporary society and its standards. You might dispute this. More practically,
by the time magistrates appointed late in life are trained and become experienced
they will only have a very few years on the bench before retirement and so it does
not seem worthwhile.

People who have committed serious offences have shown themselves to fall short
of the standards which magistrates would seek to impose upon others. Their
appointment would bring the bench into disrepute.

The position of bankrupts is more difficult because people can become bankrupt
through no fault of their own. In law, however, bankrupts are under a number of
disabilities of which this is just one. It is perhaps sensible that those who for
whatever reason cannot pay their debts should not be magistrates: at the very least
it removes them from the temptation to accept any form of bribe!

A police officer or traffic warden could not be a magistrate because there would be
a clear conflict of interest between membership of the bench and the job.

SELF-CHECK 2

It might seem that somebody who has been to prison has demonstrated a disregard
for accepted standards of social behaviour and that the inclusion of such a person
on a jury might diminish public confidence. On the other hand, having served a
sentence means that the person concerned has repaid the debt to society and may
be, from personal experience, very well qualified to determine who is guilty and
who is innocent!

It is difficuly to take exception to the list of those who are ineligible. It would be
unfair to impose the burden of jury service on someone who is mentally ill and the
mental illness might be of such a kind as to prevent the person concerned forming
a balanced view. The exclusion of those who work directly or indirectly in the

administration of justice is sensible because it eliminates any suggestion of real or imagined conflict of interest. Such people may be very conscientious as jury members but still perceived as being biased.

Those who are excusable as of right include many who could make a great contribution to any jury on which they served. The people in this category may have expertise in their particular field and have developed good judgement. Their effective exclusion can be one of the contributory causes of juries being unrepresentative.

SELF-CHECK 3

As we saw in Section Two when we discussed precedent, judges have a significant law-making role and yet they are unelected and largely answerable to nobody for their decisions. It is virtually impossible to remove them from office. If they are to command respect therefore it is important that they are chosen with care.

A major criticism of the selection procedure is that it is secret. Is there any real need for this? Why can't people simply apply for judgeships at all levels of the judiciary and submit to normal selection procedures, for example, a series of interviews and aptitude tests? If the judges are convinced that they are the right people then they would doubtlessly still obtain their appointments by this method. The present system does not give the public the confidence it should have.

A more open selection procedure might also help redress some of the imbalances by leading to the appointment of more from the under-represented minorities. If it did not do so then it would be easier to justify such under-representation on the grounds that all applications were subject to equal, open and objective scrutiny.

The present system does bring forward good people but it may exclude others who have a lot to offer. It may be that they have alienated existing judges at some point in their careers or simply have not come to the attention of those who make decisions: nobody knows. Greater openness would inspire greater confidence.

It seems strange in a late 20th century democracy that such important appointments should be left within the gift of a small closed inner circle of people whose very identity is unknown.

SELF-CHECK 4

From the tax payers' point of view it may be thought desirable that the cost of legal aid should be contained and that it should only be granted in really deserving cases. To accept this view entirely means that access to law is denied to many who are poor but in similar circumstances in which the rich would proceed regardless. You could argue that the State should seek to eliminate such inequality in the interests of social justice.

On the other hand, if legal aid is too freely available there is a danger of wasting money. Frivolous actions could be brought which waste resources and court time.

Having to pass a merits test may seem rather like a mini-trial but it can provide a useful sifting purpose. The Legal Aid Board with its accumulated experience will eliminate those cases which would be unlikely to succeed if they went to court thus saving everyone a great deal of trouble.

If people have a belief in their case then they should be prepared to back that belief with their own money. Making legal aid hard to obtain obliges would-be litigants to think about their position very carefully.

It is however difficult to justify imposing such financial limits upon legal aid that, even where a case has merit, the applicant cannot afford to proceed.

Unit 1: additional questions

These additional exercises are in some cases more demanding than the self-checks found in the unit itself.

In order to complete them it will be necessary for you to spend at least half an hour on each of them. The exercises require some careful thought and the application of the information that has been gained whilst working through the unit. In order that you really benefit you should refer to at least some of the books in the reading list: this will both broaden and deepen your knowledge and appreciation of the topics covered by the unit.

1.   Civil and criminal law share certain broad characteristics. What are they? Both civil and criminal law have some common functions. What are they? Why do you think people obey the law?

2.   Explain the differences that still exist between common law and equitable remedies and see if you can discover and describe what are regarded as the two new equitable remedies which have come into being in the last twenty years.

3.   Describe the essential differences between primary and delegated (or secondary) legislation. Consider if delegated legislation is in any sense 'inferior' to primary legislation. See if you can discover the various ways in which control is exercised over delegated legislation.

4.   Discuss whether approaches to statutory interpretation which are referred to as rules but which allow different judges a wide discretion as to which to adopt are to be regarded as being rules at all? What considerations might influence a judge in deciding whether to adopt a particular approach?

5.   'The natural and reasonable desire that statutes should be easily understood is doomed to disappointment. Thwarted, it shifts to an equally natural and reasonable desire for efficient tools of interpretation. If statutes must be obscure, let us at least have simple devices to elucidate them'. (F.A.R. Bennion).

Discuss this statement and, in particular, whether there are 'simple devices' to elucidate statutes.

6. Imagine that in the interests of promoting tourism it has been decided that London must be made to look cleaner and smarter. As a part of this programme attempt to draft a law to prevent dirty motor cars being driven within the vicinity of Buckingham Palace.

   You will find this far more difficult than at first appears but it will help you appreciate the problems of both parliamentary draftsmen and judges.

7. Do you agree with the proposition that the advantages of the doctrine of precedent far outweigh the disadvantages? Are there any legitimate means by which a judge who does not wish to apply an apparently binding precedent may avoid it?

8. 'Their Lordships regard the use of precedent as an indisputable foundation upon which to decide what is the law and its application to individual cases ... Their Lordships nevertheless recognise that too rigid adherence to precedent may lead to injustice in a particular case and so unduly restrict the proper development of the law.' (Practice Statement – Judicial Precedent [1966] ALL ER 77)

   With reference to decided cases, discuss the various reasons for the issue of the 1966 practice statement and illustrate its subsequent use by the House of Lords.

9. 'Let it not be thought from this discussion that I am against the doctrine of precedent ... All that I am against is its too rigid application – a rigidity which insists that a bad precedent must necessarily be followed.' (Lord Denning)

   Examine this statement and discuss the extent to which you agree with it.

10. Discuss whether, as a result of the United Kingdom's membership of the European Union, Parliament can no longer be regarded as being supreme having surrendered significant power to make law to Europe.

11. Hamish has been charged under Section 20 of the Offences against the Person Act 1861 of an offence triable either way.

    The incident giving rise to the charge occurred when Patrick mocked Hamish's claim to have discovered a new porridge formulation guaranteed to increase energy and improve health and Hamish then allegedly attacked him.

    Hamish denies the accusation and seeks advice stating he has faith in British justice and that he will go to any lengths to clear his name.

    Advise him as to:

    a) any choice he may have concerning the courts before which he will appear and what factors he should take into account when exercising that choice, and

b) any avenues of appeal that might be available to him.

12. Harjinder is displeased with the quality of work done in her house by Rajvir. He has sent her a bill for £450 which was the sum quoted before the work was commenced. Far from being willing to pay Hajinder wants to claim £650 from Rajvir. She says this is what it will cost her to undo the work which he has done and to have it done properly by someone else.

If this dispute cannot be settled amicably and they resort to legal action, explain where the case would probably be heard and describe steps that would have to be taken and the nature of the hearing.

13. Describe the essential differences and points of similarity between the means of dispute resolution offered by the courts, tribunals, arbitration and mediation.

14. Critically assess the contribution made to the judicial system of England and Wales by the lay magistracy.

15. Discuss whether the use of juries should be discontinued or, at least, much curtailed on the grounds that they are, among other things, unreliable, inefficient and expensive and describe possible alternatives to using juries.

16. 'Questions of proof are not satisfactorily left to ignorant or untrained minds announcing decisions of major consequence in a few unexplained monosyllables.' (Prof. Glanville Williams)

Discuss whether this argument provides sufficient grounds for abolishing the use of juries, if not in criminal cases, at least in the remaining civil cases where they are to be found.

17. Having considered the difference between the two branches of the legal profession discuss whether the division only serves the interests of the lawyers and not the public.

18. Does it matter that judges are predominantly white, male, middle-aged and from the middle or upper classes? Consider whether such a situation is inevitable and, if it is neither inevitable nor desirable, what steps can be taken to remedy the situation'

19. 'To my mind none of the evidence, general or specific, adds much to the inherent probability that men and women of certain age will be inclined by nature to favour the status quo. Is it displeasing to the public at large that the guardians of the law should share this common tendency?'

Discuss by reference to decided cases whether judges do tend to favour the status quo and, if so, whether this is a desirable tendency.

20. Do the present sources of legal aid and assistance provide adequately for those who cannot afford to pay for legal services for themselves? Consider both the statutory scheme and other non-statutory sources of help.

Additional questions: guidance

1. This first exercise is straightforward and should help to give you confidence although the third part of the question is more demanding.

   The common characteristics of civil and criminal law. Both must be made by some body which has proper authority whether it be Parliament or the courts through the doctrine of precedent. The power might have been delegated to, for example, a local authority, but nonetheless comes from a recognised source. Equally both must be enforceable with the imposition of a sanction if necessary. Both must be applicable to all members of society. In other words there must be no possibility of the avoidance of a law on an arbitrary basis.

   The common functions are concerned with the creation of some order in society. People should be able to plan their lives in the knowledge of the probable consequences both of their own actions and of those of their fellow citizens.

   The reasons that laws are obeyed range from the simple fear of sanction to an absolute belief that it is morally right to do so.

2. Although equity and the common law are administered in the same courts, they remain separate. You should refer to the purpose of the Judicature Acts 1873-1875.

   When the circumstances are correct common law remedies are available as of right whereas equitable remedies are discretionary. This does not mean that the individual judge can act in a capricious or arbitrary manner since there are rules. Your answer should explain the relevance of the maxims of equity in this connection.

   If you refer to almost any of the books on the reading list (except Griffith, 1991 for this purpose) you will quickly focus on Anton Piller orders and Mareva injunctions as examples of recent equitable developments.

3. Primary legislation emanates directly from Parliament and is complete in itself. No further legislation is needed to give effect to what the Act sets out to achieve. What primary legislation may set out to achieve is the delegation of the task of detailed law-making to another body. The set of rules made by that other body is secondary legislation.

   You should give one or two examples of such secondary legislation, perhaps, the by-laws of local authorities or regulations made by the Health & Safety

Executive. Who else has delegated powers? Government departments? What are statutory instruments? Such rules have the force of law but are created at one remove from Parliament.

Control is exercised by the courts. Your answer should give an explanation of *ultra vires*. Parliamentary control through ministerial answerability and by the various degrees of scrutiny applied to statutory instruments when they are first made.

4. Each of the three so-called rules, ie., literal, golden and mischief should be illustrated by two or three cases since there are plenty of examples in the books on the reading list. Provided you are not judgmental you should find merit in each of the approaches and so realise that a judge must have a discretion as to which to adopt in the circumstances of each case. Will feeling that judges should be interpreters rather than makers of law tend to make them more circumspect? You should give examples of judicial creativity. Are judges now prepared to adopt a more obviously creative approach to interpretation? Does the decision in **Pepper v Hart** really help or does it create a new problem of having to seek out the meaning of Hansard?

Useful material in Zander (1994).

5. This question covers the ground discussed in relation to Question 4 above but with less emphasis on the attitudes that might be taken by the judges. Your answer will probably refer to assistance provided by the various presumptions made when interpreting a statute, to other external sources of help such as the Interpretation Act, and to internal help such as the title, marginal notes, definition sections etc. How much help are they? It should refer to the help that is provided by, for example, the *ejusdem generis* rule.

Ingman (1994) is strong on this.

6. You should begin by going to a library and looking at the way an Act of Parliament is set out. Almost any Act will do. You should start the fictitious Act in the same way as a real Act begins and then try to encompass what you hope to achieve in no more than three or four sections with appropriate sub-sections.

Your problems will be mainly associated with definitions, for example, what is 'dirty', what is a 'motor car' and what is 'within the vicinity of Buckingham Palace'? You must always keep before you the purpose of the legislation which you should, in effect have stated early in your drafting.

7. Having defined terms your answer should give a conventional listing of the advantages and disadvantages of the use of the doctrine of precedent which can be extracted from the textbooks.

There will have to be a discussion of the meaning of 'distinguishing' which in turn will depend upon a proper explanation of the meaning of *'ratio decidendi'*.

Although the events took place in the 1970s you will find interesting Lord Denning's activities in attempting to free the Court of Appeal from the obligation to follow its own precedents and, indeed, to free it from the need always to follow the House of Lords.

8. Either Zander, (1994) or Ingman, (1994) will give you the useful background.

The terms of the practice statement will reveal the stated reasons for its issue.

There are a wealth of cases in the textbooks to illustrate the generally cautious use that has been made of the practice statement and how particularly at first, their Lordships had many reservations. Since its use has been comparatively limited it is possible to find cases illustrating it specifically outside its terms. There have been instances of quite prompt use being made of the licence that it gives.

Has its use been generally in accordance with the terms of the press release that was made at the time? Has its use been generally beneficial?

9. Essentially this question covers the same ground as that in Questions 7 and 8 above. Look at the cases and see how Lord Denning sometimes attempted to avoid a precedent which would have lead to a result with which he disagreed.

Although he expressed views that were sometimes not in keeping with current social thinking he was generally motivated by a wish to dispense 'justice'. Was he right to do so? Did his approach risk the introduction of a lack of certainty and an arbitrariness that struck at the heart of the doctrine? If such discretion was to be allowed him then why not to others in other courts?

10. Look for a straightforward answer.

You should explain first what has happened as a consequence of our membership of the European Union, for example, our mandatory obedience to the terms of the treaties and the effect of regulations and directives. Consider the respect that courts must give to European legislation. Can European law be disregarded? Can the UK ultimately only reassert the supremacy of its Parliament by legislating to withdraw from the Union?

11. Hamish will appear first before magistrates. If they determine that the case should be heard in the crown court then Hamish has no choice. The magistrates will commit for trial. If they decide the case is one they should hear themselves then Hamish must be told that he can elect trial by jury. He must also be warned of the power of the magistrates to commit for sentence. It is then necessary to discuss the advantages and disadvantages of jury trial, for example, the popular conception that there is a better chance of acquittal or the risk of a greater sentence if convicted as a punishment for having wasted the court's time, etc.

You will need to distinguish between an appeal proper and when the court is asked to state a case. Consider what the appeal is against: conviction or sentence. Consider the grounds: fact, law or mixed fact or law. When is leave to appeal required?

12. You should briefly explain the allocation of business between the High Court and the county court. This is clearly county court. Size of claim means automatic reference to arbitration in small claims court. There are no grounds for rescission in this case. Brief reference should be made to the commencement of proceedings.

Discuss the nature of the hearing in terms of informality, cost, speed etc. No legal aid, discouragement of legal representation. A more inquisitorial approach–how far can this be taken?

13. You answer should outline essential differences. For example, both courts and tribunals are provided by the State for the resolution of disputes whereas arbitration and mediation are arranged by the parties themselves. In the case of the courts, tribunals and arbitration the parties have the decision taken by a third party whereas with mediation it is the parties themselves who determine the final outcome. The differences should emerge from a discussion of the relative advantages and disadvantages in terms of costs, time, formality, satisfaction with outcome etc.

14. First examine the contribution made. Your answer could look at the workload in criminal cases both in terms of trial and of committal, consider the magistrates' function in connection with domestic matters and with children and discuss their administrative role in such matters as licensing.

Issues to consider include: Who are the magistrates? How well are they equipped to deal with all this work? Would it be better if it were undertaken by a smaller number of professionals? Evidence suggests that stipendiaries despatch cases far more quickly and with few causes for complaint and so would their use cost more. Do lay magistrates have the same appeal as jurors simply because they are lay?

15. Your answer could describe the jury in terms of being comprised of ordinary people who are selected at random without regard to any kind of aptitude etc. Are they easily led or do they bring their shrewd judgement and common sense into play? There should be a discussion of the advantages and disadvantages of the use of jury. Why isn't it possible to find out more about the working of juries?

Are they costly and inefficient? Consider 'perverse' verdicts: do they vindicate or condemn the jury system? You could discuss recent attempts to restrict the rights of the accused to elect jury trial – a civil liberties issue? But in any case hasn't the right to jury trial been much reduced since the war?

Replacement? A single judge, a bench of judges, a judge with two lay assessors, a specially selected jury, etc.

16. This covers essentially the same ground as Question 15 with emphasis on whether it is reasonable to present ordinary people with the task of considering complicated and often technical evidence. Are the physical and intellectual demands too great? Should it be possible to monitor jury performance? Is there a significant difference between jury trial in civil and criminal cases? In both the jury depends upon proper guidance from the judge and in both much depends upon character assessment. In a criminal case, the jury having determined the issue is not concerned with sentence. Why in a libel case should a jury determine the quantum of damages?

17. You should discuss the different roles assumed by solicitors and barristers and their different practices. What does a typical solicitor do and what does a typical barrister do? You could consider the different rights of audience and matters such as rights of direct access to the client. Have these traditionally worked for or against the client? Discuss the problems of communication with the client, the danger of lack of familiarity with the case, the late returned brief, unnecessary double manning, etc., set against the acquired advocacy skills of the barrister and the barrister's objectivity and duty to the court.

    You could discuss whether the division will soon be of only academic interest as solicitors have now acquired greatly increased rights of audience or whether the profession will choose for the most part to continue as before.

18. Griffith, (1991) will provide interesting material.

    You will first need to ascertain whether it is true that the judiciary is predominantly white, male, middle-aged...' etc.

    Issues include: Given the task that judges are asked to perform, can they be drawn from any group other than that which displays those characteristics? Is the under-representation of, for example, women and members of the ethnic minorities a cause for concern? Should there be positive discrimination in selection? Should the whole selection process be far more open with appointment decisions being taken by panels which include appropriate lay representation? Should all judicial vacancies be advertised and applications sought? Is it inevitable whatever cosmetic changes are made in the selection process that the Lord Chancellor's Department must have the last word since it alone is privy to 'inside' information?

19. As with Question 18, you will need to review the characteristics of the judiciary and the career that will have led the typical judge to the bench. Do judges tend to have a common outlook and view of society?

    Should judges respond to every change in contemporary society? Is it best for them to put a brake on hasty and ill-considered change and for them to be one-step behind society at large?

    Also consider how great the influence of the judiciary is in reality. It only interprets and applies the law and does not make it and in consequence it's influence is marginal.

20. Rozenberg in (1994) is very good on this topic. He presents the topic without becoming embroiled in detail.

Your answer should set out the basic concept of legal aid and what the present system can offer, for example, 'green form' assistance by way of representation (ABWOR), legal aid. You should refer to the means test and the merits tests in both civil and criminal cases. Significance of contributions and the statutory charge. Are the tests for eligibility far too restrictive at present?

The legal aid scheme is arguably in retreat and none of the alternatives seem to fill the gap it is leaving. Your answer could consider the role of the CAB, legal insurance, law centres, organisations such as the AA or trade unions etc. Do they come together to answer the need?

Reading list

Law is a fast-changing subject and, in consequence, textbooks tend to become quickly out-of-date. When referring to a book always check that it is the latest edition and that it is of recent date. There are many books which discuss the English legal system but you may find the following particularly helpful.

Bailey S.H. and Gunn, M. J., 1991, *Smith and Bailey on The Modern English Legal System*, Sweet and Maxwell.

> This is a full and thorough textbook which is useful for reference. It is very clearly written.

Ingman T., 1996, *The English Legal Process,* Blackstone Press, 6th edition.

> Clearly and concisely written.

Keenan D., 1995, *English Law*, Pitman Publishing, 11th edition.

> An accessible book which has considerable width and discusses, for example, contract and tort as well as the legal system. The second part of the book is dedicated to the presentation of cases and materials.

Zander M., 1994, *The Law-Making Process*, Weidenfeld and Nicolson, 4th edition.

Zander M., 1996, *Cases and Materials on the English Legal System*, Butterworths, 7th edition.

> Both Prof. Zander's books have interesting and thought provoking material and comments.

> All the above books are useful both to provide fuller explanations of the topics covered in this unit and to be used as works of reference.

> If you wish to read about the legal system generally then the following are worth considering.

Rozenberg J., 1994, *The Search for Justice*, Hodder and Stoughton.

Rozenberg is the BBC's legal correspondent and a solicitor. His book is very readable and entertaining. It contains a lot of pertinent observation and comment.

Griffith J A G., 1991, *The Politics of the Judiciary*, Fontana, 4th edition.

A challenging book which considers whether there is a detectable and consequential bias to be found in members of the judiciary.

A legal dictionary is sometimes useful. There are several available at quite low prices. The following is as good as any.

Mozley H., and Hardy Ivamy, E.R., 1993, *Law Dictionary*, Butterworth and Co., 11th edition.

Finally read the newspapers! Topics covered in this unit are frequently the subject of press reports. Try and get into the habit of looking at the so-called quality press, *The Guardian, The Daily Telegraph, The Independent* or *The Times. The Times*, for example, has an informative law feature every Tuesday and articles dealing with aspects of the English legal system are the most commonly featured. The newspapers will help you stay up-to-date.

UNIT 2

LEGAL

RELATIONSHIPS

Introduction to Unit 2

In Unit 2 you will be introduced to a range of legal relationships. The term 'legal relationships' is used here to mean those associations which arise in commercial situations. There are obviously other relationships, such as marriage, which are legally based, but these are outside the scope of this course. It is interesting to note though that until quite recently it was possible to sue for breach of a promise to marry!

At the end of your study of Unit 2 you will be able to:

- distinguish between different forms of business organisation
- explain the advantages and disadvantages of each form in a given business situation
- identify the main features of an agency relationship
- explain the importance of the contract of employment and identify its existence in a simple factual situation
- apply your understanding of the legal rules governing legal relationships to factual situations.

The objectives listed above summarise the relationships which we will be considering in this unit. Possibly the most important legal relationship which exists commercially is the contract. This subject is dealt with fully in Unit 3 but the main issues summarised below as contracts form the basis of the issues which are discussed in this unit.

Contract

A contract is a form of agreement which is legally binding. An agreement for example to purchase goods from a shop is a contract. We can identify some important features of this relationship:

- the buyer and seller will agree what is to be purchased and the price to be paid
- both of them will exchange something, this is termed consideration
- both parties will intend that the transaction is legally binding.

The relationships which are the subject of this unit are briefly discussed below.

CONTRACTS OF EMPLOYMENT

One important type of contract is the contract of employment. This is the relationship which exists between employer and employee. Again we can see the same essentials as in a contract for the sale of goods:

- the employer and employee will negotiate terms and conditions
- the employer will pay a wage and the employee provide a service
- if either party is in breach of the agreement the other can take action in the courts.

Employees sometimes work for individuals but more often they work for companies. We need to be able to distinguish between those firms which operate as companies and those which take some other form; that is partnerships or sole traders.

LEGAL FORM OF ORGANISATIONS

The choice of legal form adopted by a firm is important for a number of reasons and we need to be able to identify the advantages and disadvantages of each.

For example if you operate as a sole trader and your business becomes insolvent then you are personally liable for any losses suffered by creditors. If on the other hand you form a limited company to trade under then you have limited liability and normally your creditors cannot sue you personally for loss they have suffered. Between the sole trader and the limited company lies the partnership. This consists of at least two people trading together. Like the sole trader, partners normally have unlimited liability, that is they are personally liable for the debts of the firm.

AGENCY

Irrespective of the type of legal form adopted organisations have to operate through human beings. Individuals therefore enter into negotiation and into agreement on behalf of a firm. Sometimes this will be a firm which they own either wholly or in part, for example a sole trader or partnership. In other cases they may be employees or directors of a company. We need therefore to understand the ways in which individuals can make firms liable for agreements entered into. This takes us into the law of agency and we will see that this is important in looking at both partnerships and limited companies. Agency is the relationship which arises where one person (the principal) allows another to contract on his/her behalf in a situation where the agent can enter into a contract binding on the principal.

SCENARIOS

This unit contains four linked scenarios which show the development of a business. Additional questions linked to the business are given at the end of the unit. You should use the scenarios to test your understanding of the issues discussed in the unit. They will also be used to help you apply legal principles to factual situations. You should therefore attempt to justify your answers to the questions by bringing in the relevant legal principle. When answering legal problems you need to remember that your reasoning is as important as the conclusion you reach. This means that you need to provide reasons for your answers to the questions you will meet in this unit.

SECTION ONE

Liability for Employees and Agents

In Section One you will find material to help you learn about and understand the following things:

- what a contract of employment is
- the difference between an employee and somebody who is self-employed
- when an employer is vicariously liable for an employee's actions
- the nature of the agency/principal relationship
- when a principal is liable for the actions of an agent.

The employment relationship

Of the legal relationships which we will describe in this unit, the one which is most common is that between employer and employee. You may be working while you are studying this unit on either a full-time or a part-time basis. In either case you are likely to be an employee. On the other hand you might work or have worked for yourself, that is been self-employed. The term **'independent contractor'** is used by the law to describe those who are self-employed. Such people are also said to work under a **'contract for services'**. This should be contrasted with an employee who works under a **'contract of service'**. In the case of the employee there will be a **'contract of employment'** between the employer and employee.

In most cases it is easy to tell whether a person is an employee or self-employed but problems can arise. The increasing use of short-term contracts, sub-contractors and agency workers by firms means that we need to be able to determine whether a person is an employee or not. The discussion below is expanded upon in Unit 4 but we think it is important that you have some knowledge of it at this point.

There are a number of reasons why this is important. The rules governing income tax and national insurance payments differ between the two groups. Firms might give their employees holiday or sickness pay or pension benefits. The State certainly gives employees rights, for example to claim for unfair dismissal or maternity benefit. These rights tend to be available only to employees. Finally employers can be made responsible for torts committed by their employees which arise during the course of their employment.

This last point is termed **'vicarious liability'** and is covered in detail in Unit 4 but will be briefly explained here.

ACTIVITY 1

The term 'tort' is sometimes referred to as a 'civil wrong'. This is where one person injures another in such a way that the law requires the wrongdoer to pay damages. Some torts may be deliberate and can also be a crime. Others may be un-intentional. Using this brief explanation as a guide, write down four types of situation which you think might be covered by the law of tort.

1.

2.

3

4.

The term 'tort' applies to circumstances where a person has caused harm to another through the breach of a duty imposed by law. It excludes contractual duties although it is possible for the same action to give rise to both a breach of contract and a tort. **Trespass** to the person and trespass to goods are examples of torts. Hitting somebody deliberately is a criminal offence. It is also a tort. Another you will have read of in the newspapers is **defamation**. The most common tort is **'negligence'**. This arises where one person owes another a duty of care and causes injury to that person by an act or omission which constitutes a breach of that duty. The same act can be both criminal and tortious. For example, dangerous driving is a criminal offence but can also lead to an action for negligence if it causes damage to somebody else. Finally there is a tort known as **nuisance**. This arises where you do something on your property which adversely affects another person on his/her property. Causing pollution would be an example of this.

Vicarious liability

Where an employee commits a tort during the course of his/her employment the employee will be made financially responsible. This means that an employer who is not at fault will still have to pay damages. Damages will however only be payable if it can be shown that the employee committed a tort. An employer is not made responsible for the criminal actions of an employee, unless of course the employer was also involved.

For an employer to be made vicariously liable the employee must be acting within the course of employment. Provided that the employee is doing basically what he/she is employed to do then there will be liability even if the employer has expressly forbidden the act which is the source of the complaint.

SELF-CHECK 1

Two cases are given below to illustrate this point. In each case state with reasons whether you feel that the employer will be liable for the worker's actions.

In **Lloyd v Grace Smith & Co** [1912] a solicitor's clerk was entrusted to deal with client's property. He used his position to steal some of the money. Did the solicitor have to reimburse the client?

Heasmans v Clarity Cleaning Co Ltd [1987] involved an office cleaner who used the telephone at the office he was cleaning to make a number of expensive long-distance calls. Did the employer of the cleaner have to reimburse the firm whose telephone was used?

SELF-CHECK 2

Earlier we discussed why it is important to distinguish an employee from an independent contractor. Give three reasons for drawing this distinction.

1.

2.

3.

EMPLOYEE OR INDEPENDENT CONTRACTOR?

As we said earlier it is usually easy to tell the status of an individual worker. One obvious way is to look at how the parties have referred to the arrangement. This is not always conclusive for the courts have in the past declared a worker to have one particular status when the contract between the two states something different.

An early attempt by the courts to distinguish between the two focused on control. The control test looked at the extent to which the 'employer' directed the work. If a person was told not only what job to do but also the way in which to do it then he/she was regarded as an employee. This test might be appropriate for manual jobs or some clerical jobs but falls down where the worker is a skilled or professional person.

The question which the courts try to answer now is whether or not the person is in business on his/her own account. This requires looking at all the factors affecting the relationship before coming to a conclusion. This is sometimes referred to as the **'multiple test'**. Try to decide the court's view of the following relationship.

ACTIVITY 2

The case **Ready Mixed Concrete Ltd v Minister of Pensions and National Insurance** [1968] required the courts to decide whether drivers of cement trucks were employees or self-employed. The drivers purchased their own vehicles using loans provided by the company. The trucks had to be painted in the company's colours and could only be used to carry their cement. The company paid the drivers a set sum per mile driven and specified the route to be followed. The drivers made their own arrangements for tax and national insurance payments. They did not receive holiday or sick pay but could appoint a substitute driver.

Using the multiple test the courts will take a common sense view and weigh the factors which suggest the person is an employee against those suggesting self-employment. These will then be balanced to reach a conclusion. From the Ready Mixed case identify the factors which suggest employment and self-employment and decide what the status of the drivers is.

The fact that the drivers have to follow the company's routes and carry only their product suggest an employment relationship. The mileage payment is not conclusive either way nor is the method of payment of tax. The fact that the drivers own their own vehicles suggests that they are self-employed. This suggestion is reinforced by the fact that the drivers can appoint substitutes, a fact which the courts felt was inconsistent with the employment relationship. Accordingly the workers were held to be self-employed.

The contract of employment

It is not uncommon to hear somebody say that they have 'just received their contract of employment'. The term is frequently used to refer to a written statement given by an employer to an employee. This written statement contains the terms of the agreement, usually only the main terms, and is not strictly the 'contract' at all. Once a person starts working as an employee then he/she has a contract of employment irrespective of whether or not they have received anything in writing. The written statement of terms is just that, a written statement of the main terms of the contract rather than the contract of employment itself.

The giving of a written statement by an employer is a requirement of Section 1 of the **Employment Protection (Consolidation) Act 1978.** This states that within 13 weeks of commencing work an employee should receive a written statement giving details of specified terms and conditions. These need not all be contained in one document and in some cases all that need be done is give the employee access to the details. Frequently this provision will be satisfied by giving an employee a letter of appointment, a copy of a works handbook or even the pinning up of leaflets and notices on a notice board.

ACTIVITY 3

The matters which have to be written in the statement are the most important terms of the employment relationship. List six matters which you think should be included in the written statement.

1.

2.

3

4.

5.

6

Matters which you could have listed include: pay; hours of work; holiday entitlement; sick pay entitlement; provision of pension scheme; notice period required; and disciplinary and grievance schemes.

Terms which are actually stated by the parties to a contract are called express terms, that is they are expressed by the parties. In the employment relationship these express terms would be in the written statement but might also be found in the letter of appointment, company handbook or even on the office notice board.

IMPLIED TERMS

The written statement contains most of the express terms of the contract. As with other types of contract there are also implied terms. Implied terms are those which are not specifically included by the parties but which the law inserts. These may come from statute, custom and practice or be inserted by the courts to make the contract work in problem situations.

For example, the employee is required to give faithful service and to obey the lawful orders of the employer. He/she is not allowed to compete against the employer while in service but unless there is an express stipulation in the contract (usually referred to as a restraint of trade clause) may do so on leaving. An employee is prohibited from accepting bribes or secret commissions in much the same way as we will see an agent is.

There are few equivalent duties placed on employers. There is an obvious obligation to pay agreed wages in return for work but no general duty on an employer to provide work. Statute imposes a number of obligations on employers. These are beyond the scope of this unit but examples include obligations to look after the health and safety of workers; not to unfairly dismiss employees; and the obligation to pay maternity benefits. In most cases these are framed in terms of employee rights but clearly there will be reciprocal duties. Where an employee feels that statutory rights have been infringed, complaints are made in most cases to an industrial tribunal rather than the courts. Tribunal cases are heard by a panel of three. The panel is chaired by a lawyer and support given by two lay members who have relevant industrial experience.

SELF-CHECK 3

Peter is a recently appointed appointed confectionery salesman employed by Whizzo plc. He receives a letter which states that it should be considered as a written statement of the terms of his contract of employment. While visiting customers he attempts to sell them confectionery items made by his sister Mary. Whizzo plc discover this and he is dismissed for breach of contract of employment. The letter of dismissal states that Peter will be sued for breach of contract if he visits Whizzo plc clients again. Peter's letter of appointment did not prohibit the selling of other goods to clients. Peter wishes to know whether he was acting in breach of contract and also whether he can visit Whizzo customers now that he has been dismissed. Advise him.

Agency

An agency arises where one person is authorised to enter into contracts on behalf of another. In this section we will look at the legal rules governing the agency relationship.

ACTIVITY 4

Imagine that you booked a holiday through a travel agent. Identify below all the parties to the transaction. When you have done this state who it is you have made a contract with.

The obvious people to list are yourself, the travel agent and the holiday company. You might also have included the airline, hotel, bus company, or railway company. In buying your holiday the only people that you are likely to deal with are those in the travel agents. It is also likely that the price of the holiday is paid to the travel agent and your tickets are sent to you from the travel agent.

You could be forgiven for thinking that it is this firm with which you have a contract but this is not the case. What would happen, for example, if when you arrived at your destination the hotel was fully booked? Who would you expect to be responsible for this? Although you booked the holiday through the travel agent the agent had little control over the arrangements. These were made by the tour company yet you did not deal with them. How does the law handle a situation where the person who made the deal or the contract is not liable yet somebody who was not involved in the transaction is to be made liable?

The answer is given through the law of agency. The travel agent is an agent for the holiday company and enters into contracts on behalf of that company. Once the contract is made it exists between the holiday maker and the holiday company. The travel agent has no part in that relationship, it simply brings about the contract and then fades away into the background. This means that if there is a problem with the contract it is the tour company who is sued and not the travel agent.

The previous paragraph identified three main parties: the holiday company; the travel agent; and the holiday maker. The travel agent acts on behalf of the holiday company. In this example, the travel agent is the termed the **agent** and the holiday company the **principal.** An agent acts on behalf of a principal. The holiday maker is the **third party** to this arrangement, that is the other person in the contract. The agent acts on behalf of the principal in making the contract. The ultimate contract exists between the principal and the third party. An important feature of the agency situation is that the agent has the ability to enter his/her principal into a legally binding contract.

It would be a major problem for a principal if the agent could enter him or her into any contract. What if the travel agent had agreed with the holiday maker to vary the day or time of a specific flight? Would we expect the tour company to honour this arrangement? Common sense suggests that the tour company would not be bound by this agreement but how does this fit with our earlier statement that the agent can bind the principal into a contract? The answer is that an agent does not have unlimited powers and the principal is only bound by contract which the agent has the power to enter into. Different types of agent will have different amounts of power. We will now look at the types of agent which can exist; the way in which they are appointed; and the power they are able to exercise.

Types of agent and formation

We can identify three general types of agent.

Special agent: someone appointed to perform one specific act, once this act has been completed then the agency is terminated. An estate agent is an example of this type of appointment.

General agent: a general agent has more power. He or she will have a specific range of duties. The extent of the power will be limited by the usual scope of the person's position. A purchasing officer in a company will be able to enter into a range of contracts on behalf of the company.

Universal agent: agents of this type are appointed by a special type of deed known as a power of attorney. Universal agents have the power to do anything which their principal is legally able to do.

Usually when the agent makes a contract on behalf of the principal he or she will have no liability in respect of it. There is one type of agent, termed a *del credere* agent who does guarantee to the principal that payment will be made. In such a case if a buyer found by the agent does not pay the agent is personally liable to the principal.

FORMATION

An agency relationship is normally based on agreement between the agent and principal. There are similarities therefore between the formation of a contract and the formation of an agency. There are however situations in which an agency may be created without specific agreement by the principal. Before looking at how an agency is made we need to consider who may become an agent. The answer is that virtually anybody can become an agent. This applies both to individuals and to companies. Basically an agent may do anything which a principal has the power to do him or herself.

There are four different ways in which an agency can be created. These are by:

- express agreement
- implied agreement
- ratification
- necessity.

We will examine each of these in turn.

Express agreement

This is the most obvious case and arises where the principal specifically appoints the agent. This will usually be by some form of contract which will specify the power of the agent and provide details of remuneration.

Implied Agreement

This arises from a set of circumstances. Even if no formal agency relationship has been entered into it is open to the courts to say that one exists from the conduct of the parties. In addition there are some relationships from which an agency will be implied. Partners acting within the usual business of the partnership will usually be classed as agents of the other partners.

Ratification

This covers the situation where a person acting as an 'agent' does not have the power to do so. In this case the person who is the 'principal' may ratify the contract. This means that the principal gives retrospective approval to the contract made on his or her behalf by the agent.

Not all contracts can be ratified. A number of requirements must be met.

- The existence of the principal must be disclosed at the time the contract is made. Thus if it appears that the agent has acted purely on his/her own account then the principal may not ratify.

- A principal can only ratify a contract that he/she had the power to enter into at the time the contract was made. For example if the contract in question was for a minor to purchase non-necessaries this could not be ratified on reaching adulthood. This is because at the time the contract was made the principal was a minor. This point is important in the area of pre-incorporation contracts. These are contracts which are made on behalf of a company which is in the process of formation but has not yet been formed. The case **Kelner v Baxter** (1866) illustrates this. In this case a person purchased some wine claiming to act as agent for a company. The company was in the process of formation and once it was formed it attempted to ratify the contract. The courts decided that this attempt failed. The reason for this was that the company did not exist at the time the contract was entered into.

- The principal must have full knowledge of all the facts before ratifying or alternatively make it clear that ratification will occur under any circumstances.

Necessity

This arises where a person having some responsibility for the goods of another is faced with an urgent situation which threatens these goods. Provided that the person acts in the best interests of the owner actions taken will bind the owner. It is important that the agent in this case attempts to obtain instructions from the principal.

Two railway cases illustrate this. In **Springer v Great Western Railway** [1921] a carrier sold a consignment of fruit because it was becoming bad. The court declined to find an agency of necessity since the carrier had not attempted to obtain instructions. Contrast this with **Great Northern Railway Company v Swaffield** [1874]. Here a carrier of a horse was forced to stable it when it was not collected. The owner could not be contacted and so the court concluded that an agency of necessity had arisen.

SELF-CHECK 4

In the following situations you are required to state whether or not an agency relationship exists. If an agency exists you should state how it has been formed, that is whether it is express, implied, by ratification or through necessity.

(a) Amy asks Barbara to sell her car for her and agrees to pay a commission of ten per cent.

(b) Charlie is looking after Dan's pet dog while Dan is on a walking holiday. The dog becomes ill and Charlie incurs vet bills.

(c) Eric and Fiona agree to work together as window cleaners. Eric enters into an agreement with a company that they will clean an office block for £100, a ridiculously small sum for the size of the task.

(d) Gwen and Harry decide to form a company called Jay Ltd. Gwen leases an office on behalf of the company. After the company is formed Harry discovers this and refuses to pay.

(e) Keith, a neighbour of Laura, sees that Laura's car has been vandalised. He calls for a garage and arranges for the car to be repaired.

Responsibilities of the parties

As the agency relationship is based upon agreement it follows that the parties should keep to this agreement. Usually the agreement will specify the powers of the agent but what happens if these are exceeded? In some cases the principal may still be liable. This requires us to consider the nature of **authority**. A reverse situation may exist where the agent has authority but the third party does not know of the existence of the principal. In some cases it may be that there is no contract. This type of situation is referred to as the **undisclosed principal**. The section will then look at the duties of the parties to the agency agreement.

AUTHORITY

We pointed out earlier that there must be some limits to the power of an agent. If not then the principal could be bound by contracts which he/she would not want to enter into. The power of an agent to bind a principal is known as authority. When an agent is appointed then he/she will be given authority by the principal but this is not the only source of this.

Actual or express authority

This is the specific power given to the agent. For example a travel agent will be

authorised to sell holidays but will have no express **authority** to change the time
or routing of the holiday company's flights.

Implied authority

This may arise in one of two cases. The first is that an agent has implied authority
to do those things which are necessary to achieve the purpose of the actual
authority. For example if you authorise somebody to sell your car then they would
have implied authority to advertise it and charge you for the cost.

Implied authority can also arise where a person is employed to undertake a specific
job. In such a case that person has the implied power to do the things which are
usually done by people in that situation.

SELF-CHECK 5

In **Watteau v Fenwick** [1893] the manager of a public house was specifically
told by the owner that he could not purchase tobacco on credit. The manager
disobeyed the instruction. State with reasons whether you think the owner had
to pay for this.

Apparent or ostensible authority

This arises where the principal does something which suggests that a person is
operating as an agent. Where a third party relies on this then he/she can bind the
principal to any contracts made which seem to be within the power of the agent. It
should be noted that in this type of case there may not be an agency existing
between principal and agent. Despite this, the law states that if a person acts as if
he/she has an agent then he/she is bound by the actions of the supposed agent. This
type of situation might arise where a person is appointed as an agent over a long
period by a principal. If the agency is ended, the principal may still be liable on
contracts made by the agent with people who had previously dealt with the agent
where they did not know the agency had ended.

In cases where an agent has acted outside powers granted or implied by the principal
it may be possible for the principal to sue in respect of any damage which has
arisen. This means that even though a principal may be bound by the agent doing
something which is forbidden, damages may be recovered from the agent.

Duties of the agent

Agents are in a special position as regards their principal. They can bind the
principal to contracts and will frequently have control of assets. It is therefore
important that they act properly. This means that they should exercise appropriate
skill and care and also act in good faith. The duty to act in good faith is sometime
referred to as a **'fiduciary duty'**.

Skill and care

An agent has the following duties:

- to obey the lawful instructions of the principal
- to exercise reasonable skill and care
- to carry out the purpose of the agency.

Fiduciary duties

- to avoid a conflict of interest
- not to make secret profits or accept bribes.

SELF-CHECK 6

In each of the following cases an agent was shown to be at fault. State which of the duties listed above were broken, and why you think this was the case.

- **Lucifero v Castel** [1887], in which an agent appointed by a principal to purchase a boat, bought it himself and then re-sold it, at a profit, to the agent.

- **Turpin v Bilton** [1843], where an agent instructed to insure a ship failed to do so and the ship was lost at sea.

- **Chaudhry v Prabhakar** [1988], where a person bought a car in reliance on the advice of a friend, who was knowledgeable about cars. The car was actually an insurance write-off which ought to have been spotted.

- **Armstrong v Jackson** [1917], in which a stockbroker engaged to buy some shares for a client sold the client his own shares.

Duties of the principal

The duties imposed on the principal may seem less severe than those which the agent is subject to. The principal is responsible for paying the agent the agreed fee for the work. In addition an indemnity should be provided for any losses which the agent has suffered. This means that where the agent incurs expenses in undertaking the principal's instructions, then the principal should provide recompense for this.

The undisclosed principal

The point of an agency is that a contract is made on behalf of one person by another. One question which we need to ask is, does it matter if the third party is unaware that he/she is dealing with an agent? This may be important in some cases. What, for example, if you were selling something and did not want a competitor company to purchase the item? If you dealt with an agent you could find that there was a hidden principal who obtained the item.

The basic rule is that if you contract with an agent, the principal is able to sue on the contract and be sued on it, even if you are unaware of the principal's existence. There are some exceptions to this rule and the most important are given below:

- the principal must have capacity (that is have the legal ability to enter into the contract)
- the contract must not exclude the right of the purchaser to be acting as an agent
- where the existence of an agent would worsen the third party's legal position
- where the third party wished to rely on the skill of the agent personally rather than another person
- where the agent has misrepresented the identity of the principal.

SELF-CHECK 7

We asked the question above, 'what if you were selling something and did not want a competitor company to purchase the item?' If you are selling to an agent you may not know the identity of the principal. What if you subsequently found that the person you had sold to was an agent of the competitor company. Could you avoid the contract?

Terminating an agency

An agency is a form of contract. For this reason all the rules which apply to ending a contract will apply. In addition if either party dies or becomes insane the agreement will be terminated. Where agent or principal becomes bankrupt the matter is not so clear cut. The principal's bankruptcy will end the agreement but the agents will not (unless the contract provides to the contrary).

ACTIVITY 5

State and briefly explain the ways in which a contract can be terminated.

You should have listed: **agreement**; **breach; frustration**; **and performance**.

Where the agency ends by **agreement** this effectively is the replacement of one contract to perform a task being replaced by one not to act. The parties may jointly agree to end the contract or could provide for this in advance. The contract could, for example, give either party the right to withdraw.

Breach would end the agency if either party broke a fundamental term of the contract, for example the agent broke the fiduciary duty.

Frustration arises where, due to some unforseen event outside the control of the parties, the contract cannot be performed. A long-term sickness by the agent could fall into this category. If the principal sells a business such that the agency must come to an end this will not be frustration. Whether damages could be recovered depends upon the facts.

Frequently an agency will exist for a set time or for a set task. Expiry of either time or task will end the agency through **performance**.

THE EFFECT OF TERMINATION
We would expect that terminating an agency ends the powers of the agent. It will certainly end the express powers but you will remember that principals can be bound by their agent's actions even if they did not want to be. If a principal does not make it clear to potential third parties that the agency has come to an end then apparent or ostensible authority could arise.

POWERS OF ATTORNEY
These are a form of agency given by deed. They allow an agent to do anything which legally the principal could do. They are quite common in domestic circumstances where one person wishes to give a relative control over his/her affairs. This may be because they are working overseas or are infirm.

Two points need to be made about terminating these. First, where the power is given to secure an interest of the agent then it can be expressed to be irrevocable. (See the **Power of Attorney Act 1971**.) This might include a power over shares given to secure a loan. Second, it is also possible to express some powers as being 'enduring'. This means that if the principal becomes insane or otherwise mentally incapable, the power continues. (See the **Enduring Powers of Attorney Act 1985**.) This is of use where the power is given in respect of the affairs of an elderly person who becomes senile. Without being made enduring the power would end, just at the time when it was most needed.

The commercial agents regulations

The increasing influence of the Single European Market and the desire to encourage trade within Europe have led the European Union to draw up rules governing some aspects of agency. A common way of making law within the European Union is for the passing of a directive. This lays down the objectives of proposed legislation and orders member States to enact their own rules to comply. **EC Directive 86/653** required all Member States to introduce standard rules on commercial agents. For the UK these were introduced on 1 January 1994 in a statutory instrument, **The English Commercial Agents (Council Directive) Regulations 1993.**

The regulations do not apply to all agents. They apply to agents employed to negotiate or agree the sale or purchase of goods. Thus they do not apply to service agencies. The principal's business must be in the sale or purchase of those goods and the transactions must be on a commercial basis. Agents selling to domestic consumers are therefore excluded. In addition it is anticipated that transactions will normally be the subject of individual negotiations. In addition the principal will have an interest in developing the particular market the agent is working in. This would seem to exclude 'one-off' transactions.

The aim of the regulations is to imply into agency contracts some specific terms. It is possible for the parties to vary them but in the absence of this the terms will apply to all commercial agencies. The regulations give the agent greater rights than were previously provided by English law. It is beyond the scope of this work to consider these regulations in detail.

SELF-CHECK 8

Define the term 'commercial agent' in your own words.

Summary of section one

- employees have a contract of employment with their employer
- the most important terms of this contract have to be contained in a written statement of terms required by the **Employment Protection (Consolidation) Act** 1978
- in addition some terms may be implied by the courts
- employers are vicariously liable for the torts committed by their employees during the course of employment

- agencies may be created expressly, by implication, through ratification or through necessity
- an agent has to have authority before entering into a contract if the principal is to be bound by the contract
- authority may be express, implied or ostensible
- an agent owes a number of fiduciary duties to the principal
- special rules introduced by the European Union apply to commercial agents.

Suggested answers to section one self-check questions

SELF-CHECK 1

In the first case the court concluded that the clerk was doing his job. He was trusted by his employer to look after the money and so the abuse of his position came about while he was in the course of his employment. The cleaner on the other hand was employed to clean the office and not make telephone calls and so his employer was not found to be liable.

SELF-CHECK 2

It is important to be able to draw the distinction for reasons of tax and national insurance payment; statutory employment protection rights; determining whether an employer is vicariously liable; and for employment benefits given by the employing firm.

SELF-CHECK 3

Peter's letter of appointment may have met the requirements of the Employment Protection (Consolidation) Act but would not have contained all the terms of his contract. There are a number of implied terms which will apply. In particular there are requirements to give faithful service; not to compete; and not to accept commissions other than those paid by the employer. It would seem from the facts above that Peter breached at least one, and possibly all, of these. There is no implied term not to compete on leaving. Thus unless Whizzo plc had included a restraint of trade clause in Peter's contract they may have trouble preventing him from visiting their customers. They would be able to stop him taking lists of customers or other data with him when he left.

As a final point, even if Peter was not in breach of contract when dismissed there is probably little he can do about his position. This is because the law governing unfair dismissal requires that an employee has two years continuous employment before a complaint can be lodged with an industrial tribunal. There are some exceptions to this. Dismissals on the grounds of sex or race, pregnancy or carrying out trade union activities do not need the two-year qualifying period. We do not know how long Peter was employed by Whizzo plc but as we are told he is a recent employee the inference is that it was not for two years.

Self-check 4

(a) This is an example of express agency.

(b) Assuming that Dan cannot be contacted, this is an agency of necessity.

(c) Partnerships create an implied agency as regards those matters which relate to the partnership business. This means that Fiona is bound by the actions of her partner.

(d) As the company does not exist when Gwen enters into the lease there is no agency. In fact no agency would exist even if the company attempted to ratify the agreement.

(e) Here the neighbour has no existing duty towards Laura and so this would not be an agency of necessity. This question can be contrasted with (b) above.

Self-Check 5

If you answered 'yes' then you were correct. The court felt that purchasing tobacco on credit was something that publicans commonly did. As the seller was unaware of the restriction he was able to force the principal to pay. This points to a problem for it shows that a principal cannot fully control the actions of an agent.

Self-Check 6

(a) There is a clear secret profit here (the principal was unaware of the agent's action).

(b) This is an example of failing to carry out the purpose of the agency.

(c) Here, even though the agent was not a mechanic he was still found to have not exercised proper care.

(d) This is an example of a conflict of interest and the client was able to rescind the contract.

Self-Check 7

It would seem that unless you could show that you had made it clear that you would not contract with a specific person or company, then you would be bound by contract to the undisclosed principal. This is subject to the exceptions above, for example if you specifically asked if there was a principal and were told, 'no', this would be a misrepresentation.

Self-Check 8

A commercial agent is one who enters into individual negotiations for a principal for the sale or purchase of goods, normally transacted in by that principal, where the principal has an interest in developing the particular market in which the agent is working.

SECTION TWO

Sole Traders and Partnerships

In Section Two you will find material to help you learn about and understand the following things:

- different types of business organisation
- the legal benefits and problems of trading as a sole trader
- the definition of a partnership
- how a partnership is formed and ended
- the relationship of the partners to each other.

Business organisations introduced

ACTIVITY 6

Business organisations exist in the public and private sectors of the economy and in service and manufacturing. From your own knowledge list below four types of business organisation.

1.

2.

3.

4.

Businesses come in many shapes and sizes. The largest private sector employers are the major public companies such as British Telecom, ICI, and the large banks and retailers. Many people also work within the public sector, for example in the health service or for local or central government. In this unit we are not concerned with public sector organisations. They are established by statute and their rights and duties set out in law. This unit is looking at the possible choices of form open to commercial organisations. It is recognised that the two sectors may both have commercial goals but there are distinct differences in their legal form. You may have referred above to bodies such as building societies or insurance companies. Although they are part of the private sector they are subject to special rules as regards their legal form. These bear many similarities with companies but legally building societies are a special class of organisation.

So far we have concentrated on larger companies but you may have made reference to smaller forms of organisation. The one-person firm, for example a shopkeeper or market trader, may be a type of organisation commonly referred to as a **sole trader**. The term is obviously descriptive of the business type. Looking at slightly bigger firms we come across the **partnership** which by definition will have at least two owners. Sole traders and partnerships may be formed quite easily. There is no need for legal formalities to be completed. As such they are referred to as **unincorporated organisations.** Companies on the other hand must go through a formal creation process, termed incorporation, thus they are referred to as **incorporated organisations**. For large undertakings there is little choice but to act as an incorporated body. For smaller entities there is a real choice as to form and at the end of this unit you will be able to outline the factors to consider in making the choice.

Sole traders

A sole trader is a one-person firm, that is the firm has only one owner. This person will receive all the profits of the firm and be responsible for its losses. Note that it may have employees. There are some obvious practical problems for the sole trader. These include problems caused by sickness, holidays and succession. More importantly there are limits to the size of such firms as they will have access only to the personal capital of the owner and anything which he/she can borrow. There are in addition a number of legal problems which sole traders face. One of these is that a sole trader has unlimited liability. This is explained later but means that the proprietor is personally liable for all the debts of the business.

SELF-CHECK 1

This is the first of four linked scenarios in this unit. It will help you learn the skills of analysing legal problems and applying legal principles to factual situations.

Scenario One

Alan Tracy is a graduate in computer science. Having recently lost his job he has started to work as a freelance consultant solving the information technology problems of small companies. He works from home but has had notepaper printed with the logo 'Alan Tracy IT Consultant'. The business has been moderately successful and Alan has built up a number of clients who employ him on an hourly or daily basis to give them advice and help them with problems.

Alan has recently been approached by Farnsley Engineering Ltd (FEL). The company has decided to invest in some new integrated software to control its operations and this will necessitate the purchase of some new personal computers (PCs). FEL want Alan to advise them which of three competing computer programmes they should purchase. In addition they want him to select appropriate PCs and install the new system. The contract would be the largest that Alan had undertaken and the most lucrative. A detailed specification is set out under which Alan is required to:

(a) advise the company which integrated software package they should purchase;

(b) acquire on behalf of the company 25 PCs which will be capable of operating the chosen software;

(c) install and test the new PCs; and

(d) provide a maintenance and trouble-shooting service in respect of the PCs for twelve months after their installation.

The specification is presented to Alan by FEL's company secretary with the request that he sign it as part of a legally binding contract. On reading the document Alan discovers that it would make him liable for any loss suffered by the company as a result of any default on his part. In addition the contract stipulates that before ordering the PC's Alan must advise the directors of FEL of the details of the purchase.

After spending some time reviewing the needs of the company, Alan recommends which of the software packages to buy. He then begins to look for machines to run the programmes. During the course of his enquiries he meets Betty Parker. She works from a small workshop producing PCs to customer specifications using parts purchased from a number of dealers. The end products are not 'branded' but she offers a guarantee and appears to have a good reputation. Her prices are much lower than those asked by dealers who sell better known makes. Alan decides to purchase the PCs from Betty.

1. What type of business organisation is Alan trading as?

2. What is Alan's relationship with FEL?

3. Would FEL be bound by a contract to purchase machines from Betty if Alan entered into it on behalf of FEL without seeking the consent of the Board?

4. The clause making Alan liable for default could expose him to a claim for damages which would exceed the assets of his firm. What additional risk does this expose him to?

5. Betty supplies the machines to FEL. She is so pleased with the contract that she offers to sell equipment to Alan at a five per cent discount on her normal prices. Can Alan accept this offer?

6. What would Alan's liability be to the company if the machines supplied by Betty proved to be of poor quality?

Partnerships

Section 1 of the **Partnership Act 1890** defines a partnership as the:

'relationship which subsists with persons carrying on a business in common with a view to profit'.

The maximum number of people who can form a partnership is 20. In the case of some professional occupations, for example accountants and lawyers, the limit is relaxed. It is not essential that the business is profitable but there must be an aim that it will be. It is not always clear whether a partnership exists. Commercially, it is sensible to prepare a partnership agreement in writing but this is not strictly necessary. The partnership relationship is based upon contract and thus may be written or verbal.

SELF-CHECK 2

In the case **Keith Spicer Ltd v Mansell** [1970], two people decided to form a company to operate a restaurant. Before the company was actually formed one of the people ordered goods. As the company did not exist at the time of the order it could not be made liable to pay for the goods when it was formed. (This is termed a pre-incorporation contract and is dealt with in the next section.) In such cases, the person who actually ordered the goods is made personally liable. In addition if it could be shown that the two people were in partnership the person who did not order the goods would also be liable. Explain whether you think a partnership existed in this case.

Liability of partners

Self-check 2 introduced an important aspect of partnership. This is that partners are regarded as agents of each other and the partnership. This means that where a partner enters into a contract or incurs a debt then all the other partners are liable to meet it. This applies only in respect of contracts entered into within the authority of the partner. The word authority should remind you of our earlier discussion of agency. The rules which determine the authority of agents also apply in this case. This means that if a partner acts within express, implied or apparent authority then the other partners will be liable for any debts incurred. In addition to the normal agency rules, the **Partnership Act** Section 5 provides an additional type of liability. This says that where a partner enters into a contract which is within the usual way of business of firms like that which that partner belongs to then it will be binding on the partnership. The only exception to this is where the other party knows that the partner lacks authority or does not believe him to be a partner.

SELF-CHECK 3

In **Mercantile Credit Co v Garrod** [1962], P and G operated a garage business. They agreed that they would not sell cars. P sold a car which he did not own to the finance company. As P had no title (that is he did not own the car) neither did the company and they had to return the car to its true owner. If P had authority to sell the car then the partnership, and thus G, would be liable. Explain whether you think G had to repay the finance company.

UNLIMITED LIABILITY

Reference to personal funds in the previous section is important. Where a partnership incurs debts which exceed its assets then the personal assets of the partners are at risk. In the final analysis the law draws no distinction between partnership and personal assets. This is even more important when you consider the relationship of the partners to each other. Imagine a simple two-person partnership where the partners agree to share profits and losses equally. If losses arise which exceed the partnership assets then either partner may be sued by a creditor for the full debt. He/she would not be able to argue that only half the debt should be paid. Each partner is personally responsible for the full debt. This means that if one partner had the assets to meet the liabilities then he/she could be called upon to do so. The other partner would then have to be sued to provide his/her half of the debts. If that other partner had no money the solvent partner would have had to meet the full debts personally.

It is possible for a person to be designated a **limited partner**. Such a person only contributes capital to the firm. In this case liability is limited only to that capital. Limited partners are sometimes referred to as sleeping partners. This is an apt description as they cannot take part in the management of the firm. Once they do, their protection is lost. A partnership must always have at least one unlimited partner so not all partners can take advantage of this.

PARTNERSHIP PROPERTY

The fact that the personal assets of the partners can be seized to meet the firm's debts suggests that there is a confusion between partnership and personal property. In theory this is not the case although in practice it is often difficult to draw clear distinctions. One point which must be made here is that **legally a partnership does**

not have an existence distinct from that of the persons making it up. The process of incorporating a company actually produces a distinct legal entity which is recognised by law. Partnerships do not have this recognition. This means that partnership property is not exactly property owned by the partnership as a separate entity but by the partners jointly. In the same way, a partnership strictly cannot sue or be sued. Actions are brought by or against the partners collectively. Frequently the partnership name may be used in any legal action but this is simply as a form of shorthand.

Some specific points may be made about partnership assets:

(a) property purchased with the partnership's money is presumed to belong to the partnership;

(b) any assets acquired by the firm or taken into the accounts of the firm for the purposes of the business are regarded as partnership property;

(c) partnership property belongs to all the partners; and

(d) if an individual partner becomes insolvent then the partnership assets cannot be used to meet these debts (although that partner's share may be withdrawn for this purpose).

SELF-CHECK 4

Scenario Two

Alan and Betty spend a considerable time together over the Farnsley Engineering Ltd contract. They like working together and decide that their skills are complementary. Alan is more interested in dealing with customers directly and problem-solving while Betty prefers the workshop. In addition they are capable of assisting each other directly. They decide that they will keep their separate businesses but where they are offered work which requires both their expertise will collaborate with each other. They have some notepaper printed which is headed 'T & P Computers'.

Alan and Betty work together on several occasions over the following months. Their activities receive a boost however when an article in the Farnsley Chamber of Commerce Journal is published showing the savings which FEL have made following their investment in their new computer system. The article mentions both Alan and Betty by name and states that they work together. Following its publication the two receive a number of enquiries from potential customers.

Sufficient work is generated from these approaches to keep them both in work for three months. During this time they decide that they could earn more by working together and offering customers a complete service than working separately. They decide to pool their resources and expertise to form a partnership trading as 'T & P Computers'.

Questions

1. When Alan and Betty first begin collaborating are they a 'partnership'?

2. If Alan ordered some software for his personal business on the 'T & P Computers' notepaper before they decided to trade as a partnership, would Betty have been liable to meet the cost of this?

3. When they eventually decided to form a partnership they would both bring some assets into it. Which of the following assets originally belonging to Betty would become partnership assets:

    (a) her building society savings account;

    (b) stocks of computer hardware to be used in the new venture;

    (c) outstanding debts owed to Betty for goods supplied;

    (d) a car used for the business?

The partnership agreement

ACTIVITY 7

We have already said that partners enter into an agreement with each other. This is a contract and like most others can be verbal or written. It is sensible to use a written agreement. Many of the terms which are included are a matter of common sense, others of law. Using the information you already have and your own knowledge and experience, list six matters which you would expect to be included in a written partnership agreement between Alan and Betty.

1.

2.

3.

4.

5.

6.

We have already considered some of the important issues which would be included. These include:

- the division of profits and losses
- the capital contribution, including non-cash assets transferred to the firm
- the express authority of the partners.

There are a number of practical considerations you might have mentioned:

- the payment of wages and interest
- how new partners can be admitted
- the circumstances in which the partnership can be dissolved
- a restraint of trade clause to stop partners competing against the partnership once they have left
- methods of resolving disputes.

It must be emphasised that there is no legal requirement to have a written agreement. A verbal agreement is just as valid but the more complicated it becomes the more practical it is to write down. The **Partnership Act** 1890 actually deals with some of the issues which we have listed above. In the event of a partnership agreement not making reference to specific issues then the Act applies to the agreement. These include the following:

(a) all partners share profits and losses equally;

(b) interest is not paid on capital;

(c) no wages are payable;

(d) all partners have rights of management (note this does not apply to limited partners);

(e) a partner is entitled to recover from the other partners liabilities incurred in the proper course of the business; and

(f) decisions are taken on the basis of a majority vote except for major changes to the partnership such as introducing a new member.

It is important to remember that all these points can be varied by the agreement.

Ending the partnership

There are a number of ways in which a partnership may come to an end. Some firms may be established for a specific venture. Once that has been achieved then dissolution should occur. The same applies to a firm established for a specified duration. The most fragile type of partnership is a **'partnership at will'** which allows any partner to withdraw and require the dissolution of the firm.

It is sensible to provide in the agreement how the partnership could be dissolved, for example by the giving of notice. In addition there may be some circumstances specified where this occurs automatically, for example on the death or insolvency of a partner. Conversely an agreement could state that the survivors could continue with the estate of the deceased or insolvent partner operating as a replacement partner. Situations of physical or mental incapacity, the commission of a criminal offence or some other problem may also be specified as terminating the agreement.

Even where the agreement does not provide for termination it is possible for a partner to ask the courts to terminate the relationship and wind up the partnership. Death or bankruptcy will always be grounds for this, unless the agreement specifies the opposite. In addition there are also grounds under which the court may terminate the agreement. These are:

(a) incapacity which prevents a partner acting as such, for example mental illness;

(b) conduct by a partner which adversely affects the firm, for example a criminal conviction for dishonesty;

(c) collapse of trust between the partners or breach of the partnership agreement;

(d) that the business can no longer be carried on at a profit; and

(e) that it is 'just and equitable' to dissolve the partnership.

Where a partnership is wound up then the partners have a right to a share in the assets of the firm, after payment of liabilities, according to the partnership agreement. In the event of an individual leaving the firm but the firm carrying on then he/she is entitled to an appropriate share of the net assets based on the agreement. There is an additional problem for such a partner since liability for the debts of the firm may continue beyond the date at which he/she left.

The general rule is that a leaving partner is responsible for debts incurred during the time in which he/she was a partner. This is the case even if the remaining partners agree to the contrary. The only exception is where creditors enter into a new agreement with the remaining partners which excludes liability for the person leaving. This is known as **novation.** A new or replacement partner is not liable for debts incurred before joining.

The problems of a leaving partner do not simply end on the withdrawal. If third parties dealing with the firm still believe that person to be a partner then liability will continue. It is therefore sensible to advise all creditors of a withdrawal and to place appropriate advertisements in the press. This should include the London Gazette (or Edinburgh or Belfast) which is an official publication for notices of this type. Liability may still not be evaded if the partner is aware that the firm continues to 'suggest' that the withdrawn partner is still active. It is probably also sensible to ensure that old stationery is destroyed to make absolutely sure that mistakes do not occur.

SELF-CHECK 5

In **Tower Cabinet Co v Ingram** [1949], Ingram was a former partner in a firm which traded under the name Merry's. After he left the remaining partner operated as a sole trader and ordered goods from a new supplier which he could not pay for. This was confirmed, in error, on a form which had Ingram's name on. The owner of Merry's could not pay and so the supplier sued Ingram on the basis that his name appeared as a partner on the order form and they did not know he had left. State with reasons whether you think Ingram was liable to make the payment.

Summary of section two

- a sole trader has unlimited liability
- usually a partnership cannot have more than 20 members
- partnerships are formed by agreement, either written or verbal
- the Partnership Act 1890 puts terms into any partnership unless the partners agree to the contrary
- partners have authority to bind the partnership in respect of matters within the usual business of such firms
- partners have unlimited liability, unless classed as limited partners
- individual partners may be made liable for all the partnership debts
- a leaving partner can in some cases be made liable for debts incurred after he/she has left the firm

Suggested answers to section two self-check questions

SELF-CHECK 1
1. Alan is clearly trading as a sole trader.

2. He is not an employee of FEL. Legally he is classed as an independent contractor. In addition he is also acting as an agent for the company as regards the purchase of the equipment.

3. As an agent, Alan has authority. This may be express, implied or apparent. By purchasing equipment without asking for approval, Alan is outside his express authority and also implied authority. The issue to consider therefore is whether he is within his apparent authority. This would depend on what people in Alan's position are usually able to do. If it is common for consultants to purchase on behalf of companies then FEL are bound. If it is not, then they will not be. Alan would be liable to them for breach of duty if they were bound by a contract outside Alan's authority.

4. A sole trader has unlimited liability. This means that if claims against the firm exceed its assets, the personal assets of the proprietor are at risk.

5. Another form of liability relates to making additional gains from a transaction entered into as an agent. The rules are strict and an agent cannot retain any additional benefits received by virtue of acting as an agent. Strictly he would be accountable to FEL for any benefits received as a result of Betty's offer.

6. If the machines were of low quality then Betty would be liable to FEL for breach of contract. Alan has no liability on the contract. He is however obliged to exercise appropriate skill and care in his work. If it could be shown that he did not take proper care in deciding to buy Betty's machines then he could be sued for breach of his duty as an agent.

SELF-CHECK 2

This certainly looks like a partnership but the court questioned why the two were operating together. It concluded that they were not operating a business in common with a view to profit but were acting with the intention of forming a company. Thus they did not intend to be a partnership.

SELF-CHECK 3

The answer is that G did have to repay the company. Selling cars is a normal function of a garage business, although not a function of this particular business. The consequence of cases like this is that, as with agency, it is very difficult for a partner to prevent another partner from acting outside the partnership agreement. Where this happens it is possible for partners to sue each other to make the one who acted improperly liable. This is only of value if that person has sufficient personal funds.

SELF-CHECK 4

1. Alan and Betty seem to meet the statutory definition of a partner contained in the Partnership Act. The fact that the business is not their sole commercial activity is not critical. They seem to be carrying on a business in common as regards their joint activity.

2. If (1) above is correct then the answer to the second question should be that

Betty is liable provided the seller had no reason to believe that Alan had no authority to purchase the goods supplied. Betty would have a claim against Alan as he has acted outside their agreement.

3.   As regards Betty's property it seems that:

(a)   it is purely personal and nothing to do with the partnership;

(b)   the computer equipment seems to have been transferred into the partnership and so will become partnership property;

(c)   as the debts relate to her previous personal business, in the absence of any agreement to the contrary, they would remain hers; and

(d)   the car seems similar to the computer hardware at (b) and would seem to be now partnership property.

It would be sensible for both of them to list the assets transferred into the partnership and value them. This input could then be regarded as part of the capital contribution. If a partner wants to retain title to an individual asset then he/she could lend it to the firm but would need to make this clear.

SELF-CHECK 5

The court decided that Ingram was not liable. As Tower Cabinet was not a supplier when he left he could obviously not have advised them of this fact. The answer may have been different if Ingram had known that the old stationery was used, but he did not and so was found not to be liable for the debt of his old partner.

SECTION THREE

Forming a Company

In Section Three you will find material to help you learn about and understand the following things:

- the different types of company which may be formed in the UK
- how the concept of limited liability protects shareholders
- the way in which the law separates a company from its shareholders
- how to form a company

- the contents of the Memorandum of Association
- the purpose of the Articles ofAssociation
- how to amend the Memorandum and Articles.

Basic principles

Operating as a partnership has some attractions in that there are few formalities to observe. The problems of limited liability and the relative ease with which partners can withdraw present problems however. These may be resolved by choosing to operate as a company although as we will see this provides its own set of problems.

Companies are a type of **incorporated organisation**. This term can be applied to a number of bodies. Building societies, insurance companies and friendly societies fall within it, as well as companies which are the subject of this section. Creating organisations of this type requires that a formal process, laid down in a statute, is followed. The result is a body which is recognised by the law as having an **existence separate from its members.** This should be contrasted with a partnership which does not enjoy this separate legal personality.

Forming a company usually achieves another object. That is conferring on its members **limited liability**. This means that in the event of the company's assets not being sufficient to meet its liabilities, the individual shareholders are not liable. As we have already explained, this protection is not conferred on partners.

Whole (and rather large) textbooks are written on company law. The discussion below cannot therefore be complete and is intended as an introduction to the subject. This means that we are concentrating on basic principles only.

Separate legal personality

The importance of the concept of separate legal personality cannot be underestimated. The leading case in this area is **Salomon v Salomon and Company Ltd** [1897]. The owner of a business decided to convert it into a limited company. He formed the company and sold the business to it. Part of the payment was in the form of a debenture, that is a loan secured on the assets of the company. Shortly afterwards the company went into liquidation and the court had to decide whether the debenture could be enforced. The importance of this was that in the liquidation the debenture would be paid off before the debts of unsecured creditors. The House of Lords decided that the debenture should be paid off. Although Salomon effectively was the owner of the company, a line was drawn between the company and its shareholders. The company had an existence separate from that of its shareholders, a decision which still applies today.

SELF-CHECK 1

In **Macaura v Northern Assurance Co Ltd** [1925], the owner of a timber plantation sold it to a company of which he owned virtually all the shares. He insured the timber in his own name and sought to recover compensation from the insurance company when it was destroyed by fire.

Apply your understanding of the Salomon case and explain whether you think that Macaura was successful.

THE CORPORATE VEIL

It is sometimes said that shareholders are separated from their company by a 'corporate veil'. The use of the corporate veil can lead to problems, for unscrupulous individuals could hide behind this as protection for their wrongdoing. Because of this there have been a number of exceptions to the rule which have been developed. Some of these have been developed by the courts, that is they are common law rules, others have come from statute.

COMMON LAW EXCEPTIONS
Sham companies

Where an individual uses a company as a 'sham' then it is open to the courts to pierce the veil and impose obligations on the shareholders. An example of this is the case **Gilford Motor Co Ltd v Horne** [1933]. In this case Horne sold his business and promised not to compete against it. He attempted to evade this by getting his wife to form a company and using this as a vehicle to compete. The court took the view that the company was formed solely to do something which the seller would have been stopped from doing if he had acted under his own name. The court stopped the company from breaking the agreement entered into by Horne.

Agency

The concept of agency has also been used to pierce the veil. This is a difficult issue but an illustration is given below. This involves a parent and subsidiary company. A parent company owns its subsidiaries, that is it is a shareholder. In the same way that a company is distinct from its shareholders, a subsidiary is also distinct from its holding company.

In **Smith, Stone and Knight Ltd v Birmingham Corporation** [1939], the company owned a waste paper business which it operated through a wholly owned subsidiary. The subsidiary operated on land owned by the company. The land was compulsorily purchased and the issue was whether or not the company could obtain compensation for damage to its business. The Corporation argued that it was not entitled because the business belonged to the subsidiary and not the parent. Note that the owner of the land can get compensation for the loss of the property and loss of business. The court decided that there was entitlement. The subsidiary was regarded as an agent of the parent company. Crucially, the business had never been formally transferred from the parent to the subsidiary.

The subsidiary/parent relationship presents a problem for company law. Smith, Stone and Knight may seem a fair decision but also appears to run counter to the basic principle of separate legal personality. In **DHN Food Distributors Ltd v Tower Hamlets London Borough Council** [1976], the Court of Appeal did seem to suggest that in some cases it was possible to consider the concept of the 'economic entity' of a group. This view has not been developed and in fact the House of Lords declined to apply it in a later case, **Woolfson v Strathclyde Regional Council** [1978]. You should be aware of the problems in this area. It is safe to begin from the position that parent and subsidiary are distinct unless there are exceptional circumstances, such as the agency in Smith, Stone and Knight, which suggests the contrary.

STATUTORY EXCEPTIONS

Strictly speaking the exceptions which are listed below do not really amount to a piercing of the veil. What they represent are situations in which Parliament has decided that individuals should be personally liable for the debts of the company. This is really more a denial of limited liability (discussed in full below) than a piercing of the corporate veil.

(a) **The Companies Act 1985** Section 84 states that where a public limited company carries on business with only one shareholder (the minimum requirement is two) for a period of over six months, then the individual shareholder becomes liable for the company's debts.

(b) Section 117 of the same Act states that where a public limited company fails to obtain a **trading certificate** (discussed later) the directors are liable for any loss caused to a third party.

(c) Section 349 of the 1985 Act states that where anybody enters into certain transactions on behalf of the company without identifying the company then he/she is personally liable if the company defaults. This covers the making of orders and the signing of cheques, bills of exchange or money orders.

(d) **The Insolvency Act 1986** Sections 213 and 214 impose liability for **fraudulent and wrongful trading** respectively. These arise where the company has gone into liquidation and losses have been caused as a result of misconduct or default. In the first, individuals are running the company either deliberately fraudulently or recklessly. Any person involved may be made liable. Wrongful trading arises where a company is insolvent and has traded where the directors either knew or ought to have known that the company was insolvent. Only the directors can be made liable for wrongful trading.

SELF-CHECK 2

The sentences below summarise some of the points discussed above. Complete the blanks.

1. The leading nineteenth century case of   v   shows the significance of the corporate veil to company law.

2. The courts have developed a number of exceptions to this rule. Gilford Motor Co v Horne is an example of the veil being pierced in the case of a   company.

3. Where a subsidiary is carrying on business on behalf of a parent company, the courts have also found there to be an   relationship.

4. Statute also imposes liability on individuals for the debts of the company in some instances. Section 117 of the 1985 Act places liability on directors where the company does not obtain a

5. In addition somebody signing a cheque which does not show the company name in full can also be made liable under   if the company defaults.

6. Where a company becomes insolvent then the directors may in some circumstances be made personally liable for   under Section 214 of the Insolvency Act 1986.

Company membership and limited liability

The term 'members' is an important one. When we looked at partnerships we saw that these were made up of individual partners. Companies are made up of individual members. If you have a savings account with a building society, for example, you will be a member of that society. As such you have rights to vote at its **annual general meeting** and to receive a copy of its annual accounts. You may have received such documents yourself. For commercial companies membership requires that a person has shares in the company. The more shares that are owned the more power that member has. Usually one vote is given for every share held. The amount of **dividend** paid is also related to the shares held. When companies make profits they distribute part of them to the shareholders. This is usually expressed as an amount per share.

Not all companies issue shares. There are some which are termed **'guarantee companies'.** In this case the members do not buy shares in the company but instead promise, or guarantee, to provide money to the company in the event of its becoming insolvent. The limit on their liability is the amount which they have guaranteed. Companies of this type are usually charitable bodies or other non-commercial enterprises.

Companies which have shareholders also provide a **limit to the liability** of members. In this case the limit is the amount subscribed for the shares. Once a shareholder has paid for his/her shares in full then if the company becomes insolvent there is usually no further obligation to pay money to creditors. If shares are only **partly paid** then the liability to make up the full amount can be enforced, even if the company is in the process of winding up. The existence of limited liability and the fact that companies have a separate legal existence are important differences when compared to partnerships. It should be noted that there are some companies which do not give their members limited liability. It is possible to form an unlimited private company but we will not consider these, or guarantee companies, in this unit.

Types of company

The previous paragraph referred to **'private companies'**. Limited liability companies fall into two categories. **Public limited companies (plcs) and private companies (Ltd).** There are a number of differences between the two but for the moment we will look only at one. This is that only plcs may sell their shares directly to the public. Private companies cannot make public offers of their shares. This means that all companies which sell their shares on the Stock Exchange are plcs. The reverse however does not hold true. Not all plcs are listed on the Stock Exchange.

SELF-CHECK 3

List four types of company.

1.

2.

3.

4.

Forming a company

The process by which a company is formed may seem complicated but is relatively simple in practice. A number of firms specialise in selling **'off the peg'** companies.

These firms form companies of which they are the shareholders and then sell them simply by transferring their shares to the new owners. Usually the new owners will change the name and there will be a need to appoint new directors but the process takes only minutes. Such companies will tend to have standard constitutions. If anything unusual is wanted then it may be easier to form a company, using a lawyer or accountant for assistance. Costs are quite low and it is possible to acquire a company for about £200.

The formation process requires that the **promoters** of the company send to the **Registrar of Companies** a number of documents. These are set out below. They are self-explanatory in the main. The first two require greater discussion and these will be considered later in more detail.

The documents are:

- Memorandum of Association
- Articles of Association
- statement of the personal details of the directors and their signed consents to act as directors
- address of the registered office
- statement of the capital of the company
- declaration of compliance which states that all the formalities of the Companies Act 1985 have been complied with
- registration fee.

Assuming that the Registrar is satisfied with the documents then a **Certificate of Incorporation** is issued. This is conclusive evidence that all the formalities have been complied with. The company has no legal existence until such time as this is issued. The date on the certificate is therefore the birthdate of the company.

PRE-INCORPORATION CONTRACTS

ACTIVITY 8

The case **Kelner v Baxter** [1866] was discussed earlier when we considered the point of ratification in agency. State briefly the facts of this case as they relate to ratifying pre-incorporation contracts.

In this case a person purchased some wine claiming to act as agent for a company. The company was in the process of formation and once it was formed it attempted to ratify the contract. The courts decided that this attempt failed. The reason for this was that the company did not exist at the time the contract was entered into. Thus it is not possible for a company to ratify a pre-incorporation contract. The only way in which the company can be bound is to enter into a new contract by novation.

This may seem a harsh rule to apply to an innocent third party. To provide some remedy, Section 36c of the **Companies Act 1985** states that the individual who entered into the contract is personally liable unless the contrary is stated in the contract. The only contrary stipulations which may be made are that the promoter will be exempted from liability when the company is formed and a new agreement made or that either party may rescind if the company fails to enter into a new agreement within a specified period.

THE DUTIES OF PROMOTERS

The term promoter is applied to anybody involved in the formation of a company. In undertaking this work, the promoter owes a fiduciary duty towards the company.

SELF-CHECK 4

The term 'fiduciary duty' was discussed in the context of agency. You will remember that the duty imposed limits on the profits which agents could make from dealing on behalf of the principal and set standards of skill and care which had to be observed. From your understanding of that part of the unit and the discussion of pre-incorporation contracts answer the following questions.

1. Can a promoter make a profit by selling assets to the new company?

2. A promoter sells land to a company and advises a sub-committee of the board of directors of this. Is this acceptable?

3. An accountant is promised £500 for helping in the formation of a company. Following incorporation, the company refuses to pay. Can the company be made to pay?

The constitution: memorandum and articles

The constitution of a company is made up of two documents, the **Memorandum of Association** and the **Articles of Association**. The Memorandum deals with those matters which are of importance to the outside world. The Articles look at the internal regulation of the company.

Section 14 of the **1985 Act** states that the two documents bind the members of the company both to each other and to the company as if they had entered into a deed to this effect. This means that members may sue to enforce rights in the Memorandum and Articles. These rights must though arise in the plaintiff's capacity as member of the company.

ACTIVITY 9

In **Eley v Positive Life Assurance Co** [1876], the complainant had been appointed as solicitor for life of a company by its Articles. The company then appointed somebody else and so Eley brought an action to enforce the article appointing him solicitor. State with reasons whether you think he was successful.

The court decided against Eley. Even though he was a shareholder he brought his claim in his capacity as solicitor and not as member. Contrast this with **Rayfield v Hands** [1960]. In this case the complainant was a member of a company, the Articles of which stated that the directors should buy the shares of any member wishing to sell. The directors refused and the court granted an order compelling them to fulfil their obligations. Clearly the right to sell shares is one associated with membership. Whether this decision can be taken much further is a matter of debate since the judge made the point that the company in this case functioned similarly to a partnership. As such the Section 14 provision may have been interpreted generously.

The Memorandum of Association

The Memorandum contains the following clauses.
- company name
- registered office or domicile
- objects
- statement that the company members have limited liability
- statement of the company's capital
- association clause.

COMPANY NAMES

There are several firm legal rules which govern the choice of a company's name. These apply whether it is the first name being selected or a proposed change of name.

ACTIVITY 10

There are a number of legal rules which prohibit a company's choice of name, for example, the name must end in limited (or Ltd) or public limited company (plc). We have not yet discussed these but most of them are a matter of common sense. The following names all infringe legal rules. State under each what you think is the problem with them.

(a) A public limited company called 'The XYZ Corporation'.

(b) A company which sells mountain gear called 'Boy Scouts Ltd'.

(c) A company which operates as a travel agency called 'The Foreign Office Ltd'.

(d) A company which sells lingerie called 'Marks and Spencer Ltd'.

Of these (a) is probably the most difficult to appreciate. A list is given below of the rules which must be adhered to in choosing a name.

1. The name must end in 'limited' or 'Ltd' in the case of a private limited company. For a public limited company it must end in 'public limited company' or 'plc'. The name in (a) infringes this rule. Note that the Welsh equivalent of plc is ccc.

2. Certain names are prohibited and their use constitutes a criminal offence. The names of many leading charitable bodies such as the Red Cross fall into this category. Words like 'bank' or 'building society' can also only be used by bodies of this type. The Boy Scouts Association falls into this category so making (b) an unlawful name.

3. Related to this is the fact that certain words may only be used with consent. This includes names which suggest a connection with the Government. (c) therefore infringes this rule. Names of other Government departments or those suggesting connections with local authorities would be other examples.

4. A company cannot be registered with a name which has been taken by another company. Using 'the' in the name or other cosmetic changes do not evade this rule. Thus (d) would be unacceptable.

5. Names which are considered offensive by the Registrar will not be permitted.

Before a name is selected it is sensible to check the index of names maintained by the Registrar. Even if a name is accepted the Secretary of State can ask a company to change it if it subsequently appears to have infringed the rules.

Passing off

If the name in question (d) above was accepted this would obviously annoy the real Marks and Spencer. Perhaps more importantly it might damage their business and so the restriction is justified. What however if the name chosen was similar, say 'Morks & Spancer', how would this be treated? There is a possibility it would be accepted but this would not be the end of the story. If the original company felt that the newcomer was attempting to cash in on its name then it could bring an action for 'passing off'. The term appropriately describes what it is intending to prohibit. Such an action would allow recovery of damages. This could be the profits made by the guilty party.

An example of this is the case **Ewing v Buttercup Margarine Company** [1917]. Here the owner of a business called the 'Buttercup Dairy Company' was able to obtain an order prohibiting the defendants' use of their name on the grounds that the public might think the two firms were connected.

This provision is meant to protect a company's goodwill. Thus if it has no interest to protect then no action will be possible. For example a local Newcastle firm would not be able to sue a local Bristol firm. In addition there must be the potential for public confusion. If there is not then no action may lie.

Trading names

What if a company decides for some reason to trade under a name different from that which it is registered under? For example it might want to diversify and somehow differentiate the new business form the old. Using a different trading name would help this. Where a name is used which is different from the registered name, this is termed a 'business name'. In this context 'different' can be as little as dropping the 'plc' or 'Ltd'. Thus by advertising itself as 'Marks and Spencer', Marks and Spencer plc is using a business name.

Where business names are used the law requires that the registered name be displayed on all stationery and in every place of business. Next time you are in Marks and Spencer see if you can find the plaque which has its full name on. The laws governing this are contained in the **Business Names Act 1985**.

Registered office

The address of the registered office is not shown in the Memorandum. What is given is the company's domicile. That is whether it is an English, Scottish or Irish company. Once this domicile has been chosen it cannot be altered. This does not mean that an English company cannot operate in Scotland. What it means is that the registered office must remain in England and its public file will be kept at the English registry. For this purpose Wales is regarded as part of England. Within its domicile a company is free to move its registered office.

Objects

If we had been writing a few years ago this would have been a much more difficult topic. The position was illustrated by a case, **Ashbury Carriage Company v Riche** [1875]. In this case a company with the object of making railway carriages entered into a contract to develop a complete railway system. The court concluded that this went beyond the objects of the company and so it was an invalid contract. The term used to describe such acts is *ultra vires*, meaning 'beyond the powers'. The fact that the act was in the best interests of the company and even approved by the shareholders was no defence to such actions.

Being constrained by an object written into the constitution at the start of a company's life does not assist the development of the firm. Over time, lawyers found ways to get around this and so few problems actually arose. Long multiple objects were commonly used which seemed to allow the company to do anything. The original idea behind the concept of *ultra vires* was to protect shareholders by stopping the company using their money for a purpose the shareholder did not wish. The way in which this was eventually applied by the courts can hardly be described as protecting shareholder interests. In Ashbury Carriage Company, for example, the company could not enter into a profitable contract which the majority of shareholders approved because it was *ultra vires*.

This case and brief introduction give you some idea of the problems which existed prior to the passing of the **Companies Act 1989** which amended this area of law.

COMPANIES ACT 1989 REFORMS

Before we consider these, a brief point of referencing. The 1989 Act operated by modifying the Companies Act 1985. Thus references here are to the Companies Act 1985, as amended by the Companies Act 1989. You may be forgiven for thinking that the Parliamentary draftsman did not have you in mind when framing this legislation. In an attempt to help and to stop repeating the derivation of these provisions, sections which were introduced in this way will use the term 'new section' to describe them.

The 1989 Act made the following changes to the law.

1. New Section 35 states that an act done by a company cannot be called into question on the grounds of anything in its Memorandum or Articles (including the absence of any specific provision). In this context, an act would include the making of a contract. What this means is that if a company enters into a contract then it will be valid, even if not authorised by the memorandum.

2. Under new Section 35, a shareholder may take legal action to prevent a company from undertaking an *ultra vires* act as long as this is done before a contract is entered into. Once a contract exists then it cannot be stopped. Where a contract has been made which contravenes the objects clause it may be ratified by the members by means of a special resolution (explained later in this section). Ratification is a process of retrospective approval. If not ratified the directors may be sued for breach of duty and so would become personally liable for any loss the company made.

3. A company may, under new Section 3A, have the single object of being a **'general commercial company'**. This gives the company the power to carry on any trade or business and to do those things incidental to such trade or business.

Having an object such as that in (3) above effectively means that a company cannot act *ultra vires*. In other cases it is still possible for a company to undertake an *ultra vires* act but it will be valid. The directors who approved the act can however be sued for any damages suffered by the company. A member can only prevent the commission of an invalid act if he/she has sufficient notice to go to court before a legally binding contract is made.

LIMITED LIABILITY

ACTIVITY 11

We discussed earlier the way in which the concept of 'limited liability' conferred protection on shareholders. Give a brief explanation of your understanding of the term limited liability.

When a company has limited liability this means that the members are not normally required to meet the debts of the company. Their liability is limited to the value of the capital they have subscribed to the company. If shares are not fully paid up then a liquidator may compel shareholders to pay outstanding amounts.

STATEMENT OF CAPITAL

The statement of the company's capital is simply a statement of the amount of capital which the company can issue and how this is sub-divided. This may be something like; 'the capital of the company is £1,000,000 divided into £1 shares'. Note that this is the authorised capital of the company, what it is allowed to issue. It is not necessarily what has been issued.

ASSOCIATION CLAUSE

The association clause is a formal statement that the founders intend to be formed into a company. It will also say how many shares the founders are taking and be signed by them. It will take the following form.

> We, the subscribers to this Memorandum of Association, wish to
> be formed into a company, pursuant to this Memorandum, and we
> agree to take the number of shares shown opposite our
> respective names.
>
> | Names and addresses of subscribers | Number of shares to be taken by each subscriber |
> |---|---|

Finally each subscriber, and at least one witness, must sign the document.

In the case of a plc there must be at least two shareholders. Large listed companies might have a share register in hundreds of thousands or even millions. Two might therefore seem a low number. Until recently the same rule applied to private companies but it is now possible to have single member private companies. This means that even sole traders can form companies. In reality they have always been able to do so. They could for example, own 1,000 shares in a new company and be taking 999 themselves and giving one to another person keep effective control and still have two shareholders.

The changes were introduced through a statutory instrument the **Companies (single member private limited companies) Regulation** 1993.

The clauses we have discussed above limited liability; domicile; capital; and association are all quite formal. This leaves us with two clauses to consider further. The name and objects are worthy of detailed discussion and we will consider them now.

SELF-CHECK 5

Andrew, Brian, Charlotte and Diane decide to form a private limited company in Birmingham. The name of the company is to be made up of their initials. They intend to have an authorised share capital of £100,000 divided into 1,000,000 shares and will take 100 shares each. They also intend to have as wide objects as possible. Draft a Memorandum of Association for them. (There is no need to write out the association clause in full.)

The Articles of Association

We stated earlier that the Articles dealt with 'internal' matters. By this we mean those issues which regulate the relationship between the shareholder and company.

Matters covered by the Articles includes: convening meetings; voting; appointment of directors; shares; and payment of dividends. In Self-check 5 you were asked to draft a Memorandum. This is a relatively easy job and the answer given at the end of this section would be workable in practice. This is not the case for the Articles. They will need to cover a wide variety of situations and detailed rules will be needed to provide that problems which arise can be dealt with.

Drafting Articles is therefore a major job and most company founders will not be able to do it. To help them there are standard sets of Articles which can be adopted instead. For limited companies the model set is referred to as **Table A**. This is updated periodically, the last time in 1985. It is published in a statutory instrument after consultation and as such represents over a century's experience of company regulation. Larger, listed companies are much more likely to draft their own Articles. It is also possible to have a hybrid position. This is adopting **Table A** with appropriate amendments.

SELF-CHECK 6

A new company drafts its Memorandum but fails to create any Articles. What is the consequence of this as regards the company's constitution?

Changing the constitution

THE MEMORANDUM

Of the clauses in the Memorandum, all but one can be changed. The odd one out is the domicile clause which is fixed. The authorised share capital clause can be altered by means of an ordinary resolution. The rest, with one exception, by means of a special resolution. Changes to confer unlimited liability on a private limited company need unanimous consent. A plc cannot be unlimited. Note that as the association clause is simply a statement then it is never necessary to change this. The fact that the founders give up their shares is not relevant.

We need to define the two types of resolution which we have mentioned.

Special resolution

This is a resolution passed by three-quarters of the members attending a general meeting in person or by proxy at which notice to move the resolution has been given at least twenty-one days earlier.

Note that votes are usually one per share. Thus a person who holds seventy-five percent of the shares in a company could always pass a special resolution. The three-quarters figure relates to the shares actually voted and not the total number in circulation.

Ordinary resolution

This is passed by a simple majority. Strictly no notice is needed but as a general meeting requires at least fourteen days notice this will be usually given for ordinary resolutions.

There is one final type of resolution to consider here. The **extraordinary resolution** is similar to a special resolution but requires only fourteen days notice.

In some cases it is possible to have less than the required notice but this normally requires the consent of the holders of at least 95% of the shares in the company.

SELF-CHECK 7

List the clauses of the Memorandum and state alongside each the type of resolution which can be used to alter it.

For changes to the name the rules which applied to the original selection must still be met. Changes to the objects can be subject to a challenge in the courts by shareholders who opposed the measure provided that they hold at least fifteen per cent of the company's shares and apply within twenty-one days. The court would then decide whether or not the change should come into effect. Where a plc re-registers as a private company then the holders of five per cent of the shares may object to the court within twenty-eight days.

Where changes are made they must be notified to the Registrar within fifteen days and a copy of the altered Memorandum enclosed.

THE ARTICLES

The Articles may be altered by means of a special resolution. Within fifteen days of any changes the Registrar must be notified and an amended set of Articles forwarded. Once altered the Articles bind members in their altered form.

The law places some limits on the power of alteration. The Articles must be consistent with the Memorandum and with the Companies Acts. Section 16 of the **1985 Act** specifically states that a shareholder cannot be forced to subscribe for extra shares because of the Articles.

There may be cases where the Articles are a contract between the company and an individual. For example they may state that a named individual should be a director for a period of time. What if the Articles are changed to remove this provision? The consequence could be that the director might now be dismissed. The courts will not prevent a change like this taking place but in the event of the contract being ultimately breached, for example when the director is dismissed, damages may be payable.

Finally there are some changes which seem to fit in with all the criteria above but which some members think is unfair to them. Discussion of this point is beyond the scope of this course but you should be aware that the courts can strike out a change which they feel is not for the benefit of the company as a whole.

SELF-CHECK 8

Axe Ltd has an issued share capital of 100,000 £1 shares. A special resolution is proposed to change the Articles. The holders of 50,000 shares cast their votes at the meeting and 40,000 shares vote in favour of the change. Zoe, a shareholder with 100 shares objects to the change. She claims it is not binding on her since she is bound only by the Articles in force when she purchased her shares and that the change was approved by only forty per cent of shareholders. Advise her whether her view is correct.

Summary of section three

- companies are normally either public limited companies or private limited companies
- to form a company a process of incorporation must be undertaken
- incorporation requires the filing of specified documents with the Registrar of Companies
- once incorporated a company is legally distinct from its members
- the members of a limited company have the protection of limited liability
- the constitution of a company comprises the Memorandum of Association and the Articles of Association
- these documents effectively create a contract between the company and its members and between the members
- subject to some limitations, both the Memorandum and Articles may be changed with the approval of a majority of members.

Suggested answers to section three self-check questions

SELF-CHECK 1

If you said 'no' to the question, you are correct. The timber did not belong to Macaura but to the company. This meant that only the company could recover compensation for its loss. Macaura, as an individual had not suffered directly, it was the company which lost part of its assets. Insurance companies will only pay where a person has an 'insurable interest', that is some right over the asset. In this case the corporate veil, as it is sometime called, worked against the shareholder.

SELF-CHECK 2

1. Salomon v Salomon;

2. sham;

3. agency;

4. trading certificate;

5. Companies Act 1985 Section 349; and

6. wrongful trading.

SELF-CHECK 3

You should have listed: public limited company; private limited company; guarantee company; and unlimited private company.

SELF-CHECK 4

1. The answer to this question is that a promoter can make a personal profit provided that there is full declaration to the company. This would mean the full board of directors.

2. Using the answer in (1) above, the situation here is unacceptable and the promoter would be liable to pay any profit he/she made to the company.

3. Here, the accountant has a problem. As this was a pre-incorporation contract the company is not liable to pay. In practice it will pay such debts. If it fails to pay then the remedy is to sue the individuals who arranged for the service and make them personally liable.

SELF-CHECK 5

Your answer should look something like this:

MEMORANDUM OF ASSOCIATION

1.   The company's name is 'ABCD Limited'.

2.   The company's registered office is to be situated in England and Wales.

3.   The object of the company is to be a general commercial company.

4.   The liability of the members is limited.

5.   The company's share capital is £100,000 divided into 1,000,000 shares of 10p.

   We, the subscribers to this Memorandum of Association, wish to
   be formed into a company, pursuant to this Memorandum, and we
   agree to take the number of shares shown opposite our
   respective names.

Names and addresses of subscribers	Number of shares to be taken by each subscriber
Andrew	100
Brian	100
Charlotte	100
Diane	100
Total number of shares taken	400

   Witness signature (and name and address)

   Date

If the company had been a plc, the only difference would have been the inclusion of a clause to this effect. This states simply that 'The company is a public company'.

SELF-CHECK 6
The position is that the company has a set of Articles. It is deemed to adopt Table A except insofar as this is excluded either in whole or in part.

SELF-CHECK 7

1. Name	Special
2. Domicile	Not alterable
3. Objects	Special
4. Liability	
Limited to unlimited	Unanimous consent
Unlimited to limited	Special
5. Share capital	Ordinary
6. PLC	Special

SELF-CHECK 8

Zoe is wrong in her claim. She is bound by the Articles in their amended form, not by those existing when she became a shareholder. In saying that only forty per cent of shareholders approved the change she is factually correct but this is not important. A special resolution is needed to change the Articles. This requires a three-quarters majority of those voting. In fact eighty per cent of those voting approved the change and so it is valid.

SECTION FOUR

Managing the Company

In Section Four you will find material to help you learn about and understand the following things:

- the difference between shares and loans
- the definition of charges over company property
- the decision about whether to trade as a company or a partnership
- some of the special rules applying to small companies
- the obligations owed by directors to their company.

Capital

The discussion in Section Three has already introduced you to the concept of limited company shares and you will look now at some of the important characteristics of these. Companies need share capital but in addition may wish to borrow money. This can be achieved by using bank overdraft facilities or by raising long term debt. Large companies issue debt stock. This may be bought and sold on the stock exchange in a similar way to shares. Whether debt stock is issued or an overdraft raised, a creditor may want some form of security. This will typically be by having some 'right' over all or part of the assets of the company. The aim of this section is to consider the legal rules governing this and the issue of shares. If you are studying accounts as part of your programme of study you will become familiar with the idea of the **balance sheet.** Put simply this is a statement of all the assets and liabilities of the company. You will find details of the company's capital on the **liabilities** side of the balance sheet. Capital is a liability since it does not belong to the company. Money raised as capital is used to purchase assets and so you can see that liabilities and **assets** will be equal.

Shares

You are probably familiar with a number of points regarding shares. News bulletins give details of share prices and fluctuations in measures such as the Stock Exchange Indices. It is important that you have some understanding of share prices and we will consider this now.

Imagine that a new company needs to raise £1,000,000. It could sell issue shares to generate this amount. One obvious way would be to issue 1,000,000 shares at £1 each. Equally it could issue 2,000,000 shares at 50p or even 100,000 at £10. Whichever price it fixes is to some extent irrelevant. We will assume that it issues the £1 shares. Every share has to have a face value. This is called the **nominal value** and in our example it is £1. If you look on the balance sheet of a company there is a figure termed **'paid up share capital'**. This is the total of the nominal values of all the shares issued.

Now we know that shares fluctuate in value. We do not need to understand how but simply we can say that if the company prospers its shares will increase in value and decline if the company fails. Now imagine that the price of our shares has increased to £1.50. We need to make several points. The first is that the company will not change the value of shares in its balance sheet. The second is that the face value will not change. Thus we have a share which states it has a £1 nominal value with a market value of £1.50. If an investor wishes to sell some shares then he/she must find a buyer for them. The company will not refund the money paid for them.

What if our company now needs to raise another £1,000. Its shares have a nominal value of £1 but it would be unfair to sell them for this since existing shares have a market value in excess of this. There is no reason why the company cannot issue new shares for a price above their nominal value (although it cannot issue them for less). Thus if it charged £1.50, to raise £1,000 would only require the issue of 667 shares. The amount paid in excess of the nominal value is termed **share premium**. It is shown under the heading **'share premium account'** on a company balance sheet.

SELF-CHECK 1

Your grandfather has found some old share certificates in Redox plc a company listed on the London Stock Exchange. He vaguely remembers buying them but lost touch with the company when he moved house ten years ago. The shares have a nominal value of ten pence. He shows these to a neighbour who tells him that the company will not repay the money and as the shares are old they are probably not worth much. The neighbour offers to buy them for their face value. What advice would you give to your grandfather?

TYPES OF SHARE

Ordinary shares

The type of share which we have been describing is an ordinary share. These entitle their holder to voting rights and to a share in any dividends announced. Ordinary shareholders provide risk capital. If the company is profitable they will receive a good return. If it fails they are likely to lose all their investment. When a company becomes insolvent, ordinary shareholders are repaid last.

Preference shares

Companies may offer other types, or classes, of shares. Preference shares entitle their holder to a fixed rate of dividend. This is usually cumulative which means that if a dividend is not paid in one year it becomes payable the next year. Preference shareholders cannot sue if they receive no dividend. Their protection is that ordinary shareholders cannot receive anything until they have been paid in full. Typically preference shares do not carry voting rights at general meetings.

Redeemable shares

Companies may issue either ordinary or preference shares as redeemable. Usually shares are permanent but in some cases they can be issued in such a way that the company has the right to redeem them, that is buy them back, at a given time. This is useful if, for example, a company needs to raise money for a specific project which has a definite life span.

Founders' shares

As a final point it is possible to issue shares with other rights attached. Small companies may want to give their founders extra votes and so can issue them shares with higher voting rights. Conversely shares can be issued without voting rights.

ISSUING SHARE CAPITAL

The number of shares which a company can issue is given in the memorandum. If the company has issued all these it will need to pass an ordinary resolution to increase the authorised share capital. To actually issue shares, the directors of the company need authority from the members. This is given by means of an ordinary resolution. The resolution must specify the number of shares which can be issued and the time period of the authority. This cannot normally exceed five years.

Where shares are issued they are subject to **pre-emption rights**. This means that existing shareholders are allowed to purchase new shares in proportion to their existing holding. Thus a shareholder who has ten per cent of the company's shares can buy ten per cent of any new ones. A private company can have an Article which states that these rights will not apply. A plc cannot do this but either type of company can pass a special resolution to disapply them. This resolution cannot last longer than the directors' authority to issue shares.

Where shares are offered to the public then a **prospectus** must be issued setting out the terms of the offer and giving information about the company. If the company is to be listed on the Stock Exchange a similar document, referred to as **Listing Particulars**, is published.

A company may sell shares for a price in excess of nominal value but not for less. It is possible to issue shares for less than their full price but the amount received must be at least one quarter of the nominal value plus all the share premium. Companies may accept non-cash assets in exchange for shares. Strict rules apply to plcs acting in this way. Assets need to be valued under the supervision of a company auditor and must be transferred within five years. A promise to perform a service cannot be accepted.

SELF-CHECK 2

The directors of Beta plc propose to issue 10,000 shares to Yasmin in exchange for a plot of land which she owns. List the legal considerations they must take into account in doing this.

Borrowing

Strictly what we are concerned with in this section is the giving of **charges**. Unlike the issue of shares there are few legal rules governing borrowing. Usually there will be a specific power in the memorandum (although this is not necessary where a company opts to be a 'general commercial company'). Where a company gives a charge over its assets however then there are some rules which need to be considered.

You are probably familiar with the idea of a mortgage over a house. When we borrow money for house purchase we grant the lender a mortgage of our property. In the event of us not repaying the loan, the lender has a number of remedies. The most extreme is to take possession of the house and sell it. A mortgage is a type of charge and companies can give charges over their property in the same way.

Where the charge is over a specific asset, this is usually termed a **fixed charge**. The grant of a fixed charge stops the borrower from disposing of the property without the consent of the lender. This is fine where the asset is a factory but it means that a fixed charge over stock, for example, would not be possible. To get around this problem companies can give a **floating charge** over their assets. It should be noted that only companies can create this type of charge.

A **floating charge is a charge over all or a class of the assets of a company**. The assets in the charge will usually alter and the company is able to use them without the consent of the lender. In the event of the company defaulting a floating charge

crystallises. This means that it is converted into a fixed charge. At this point the company loses the right to use the assets covered. Crystallisation can occur in other circumstances specified in the contract which created the charge.

REGISTERING CHARGES

There are two registers of charges. One is kept at the company's registered office. Failure to register is a criminal offence on the part of the company. Of greater importance is the register maintained by the Registrar of Companies. Charges must be registered within twenty-one days of creation. If this does not happen the charge is invalid against all other creditors. This does not mean the company does not have to repay the loan. But if the company becomes insolvent the unregistered charge is repaid after all other creditors. Any person may register the charge. Details to be given are the date of creation; the amount borrowed; the property charged; and the lender.

Late registration is possible but any rights which arose after creation but before registration will take priority. For example if charge A is created on 1st January it will be valid from this date provided it is registered by 21st January. If it is not registered until 1st February it will be valid from this date. If no other charges are created this is not a problem but assume now a second charge, B, over the same property is created on 15th January which is properly registered. If charge A was properly registered then it will take precedence over B as usually charges rank in the order in which they are created. Charge A however was not registered correctly and so B takes precedence.

PRIORITY OF CHARGES

The rules on priority of charges were introduced in the previous paragraph. It may seem odd to have more than one charge over the same assets but this is quite normal. Imagine a factory valued at £500,000. The company could use this to secure a loan of, say £200,000. This would be the first charge. If it then used the factory to secure another loan of £200,000 this is a second charge. A further charge for another £200,000 could also be created but now the asset is worth less than the loans secured against it. What happens now if the company defaults on its loans? Where a lender ranks in priority determines whether the loan is repaid.

The rules are quite simple but their application can seem complicated.

1. Assuming they are correctly registered, charges rank in their order of creation.

2. Fixed charges always rank over floating charges even if made afterwards.

SELF-CHECK 3

Cheeta plc has a factory valued at £600,000. It gives a fixed charge over this to Bryn Bank to secure a loan of £300,000 on 23rd March. This is registered on 1st April. On 3rd April it gives a charge over the factory to Smith to secure a loan of £100,000. This is registered on 1st May. On 15th April a floating charge over all the assets of the company is given to Jones to secure a loan of £150,000. This is registered on 22nd April. Finally a fixed charge over the factory is granted to Brown to secure a loan of £100,000. This is created on 29th April and registered on 2nd May. Cheeta plc has now been declared insolvent. It has no assets other than the factory. The best price which this can be sold at is £500,000. Explain to the four creditors how much they will receive.

From this we see the importance of the priorities as Jones is not repaid in full and Smith receives nothing.

The situation is further complicated by the fact that there are other creditors. Unsecured creditors rank last of these. There is an intermediate class known as **preferential creditors**. These are a special group and include employees as regards unpaid wages and the State in respect of certain unpaid taxes. They rank ahead of floating creditors. Thus in our example, Jones would receive even less. Where there are other assets the first charge on them is to pay the costs of the liquidation.

REMEDIES

For a fixed creditor the usual remedy is to take possession of the asset and sell it. If this realises a surplus then this is given either to the next fixed charge holder or, if none, to the liquidator. If there is a deficit then for the balance the fixed chargeholder becomes an unsecured creditor.

The usual remedy of a floating chargeholder is to appoint an **administrative receiver**. This person has effective powers of management of the company and has the role of realising sufficient funds to repay the floating charge. This is subject to the priorities discussed above.

SELF-CHECK 4

Scenario Three

The partnership, T & P Computers has now been trading for a year. During this short time business has been good with customers generally pleased by the service they have received. After their first year together Alan and Betty decide that they will try to make a plan for the future. This has been prompted by a number of events.

1. They have become overdrawn at the bank due to their need to carry an increasing level of stock and delays in payment by clients. They anticipate that they will need more cash to run their business.

2. Currently they are operating from Betty's small workshop but need more space.

3. They are finding it increasingly difficult to respond to service requests by customers and need some assistance.

4. Winding-up proceedings have been started against a customer. He is insolvent and it is unlikely that creditors will receive more than fifteen pence for every one pound owed. Alan and Betty have lost £3,500. This fact combined with their overdraft has set them thinking about the personal implications of T & P Computers becoming insolvent.

5. A new van is needed to replace the old vehicle currently used by the partnership.

Following discussions with a number of people they find a small shop which could be used as a base for their operations. This would cost £75,000 to purchase. Their bank manager tells them that they also need at least £15,000 more working capital. With the new van they estimate their cash needs at £100,000.

The bank offers to lend up to £65,000 'provided that it can have a charge over all the assets of the firm'. Alan is not sure what this means but feels that this loan is not needed as his mother will lend them £50,000 provided that she has some security. Several of Alan's rugby club friends say that they would invest some money in the partnership and Alan thinks that they could put an advertisement in the newspaper offering shares for sale. Betty is concerned about 'working for somebody else' and does not want to lose her half share in the business. She is happy to accept the loan from Alan's mother with the balance from the bank.

Question

State with reasons based on the scenario above and your understanding of the law whether Alan and Betty should form a limited company or remain as a partnership.

Company management

This is a huge subject and only a brief overview can be given.

MEETINGS

There are several organs of management in a company. We have already considered the general meeting which has the power to pass the resolutions needed to achieve some specific ends. Companies hold two types of general meeting. The **annual general meeting** (AGM), which is held once each year, and **extraordinary general meetings** (EGMs). Any general meeting which is not an AGM is classed as an EGM.

Members entitled to vote must receive notice of meetings. Usually fourteen days notice is required unless a special resolution is being moved in which case twenty-one days is needed. Twenty-one days notice for the AGM is also needed. Short notice is possible. For an AGM short notice requires the consent of all members. Short notice of an EGM requires the holders of ninety-five per cent of shares to agree. Where a member does not receive notice then the meeting is invalid. Under Table A if an accidental omission occurs the meeting is still valid. Usually the quorum is two, that is there must be two people present for the meeting to start. In the case of single member companies this will obviously only be one person.

Meetings will usually be convened by the directors but there is provision for the holders of ten per cent of the shares in the company to demand that a meeting be held. In addition, if the directors fail to hold an AGM any shareholder can ask the Secretary of State to convene one.

The AGM has some standard items of business. These include: laying and approval of annual accounts, directors' report and auditor's report; re-appointment of auditors; and appointment of directors. EGMs will deal with non-standard business. Again these will usually be initiated by the directors but members holding five per cent of the shares can insist on putting a resolution to a meeting. Note they need ten per cent to actually convene the meeting.

DE-REGULATION OF PRIVATE COMPANIES

Many small private companies as a matter of practice do not hold general meetings or deal with resolutions in the way in which the law strictly requires. This was recognised in the Companies Act 1989 which went some way to relieving the burden on these firms.

Written resolutions

Instead of holding a general meeting and passing a resolution, private companies can use the written resolution procedure. This allows the members to pass a resolution by signing a document on which the text of the resolution is printed. The resolution is effective when all members have signed it. The procedure cannot be used to remove either an auditor or director from office as they have a right to address a meeting.

Elective resolutions

Where a private company passes an elective resolution it is exempted from some of the more formal rigours of company law. An elective resolution may exempt a private company from all or any of the following:

(a) duty to hold an AGM;

(b) duty to lay accounts before AGM;

(c) duty to re-elect auditors annually at AGM;

(d) allows directors to be given power to issue new shares without time limit (usually it is a five year maximum);

(e) allows short notice of EGM to be given with the consent of holders of ninety per cent of shares.

DIRECTORS

Appointment

Every company needs at least one director. In the case of a plc the minimum is two. The first directors are appointed on formation of the company, thereafter there are a number of ways in which they can attain office. Appointment is by ordinary resolution at the AGM. In plcs it is common for directors to serve for three years and then stand down for re-election. In private companies continuing appointments are more usual. Casual vacancies can be filled between AGMs by co-option. In this case the appointee must stand down at the next AGM and submit to election.

Virtually anybody can become a director. No formal qualifications are needed although some people are disqualified from taking office. The main disqualifications are listed below.

1. For plcs there is a retirement age of seventy. This is not however mandatory and unless the Articles provide otherwise re-election is possible provided the other directors give notice to the members justifying continuation of appointment.

2. The **Company Directors Disqualification Act 1986** provides some exclusions. These include:

- bankrupts
- those who have committed an offence with regard to the formation or management of a company
- those who have persistently defaulted in filing returns to the Registrar; and
- those who have committed fraudulent or wrongful trading.

3. Under the 1986 Act the court may disqualify a person where they regard him/her as unfit to be a director.

Removal

Directors may be removed by means of an ordinary resolution. It is not possible for a company to contract out of this by a clause in a contract or in the Articles or Memorandum. A director who has been removed may receive damages if this causes a breach of contract.

Directors who are subject to disqualification must also resign. In addition Table A states that a director should stand down in a range of circumstances. These include the director: becoming bankrupt or making an arrangement with creditors; becoming of unsound mind; or being absent from meetings for six months without the consent of the board.

Duties and powers

Directors have wide powers of management. If abused these could result in them furthering their own interests instead of those of the company. To ensure that this does not happen their powers are balanced by legal duties. The duties are similar to those we discussed earlier in this section when we considered agency. Directors, like agents, owe a fiduciary duty to their company. Thus they must not make secret profits or put themselves in situations where there is a conflict of interest. To some extent conflicts of interest may be unavoidable but where they arise there should be prompt and full disclosure.

In addition to their fiduciary duty, directors need to act in good faith and exercise their powers for a proper purpose. They also owe duties to act with a reasonable degree of skill and care.

SELF-CHECK 5

The following cases consider aspects of directors' powers and duties. Using your knowledge gained earlier in this section you are required to state, with reasons, what you think the outcome of the cases was.

(a) **Freeman & Lockyer v Buckhurst Park Properties** [1964], in which a director of a property company assumed the role of managing director despite not having been appointed to this position. He entered into a contract with an architect on behalf of the company which subsequently refused to pay the fees. The company would be liable if it could be shown that the director had authority to act as he did. 'Authority' in this sense has the same meaning as it has when considering the power of a partner. Was the architect successful in recovering the fee?

(b) **Industrial Development Consultants v Cooley** [1972], concerned a director who attempted to negotiate a contract on behalf of a company (IDC). On discovering that the company could not get the work (which was accepted by the courts) but that he personally could, he feigned illness, was released from his post and did the work himself. Could IDC claim the profits he made from the contract?

(c) **Hogg v Cramphorn** [1967] involved an issue of shares by the directors of a company which was done to defeat a takeover bid. The directors genuinely believed that the bid was not in the company's best interests. Could the transaction be ratified by the members?

In addition to the common law rules on directors, illustrated in the last Self-check, there are some statutory rules. These are listed below.

1. Where directors have a personal interest in a contract being discussed by the board they must declare their interest. Failure to do so renders the director liable to a fine and the contract can be rescinded by the company.

2. If a director sells to or purchases from a company an asset over a specified amount then this requires the consent of the members by ordinary resolution. The amount is the lower of ten per cent of net assets or £100,000. Such arrangements are termed 'substantial property transactions'. Transactions for less than £2,000 are excluded. If this rule is broken the contract is voidable and the director concerned is liable to pay to the company any profits made and indemnify it against losses incurred.

3. Generally loans to directors are prohibited. There are some exceptions to this. Loans under £5,000 are allowed as are those which fall within the normal course of the company's business, for example if it is a bank. In addition it is permitted to make loans to allow the director to perform his/her duties, for example an advance on expenses.

4. Where a company enters into a service contract with a director for over five years this must be approved by an ordinary resolution. If this does not happen the contract is void.

SELF-CHECK 6

Scenario Four

Following the formation of the company Alan and Betty decide to employ a maintenance engineer. He/she will assist Alan and Betty and also provide a call-out service to customers experiencing problems with machines purchased from the company. Following an advertisement in the local newspaper they decide to offer the job to Charles Hood. Charles formerly ran his own computer firm but had been forced out of business when two major customers defaulted on payment. He agreed to join the company on the condition that he would be given some shares in it after one year of employment and that he was appointed as a director. Although this was not the arrangement which they envisaged both Alan and Betty were impressed with Charles and felt that his joining them would increase the potential of the company. They offered him a six-month trial period as an employee with a directorship then and the issue of shares after two years. Charles accepted this. Shortly after Charles' arrival the working relationship between Alan and Betty suffered a setback. Betty placed an order for some computer monitors without discussing it with Alan. The two had agreed that all contracts over £500 in value be jointly agreed but the cost of the monitors was £3,800. Although Alan agreed that this was a very competitive price, he was concerned that they already had sufficient monitors in stock and so he refused to accept delivery of the goods when they arrived. The seller, Compusave plc, is now threatening to sue T & P Computers Ltd.

Alan reluctantly accepts the order to protect the reputation of the company although feels that he does not need to do so. In order to ensure good relations with Betty he also agrees to let the matter drop provided that Betty promises it will not happen again. She agrees to this.

Questions

1. If Charles was appointed how easy would it be to:

    (a) dismiss him within the initial six months if he proved to be unsuitable; and

    (b) dismiss him after two years on the assumption that he had been made a director?

2. It is subsequently discovered that Charles has kept in contact with some of his old clients and is doing some work for them on his own account. Can Alan and Betty prevent this?

3. Alan agreed to pay for the computers from Compusave plc, but was the company legally bound to do so?

4. What rights does Alan have against Betty if she enters into contracts again such as the one with Compusave plc?

Summary of section four

- companies raise finance from shareholders and through loans
- where shares are issued a company may charge more than the nominal value but not less
- existing shareholders have pre-emption rights and can buy shares in proportion to their current holding
- shares can be issued for non-cash consideration provided statutory procedures are followed
- where companies give charges over their assets these may be fixed or floating
- to confer protection on lenders charges must be registered
- special statutory rules apply to reduce the burden on small companies
- strict rules apply to directors' relationship with their companies.

Suggested answers to section four self-check questions

SELF-CHECK 1
The neighbour is certainly correct to say that the company will not redeem the shares. Assuming that the company still exists however the shares are unlikely to be worth 10p. They will have a market value which can be found easily by looking at the Stock Exchange prices in a newspaper. Your grandfather could then sell them to a broker at their market price. It might also be worth checking to see if there are any unclaimed dividends for the ten years since he moved house.

SELF-CHECK 2
The directors need to determine whether:

(a) they have any share capital to issue;

(b) whether pre-emption rights have to be dis-applied;

(c) they must have the land valued;

(d) the land must be conveyed to them within five years; and

(e) the value must be equal to the shares issued.

SELF-CHECK 3

As the Bryn Bank charge is a first fixed charge and was properly registered then this will·be repaid in full. The Smith charge is registered late and so ranks from the date of registration, that is 1st May. The Jones charge is properly made and so takes precedence over Smith. Finally the fixed charge in favour of Brown would take precedence over Jones as fixed charges take preference over floating. The order therefore is

	Receives	Balance remaining
Bryn Bank	300,000	500,000
Brown	100,000	200,000
Jones	100,000	100,000
Smith		0

SELF-CHECK 4

The usual advantages of a limited company are limited liability; the separation of the company from its shareholders; the ability to attract capital from selling shares; and the ability to grant floating charges. Against this are the facts that there are set -up costs to pay; companies have to have annual accounts prepared and audited; there are general meetings to hold; decisions may need the passing of resolutions; some control is given away if shares are sold; and the freedom to dissolve a partnership is removed. Some of these practical problems have been addressed in the 1989 Companies Act which are discussed below.

From the question it is clear that Alan and Betty need a large injection of capital. The van and shop will represent an investment in the business but would also provide assets which could be used as security. If the bank wanted a charge over all the assets this would be a floating charge and so would necessitate them forming a company. Alan's mother could be given a fixed charge over the shop. Selling shares to friends is acceptable for a private company but to advertise they would need to be a plc. There are more stringent requirements for a plc in terms of accounting, issue of shares and control of directors and for a firm this size the benefits are less than the disadvantages. Selling shares would dilute Betty's interest but if debt is raised this would have to be repaid before any profits were taken from the business. Forming a private limited company would seem the best option. This would confer some protection on Alan and Betty in the form of limited liability. A fixed charge in favour of Alan's mother and a charge to the bank to secure the balancing loan would meet their capital needs.

The above assumes that the bank will accept this arrangement. Commonly the directors of small firms give personal guarantees to secure the company's debts and so often limited liability is more an illusion than reality. It is also likely that the bank would insist on a first charge.

SELF-CHECK 5

(a) The architect in Freeman & Lockyer was successful. Although not appointed formally as managing director, the director acting out this role had ostensible authority. As the contract made was one which would normally be made by a director in that type of company it was binding.

(b) IDC v Cooley was decided in favour of the company. Although the company could not itself have benefited from the contract the director became aware of it while acting as director. He was therefore subject to a conflict of interest and as he did not have the company's consent to proceed had to pay over to it the profits he had made.

(c) Finally in Hogg v Cramphorn the directors were in breach of their duty. Issuing shares should only be done to raise finance and this was therefore an act done for an improper purpose. It could however be ratified provided that the newly created shares did not join in the vote.

SELF-CHECK 6

1. When we looked at the contract of employment at the start of this unit we stated that the right to claim for unfair dismissal required two years continuous employment. In (a) Charles would not have this and so could be dismissed easily. Once appointed as a director he ceases to be regarded as an employee unless he has a separate service contract. It is likely that this could be implied from the conduct of the parties. He could be dismissed as a director by an ordinary resolution but may then be able to claim compensation. The company would not be able to force him to sell shares.

2. As an employee there is an implied term in Charles' contract not to damage the employers business. Thus unless they gave him permission to work for himself his actions would be breach of contract. This would also apply if he was appointed a director before the problem was discovered.

3. The company was almost certainly legally obliged to accept the order. Betty has apparent authority to enter into contracts of this nature as it would be expected that the director of a computer firm would be able to buy computers. The action would though be a breach of duty by Betty. This appears to have been ratified by Alan and so she will not be sued but if the situation recurred she could be sued for any losses made by the company.

Unit 2: additional questions

Each of the following problems is free standing and is in no way connected to any of the others, each part of each question is also free standing.

1. T & P Computers Ltd have encountered the following problems.

    The company requires a new car park to be constructed for its customers to use.

This requires the foundations to be dug out and the surface to be laid down. For the former they employ Digit Ltd, who supply a mechanical digger and driver. For the latter they employ Smooth Ltd who supply a gang of workers and a small mechanical roller. Digit's digger injures some of Smooth's gang. It turns out that Smooth only employs the workers on a daily basis and that Digit does not own the digger. This is owned by another person who sometimes drives it but on this occasion he has provided another driver, Tommy. Smooth's gang cause an injury to a T & P employee, Sally, who falls over a barrow left in the path to the main door.

2. James, who has worked for the company for three years, was dismissed by T & P after they discovered that he had been using a high resolution colour copier at a client company where he did the computer maintenance at night. He had not been paying for the use of the copier. The materials copied were in fact brochures advertising the 'James Computing Services Company' (of which James is the sole proprietor).

    Advise the parties regarding:

    (a) liability for the injuries caused during the construction of the car park;

    (b) whether James is in breach of his contract of employment; and

    (c) a claim by the client company against T & P for the cost of the copying done by James.

3. Alan Tracey took his company-owned car to Dotty's Garage Ltd to have some repair work carried out, as well as having the scheduled service done.

    As he left the car he said to Dotty 'By the way, we are thinking of getting rid of this car, if you can get in the region of £4,000 for it, take it. We will see you right'.

    The same afternoon Dotty is offered, and accepts, £3,200 for the car from Carol.

    Alan now:

    (i) claims there was no intention to sell, and

    (ii) claims that the car still belongs to him, and

    (iii) seeks to reclaim the car from Carol who has possession of it.

    Advise:

    (a) Alan Tracey;

    (b) Dotty's Garage; and

    (c) Carol,

as to their legal positions regarding ownership of the car and liability to each other.

4.   T & P Computers Ltd. had instructed Brian, a specialist purchaser of computer equipment, to purchase some equipment on its behalf to a total price of £20,000. Brian had a great deal of business at that time and so instructed Charles (with whom he did a great deal of business) to negotiate and deal on his behalf.

Charles negotiated the purchase in his own name getting all the required goods but for £22,000. The seller of the goods (Byte) was pleased with the deal and gave Brian £1000 "for his efforts". Since the deal was completed there has been an upturn in the market and Byte could get more for the goods by selling them elsewhere.

Byte now refuses to deliver the goods to T & P Computers Ltd claiming he only intended to deal with Brian. Brian now claims the benefit of the contract is his.

Advise:

(a) T & P Computers Ltd;

(b) Brian; and

(c) Byte,

   as to their legal positions.

5.   Alan Tracey has been employed by Third Ltd, to act as a consultant regarding the purchase of some computer hardware. He has known Betty Parker for a number of years, she is a computer engineer and has a small business buying in parts and assembling them into fully operational computer units. Alan approaches Betty and they work together to get the required number of computers for Third Ltd.

Alan supplies the computers to Third Ltd and shares the commission with Betty.

Alan and Betty decide to continue operating together in this way and subsequently obtain a number of orders which they complete and once again share the profit. As time goes on they decide:

(i)   that they will trade as Tracey & Parker;

(ii) that they will share the profits on a 55%/45% basis;

(iii) that they will lend to the business a total of £10,000 in the same proportions as they share the profits; and

(iv) that Betty's son will join the firm as 'an equal partner'.

Advise regarding the following issues:

(a) the consequences for Alan if due to the negligence of Betty in dealing with Third Ltd, she is successfully sued by Third Ltd but cannot pay the damages;

(b) the effect of the oral agreements reached in (i), (ii), (iii), and (iv) above; and

(c) how the position of each partner could have been safeguarded in law.

6. Alan and Betty are partners of a firm selling office computing equipment. Chris had been a partner in the business but retired from the firm last year.

About three months before Chris retired the firm had entered into a contract with Circuits Ltd for the supply of '2,000 circuit boards per year at a fixed price of £10 per board' over a period of 3 years.

Shortly after Chris had retired Alan and Betty borrowed £10,000 from Blacktown Bank. All correspondence took place on old notepaper bearing the names of all three partners (Alan, Betty and Chris).

Chris has now been approached by:

(i) Circuits Ltd, because Alan and Betty have failed to pay for the circuit boards and are being sued by the company for breach of contract; and

(ii) Blacktown Bank because Alan and Betty have failed to make the scheduled repayments on the loan.

Advise Chris as to his possible liability on the contracts with Circuits Ltd and Blacktown Bank.

7. Alan and Betty, trading in partnership as Tracey & Parker intend to form a limited company to carry on business in computing and so instruct their solicitor to form a company to be named T & P Computers Limited. The solicitor prepared the necessary documents and these were delivered to the Companies Registration Office on May 6 this year. Alan and Betty intend to be the first directors of the company and have told the solicitor to see to this.

On the 21 May, Alan negotiated a deal with, and then agreed to purchase a large quantity of microchips from, Bytes plc in a letter which he signed 'For and on behalf of T & P Computers Ltd, Alan Tracey, Director'. The chips have not yet been delivered and Bytes plc deny any liability on the contract (finding that they can sell them for more elsewhere).

On July 3 (this year) Betty agreed, on behalf of T & P Computers Ltd, to supply Zen plc, a large chemical manufacturer, with all of their computer spare parts and servicing for a period of five years. In order to obtain the contract she had to agree to very competitive prices.

The certificate of incorporation of the company, dated July 1, was received by Alan and Betty on July 4.

They now consider that the agreement with Zen plc will not be profitable and have told Zen that they will not honour it. They claim that Betty had no authority to bind the company to the agreement.

Advise T & P Computers Ltd as to its legal position on the agreements with Byte and Zen.

8. Alan Tracey and Betty Parker are concerned at the recession in the computer supply business. As the only directors of T & P Computers Ltd, they decide that the company should diversify into the transport business. Writing on notepaper which described the company as computer manufacturers Alan ordered a quantity of heavy transport maintenance equipment for the new garage they have had built. The equipment was delivered but T & P Computers Ltd now decide this purchase would be an error as the equipment could be obtained cheaper elsewhere. They have refused to pay for the equipment on the grounds that the contract was outside the scope of business for which the company was established and was in law *ultra vires*.

Meany, a minority shareholder in T & P Computers Ltd, is now anxious that the company should close down the transport part of the business as soon as possible.

Advise:

(a) the supplier of the maintenance equipment whether the contract with T & P Computers Ltd is valid;

(b) Meany whether he may restrain the company from carrying on the transport side of the business; and

(c) Alan and Betty how in the future they could avoid these apparent problems with the *ultra vires* rule.

9. T & P Computers Ltd has been established for some time and the directors realise that more capital is needed if the company is to be able to expand at all. The directors agree that they need to issue new shares and to borrow to raise the amount needed for expansion.

It is agreed that a further £100,000 be raised by the issue of a further 200,000 50p ordinary voting shares and a further £600,000 by borrowing. The borrowing is to be achieved by the issue of three £100,000 debentures (A, B and C).

Debenture A is issued to Big Bank plc on February 1, secured by a charge on surplus land owned by the company. This charge is registered on April 10. Debenture B is issued on March 1 to Huge Bank plc secured by a charge on the same land. This charge is registered on April 1. Debenture C is issued on February 26 to Enormous Bank plc secured by a charge over the stock of the company. This charge is registered on April 8.

On April 1 the company placed an advertisement in the local newspaper to sell 100,000 of the shares, having already sold 100,000 to their relatives.

On May 1 the company fails to make the interest repayments due on the debentures because it is suffering from a cash flow problem.

Advise:

(a) as to the order of priority of the charges attached to the debentures, in the event that T & P Computers was wound up; and

(b) as to the legality of the issue of the shares.

10. T & P Computers Ltd do a great deal of work for Xanadu plc. The managing director of Xanadu (Ellie) owns a number of shares in T & P Computers Ltd. The following events have taken place:

1. Ellie sold a piece of land to T & P Computers Ltd at a price of £60,000. This land was then sold to Xanadu plc at a price of £100,000. The actual value of the land was £60,000 and Ellie, Alan and Betty (the directors of T & P) share out the £40,000 profit between themselves.

2. Xanadu plc enter into a large long-term contract with T & P Computers Ltd. Ellie was primarily responsible for setting up the deal and argued very strongly for it at the Xanadu Board meeting at which it was finalised.

Advise:

(a) the shareholders of T & P Computers Ltd about the profit sharing;

(b) the directors of Xanadu about Ellie's involvement in the profit sharing; and

(c) the directors of Xanadu who have now found out about Ellie's shareholding in T & P Computers Ltd and also that it appears that Ellie is a director of T & P.

11. T & P Computers Ltd. has two directors, Alan and Betty, who are also the majority shareholders in the company. There are a further 20 shareholders in the company.

When the company was formed Alan and Betty sold their existing business to the company for £50,000. The Articles of Association of the company state that Alan and Betty are directors of the company and that they hold executive positions that 'may from time to time be alternated between them by agreement'. Since formation they have held regular directors' meetings. Initially the company held an annual general meeting and general meetings of the membership, recently they have taken advantage of the written and elective resolution procedure.

A number of the minority shareholders are now concerned by the following issues:

(a) they believe that the original business purchased by the company was in fact only worth £30,000;

(b) some shareholders wish to remove Alan from his post as director but have been told by him that they cannot do this because of the clause in the articles;

(c) a shareholder wishes to remove Betty from her post as director and is proposing to use a written resolution for this;

(d) a shareholder wants to know why they do not have an AGM and why they do not therefore get to see and discuss the annual accounts of the company together. The shareholder wishes to requisition an Extraordinary General Meeting;

(e) a shareholder wishes to know whether it is lawful for Alan and Betty to have contracts of service for their executive duties as directors for a period of 10 years.

Advise regarding all the above issues.

Additional questions: guidance

Each of the following outlines indicates the areas of law that might need to be addressed in order to reach some form of reasoned conclusion and advice. As with many aspects of law there is often neither a 'right' answer nor a 'wrong' answer it might amount to who wins the argument and therefore carries the day or it might merely depend upon who carries the day in court.

It is always useful in law to refer to decided cases that support the point you are making.

1. (a) The nature of the employment relationship and the distinctions to be made between employees and independent contractors. This might include the various tests that can be used by the courts to determine the relationship.

    See: **Ready Mixed Concrete v Minister of Pensions & National Insurance.**

The nature of liability in employment situations–again the distinction to be drawn between possible vicarious liability (an employer for negligent acts of an employee during the course of employment), and the liability of an independent contractor.

See: section on the employment relationship and also Unit 4.

Definitions should be given for terms used such as vicarious liability, negligence, course of employment.

b) The contract of employment and its termination – unfair dismissal (some might draw the distinction between this and wrongful dismissal). Conflict of interest and exclusivity.

See: **Lloyd v Grace Smith & Co and compare this with the decision in Heasmans v Clarity Cleaning Co Ltd.**

(c) Responsibilities of the employer for actions of the employee during the course of employment.

2.   Alan Tracey: will seek to argue that no authority was given to Dotty's Garage to sell and therefore no title can pass to a third party. If this is the case then the car does still belong to Alan and possession can be claimed.

Dotty's Garage: will claim that an agency was created by Alan's words 'By the way .... etc.' This would be a commercial agency (factor) and would carry with it the right to the remuneration promised. If this is the case then the garage can pass a perfectly good title to Carol (garage in possession with the owners consent, innocent third party, authority to sell).

Carol: will wish to back Dotty's claim. If there was an agency then a valid title will pass to Carol.

See: the section on agency.

3.   T & P Computers Ltd: the nature of agency. Creation through ratification and the notion of ostensible authority. Can authority be delegated? What is a secret profit and what effect does it have (duties of agents)?

Brian: is Brian the principal – if so what effect might it have? Is Charles in fact the principal (rather than operating for an undisclosed principal)? What effect might the secret profit have?

Byte: who has Byte contracted with? Does it matter who they think the contract is with?

See: the section on agency. Consider **Watteau v Fenwick** and **Kelner v Baxter**, what is an undisclosed principal, the notion of the commercial agent.

4.   a) A partnership is a function of behaviour not legal formality. If the original contract was carried out 'by persons acting in concert with a view to profit' then the law may well decide that it was a partnership at that time. If that is the case it predates the partnership agreement and so will be subject to the Partnership Act 1890 (basic rule being one of equality).

b) Did these amount to a partnership agreement? If they did they will overrule the **Partnership Act** 1890, if they do not amount to an agreement or deed of partnership then the Act will remain as the guiding principle for the partnership, that is equality.

c) Articles of partnership, or a partnership agreement or a deed of partnership should have been properly drafted giving effect to, and detailing, the wishes of the partners.

See: the section on partnership creation, and agreement.

5.   a) Nature of a contract. Agency and the contracting parties. Contractual liability of partnerships, especially the liability of a partner for contracts made during their period as a partner 'contracts of a continuing nature'. Had any attempt been made to exclude Chris from liability? Could the attempt have been successful?

b) Possible liability of a retired partner for contracts entered into after retirement—notion of ostensible authority. Cessation of partnership and measures that should be taken to terminate authority and liability.

See: the section on partnership. Consider the outcomes of **Keith Spicer Ltd v Mansell** and **Mercantile Credit v Garrod**. How could the decision in **Tower Cabinet v Ingram** apply to these facts?

6.   Byte: notion of pre-incorporation contracts and liability resulting from this. Inability to ratify such a contract (principal not in existence). Liability therefore falls on the partnership that existed prior to the formation of the company.

Zen: certificate of incorporation is the 'birth certificate' of the company. Date on the certificate is conclusive evidence. Company therefore has capacity as from July 1st. T & P might try to argue that there was a lack of authority but Zen can rely on ostensible authority as well as the rules of director's duties.

See: the section on incorporating organisations, and the requirements for formation. Consider **Kelner v Baxter**, and cross refer to partnership and agency.

7.   (a) The role of the objects clause of a company as contained in the Memorandum of Association. The notion of *ultra vires* and the legislative effect of the Act 1989, Companies Act 1989. Remedies possibly available including tracing.

(b) The powers of a minority shareholder to restrain a company from taking action.

(c) Companies Act 1989 and the objects clause 'to carry on business'.

See: the section on the Memorandum of Association, and the objects clause. Consider the relevance of **Ashbury Railway Company v Riche** to modern commercial practice.

8. a) Scope for a private limited company to raise capital through the issue of shares – meaning of to the public. Role of the Memorandum of Association – capital clause, liability clause. Scope to change the Memorandum and the status of the company.

   b) Distinction between fixed charges and floating charges and legal and equitable. The notion of priorities and registration (including late registration).

   See: the sections on capital and company formation, also the section on borrowing.

9. (a) Directors duties in particular the notion of secret profits and to act in good faith. Effect of breach of duty. Possible courses of action to be initiated by the company or is it possible for the shareholders to do this? Idea of the 'proper plaintiff'.

   (b) Powers of directors to issue shares. The scope of, and any time limit applicable to, an elective resolution.

   (c) Conflict of interest.

   See: the section on company management.

10. (a) The nature of the relationship between a promoter and the company about to be formed. No secret profits.

   (b) A director can be removed by an ordinary resolution with special notice. It is possible to have weighted voting rights laid down in the articles, but a mere statement that 'X is a director' will not protect that person from dismissal from the post.

   (c) When can a written resolution be used and for what purposes?

   (d) Rules regarding AGMs, alteration under the 1989 Act, powers of requisition.

   (e) Nature of the maximum length of service contracts.

   See: Duties of promoters. **Eley v Positive Life**. De-regulation of private companies.

UNIT 3

BUSINESS
CONTRACTS

Introduction to Unit 3

In Unit 3 you will be introduced to the law of contracts. If there is one pervasive activity in the world of commerce it is involvement in contract. All of the following are achieved through the medium of contracts. It is essential, therefore, that you learn and understand the basic rules which govern contractual relationships.

- sales of goods and the provision of services
- the employment of workers
- the occupation of premises
- transportation of materials and goods.

At the end of your study of Unit 3 you will be able to:

- define what a contract is
- describe how the agreement which is the basis of a contract is achieved and signified
- recognize when agreements will be legally binding
- explain how the parties make their agreement legally enforceable
- explain the effect on the contract of flaws in the making of that contract
- evaluate the impact on a contract of problems concerning certainty, lack of capacity and lack of formality
- recognize the effect on a contract of untrue statements made during its negotiation
- identify the contents of a contractual agreement and the various types of contractual terms
- explain the controls imposed on the exclusion or limitation of liability for breaking the terms of a contract
- describe the various ways contracts can be brought to an end at some point prior to complete fulfilment of the parties' obligations
- consider and evaluate the factors which influence the availability of compensation for losses suffered from a breach of contractual obligations
- identify and describe remedies other than damages which may be available to the victims of a breach of contract.

Making a Contract

In Section One you will find material which will enable you to learn about and understand the following things:

- what a contract is
- the role **offer and acceptance** play in the formation of a contract
- what does and what does not amount to an offer
- how offers are brought to an end
- what is required for an offer to be accepted
- the importance of the **intentions of the parties** about the legal significance of their agreement
- the **exchange of benefits and obligations** between the parties which makes the agreement enforceable.

What is a contract?

A contract is an **agreement** between two or more people (or it can involve entities such as corporations, which are deemed to have a legal personality). But it goes beyond a mere agreement in that it involves a **bargain** between the parties. Each of the parties to a contract wants or needs something the other party has in its power to give; and each of the parties is willing to give up something of its own in order to secure what the other party has. Generally the parties to a contract will only conclude their agreement if each feels that they are getting about as much as they are giving. But there does not have to be an equal exchange of burdens and benefits between the parties. If you make a bad deal usually you will still have to honour it if it is embodied in a contract. For a contract also differs from a mere agreement in that it is **legally binding**. Whatever is agreed between the parties, each can go to court to ensure that the other actually shoulders the obligations or delivers the benefits arising out of the agreement.

We all enter into myriad contracts daily:

- purchasing a newspaper or chocolate bar from a newsagents
- taking the bus to work or school
- doing a part-time job
- buying petrol for the car or a pint of beer in the pub.

We generally don't think of contractual obligations in connection with these types of activities because in most cases there is no formal indication that there is a contractual relationship. For example, you and the shopkeeper do not write down that you will pay a certain price for a Mars Bar and that if you tender that amount the shopkeeper will give it to you. This leads many people to believe that contracts are limited to, and always involve, some sort of written agreement. It is true (as we will see later) that contracts concerning a limited number of activities are valid only if written down. But for the most part a valid and binding contract can be created as readily orally as in writing. It is even possible to create a contract just by acting in a certain way. This amounts to **implying** a contract from **conduct**.

Most business activity is based on contracts:

- employing workers
- leasing or purchasing premises
- buying and selling goods and services.

EMPLOYMENT CONTRACTS

All employees have a contract of employment. This is true even if the employer never gives them a piece of paper spelling out the terms and conditions of their employment. Rates of pay, duties, hours of work, holidays – all of these form the **terms** of your contract of employment whether they are written down or merely agreed in a discussion with the employer before starting to work. There may be terms in your contract of employment which you and your employer never discussed. For example, the **Equal Pay Act 1970** inserts into every contract of employment a right for the worker to receive pay equal to that received by other workers doing the same work, or work of equal value. The common law – the law made up out of the cases which have been decided by judges – implies into every contract of employment an obligation on the employer to protect the health and safety of the employee. If the employer fails to do that the employee can sue him or her for any injury suffered as a result. The **Health and Safety at Work Act 1974** even makes it a criminal offence to fail to take reasonable steps to secure the health and safety of workers.

SELLING GOODS AND SERVICES

Most businesses have as their objective the sale of some type of goods or service for a profit. These transactions are effected through a contract between the buyer and the seller. This enables each side to be sure that the other will honour its obligations:

- SELLER – to deliver the goods or provide the service.
- BUYER – to pay for the goods or service

There is a specialized body of law, based largely on the provisions of the **Sale of Goods Act of 1979** and the **Supply of Goods and Services Act 1982**, which regulates many commercial transactions. But, in addition, these must conform to the general principles of contract law. In this unit we will not examine in detail all of the special rules relating to sales of goods and services; but business dealings will be used frequently to illustrate the general principles of the law of contracts.

ACTIVITY 1

Using your own words, and without looking back in the text, write down a definition of a contract.

You should have written down that a contract is a legally binding agreement. You might also have put down that it normally encompasses some sort of bargain between the parties – ie. each one gives up something to get something from the other.

Creating the contract

Just as before you can successfully bake a cake you must assemble the necessary ingredients, before a contract can come into being, a certain number of requirements must be satisfied. For example, all contracts represent agreements, but not all agreements are contracts. If I offer to meet you in the pub tonight for a drink and fail to show up, do you think you can sue me for not being there? The answer is almost certainly that you cannot. Why? Because there was no **intention** on my part to create a **legally binding obligation** when I promised to meet you.

A contract is created only where certain essential criteria are fulfilled:

- a definite **offer** is made (to sell something, to buy something, to provide some service, etc.)
- that offer is **accepted**
- the parties to the contract each give the other something as consideration for the benefit they receive under the contract
- the agreement is concluded in circumstances which make it clear that the **parties intend that the agreement is to be legally binding.**

In Section One we will be looking in detail at each of these requirements for the formation of a contract.

After you have studied the material in Section One you should be able to do the following things:

● decide whether or not an offer has been made

● establish whether the offer has been accepted; or if it has suffered some other fate, such as revocation, before acceptance

● outline the rules determining whether or not the parties intended to create a legal relationship

● decide whether each of the parties has furnished consideration to the other – ie. has each party given the other something in exchange for what they themselves received under the contract?

Before we begin our study of what is required to make a contract, see if you can do the following activity.

ACTIVITY 2

Write down four essential ingredients of a contractual agreement.

1.

2.

3.

4.

You should have listed:

● offer

● acceptance

● an intention to create legal relations

● consideration.

Agreement – offer

Agreement is a fundamental aspect of a contract. The agreement required is sometimes referred to as a *consensus ad idem* or meeting of the minds. The necessary meeting of the minds is said to occur when an offer made by one party is unreservedly accepted by the other. We will see later that in some cases the courts have held that contracts have been made even though it is difficult to see any point at which there was truly a meeting of the minds of the parties. But, generally, unless the parties have agreed (or acted in such a way as to make it clear they were in agreement) about what benefits and burdens each is to derive from their relationship, the courts will not say a contract exists.

The importance of agreement in establishing a contractual relationship means that it is essential to be able to define when an **offer** has been made and when that offer has been **accepted**.

REACHING AN AGREEMENT – THE OFFER

There are four important issues to be dealt with:

- what amounts to an offer?
- what does not amount to an offer?
- how can an offer be made?
- what is the result of making an offer?

What amounts to an offer?

An **offer** is made when one of the parties involved in a set of **negotiations** states the terms on which, without any further changes, he or she is ready to be bound into a **legally enforceable agreement** with the other party. The party making the offer is signalling that as far as they are concerned no further negotiations are necessary. The offeror – the person making the offer – is presenting the other party (the **offeree**) with a set of terms which can be accepted or rejected, but which is not open to further bargaining.

Does the offer have to be made in so many words? For example, 'I offer to buy your car for £250.' In **Gibson v Manchester City Council [1979] 1 All ER 972, HL** judges in the Court of Appeal and in the House of Lords who heard the case disagreed about this point. Lord Denning, speaking for the majority of the judges who heard the case in the Court of Appeal, argued that there was no need to look for words that explicitly stated an offer was being made. An offer could be inferred from the totality of the correspondence or transactions between the parties. This assertion was rejected by the Law Lords when the case came on a further appeal to them. In their opinion, specific phrases of offer (and acceptance) are required Since a decision of the Judicial Committee of the House of Lords binds all the lower courts, it is clear that something recognizable as an offer has to be found. But remember, an offer can be made and accepted even if no words pass between the parties. It is enough that their conduct amounts to one having made an offer and the other having accepted it.

ACTIVITY 3

Write down in your own words what it is that distinguishes an offer from negotiations.

Negotiations lead up to the conclusion of a contract. They are the way the parties define what they want the terms of the contract to be. An offer is a statement by one party (whether made expressly or not) that those negotiations have generated a set of obligations on his/her part which s/he is happy to be bound legally to honour.

What does not amount to an offer?

Let's look at some things which are not offers:

- supplying information about the subject matter of a potential contract.
- advertisements
- displays of goods
- tenders.

Advertisements, displays of goods, and tenders are all what are known as **invitations to treat.** They each amount to a request for someone else to make an offer.

SUPPLYING INFORMATION ABOUT THE SUBJECT MATTER OF A POTENTIAL CONTRACT

Responding to a query about, for example, the price or quality of goods does not amount to an offer to sell the goods.

Harvey v Facey [1893] AC 522, PC

The plaintiff sent this telegram to the defendant: 'Will you sell us Bumper Hall Pen? Telegraph lowest price. ' The defendant replied: 'Lowest price £900. ' The plaintiff cabled back: 'We agree to buy for £900.' The court held that the defendant's reply was not an offer to sell for £900. The owner of Bumper Hall Pen was merely furnishing an enquirer with information which later might or might not be used in negotiations leading to the sale of the property.This case makes it clear that the actual wording used in negotiations is very important in establishing when an offer has been made and accepted. (See the discussion about the 'battle of forms'.)

ADVERTISEMENTS

An advertiser is seeking offers for the goods or services advertised. The advertisement may indicate a price for which they are for sale but this is no more than a guide to the reader/viewer/listener as to what price, if offered, is likely to be acceptable to the advertiser.

Partridge v Crittenden [1968] 2 All ER 421, QBD

The defendant inserted an advertisement in a magazine for caged bird enthusiasts. The ad said that he had finches for sale at 25 shillings each. The defendant was prosecuted and convicted for an offence under the Protection of Birds Act 1954 which makes it illegal to offer this type of bird for sale. The defendant appealed to the Divisional Court of the Queen's Bench against his conviction.

Did the Divisional Court think he'd been wrongly convicted? Yes.

The conviction was overturned on the ground that no offer to sell the birds had been made. The advertisement amounted to no more than an invitation to treat. The court reasoned that the advertisement could engender an unlimited and unknowable number of responses; while the supply of birds for sale was fixed. Common sense indicated that the advertiser could not have intended the advertisement to do more than secure offers from the readers to buy the birds at the suggested price.

But not all advertisements are merely invitations to treat. If the advertisement contains **conditions**, and if it indicates that once these are fulfilled the advertiser will be under some obligation to the reader, then the ad may well be considered to amount to an offer. Such an offer is said to be made **'to the world'**. Anyone who fulfils the stated conditions can consider themselves to have accepted the offer and the advertiser will be legally bound to meet his or her end of the bargain. Another term used to describe an offer made to the world is unilateral offer. One of the most common forms of **unilateral offer** is the offer of a **reward**.

SELF-CHECK 1

Bruno lost his pet Rottweiler, Butch, and advertised a £50 reward for his return. John, who read the ad while he was eating breakfast, was attacked by Butch while out for a walk in a park near Bruno's home. He managed to knock the dog out with his walking stick. He found an ID tag on Butch's collar and dragged the inert animal across the park to Bruno's house. When he got there he gave the dog to Bruno, threatening to sue him for the fright he had had.

Was John entitled to claim the £50 reward? Does it matter that John did not return the dog for the purpose of obtaining the reward?

DISPLAYS OF GOODS

The case which established that displaying goods on the shelves of a shop does not amount to an offer to sell them was:

Pharmaceutical Society of Great Britain v Boots Cash Chemists (Southern) Ltd. [1953] 1 A11 ER 482, CA

Drugs included in the poisons list were set out, with their prices indicated, on self-service shelves in a Boots shop. The **Pharmacy and Poisons Act** 1933 required that these drugs be sold under the supervision of a pharmacist. There was no pharmacist present by the shelves, but one was always on duty at the cash desk where customers came to pay for the goods they'd chosen. The Pharmaceutical Society claimed that the display of the drugs on the shelves amounted to an offer to sell them at the marked price; an offer which was accepted when the customer put the items into his/her shopping basket. Since no pharmacist was present when the customer selected drugs from the shelves, the Society argued that company was in violation of the Poisons Act. The Court of Appeal held that the display of drugs on the shelves was merely an invitation to treat.

The reasoning behind the decision in **Boots** is complicated. In part it stems from a long tradition that, just as the customer can choose where to shop, a shopkeeper should be able to choose who to sell to. If the display of goods amounted to an offer, the shopkeeper would lose this discretion. Anyone who picked the goods off the shelf would have a right to buy them. Another practical consideration which probably shaped the Court of Appeal's decision is that if the display of goods amounted to an offer, and taking goods off a shelf amounted to acceptance, there would be no possibility of changing one's mind about purchases while still in the shop. By locating the creation of the contract at the cash desk, the Court of Appeal made it possible for shoppers to browse without making any commitment to buy.

SELF-CHECK 2

Shifty owns a pawn shop in the Rundown district of Bigtown. He displays various unredeemed pledges in the shop's window. One item in the window is a pearl necklace. A sign says it is on special offer for £15. In fact, Shifty has made a mistake in writing the sign. He meant to put that it was for sale for £150. Mandy sees the necklace and realizing what a good bargain it is, goes in the shop to buy it. Shifty refuses to sell it to her for £15 and Mandy threatens to sue him for breach of contract.

Is Shifty bound to sell her the necklace?

TENDERS

If a company or other organisation needs some goods or services, it will often advertise, inviting bids or **tenders** to supply the goods or service. The invitation to tender is not an offer. The tender itself is.

Normally an invitation to tender will involve a specified quantity of goods or services. If the tender is accepted the tenderer will be bound to supply, and the advertiser will be bound to accept, the specified quantitites at the price contained in the tender.

The wording of the invitation to tender may amount to an 'offer to the world' if it specifies that the lowest bid or tender will be accepted. Making the lowest bid fulfils the condition and amounts to acceptance of an offer to deal with the lowest bidder.

ACTIVITY 4

What are the things which we have examined which generally are considered not to be offers?

You should have listed:

- requests for information
- advertisements
- displays on shelves in shops
- displays in shop windows
- invitations to tender.

HOW OFFERS ARE MADE

Offers can be made:

- orally
- in writing
- by undertaking some action understandable as amounting to an offer.

However it is made, to be effective an offer must be **communicated** to the offeree. Remember, John would not have been eligible to collect the reward for returning Bruno's dog if he had not known there was a reward for doing so.

WHAT IS THE RESULT OF MAKING AN OFFER?

If the offer is accepted, a contract comes into being (provided all the other ingredients are present). Remember, if you make an offer it indicates that the bargaining process is over. You have negotiated your way to what is an acceptable deal, as far as you are concerned, and you are prepared to stick by the terms of that deal if the other party is prepared to accept them.

If **rejected,** the offer immediately lapses. If I offer to sell you my car for £500 and you say you don't want to buy it, I'm under no obligation to sell it to you if a week later if you change your mind and say you'll buy it after all.

Besides being **rejected**, there are other ways in which an offer can come to an end:

- If more than a **reasonable** amount of time passes without the offer being accepted, it lapses.
- The offeror may wish to **revoke** the offer before the offeree has had a chance to accept it. An offer can be revoked at any point prior to acceptance.

- There are two important exceptions to the rule that an offer can be revoked at any point before it has been accepted. The offer cannot be revoked if the offeror promises to keep the offer open for a stated period of time and he/she is given money or some other form of **consideration** to do so. Nor can the offer be revoked if it contains a **condition** that will take some time to accomplish and the offeree has actually started to do whatever the offer requires. It cannot be revoked so long as he or she continues to go about fulfilling the condition.

- If the offeree says the offer is accepted but tries to impose new terms when doing so, they are, in fact, making a **counter-offer**, which extinguishes the original offer. This is really just a case of the original offer being rejected. The original offeror now becomes the new offeree. The original offeror will have to decide if the terms of the counter-offer are acceptable. It is important to distinguish between a counter-offer and a **request for further information** by an offeree who has yet to make up his/her mind whether to accept or reject the original offer.

- If the offeror **dies** before the offer is accepted, the offer will be deemed to have lapsed at the time of the death unless it concerns something which the executors of the estate can do as well as the offeror could have – eg. sell a piece of the dead man's property.

SELF-CHECK 3

Read the case set out below. The issue in it is whether the purported acceptance of the offer is effective with the result that a contract has been made. Write down your conclusions as to whether the offer has been brought to an end in some way before it was accepted; and, if so, how.

Case

Hyde v Wrench [1840] Beav 334, Rolls Court
The defendant offered to sell his farm for £1000. The plaintiff's agent said he would give £950 for it. The defendant asked for a few days to think it over. At the end of that period the defendant wrote back saying that he couldn't accept the lower price. When he got this letter, the plaintiff wrote to the defendant saying OK, he'd pay the £1000 originally asked. The defendant refused to go through with the transaction and the plaintiff sued for specific perfomance – ie. he asked the court to make the defendant honour the contract by accepting the plaintiff's money and turning the land over to him.

Concluding the agreement – acceptance

If an offer is accepted, then the terms contained in the offer become part of the contract. In effect, the offer disappears into the contract.

ACTIVITY 5

If being accepted is one way in which an offer is effectively closed, what are four other ways (discussed above) an offer can be brought to an end?

1.

2.

3.

4.

You should have said:

- by the death of the offeror
- by the lapse of time
- by a counter-offer
- by being revoked.

The two essential requirements for effective acceptance of an offer are:

- the terms of the offer must be accepted without any amendments or qualification
- the fact that the offer is being accepted must be communicated to the offeror.

ACCEPTANCE REQUIRES UNQUALIFIED ASSENT TO THE TERMS OF THE OFFER

If the offeree attempts to impose new terms, or seeks to modify the terms of the offer, his or her reply will amount to a **counter-offer**. As we have seen in **Hyde v Wrench,** this means the original offer will be extinguished. This can give rise to problems in a commercial transaction where each of the parties has a standard set of terms they use when entering into contracts; and there are differences between the parties' standard terms. Because standard terms are generally incorporated into order forms, the conflict over the terms on which the contract is to be concluded is known as **the battle of the forms**.

SELF-CHECK 4

Read the following case and decide on whose terms the contract was made.

**Butler Machine Tool Co. Ltd v Ex-Cell-O Corporation (England) Ltd.
[1979] 1 All ER 965, CA**

The plaintiffs were manufacturers of machine tools. They gave a quotation for
the supply of a machine to the defendants. The quotation was made on a
form which contained the plaintiffs' standard terms of business. One of these
provided that it was a condition of accepting the quotation that the goods
would be supplied at the price ruling on the date of delivery even if this was
different from the price set when the contract was concluded. The defendants
purported to accept the offer by returning their own order form. This set out
the defendants' standard terms of business which did not include any provision
for variation of the price. At the bottom of the defendants' order form there
was a tear-off slip to be returned in acknowlegement of receiving and
accepting the order. The plaintiffs signed and returned the slip. When the
machine tool was delivered, prices had risen and the plaintiffs demanded an
extra £2,000 from the defendants. The defendants refused to pay the extra
money.

Whose terms do you think the contract was made on? Why?

Is *any* divergence between the terms of an offer and the terms of acceptance
allowed?

**Yates Building Co. Ltd. v R.J. Pulleyn & Sons (York) Ltd. [1975] 119 Sol Jo
370**
An option to purchase property contained the provision that the option should be
exercised (taken up) by sending written notice by way of registered or recorded
delivery. In fact, the buyer sent his acceptance of the offer by ordinary post. The
seller claimed this rendered the acceptance invalid and refused to complete the
transaction. The court held that the impact of any divergence from the terms of an
offer must be subjected to a test of relevance. Was the term about mode of
acceptance one on which the offeror apparently placed great reliance? In this case
there was no evidence that it was. Did the acceptance fulfil the other terms of the
offer? Yes it did. In that case, the court said, the divergence could be ignored and
the offeree's reply would amount to an acceptance not a counter-offer, even though
it was sent by ordinary post.

ACTIVITY 6

What are the two essential criteria for acceptance of an offer?

1.

2.

You should have written down:

- the exact terms of the offer must be accepted
- acceptance must be communicated to the offeror.

COMMUNICATION OF ACCEPTANCE

It lies with the person who makes an offer to specify how acceptance must be communicated.

Holwell Securities Ltd. v Hughes [1974] 2 All ER 476, CA

The offer stipulated that the acceptance must be given in writing at the offeror's office by a certain date. The plaintiff posted his acceptance well before the deadline but it never arrived. He sought to enforce the contract on the basis of the postal rule – ie. that unless a reply by post is ruled out in the offer, an acceptance dates from the proven time of posting even if it never arrives in the hands of the offeror. The court held that in this case the wording of the offer made it clear that the offeror regarded it as essential to actually receive a document containing the acceptance. Since he did not receive the letter before the deadline, no contract was concluded.

SELF-CHECK 5

Read the following case and decide if the acceptance was valid.

Tinn v Hoffman [1873] 29 LT 271

The offeror specified acceptance was to be made by return of post. The offeree sent his acceptance of the offer by telegram.

Acceptance cannot be assumed or imposed

The offeror cannot assume that the offeree has accepted the offer simply because no rejection is received. Nor can the offeror pose the offer in terms that silence on the part of the offeree will be taken to mean acceptance. This is reflected in the **Unsolicited Goods and Services Act 1971** which makes it an offence to demand payment for unsolicited goods which arrive through the post.

Exceptions to the rule that acceptance must be communicated

There are only two exceptions to the rule that acceptance must be communicated by the offeree:

- the postal rule
- where the offer contains a performable condition.

The postal rule

The postal rule throws up an apparent contradiction of the general rule that a contract can only come into existence where there is a *consensus ad idem*.Where acceptance is made by post it takes effect as soon as the letter is posted whether or not the letter containing the acceptance is lost in the post and arrives past some deadline, or never at all.

The postal rule cannot be relied on where the offeror has specified that he or she must actually receive notice of acceptance [**cf. Holwell Securities Ltd. v Hughes [1974]** above]. Nor can it be relied upon where some other method of communication is specified and the offeree's use of the post would in some way disadvantage the offeror [**cf. Yates Building Co. Ltd. v R.J. Pulleyn & Sons (York) Ltd [1975]** above].

In fact, the postal rule today will normally apply only where the offer is made by post, or the offer specifies that acceptance by post is acceptable. Otherwise, more rapid means of communication will be expected to be used.

Using methods of instantaneous communications

The postal rule evolved in the 19th century when most business transactions, in which the parties were not dealing face-to-face, were carried out by exchanges of letters. Although it created certain difficulties, this seemed tolerable to the courts who felt that an offeree should not be penalised simply because of the vagaries of the post. They were prepared to accept that the postal rule put offerors into the position of being bound into a contract without knowing exactly at what point their obligations arose. It was even acceptable that a contract could arise where the offeror believed the offer on which the contract was based had been revoked.

Today parties can communicate with each other more or less instantaneously over the telephone or by using telex or fax machines. The question which arose once these technical advances had been made was whether the postal rule would apply if there were some delay in the transmission of the acceptance. The cases which have been decided have established that the postal rule normally will not apply to telephonic or faxed communications; but not all situations have been dealt with by the courts – eg. where a fax is received in the offeror's office out of office hours [**cf.**

Entores Ltd. v Miles Far East Corporation [1955] 2 All ER 493, CA; Brinkibon Ltd. v Stahag Stahl [1983] 2 AC 34, HL].

Acceptance by conduct

In most day-to-day transactions there is no need for the express communication of either offers or acceptance. You may go into a newsagent, pick up a newspaper, hand the shopkeeper the 45p or whatever the paper costs, and leave without any words ever being spoken. You have nevertheless entered into a contractual relationship as binding as one based on the exchange of detailed written terms and condtions. But in this case the contractual relationship has been created and discharged by conduct alone.

We have seen already that incorporating a performable condition into an advertisement can convert the advertisement from an invitation to treat into an offer. Where an offer contains a performable condition, the general rule that acceptance must be communicated to the offeror is waived. Simply performing the condition is deemed to amount to acceptance of the offer.

One of the most famous cases in the law of contracts concerned such an offer.

Carlill v Carbolic Smoke Ball Co. [1893] 1 QB 256, CA

The company advertised its patent flu preventative with the promise that it would pay £100 to anyone who caught the flu after using the smoke ball according to the instructions and for the specified period. The ad said that £100 had been deposited by the company in a bank in order to show their sincere intention to cover any successful claims Mrs Carlill bought a smoke ball and used it according to the directions. She still caught flu. She claimed the £100. The company refused to pay, saying that they were not legally bound by the promise made in the advertisement They claimed it amounted to no more than 'trade-puffery' aimed at persuading people to buy the product (like saying Persil washes whiter than white). The court, however, held that the advertisement amounted to an offer to the world. The company then said that, even if the ad amounted to an offer, they were not bound to pay Mrs Carlill because she had not informed them that she accepted their offer. The court held that it was accepted by anyone who bought a smoke ball and used it as directed. The mere using of the smokeball started a process of acceptance (which was completed once it had been used for the prescribed period).

SELF-CHECK 6

Who do you think the court sided with in the following case?

Errington v Errington and Woods [1952] 1 KB 290, CA

A father allowed his children to live in a house which he owned. He told them that if they paid the mortgage instalments they could continue to live there and when the mortgage was paid off he would give them the house. The children made no promise to pay the mortgage but began making payments as they fell due and carried on doing so even after the father died. The executor of the father's estate attempted to take possession of the house so that he could sell it. The children claimed they were entitled to remain in the house because of the payments they were making.

Intention to create legal relations

Just because an agreement has been reached, the parties to the agreement are not necessarily bound together in a legally enforceable relationship. For example, we might agree to meet at 8 pm for a drink in the local pub but that would not amount to a contract. If I failed to turn up you could not sue me for that. Why not? Because the court would hold that when I made the promise I had no intention to create a legal relationship between us.

An **intention to create legal relations** is an essential element of any contract. Both parties must accept that the rights and obligations which are embodied in their agreement are enforceable in court if need be.

The courts have laid down guidelines as to when, in the absence of any express statement, the parties might be **presumed** to have intended for their agreement to be legally enforceable. The presumption operates differently in:

- social and domestic situations
- the world of commerce.

Social and domestic agreements generally do not give rise to a contractual relationship because it is presumed that there was no intention to create legal relationships.

Whether or not the presumption will operate in any given circumstance depends on the calculation of the following:

- how close was the familial or social relationship of the parties?
- what was at stake?

Simpkins v Pays [1955] 3 All ER 10, QB
S was a lodger in P's house. S and P and P's granddaughter entered a competition each week. They shared the cost of the entry but it was made in P's name. One week their entry won £750. P refused to share the money with S and the granddaughter. S sued for his share. The court held that there had been a contractual agreement to

share any winnings. The presumption that no legal relations were intended to arise out of the agreement was rebutted in view of the fact that S was only a lodger, not a family member, and in view of the potential winnings which each person's share in the coupon might attract.

Commercial agreements are presumed to be made in the context of an intention to create legal relations, although this presumption is also rebuttable. Perhaps the most surprising circumstance in which it is held that there was no intention to create legal relations in making a commercial agreement is where a trade union and an employer enter into a collective agreement concerning wages or the terms and conditions of employment. Unless the collective agreement expressly states that it is to be enforceable at law (and it virtually never does) the presumption that it is not enforceable rules.

ACTIVITY 7

Why do you think the courts apply a different presumption about the intentions of the parties regarding enforceability of the promises they make when the promises are made in a social context rather than as part of a commercial transaction?

You could have said that it is because the courts believe more thought will be given to the consequences of making promises in business than in one's personal life. Therefore those promises should be taken more seriously. Another factor which may influence the courts is the fact that in our personal relationships there are a range of informal sanctions which can be applied by those who we let down, whereas in the world of business this usually is not possible. A final consideration which might figure in the courts' reckoning is a desire on their part to keep out of social or family disputes, as far as possible.

Consideration

A contract is a bargain. The essence of a bargain is that the parties each give up something they have in order to get something they want. It is this conception of what contractual relationships are about which underpins the idea that a contract can only come into being if each of the parties to the contract furnishes **consideration** to the other. So what is consideration? It is the price each party pays to get the benefit they will derive from the contract.

Remember I said that you could not go to court to make me honour my promise to meet you in the pub tonight to buy you a drink because in the context of a social arrangement there was a presumption that neither party intended that what was said would be legally binding. Another reason why a court would not make me honour that promise is that it was not **secured** – ie. matched or responded to – by any obligation on *your* part. Such a promise is what is known in the law as a **bare promise**; and bare promises are legally unenforceable unless they are embodied in a deed (the sort of formal document used for wills). What differentiates a bare promise from an enforceable promise is an **exchange of consideration** (exchange of promises, exchange of money for goods, etc.) between the parties to the agreement.

WHAT CAN A PARTY GIVE AS CONSIDERATION?

In business the consideration exchanged between the parties usually amounts to **money** on the one hand and **goods or services** on the other. Or there may be a barter arrangement where one type of goods or services are exchanged for another. But consideration is not limited to tangible exchanges. A mutual **exchange of promises** is an equally valid exchange of consideration.

SELF-CHECK 7

(i)   Ben sees Yasmin's car standing on his driveway with a 'For Sale' sign on it. He stops and offers Yasmin £100 for the car. Yasmin agrees to sell it for this amount and hands over the keys. Ben drives off in the car.

What consideration has each party furnished?

(ii) What if Ben promised to give Yasmin £100 for the car as soon as he was paid at the end of the week and Yasmin agreed to this? Has each party given consideration? What?

For something to serve as consideration it must meet several criteria.

● The thing given or promised must have some value, however small.

Read about the following case and you will see why it is said that anything of value can serve as consideration; and that value is in the eye of the beholder.

Chappell & Co. Ltd. v Nestle Co. Ltd. [1959] 2 All ER 701, HL
Chappell & Co. owned the copyright in a song called 'Rockin' Shoes'. Nestle hired a band to record this song and distributed the records as part of a promotional campaign. A copy of the record could be obtained by sending in 1s 6d plus 3 wrappers from bars of Nestle chocolate. Chappell & Co. sued Nestle for breach of copyright. They argued that the chocolate company should have obtained permission prior to making the recording of 'Rockin' Shoes'. The only time such prior permission was not required was if the music was recorded for retail sale. Chappell & Co. argued that inclusion of the requirement

to send in chocolate bar wrappers in order to obtain the record meant it was not a retail sale according to the meaning usually given to that term – ie. a sale for cash alone. Nestle argued that it was a cash sale because they simply threw the wrappers away as soon as they were received. The court held that the wrappers must have been part of the consideration furnished by purchasers because Nestle would not have sent a record to anyone who sent in only the money. Since the wrappers were part of the consideration Chappell & Co's contention that the sale of the records was not an ordinary retail sale was accepted and the court held that Nestle was in breach of copyright.

The significance of the decision in this case is that it clearly establishes that it is up to the parties to define what is of value to them. The wrappers had no intrinsic value whatever but in the eyes of Nestle they were valuable because the requirement to send them in triggered off sales of the their product.

● The thing given or promised must not be something the party was

  already obliged to give to or do for the other party.

Compare these two cases.

Stilk v Myrick [1809] 2 Camp 317
The captain of a ship promised to divide the wages of two deserters among the remaining crew if they would sail the ship home short-handed. After reaching home-port he refused to honour his promise. When the sailors sued for the money the court held that the promise was unenforceable. Their existing contracts as seamen obliged them to meet the 'normal' emergencies of a voyage and these included sharing out the duties of missing crew members. The sailors had done nothing above and beyond their existing contractual obligations. They had provided no consideration to make the captain's promise enforceable.

Hartley v Ponsonby [1857] 7 E & B 872
When a ship reached its destination so many sailors deserted that the ship was deemed unseaworthy by the port authorities. The captain offered the crew extra money if they would sail the ship home anyway. They did and once again the captain refused to honour his promise. The men sued for their money. This time the sailors' claim succeeded. Sailing an unseaworthy ship went beyond the normal contractual obligation to meet day-to-day emergencies. Taking on the extra risk was sufficient consideration to make the captain's promise enforceable.

SELF-CHECK 8

According to Stilk v Myrick, merely fulfilling already existing contractual obligation secures no right to any extra payment. But consider the following case

Williams v Roffey Bros. [1990] 1 All ER 512, CA

The defendants were the main contractors involved in the refurbishment of some flats. They sub-contracted carpentry work to the plaintiffs. Part way through the refurbishment it became clear that the carpenters would be unable to finish their work on time. There was some doubt if they would finish it at all. The defendants offered additional staged payments based on the completion of each flat. The carpenters then finished the work but the defendants refused to pay them the extra money. The defendants argued that no consideration had been given to make their promise of additional payments enforceable. The carpenters were already under contract to do the work on the flats.

Do you think the court allowed the carpenters to enforce the contractors' promise of extra payments?

● The thing given or promised must be in response to the other party offering to give up or to do something.

Re McArdle 1951 Ch 669, CA

A man's will gave his wife a life interest in a house which his children would eventually inherit. One son and his wife moved in to live with their widowed mother. The son's wife carried out a number of improvements to make the house more comfortable to live in. When the mother died all of the other children promised to pay the son's wife for the work she'd done on the house. It had increased the value of the place and as the inheritors of the property they would benefit from her endeavours. She was never paid, however, and eventually she sought to enforce their promise in the courts. The court held that the children were under no contractual obligation to pay her. Aside from any question of whether there was an intention to create legal relations when the promise was made, the fact was that she had provided no consideration for the promise to pay her. The work she had done while the mother was alive was not connected to, nor contemporaneous with, the promise to pay. She had done it of her own volition and for her own benefit.

CONSIDERATION DEFINES WHO CAN ENFORCE A CONTRACT

Only those parties who furnish consideration can enforce a contract. Even if someone would derive some benefit from an agreement, he/she can enforce it and actually secure the benefit only if they can show that they have paid some price for it – ie. that they have given consideration for it. This rule is generally expressed in the phrase 'consideration must move from the promisee to the promisor'.

Tweddle v Atkinson [1861] 1 B&S 393

The respective fathers of a young man and his bride-to-be promised each other that they would each pay a sum of money to the young man when the marriage took place. In fact, neither father gave the couple any money. When the bride's father died soon after the wedding the young man sued his estate for the promised sum. The court dismissed the claim. The fathers had struck a bargain between themselves. The young man was to benefit but he had no part in the bargain. Each father had given the other a promise to pay as consideration. The boy had given nothing. He had no standing vis-a-vis the contract between the fathers and could not enforce it. In legal terms, the bridegroom was not privy to the contract.

ACTIVITY 8

What are three things that are required for anything to serve as the consideration required to make someone else's promise legally enforceable?

1.

2.

3.

You should have listed:

- it must have some value
- it must be given contemporaneously with the other person's promise
- it must be something in addition to what you are obliged to do for that person.

Summary of section one

- a contract is a legally binding agreement
- agreement is reached when an offer has been unreservedly accepted
- an offer signals the end of negotiations: the offeror is ready to be legally bound to a particular set of terms
- invitations to treat are not offers
- displays of goods in shop windows and on the shelves of a shop are an invitation to treat
- advertisements are invitations to treat unless they contain a performable condition which may turn them into a unilateral offer
- all of the terms of the offer must be accepted
- a purported acceptance which seeks to impose new terms on the offeror is a counter-offer
- acceptance must be communicated
- the postal rule is an exception to the rule that acceptance must be communicated, where it applies

- acceptance can be made by conduct if a performable condition is undertaken
- the parties must intend for their agreement to create a legal relationship
- the parties to commercial agreements are presumed to have intended the agreement to be legally binding
- consideration is the price each party pays to obtain the benefit of the contract
- consideration must be of value
- consideration must be timely and in addition to any other obligation already owed to the other party
- only those people who furnish consideration in respect of a contract can enforce it in court.

Suggested answers to section one self-check questions

SELF-CHECK 1
Yes: John can claim the reward. It doesn't matter that he returned the dog for some purpose other than to collect the reward. He has fulfilled the condition and that obliges Bruno to honour his promise to pay. It would have mattered if John had returned the dog without even knowing there was a reward. Because no one can accept an offer of which they are not aware. Consider the following case.

SELF-CHECK 2
No: Displaying goods in a shop's window is, like displaying them on the shop's shelves, no more than an invitation to treat. The shopkeeper is hoping to entice you into the shop so that you will offer to buy the goods he/she has displayed. When Mandy offered to buy the necklace for £15 Shifty was perfectly at liberty not to accept the offer.

SELF-CHECK 3
Compare your answer with that given by the judge in each of the cases. (This will also give you some practice at reading the sometimes difficult language used by judges in their opinions!)

Hyde v Wrench
Langdale M R: 'Under the circumstances stated in this case, I think there exists no valid binding contract between the parties for the purchase of the property. The defendant offered to sell it for £1,000, and if that had been at once unconditionally accepted, there would undoubtedly have been a perfect binding contract; instead of that, the plaintiff made an offer of his own, to purchase the property for £950, and he thereby rejected the offer previously made by the defendant. I think that it was not afterwards competent for him to revive the proposal of the defendant, by

tendering an acceptance of it, and that, therefore, there exists no obligation of any
sort between the parties; the demurrer must be allowed. '

SELF-CHECK 4

The court held that the plaintiffs (the sellers) made an offer when they quoted for
the supply of the tool. The defendants' (the buyers) order was really a counter-offer
because it was made on the defendants' standard terms which differed from those
of the plaintiffs. When the plaintiffs signed and returned the tear-off slip they
were accepting the defendants' counter-offer. Therefore the contract was made on
the defendants (the buyers) terms. These did not provide for a variation of price, so
the plaintiffs lost the case.

The decision in this case reaffirms the view that it is the last set of terms which pass
between the parties before either starts to carry out obligations under the contract
which will be the terms of the contract. Although this is potentially of great
significance, in practice, businesses often ignore the fact that the other firm is
insisting on contracting on its set of standard terms and conditions, and will
commence performance of the contract assuming that it has been made on their own
terms. This can be the source of disputes later on.

SELF-CHECK 5

The court held that the person accepting an offer can use any other, equally quick,
method of communication instead of that which is specified in the offer.

In effect, the court in **Tinn v Hoffman** applied the same reasoning used by the court
in **Yates v Pulleyn**. If the divergence from the terms of the offer does not negatively
affect the offeror's interests, and if there is no reason to assume that he placed great
reliance on that term of the offer, then it can be ignored. However, if the offer
clearly states one method of communication of acceptance to be used and goes
further to specify that no other can be used, then that will amount to a binding
condition in the offer.

SELF-CHECK 6

The court held that the father's offer could not be revoked because the childrens'
actions amounted to on-going performance of the condition in the offer. If the
condition in an offer is one which is performable but completion of performance
will take some time, the offeror cannot revoke the offer so long as the offeree
continues to perfom the condition.

SELF-CHECK 7

(i) Ben's consideration is the £100 he has paid Yasmin. Yasmin's consideration
     is the car.

(ii) Ben's consideration is the promise to pay Yasmin the £100. Yasmin's
     consideration is the promise to turn the car over to Ben at the end of the week.

Where consideration is comprised of an act of some sort, it is called executed
consideration. If the parties merely exchange promises to each do something at
some point in the future, there is said to be an exchange of executory consideration.

The exchange of promises creates a binding agreement just as much as if the parties had actually carried out an exchange of goods or services and money. The contract is said to arise at the point where the promises are exchanged, not when the actions promised are carried out.

SELF-CHECK 8

On appeal it was held that the carpenters were entitled to the extra payments. The defendants clearly benefited from their renewed efforts. They were able to avoid the trouble and expense of engaging another firm of carpenters to complete the work; and they avoided having to make large penalty payments to the owners of the block of flats for failing to complete the refurbishment project on time. The Court of Appeal felt that on that basis **Stilk v Myrick** could be 'distinguished' (disregarded as a precedent).

The Court of Appeal's focus was clearly not on what extra benefits, if any, the promisor derived from the actual fulfillment of the promisee's already existing obligations, but rather on what costs the promisor's had avoided. In the court's eyes an act which allowed the contractors to avoid costs benefited them.

A businessman or woman may sometimes be confronted with a situation where they are contracted to buy or sell something and find that it can be obtained or sold at such a favourable price elsewhere that, even after taking into account any damages that may have to be paid for breach of contract, it would still be profitable to sell or procure the goods or service elsewhere. The other party, realizing that this is the case, may offer some incentive for them to honour their contractual obligation. Should the other party be able to renege on their promise to pay the extra amount once the contract has been fulfilled? The answer the law has traditionally given is yes (**Stilck v Myrick**). But is it not just as logical to say that the promise of extra payments has been 'secured,' or paid for by the business person foregoing the opportunity of securing a better price or cheaper goods elsewhere?

SECTION TWO

What Can Go Wrong During the Making of a Contract

In Section Two you will find material which will enable you to learn about and understand the following things:

- what it means when it is said that a contract is **unenforceable**, **void** or **voidable**
- the effect on a contract of a **lack of certainty about terms**
- the requirements about **formality** for certain types of contracts
- what happens if a contract is entered into by someone who does not have the **legal capacity** to contract – for example, a minor
- what types of **restraints of trade** are illegal, and the effect of embodying these in a contract
- what happens to a contract if it is entered into by one party as a result of the other party making a **misrepresentation** about some aspect of the subject matter of the contract.

What can go wrong in the making of a contract and how it affects the contract

There are a number of things which can go wrong during the formation of a contract which will mean that, even though an agreement has been reached, and although that agreement has the necessary characteristics of a contract, it is **unenforceable.** Three of the most important of these vitiating factors are:

- lack of **certainty** about what the parties' rights and obligations under the contract are
- lack of some required **formality**
- lack of legal **capacity** to enter into a binding agreement.

There are other things which can go wrong in the course of making a contract which will result in its being rendered **void** or **voidable**:

- either the common law or statute makes it **illegal** to conclude an agreeement such as the one the parties have entered into
- the agreement has been reached only as a result of one party subjecting the other to either **duress** or **undue influence**

- the offeror has **misrepresented** some aspect of the subject matter of the agreement
- one or both of the parties are **mistaken** about some fundamental aspect of the agreement – for example, the parties have entered into a contract the subject matter of which is no longer in existence.

VOID AND VOIDABLE CONTRACTS AND RESCISSION

A **void contract** is one which is flawed in such a way that it is treated by the law as if no agreement ever had been made between the parties. The Latin term applied to describe such a situation is that the contract is *void ab initio*. Neither party is regarded as ever having had any rights or obligations toward the other as far as this agreement is concerned.

Some flaws – eg. illegality – are such that the courts will always regard them as rendering the contract void. The law will not recognize that any agreement has ever existed, even if the parties would like to ignore the flaw and carry on with the contract. But some flaws only render a contract voidable. It is left to the injured party to decide if they wish to treat the flaw as having rendered the contract void or if they wish to ignore the flaw and carry on with the contract. If they do choose to take the opportunity of considering the contract to be void, it is said to be **rescinded** at that point. The effect of **rescission** is that the contract is regarded as void from the very beginning. This gives both parties a right to be restored, so far as this is possible, to their pre-contractual position as regards exchanges of money, goods or services.

Where a contract is said to be voidable some account has to be taken of what has happened so far in the relationship between the parties. For example, 'injured' parties who find out about the flaw but continue to perfom their obligations and receive benefits under the contract for some time afterwards, may be deemed to have **'affirmed'** the contract. This means they will have lost this right to rescind it. Similarly, if it is substantially impossible to restore the parties to their pre-contractual positions by the time the notice of rescission is given, the court may not uphold the decision of the injured party to rescind the contract.

After you have studied the material in Section Two you should be able to do the following things:

- explain the difference between a contract being unenforceable and being void and indicate what types of flaws can result in the contract being either unenforceable or void
- differentiate between those situations where a contract is voidable rather than being automatically void and indicate what is likely to render a contract voidable
- decide whether statements make in the course of negotiations about a contract have any legal significance and explain what significance they have and why

● explain what the consequences of rescinding a contract are and indicate
the circumstances when rescission will not be available.

ACTIVITY 9

Using your own words, and without referring back in the text, jot down the
difference between a contract being unenforceable, or voidable.

An **unenforceable contract** is one which, although it remains in being, has some
defect which means that the courts will not make the parties honour their
obligations. This may have resulted from, for example, one of the contracting
parties lacking the capacity to enter into a binding legal relationship because they
are a minor. A **voidable contract** is one which contains a flaw that is seen in the
eyes of the law as giving the party who stands to suffer as a result of the flaw a right
to regard the contract as void. If that party chooses to they can act as if no contract
had ever been made.

Lack of certainty

It is essential that the parties to a contract are absolutely clear what obligations and
rights they each have. If the terms of the agreement they have made are not of
sufficient **certainty** the contract is said to be inchoate and hence **unenforceable**.

Scammell (G) and Nephew v Ouston [1941] AC 251, HL
The defendant agreed to purchase a van from the plaintiff . The purchase was said
to be made on 'hire-purchase terms over two years.' When the plaintiff refused to
deliver the van, and the defendant sued for damages for non-delivery, the essential
question was what obligation the agreement actually imposed on the plaintiff. The
court held that the contract was unenforceable because no one could specify what
supplying on 'hire-purchase terms' meant. There was a variety of possible hire-
purchase arrangements and no way to tell which one was to be used in this case.

The courts will go to some lengths to give a contract what is known as **business
efficacy** – ie. they will do all they can to make the contract workable. Where
uncertainty as to the meaning of a disputed term or terms is concerned they can
seek enlightenment from a number of sources:

- other parts of the contract may give a **contextual meaning** to the disputed term.
- there may be some **mechanism provided in the contract** for resolving ambiguous or vague terms – for example, a provision for an arbitrator to sort out disputes
- there may be a **standard trade practice** which will flesh out the meaning of a term
- there may be a **course of previous dealings** between the parties in which the disputed term has always been taken to have some particular meaning
- where there is a question as to what the parties have agreed about the price of goods, **Section 8 of the Sale of Goods Act 1979** provides that if the parties have failed to specify a price, the buyer will pay a 'reasonable' price.

As a rule of thumb, the courts are reluctant to accept the contention of one party that the terms of the contract are too uncertain to be enforceable if that party has actually been perfoming the contract for some period before the dispute over the meaning of its terms arose

ACTIVITY 10

Why does a lack of certainty render a contract unenforceable?

The courts' function is to ensure that each party to a contract lives up to their obligations under the contract. If the courts cannot clearly ascertain what those obligations are, they cannot perfom that function. So uncertainty renders the contract unenforceable.

Lack of necessary formality

As a general rule there is no particular form which a contract must take in order to be valid. It can be **oral**, **written**, or based merely on the **conduct** of the parties. There are a few types of contracts, however, which will not be enforceable unless they meet certain formality **requirements**. Among them are:

- contracts for the transfer of shares in registered companies
- hire purchase agreements

- contracts for the sale of land
- conveyances of land
- leases of land for a period of more than three years.

Lack of capacity

Only a few 'persons' are deemed not to have the capacity to enter into a legally enforceable agreement:

- minors
- the drunk and the mentally incapacitated
- corporate bodies which enter into an agreement beyond their powers.

LEGAL CAPACITY OF MINORS

A minor is defined in law as a person under the age of 18 (reduced from 21 by the **Family Law Reform Act 1969**). The extent to which minors can enter into an enforceable contract is governed by two pieces of legislation:

- **Minors' Contracts Act 1987**
- **Sale of Goods Act 1979**

Minors can enter into all sorts of agreements but the obligations they undertake in agreements involving **loans of money** and the **purchase of non-neccessaries** on credit cannot be enforced in the courts.

Whether goods are considered 'necessary' or a 'non-necessary' depends on the facts of each case. The courts will look at factors such as:

- the minor's station in life – ie. what material standard of living he/she is accustomed to
- whether or not the goods have some 'utility' value
- what stock of the goods the minor already possesses.

The rules regarding sales to minors seem to bear hard on merchants. Apart from obvious examples such as jewellery, etc., how are they supposed to know whether the goods they sell are necessaries or non-necessaries? (Of course, they could avoid the problem – and many do – by refusing to sell goods on credit to minors.) If they do enter into a contract for the supply of non-necessaries on credit they are bound to fulfil their obligation to deliver the goods to the minor but they cannot sue for the price. This restriction on the rights of merchants who deal with minors was ameliorated to some extent by Section 3 of the **Minors' Contracts Act 1987**. Section 3 gives the court the discretionary power to order the minor to return non-necessary goods bought on credit to the merchant (or to hand over any other property or money which can be shown to have been obtained from someone else in exchange for the goods).

LEGAL CAPACITY OF PEOPLE WHO ARE DRUNK

Drunks will be bound by any contract they enter into which they could have understood the nature of at the time. In order to avoid their obligations they must not only show that they did not comprehend what they were doing, but show also that the other party was aware of this. As with minors, they will be bound to pay a reasonable price if the contract was for the supply of necessaries. They will also be bound where they actually have paid for the goods at the time of purchase.

LEGAL CAPACITY OF THE MENTALLY ILL

Their incapacity is the same as that of drunks.

LEGAL CAPACITY OF COMPANIES

A company is deemed to have a **legal personality**. It can enter into any agreement which is in conformity with its articles of association, and which does not violate statutory restrictions. The articles of association of a company set out the objects or purposes for which the company was formed. Nowadays these tend to be very widely drawn so that there are few limits on the types of activities companies can engage in.

Most companies are formed by registration under the **Companies Act 1985**. Section 35 of the Companies Act 1985 provides that any transaction directly approved by the board of directors' of a registered company will fall within the capacity of the company. This allows companies to escape any restriction imposed by the purposes section of the articles of association.

ACTIVITY 11

Can you remember what circumstances there must be before a minor will not be obliged to live up to contractual obligations?

The minor must make a **purchase of non-necessaries** on **credit**.

Illegal contracts

There are some contracts which are rendered void simply because they have a purpose which runs contrary to either the common law or statutes. Among these are:

- *common law:* any agreement to commit a criminal offence or a tort
- *common law:* a contract which will result in the Inland Revenue being defrauded

- *common law*: contracts with a connotation of immorality – eg. a bargain with a prostitute
- *common law*: contracts involving wagers or gambling debts
- *Resale Act 1976*: if suppliers agree to penalise retailers who sell goods below some minimum price set by the suppliers, then that agreement is illegal
- *Restrictive Trade Practices Act 1976*: agreements which affect goods/services must be registered with the Director General of Fair Trading. If they are not, then the restrictive agreement will be presumed to be void. The presumption can be rebutted by proof that the agreeement is beneficial to the parties and in the public interest.

Perhaps the most commonly found illegal contract is one which involves a **restraint of trade.**

CONTRACTS IN RESTRAINT OF TRADE

The restraint of trade is illegal. Therefore any contract which involves a restraint of trade is *prima facie* illegal and hence void. However, a common law **doctrine of restraint of trade** has evolved. Under the doctrine not all restraints are deemed to be so objectionable that they will render a contract void. The restraint may avoid illegality by being of a type which has 'passed into the accepted and normal currency of commercial or contractual or conveyancing relations'; or because the inclusion of the restraint can be shown to be **reasonable** and **not against the public interest.**

The essential condition in establishing reasonableness is that the person seeking to rely on the restraint has an actual interest to protect by way of the restraint. Having established this, the courts will then turn to measuring the **temporal** and **geographical extensiveness** of the restraint imposed to see if it exceeds what is required to protect the interest.

Measurement of what is *not* against the public interest is more difficult. There are competing interests to be weighed up. On the one hand lies the freedom to contract – an esential component of our view of the best form of organisation of economic life. On the other hand lies the freedom to trade. It is the great value attributed to the latter that underlies the existence of the idea that restraint of trade should be illegal in the first place.

One last general comment is necessary before we analyse the types of restraints. The cases which come before the courts generally are brought by the party who is seeking to rely on the restraint. The action will usually involve two claims: one is for **damages** for the loss of trade caused by the failure to observe the restraint; the other is for an **injunction** to prevent any further breaches of the restraint.

ACTIVITY 12

What are the three things which must be shown in order to rebut the presumption that a restraint of trade renders a contract void for illegality?

1.

2.

3.

You should have identified:

- there has to a legitimate interest to be protected by the restraint
- the restraint has to be reasonable as to its temporal and geographical extent
- the restraint must not be against the public interest.

WHERE CONTRACTS IN RESTRAINT OF TRADE ARE USED

The most common types of restraints of trade are as follows:

- An employer attempts to keep an ex-employee from setting up in competition. Most commonly employers are claiming to protect either trade secrets or business connections and customer lists.

If the employer claims that the proprietary interest for which protection is sought is a trade secret, then it must truly be a secret, not just a way of organising a business; and the employee must know enough about the secret to be able to successfully exploit it elsewhere.

An employer will only have a proprietary interest in restraining ex-employees from exploiting their knowledge of the firm's customers if it can be shown that the ex-employees not only had contact with customers, but could be said to have some influence over them. It must be possible that customers may be attracted away from the employer if an ex-employee sets up on their own.

Mason v Provident Clothing and Supply Co. Ltd. [1913] AC 274, HL
The company imposed a term in the plaintiff's contract of employment restraining him from working for any company with a similar business located within 25 miles of London. The restraint was to last for three years. The court held that the company had a legitimate interest in protecting its customer list. But it went too far in the restraint imposed regarding the area from which he was excluded from employment by one of the company's rivals. As to the suggestion that the contract could be saved by severing the illegal restraint and imposing one which was within the limits of reasonableness, the court held that

severance was possible only where the illegitimate part did not go to the heart of what the employer was seeking to do. In this case the court believed the purpose was to penalise the employee if he left the firm rather than merely protecting the firm's interests.

● Someone who has bought a business attempts to keep the seller from setting up in a new business to compete.

The courts have proved more willing to uphold restraints keeping people who sell businesses from opening up again in the same trade and/or in the same area than they have liked to do where the restraint is aimed by an employer at an employee. One reason why is their view that the parties are more likely to be of equal bargaining strength where the sale of a business is concerned. (An employee may not be in a very good position to resist the imposition of a restraint by his/her employer.)

Goldsoll v Goldman [1915] 1 Ch 292, CA
The defendant was in the costume jewellery business in London. He sold the business and in the contract of sale he agreed that for two years he would not deal in real or imitation jewellery in any part of the UK, France, Russia, or Spain or within 25 miles of Potsdamer-strasse in Berlin or St. Stefans Kirche in Vienna. The court held that the restriction on trading in the UK was reasonable because the plaintiff acquired most of his customers by way of advertisements placed in widely circulated newspapers. But the restraint on the defendant trading outside the UK was unreasonable. The plaintiff had no interest to be protected by such a restraint. Similarly, the restraint on trading in real gold jewellery was unreasonable. That was not an activity which had ever been connected with the defendant's business.

● *Solus* agreements arise where retailers agree to sell only one brand of goods. The retailer benefits from preferential prices; the wholesaler gets an assured market for his/her products. Since a restraint of trade is involved these agreements are *prima facie* void. The courts, however, will allow *solus* agreements to stand if they are reasonable in all the circumstances.

Esso Petroleum Co. Ltd. v Harper's Garages (Stourport) Ltd. [1968] AC 269, HL
The owner of two garages entered into solus agreements with Esso. One agreement was for a period of four years; the other was for 21 years. Was either agreement valid? The court held that the four-year agreement could stand because four years was a reasonable period about which to make judgements concerning the strength of one company's products in the market. The 21-year agreement was held to go beyond the bounds of reasonableness simply because realistic market evaluations could not be made encompassing such a long period. Nor was it in the public interest to tie a retailer to a supplier for such a long period. The community might be better served if the retailer had more flexibility as to whose products he sold; or even what type of products he sold.

● Restraints imposed on the members of a trade association.

The restraint must protect a genuine interest and it must not exceed what is required to do that, nor be against the public interest. The courts have focused on the fact that most agreements of this type have been entered into quite freely out of a perception that the individual participant's best interests are being served by the restraint imposed on the group as a whole.

SELF-CHECK 1

After years of playing round the pub circuit, Bonzo and his band cut and privately distributed a record which made it into the top 40. They were approached by a major recording company and after an evening of champagne-drenched negotiations Bonzo signed a contract which gave the company exclusive worldwide rights to distribute any records which the band made during the next ten years. The band would receive a royalty of 0.5p from thecompany for each record sold. The company was not obliged to promote the band's records. The agreement provided that it would automatically be extended for another 10 years if royalty payments reached a level of £10,000 in any one year. The agreement could be cancelled by the company at one month's notice; but there was no provision for termination by the band.

Two years after the contract was signed the company had still not issued any of the band's new recordings. Bonzo began to suspect that the company had signed them up simply to keep their style of music from reaching a wide audience and possibly affecting the popularity of other recording artists signed with the company. He sought to have the contract set aside by the court.

On what grounds do you think Bonzo's counsel might argue that his client should be released from his contractual obligations?

Misrepresentation

As we have seen many contracts are concluded with virtually no negotiations between the parties. You lay down your money and the newsagent gives you your newspaper. If anything is said it is more likely to be an exchange about the weather or the day's news than anything to do with the transaction. But in many contracts, especially where substantial sums of money are involved, the parties will engage in some form of pre-contractual negotiations, the purpose being to establish exactly what each party is getting and giving in the transaction. Those negotiations may involve each party making a number of assertions to the other about the subject matter of the contract – though these will usually come from the **offeror** (and in sales of goods, from the **seller** of the goods). The main purpose of such statements is to induce the other party to enter into the contract. They may give details about, for example, the quality of a car, or the durability of a pair of shoes, or the suitability of a paint for outdoor use.

There are three possible levels of significance which attach to such statements:

- if these assertions really have been influential in making the other party decide to contract then they may amount to **representations**; if they then prove not to have been true, they will have been **misrepresentations**; if a misrepresentation is made this will give the 'injured' party a right to damages or perhaps to bring the contract to an end

- it may be that the statement made is of such importance that it will actually be incorporated as a **term of the contract**, where, if it turns out to be untrue, it will give rise to a right to claim damages for breach of contract

- it may be that the statement amounts to no more than **'puffery'** or the expression of an **unfounded opinion**, in which case it will not give rise to any claim by the 'injured party' if it proves to be untrue.

What we are going to do now is to look at the effect on a contract of one of the parties making a misrepresentation.

[You may find it useful at this point to turn to Section Three (Terms of the Contract) and read what is said there about differentiating between terms, representations and statements having no legal significance.]

WHAT IS A MISREPRESENTATION?
Misrepresentations lie somewhere between statements which become terms and statements which have no legal significance. In order to serve as the basis for an action for misrepresentation the statement must have all of the following qualities:

- it must purport to be a statement of **existing fact**
- it must be made for the purpose of **inducing** the other party to enter into the contract, therefore it must be made prior to the conclusion of the contract
- the other party must have relied on the statement to the extent that it actually was influential in persuading him to enter into the contract
- the statement must not have been incorporated as a **term of the contract**; if it has then the victim's remedy lies in a suit for breach of contract, not an action for misrepresentation.

Those, in fact, are the qualities a statement must have if it is to be considered to amount to a **representation.** For the statement to amount to a **misrepresentation** there must be added the condition that:

- the statement must be **false** or, if truthful, it must be **wholly misleading** as to the true state of affairs.

SELF-CHECK 2

Bob wanted to buy an apartment block owned by Joe and Joy. When Bob asked them if the flats were all rented, they told him that they were. This was true – but what Joe and Joy did not tell Bob was that due to the high rents they had been charging, all of the tenants had given notice to give up their tenancy. They also did not tell Bob that a recent structural survey of the building had shown that it was likely to require substantial spending on reinforcement of the foundations (due to subsidence). Unfortunately, Bob, who was a novice in the property market, did not have a survey of the building made before he purchased it, so he did not find out about the foundations problem until after the sale. Although he was annoyed when he found out about the true state of the building, and that all the tenants were going, Bob was not too upset as his real purpose in buying the building had been his need to find a good way to launder huge sums of money which he was taking in through his drug dealing business. He would have bought the building even if he had known about the foundations and the tenants.

Do you think that Bob would succeed if he went to court and claimed that he had been the victim of misrepresentations made by Joe and Joy?

TYPES OF MISREPRESENTATION

The remedies for misrepresentation depend on the type of misrepresentation the statement amounts to. Misrepresentations are categorised into those which are:

- fraudulent
- negligent
- innocent.

Remedies for misrepresentation – Fraudulent misrepresentation

The definition of fraudulent misrepresentation was laid down by **Lord Herschell** in **Derry v Peek [1889] 14 App Cas 337, HL**:

'Making a statement knowing that it is false (or at least not believing it to be true) and recklessly not caring whether it is true or not.'

The common law effect of fraudulent misrepresentation is to render the contract **voidable**. This means the contract can be **rescinded** by the 'injured' party, but it does not have to be brought to an end. It is up to the injured party to decide if this is what they want to do.

Whether or not they choose to terminate the contract, the aggrieved party can sue in the **tort of deceit** for damages equal to the amount of their actual loss due to the fraudulent misrepresentation.

Innocent misrepresentations

A false statement, which the person who makes it honestly believes is true, is an **innocent misrepresentation**. If the person who made the statement had good reasons for believing it was true then it is a **wholly innocent misrepresentation**. If, however, the statement was held out to be true but the maker had no reason to believe it was, then it was an innocent, **but negligent misrepresentation**. As far as the **common law** is concerned there is no remedy for either form of innocent misrepresentation. **Equity**, however, may step in to enable the injured party to rescind the contract.

Prior to enactment of the **Misrepresentation Act 1967** no claim for damages could be made if the misrepresentation had not been fraudulent or negligent. This put a party at a severe disadvantage if he/she had suffered some consequential damage as a result of a wholly innocent misrepresentation. The injured party would want to make up their losses but might see some advantage in carrying on with the contract, rather than rescinding it. This situation gave a real impetus to judges to find that statements had become **terms of the contract** rather than remaining mere representations. If the statement was a term and proved to be false an automatic claim lay for damage for breach of contract. Section 2(2) of the Act has improved this situation by providing for damages to be recovered **in lieu of rescission** where there has been a wholly innocent misrepresentation –although it follows that if the possibility of rescission has been lost so has any right to damages in lieu of rescission.

SELF-CHECK 3

Read the facts of these two cases. Say how you think each would have been decided. Explain why the court might not have reached the same conclusion in each case.

Dick Bentley (Productions) Ltd. v Harold Smith (Motors) Ltd. [1965] 2 All ER 65

The plaintiff bought a second hand car, relying on an assurance that it had had a replacement engine and gearbox fitted only 20,000 miles earlier. In fact, although the salesman did not know this, the replacement parts had been in the car for nearly 100,000 miles. The salesman honestly believed they'd only done 20,000 miles. When the motorist found out the true position he brought proceedings against the car dealer.

Oscar Chess Ltd. v Williams [1957] 1 All ER 325

A motorist sold his car to a garage. Based on a logbook he found in the car's glovebox (the logbook was later proved to have been forged) he described the car as a 1948 Morris '10'. In fact the car was a 1939 Morris which was worth considerably less than the trade-in value the garage allowed on it. The motorist was honest in his belief that the car was a 1948 model. The car dealers went to court anyway.

Summary of section two

- a flaw in the formation of a contract can result in the contract being rendered voidable or unenforceable
- lack of certainty renders a contract unenforceable
- the courts can look outside the contract to give meaning to vague or uncertain terms – eg. by referring to standard trade practices, or by looking at the previous dealings between the parties
- most contracts do not have to take any particular form to be valid
- some contracts have to be written down to be enforceable (hire purchase agreements, share transfers) while others must be embodied in a deed (conveyances of land, long-term leases)
- minors, drunks and the mentally ill are the exceptions to the rule that anyone can make an enforceable contract
- contracts entered into by minors are enforceable unless they involve a credit sale of 'non-necessaries'
- incorporating a restraint of trade into a contract makes the contract *prima facie* void
- the doctrine of restraint of trade allows restraints to be enforced if they are reasonable and not against the public interest
- the person seeking to rely on a restraint must show that he/she has a real interest to protect – eg. a trade secret known to an ex-employee
- a representation is a statement of fact aimed at inducing someone to enter into a contract. This becomes a misrepresentation if the factual basis of the statement is false or grossly misleading
- the **Misrepresentation Act 1965** has made it possible for an injured party to obtain either damages or cancellation of the contract regardless of whether the misrepresentation is wholly innocent, negligent or fraudulent.

Suggested answers to section two self-check questions

SELF-CHECK 1

It might be argued that the contract was illegal for being in restraint of trade. But whether that will render the contract void depends on the answer to the following questions: (1) is there a legitimate interest to be protected by a restraint? (2) is the restraint applied unreasonable? (3) is it against the public interest? The decision of the court in the following case indicates that the answer to all three of those questions is yes in Bonzo's case.

A Schroeder Music Publishing Co. Ltd. v Macaulay [1974] 3 All ER 616, HL
Macaulay was a songwriter. He signed a contract with the plaintiffs giving them exclusive world copyright in all of his compositions over the succeeding five years. He would be paid a royalty for the use of his music but the company was not obliged to promote his work. If royalty payments reached £5,000 then the contract would automatically be extended for a further five years. Termination by the plaintiffs was at one month's notice. No provision was made for termination by the defendant. The court held that this agreement was void for restraint of trade. It imposed a total commitment on the defendant and virtually none on the plaintiffs. It also obstructed the development of the defendant as an artist and that was against the public interest.

SELF-CHECK 2

There are two reasons why Bob might feel he could mount a claim for misrepresentation: the assertion that the apartment was fully let; and Joe and Joy's failure to reveal the state of the building's foundations.

1   Joe and Joy's statement about the apartment block being fully let was true, but misleading in the light of the fact that they knew that all the tenants were leaving. In **Dimmock v Hallett [1866] 2 Ch App 21** an estate was being sold. A prospective purchaser was told that all of the farms on the estate were let. This was true. What he was not told was that all of the tenants had given in their notice. Normally silence does not amount to a misrepresentation. The caveat 'let the buyer beware' applies. However, in this case silence as to the real position regarding the tenancy of the farms turned an otherwise true statement into a misrepresentation.

2   Joy and Joe failed to tell Bob about the parlous state of the building's foundations. Did their silence about this amount to a misrepresentation? No. There is no indication that Joe and Joy said anything about the foundations – good bad or indifferent – and a misrepresentation can only arise if there is some representation made.

What would put paid to Bob's hopes of successfully claiming damages for misrepresentation, even disregarding the points made above, is that he was apparently not induced to enter into the contract to purchase the building by anything Joe and Joy said. He wanted the building for his own purposes and that was that. A misrepresentation can only occur if the false statement actually induces the so-called injured party to enter into the contract. So there was no misrepresentation here.

SELF-CHECK 3

Dick Bentley (Productions) Ltd. v Harold Smith (Motors) Ltd.

The court held that in view of the reasonable presumption that the salesman would know the details of the car's history, his assertion amounted to a warranty. This is one of the two types of contractual terms, thus the plaintiff could sue for breach of contract.

Oscar Chess Ltd. v Williams

The court held that the defendant's statement was a wholly innocent misrepresentation. It rejected arguments that as in the Dick Bentley case the statement should be considered a term of the contract. Why? Because the car dealer could be presumed to have sufficient expertise to determine the age of the car; plus the statement was made sufficiently far in advance of the deal being struck that he should have uncovered the true age of the vehicle. Given that this case occurred prior to enactment of the Misrepresentation Act the only remedy available for a wholly innocent misrepresentation was rescission. But in this case too long had elapsed since the contract was made: access to that remedy was closed. So the dealer was left to bear his loss.

Section Three

Contractual Terms

In Section Three you will find material which will enable you to learn about and understand:

- the sources of terms of a contract
- the basis on which terms are implied into contract
- the varying consequences of breaking the terms of a contract
- how far liability to compensate the other party can be limited if you fail to live up to your obligations under the contract .

The contents of a contract

The terms of a contract spell out what obligations and rights each of the parties has. Terms are of varying importance. Some, called **conditions**, if broken give the injured party the right to terminate the contract – ie. to consider themselves discharged of all obligations under it. Others, called **warranties**, if breached give a right to claim damages but require the injured party to continue to perfom their own obligations under the contract. Some terms, called **exclusion or exemption clauses**, are aimed at excluding any right to either damages or termination of the contract if other terms of the contract are broken.

The terms of a contract are arrived at as a result of the negotiations of the parties (or if the contract is a simple one, involving something like the purchase of a newspaper, they are implicit in the conduct of the parties). Those terms which the parties agree between themselves are known as **express terms**. But these may not embody all of the obligations and rights of the parties to the contract. Some of the contract's terms may arise out of legislation such as the **Sale of Goods Act of 1979**. Other terms may be found in customs of the trade with which a contract is concerned. And terms may be found in a contract simply because it does not make sense unless they are. All of these types of terms are called **implied terms** and they bind the parties as tightly as any of the express terms they have agreed.

After you have studied the material in Section Three you should be able to do the following things:

- differentiate between **express** and **implied** terms
- outline the sources of implied terms, and discuss the 'tests' which the courts can apply to determine if a term should be implied into a contract
- differentiate between **conditions** and **warranties**
- discuss common law and statutory controls on exemption clauses.

Terms and pre-contractual statements

However lengthy or brief they may be, it is the pre-contractual negotiations between the parties which throw up what will become the main terms of the contract. In many cases, contracts come into being and are **discharged** (fulfilled or completed) with such rapidity – contact between the parties is so brief – that it is not possible to identify any period of negotiation or bargaining leading up to an offer and acceptance. But in many other cases there is an identifiable set of exchanges between the parties: exchanges which eventually solidify into an offer and an acceptance containing the agreed-upon terms of the contract.

Not all things said or written in the course of negotiations are of the same significance so far as the contract is concerned. Some statements are of no legal import; others amount to mere **representations** (which, if they prove to be false, will become misrepresentations). These are important in persuading someone to accept an offer, but they do not become part of the parties' rights or obligations under the contract. Other statements consist of commitments or promises which do become part of the overall package of obligations and rights of which the contract is comprised.

SORTING OUT THE TERMS OF THE CONTRACT FROM WHAT HAS BEEN SAID IN PRE-CONTRACTUAL NEGOTIATIONS

Some of the things the parties say in the period leading up to the formation of the contract may be of no legal significance at all. Mostly these are assertions in the nature of 'Brand X washes whiter than white' or 'New, improved Fido, now better than ever'. Such statements are known as 'trade puffs' and they are not actionable. One of the claims raised by the defence in Mrs Carlill's case was that the company's assurances about the effectiveness of the Carbolic Smoke Ball were no more than promotional exaggerations. Therefore the product's failure to live up to the claims made on its behalf was not actionable. The company did not really expect any of its customers to take it at its word. The court agreed that in most circumstances such claims as those made by the Smoke Ball Company would not be actionable. However, the company had actually deposited £100 in a bank with the stated purpose of using that fund to defray the cost of claims and this, the court said, was enough to remove the assertions out of the category of puffery and make them into legally binding promises.

Another frequently found type of pre-contractual statement which has no legal significance is the **statement of an opinion**. Unless the opinion is based on expert knowledge, it will not serve as the basis for an action.

Compare the decisions of the courts in these two cases.

Bissett v Wilkinson [1927] AC 177, PC
A man was selling a farm. He told the potential purchaser that he believed the farm (which was in New Zealand) would support 2,000 sheep. In fact he had never seen the farm; the farm had never been used for sheep farming before; and the seller

knew nothing personally about sheep farming. The vendor's statements amounted to no more than the voicing of his opinions. There was no actual or expert knowledge to support those opinions. Therefore they had no legal significance whatsoever. A representation must be a statement of existing fact, not a mere opinion.

Esso Petroleum Co. Ltd. v Mardon [1976] QB 801, CA

M was considering taking the tenancy of a new petrol station being opened by Esso. A representative of the company told him that the station should turn over a certain number of thousands of gallons of petrol per week. In fact, once he'd leased the station, M found that the volume of petrol sold was very much lower than that estimate. The issue which came before the court when the lessee sued to have his contract with Esso set aside for misrepresentation, was whether the representative's statement was legally significant. The job of the Esso representative involved frequent appraisals of station sites. It could be assumed that he was stating an opinion based on expert knowledge. In such a circumstance the person to whom the statement was made was entitled to rely on it as a fact. If it was inaccurate, the statement was a misrepresentation. In fact, statements about such an important consideration as prospective sales volumes are likely to be incorporated into a contract as one of its terms and the remedy would be to sue for breach of contract, not to bring an action for misrepresentation.

SELF-CHECK 1

Which of these statements made by Fred is likely to be a term and which a representation (or misrepresentation) or even a statement of no contractual significance?

1. Ed wants to buy a boat capable of sailing in a race across the Atlantic. Fred shows him a boat which he says has participated in the round-the-world yacht race twice and, therefore is eminently suitable for Ed's voyage.

2. Fred says that the boat will serve Ed well in the race because 'it has the spirit of a winner'.

3. Ed is interested in the boat but the price is a bit more than he wanted to pay. Fred tells Ed he'd better hurry up and decide because someone else is coming to make an offer on the boat at 5 o'clock.

DISTINGUISHING BETWEEN REPRESENTATIONS AND TERMS

We have seen how the courts will disregard any trade puff or statement of mere opinion as being of no legal significance (unless the opinion is backed by expert knowledge). How do they distinguish between representations and terms of the contract? A number of rules of thumb are used.

● Did the person making the statement suggest it's accuracy be checked? If they did, then the statement is likely to be of no legal consequence. A recommendation that the other party should rely on their own judgement or on the observations of some third party who checks out the statement, robs it of any element of inducement by the person who has made it.

● On the other hand, if the person making a statement dissuades the other party from checking it, then the statement is likely to be a term rather than a mere representation.

● One very important consideration is whether there has been any indication by the party to whom the statement is made that they are putting **great reliance** on it. If so, then, as the case below shows, the statement will not only be legally significant, it will become a term of the contract.

Bannerman v White [1861] 10 CB (NS) 844

B was negotiating the purchase of some hops from W. Several weeks before serious negotiations began he asked W if the hops had been treated with sulphur. If they had they were unsuitable for the use he wished to make of them and he would not even bother to carry on discussions about their purchase. W assured B that no sulphur had been used on the hops. B went ahead with negotiations and eventually purchased them. The hops then proved to have been treated with sulphur. The question was whether W's assurance had any significance at all, and if it did whether it was a representation or a term of the contract. As to whether the statement had any legal significance, the problem arose because of the period of time which separated the making of the statement and the conclusion of the contract. The court considered whether the two were still intimately linked. It concluded that they were, and that the assurance was so central to the benefit which B sought to achieve from entering into the contract that the assurance must have become a term of the contract.

ACTIVITY 12

Why is it important to distinguish between statements which are representations and those which are terms? If you can't remember, look back at Section Two at the pages dealing with misrepresentation. Then see if you can give an answer to the question in your own words.

The reason why differentiation between terms and representations is so important is because of the different remedies available for misrepresentation and breach of contract.

Bannerman v White is a classic illustration of the dilemma confronting the courts in the days prior to the passage of the Misrepresentation Act 1965. They were under great pressure to find that a statement was a term and not a representation. The choice confronting the court was to:

- treat the statement as too remote from the conclusion of the contract to be legally binding. Bannerman would have no redress

- treat the statement as a representation. But, at that time, unless there had been a fraudulent misrepresentation no remedy was available to B. There was no evidence of fraud here. White truly believed the hops had not been treated with sulphur

- treat the statement as a term of the contract. Then damages could be recovered for breach of contract.

It chose to treat the assurance as a term of the contract.

SELF-CHECK 2

How do you think the court decided the following case?

Routledge v McKay [1954] 1 All ER 855, CA

R was discussing buying M's motorcycle. On October 23rd M told R that the bike was a 1942 model. He took this information from the log book. On October 30th the parties wrote out a contract for the sale of the bike but nothing about the date of the bike's manufacture was written down. Later on it was found the bike was actually a 1930 model. R sued for damages.

Contractual terms – express and implied

The terms of a contract can be broken down in two different ways:

- importance
- source.

Terms come to be in a contract either because the parties have actually agreed that they should be – these are called **express** terms – or because, even though the parties may not have agreed to embody a particular right or obligation in the contract, the courts will hold that it is an **implied** term of the contract. An implied term can arise:

- because there is a statutory requirement that it be part of the contract
- because it is necessary in order for the contract to reflect the parties' intentions
- because without the term the contract does not have what is called **business efficacy** – ie. it does not make sense. For example, the parties to a commercial transaction may have failed to expressly include a term which reflects common practices in that area of business. The contract would be deemed to include that term.

ORAL AGREEMENTS AND WRITTEN CONTRACTS

It is a general rule of evidence that where the parties have reduced their contractual agreement to writing that **parol evidence** as to the existence of additional terms which were only verbally agreed, will not be taken into consideration by the court in establishing what the obligations and rights of the parties are. There are, however, several exceptions to this 'rule':

- where there is evidence of a trade custom or practice which significantly modifies the meaning of the term which was written down
- where there is evidence that what was written down was really only an aide memoire or memorandum of a contract which consisted of verbal agreements.

ACTIVITY 13

What are the two different ways of categorising the terms of a contract? One way has to do with the source of the terms:

1. _____terms

2. _____terms.

The other way has to do with the importance of the terms:

1.

2.

The *source of terms*: express agreement and implication (by statute or common law).

The importance of terms: conditions and warranties.

IMPLYING TERMS INTO A CONTRACT — STATUTORY INTERVENTION

There are a number of statutes which impose terms into certain types of contracts. For example:

- **Equal Pay Act 1970** implies a right to equal pay and conditions into all women's contracts of employment

- **Health and Safety at Work Act 1974** implies into all employee's contracts of employment a term that the employer will take reasonable care to ensure his employees are kept from risks to their health and safety.

From the point of view of businessmen one of the most important sources of implied terms is the **Sale of Goods Act of 1979 (SOGA)**. This Act (and the **Supply of Goods and Services Act 1982**, which implies virtually the same conditions into contracts for the supply of services or the supply of goods by means of barter, hire-purchase or rental) conditions all contracts where there is a transfer of title to goods for a monetary consideration.

SOGA IMPLIED TERMS-RIGHT TO SELL

There is a **condition** that the seller has good title in the goods. This is a matter of **strict liability** ie. the seller will have to compensate the buyer (or take the goods back and give the buyer a refund) if there is any question about the title he has passed to the buyer, even if the seller did not know there was any limitation on his/her right to sell the goods.

Delivery

The seller has a duty to deliver the goods contracted for. Delivery may be acomplished by simply handing over the documents of title to the goods. Unless the contract specifies otherwise, the buyer need not accept delivery of the goods by instalments. In commercial contracts there is a presumption that any specification as to the time of delivery is a condition of the contract. If the seller fails to deliver on time, the buyer can refuse to accept the goods when eventually they are delivered.

PAYMENT

If the buyer fails to pay for the goods on time this will be treated as no more than a breach of a warranty, giving the seller the right to claim compensation for any costs or inconvenience caused by the buyer's late payment, but not allowing him/her to refuse to deliver the goods unless the contract has specified that this should be the case.

CONFORMITY TO DESCRIPTION

]There is an implied condition that the goods will correspond to their description. What the court will focus on as the words which describe the goods will be those words which give the most basic definition of what the goods are. In several cases concerning the compounding of animal feeds, the courts have said that animal feed ordered for one type of animal, but proving to be wholly unsuitable for that animal, still conformed to the description 'animal feed' because there were some animals to which it could be fed without ill-effects. (**cf. Ashington Piggeries v Christopher Hill Ltd. [1972] AC 441, HL** and **Pinnock Brothers v Lewis and Peat Ltd. [1923] 1 KB 690).**

Satisfactory quality

Except for certain limitations, *caveat emptor* – the Latin phrase which means 'let the buyer beware ' – applies regarding the quality of goods . The exceptions are:

- Where the seller sells goods in the course of a business, the goods must be of satisfactory quality. The test of whether goods are of satisfactory quality is whether a reasonable person would find them satisfactory taking into account their description, price and other relevent matters such as usability for their normal purposes, appearance, finish, freedom from minor defects, safety and durability.

- Goods must be usable for any special purpose notified by the buyer to the seller. The fact that the seller goes ahead and sells the goods knowing what purpose the buyer wants them for means they have to be suitable for that purpose even if it is not one of the normal or usual uses of those goods.

Defects

Whatever defects the seller tells the buyer about *before* the sale is concluded cannot be later on relied on by the buyer in a legal action. The law assumes the price has been adjusted to take those defects into account. But what about other defects? The Act makes it clear that a buyer has no 'duty of inspection'. Only those defects mentioned by the seller *or* those which reasonably could have been expected to be discovered in the course of whatever inspection the buyer *actually* made are excluded from complaint. Even the fact that there is a warranty which would secure the repair of minor defects at no cost to the buyer does not automatically exclude those defects as the basis of a claim that the goods are not of satisfactory quality.

Accepting goods

If a buyer accepts goods he loses the right to a refund of the price he has paid. Because of this the Act provides that goods will not be deemed to have been accepted before the buyer has had a reasonable chance after they are delivered to inspect them.

SELF-CHECK 3

Larry went into Mark's shop to buy a hi-fi system. Mark recommended that Larry buy the Boomer 12 which just happened to be on sale at a remarkably low price. Mark offered to unpack one and demonstrate it for Larry. But Larry said he was in a hurry. From the pictures and brochures it looked like just what he wanted, so he'd take one. On the way home Larry was involved in a car accident and suffered injuries which meant that he spent the next 2 months in the hospital. When he finally was able to unpack the hi-fi he found that there was a large dent in the casing. He also found that the layout of the controls was completely different from the way it was pictured in the brochure. Larry took the system back to the shop and demanded a refund. Mark said that he'd offered Larry chance to inspect the goods before buying them and since he'd not taken it he couldn't complain about any defects found when he brought the goods home. In any event, Mark said, the dent and the layout of the control panel didn't affect the way the Boomer played. And even if they did, he'd had the goods far too long to expect a refund for them.

(i)   Do you think Larry is entitled to a refund? If so, on what grounds?

(ii) If the hi-fi had not been dented but after working fine for two or three days, had suddenly stopped working, do you think that Larry could still have had a refund? What if it had worked for a month before packing up?

(iii) Assume that before Larry bought the Boomer 12 he told Mark that he needed a portable stereo so that he could use it at discos he staged in his spare time in order to earn a bit of extra money. And assume that when he unpacked the stereo at home, Larry discovered that there was a red label affixed to it warning that the system was fragile and once set up should be moved only if absolutely necessary. Would he be able to get a refund?

IMPLYING TERMS INTO A CONTRACT — COMMON LAW RULES

The common law ensures that all contracts of certain types have certain terms regardless of whether the parties agreed to them or not. This is most commonly found to be the case with **contracts of employment.**

Common law duties of the employer:

- to pay employees
- to reimburse employees for expenses incurred in the course of their employment
- to manage employees in a reasonable manner
- to take reasonable care to ensure the health and safety of employees.

Common law duties of the employee

- to take reasonable care for his/her own health and safety
- to be ready, able and willing to work
- to obey the lawful and reasonable orders of the employer
- to remain loyal and honest.

In addition to ensuring that all contracts of certain types contain certain terms, judges have developed guidelines as to when a contract of any type may be said to contain some particular term.

Recognizing a custom

There may be a local practice which is customarily followed and which, provided it is of sufficient 'certainty' and 'notoriety', the courts will recognise and incorporate into a contract as an implied term.

Sagar v Ridehalgh and Sons [1931] 1 Ch 310, CA

It was standard practice to deduct 'fines' for bad workmanship from the wages of textile trade workers in Lancashire. No provision for this was made in their contracts of employment, however. The court held that nonetheless it was a term of their contract of employment because it was such a firmly established practice that anyone who entered into employment as a weaver in Lancashire must be presumed to have actual or constructive knowledge that the practice existed; and by taking up the employment, he or she gave implied consent to the same condition affecting his or her employment.

Implementing the parties' intentions

Making sure that the intentions of the parties in entering into the contract are fulfilled is said to be giving the contract **'business efficacy'**. If this is not done, the contract may fail to secure its object. The courts will strive to see that this does not occur.

The courts will only intervene in the name of business efficacy when it is necessary for them to do so. Whether this state of affairs applies is usually determined by applying what is sometimes called the **officious bystander test**:

- does the contract make any sense at all if the term under consideration is said not to be part of it?
- was the term not expressly incorporated into the contract simply because it was too obvious to need saying?
- are the intentions of the parties fully reflected if the contract does not include this term?

The Moorcock [1889] 14 PD 64, CA

The appellants owned a wharf and jetty extending out into the River Thames. The plaintiffs owned the vessel *The Moorcock*. The parties agreed that the ship should be moored at the jetty so she could take on a cargo lying on the wharf. Both parties knew that that at low tide the ship would rest on the river bed. What neither knew was that underneath the mud on the river bottom lay a ridge of hard ground, which, when the ship pressed down on it, caused damage to the keel. There was no evidence that the jetty owners had waranted that the berth was safe. The court, however, said that this must be taken to be one of the terms of the contract. The court presumed that the parties both intended that the ship should have a safe berth. The contract would only have 'business efficacy' if those intentions were implemented in the terms of the contract. How did the court decide that the parties intended the ship to have a safe berth? It applied the 'officious bystander test'. Anyone asked, 'would that have been the parties' intention? ' would be bound to say, 'Of course. It goes without saying. '

Because it is reasonable to do so

Should the courts be confined to implying terms only where it is *necessary* that they do so? What about situations where it is merely *reasonable* to do so? Consider the following case.

Liverpool City Council v Irwin [1976] 2 WLR 562, HL

The Court of Appeal considered that it was necessary that a term requiring the landlord to take reasonable care to keep the common areas of the building – especially the lifts – in good repair was implied into the lease of a flat on the upper floor of a tower block. Lord Denning went further to say that even if it were not regarded as a necessary condition of the lease that the lifts always should be kept in working order, it still should be implied into it simply because it was reasonable to do so. The House of Lords rejected this assertion. The limits of necessity did not extend to an absolute duty to keep the lifts working. The tenants could still make their way to and from their flat, however inconveniently, via the stairs.

In fact the only contracts into which the courts will consistently imply terms because it is reasonable to do so, are contracts of employment.

Conditions, warranties and innominate terms

The terms of a contract are not all of equal importance. Some are so fundamental to the fulfilment of what the parties sought to achieve by contracting that, if the obligation or right they embody is not honoured, there may be no reason to carry on with the contract. Some have such serious consequences, that if they are not observed, then the contractual relationship cannot survive their breach. Such terms are called **conditions.** The breach of a condition entitles the injured party to terminate the contract (as well as claiming damages for the loss the breach has caused him/her). Other terms are less significant: their breach may cause a loss (recoverable by a claim for damages) but the object of the contract remains attainable and desirable, so the contract runs on past the breach. These less important terms are called **warranties**.

The effects of a breach of contract will be discussed more fully in Section Four where remedies in contract are discussed.

The following case illustrates the breach of a condition.

Poussard v Spiers and Pond [1876] 1 QBD 410

A singer whose illness prevented her from performing during the first week of an opera's run sued the opera house for breach of contract when the management refused to let her take over from the replacement singer they'd hired to cover her absence. The court held that the singer was herself in breach of her contract to perform. Actually turning up on the opening night was such an important part of the agreement between the parties, that her failure to do so, however innocently, amounted to the breach of a *condition*. This gave the management the right to consider the contract cancelled and to hire a replacement singer who would perform throughout the opera's run.

SELF-CHECK 4

A singer contracted to sing at a number of performances of an opera. Part of the agreement was that she would attend a number of rehearsals. She did not come to any of the rehearsals but came on opening night prepared to sing her role. The manager refused to allow her to perform. He claimed the contract had been brought to an end by her failure to attend rehearsals. She sued the opera company for damages for breach of contract.

In the light of the decision made in **Poussard v Spiers and Pond,** do you think she won her case?

THE PARTIES' OWN DEFINITION OF THE TERMS

Although the courts are loath to interfere with the freedom of the parties to enter into whatever contract they wish, judges will not always consider the description the parties attach to the terms of their contract as being conclusive of the status of the terms. As the case below shows, calling a term a condition will not make it one if the term is not fundamental to the purposes of the contract.

L. Schuler AG v Wickham Machine Tool Sales [1973] 2 WLR 683, HL

Schuler granted the exclusive right to sell his machine tools in the UK. The agreement contained a provision that it was a condition of the contract that Wickham's salesmen should call on at least six customers a week. Wickham's men failed to maintain this schedule and Schuler claimed to rescind the contract for breach of condition. The court held that the parties' description of the term regarding sales calls as a condition was not reasonable. Fulfilling the requirement about the number of sales calls to be made might or might not be essential to the accomplishment of the purpose of the contract which was to secure the sale of Schuler's machine tools in the UK.

INNOMINATE TERMS

In some cases the consequences of the breach of a term cannot be forecast accurately. This is the case where a term is drawn in wide, vague language. Or where the obligation is cast in words which themselves have a wide range of meanings. We have seen that if the language used to define contractual terms is too vague and imprecise the contract will be unenforceable due to uncertainty. In many cases the courts will regard terms as being **innominate** in character. In other words, it is only following a breach, when the actual consequences can be assessed, that the true status of the term is established.

Hongkong Fir Shipping Co. Ltd. v Kawasaki Kisen Kaisha Ltd. [1962] 2 QB 26, CA
The contract for a two-year charter of a ship provided that it should be 'in every way fit for ordinary cargo service.' In shipping language this meant the ship was to be 'seaworthy'. When the ship was delivered at the start of the charter it was found to be unseaworthy. After its first voyage, repairs which took four months were required. The charterer claimed there had been a breach of condition amounting to a repudiation of the contract on the part of the owners. This gave the charterers the right to rescind the contract. The owners contested the rescission in court. The court held that the scale of disruption was not enough to entitle the charterer to consider the contract to be terminated. True, the ship had not been seaworthy, but that word encompassed everything from the ship's first aid cabinets being fully stocked, to its engines being in good working condition (which, in this case they were not). It could not be said whether a breach of the term regarding seaworthiness amounted to the breach of a condition or the breach of a warranty until the consequences of the ship's unseaworthiness were actually apparent. In this case four months' use out of a two-year charter had been lost to the hirers. They could still secure the bulk of the benefit they had envisaged from hiring the ship. Therefore, the court held the breach as to seaworthiness amounted in this case to the breach of a warranty only. The hirers had been wrong to rescind the contract and had to pay damages to the owners.

ACTIVITY 14

Can you remember what the difference is between a condition and a warranty, both as to *their nature* and as to the *consequences of their breach?*

A **warranty** is a minor term of the contract – for example, there is a warranty with a new single engine aircraft that the radio will work – and the consequence of the breach of a warranty of this warranty is to give the injured party a right to claim damages in compensation. A **condition** is an important term of the contract: one which embodies the very purpose of making the contract in the first place. For example, it is a condition that a new aeroplane's engine will work. If it does not then the whole purpose of the contract would normally be said to have been thwarted. The aircraft cannot be used as a means of transportation. Logically then, the consequence of breaching a condition of a contract is more dramatic than where a warranty is breached. The injured party can treat the contract as non-existent and obtain from the party in breach full restitution of any money or other forms of payment made.

EXTERNAL DETERMINANTS OF THE STATUS OF TERMS

Whether or not a term is a condition or warranty may not be left to the choice of the parties. Statute may intervene to define the status of the term. For example, the terms implied into all contracts for the sale of goods by the Sale of Goods Acts of 1979 and 1994 are said to be conditions, but note that the parties are allowed to treat a condition as a warranty if the victim wants to.

Other external determinants of the status of terms are:

- trade custom
- the previous course of dealing
- legal precedents.

Terms which exclude or limit liability

The parties' freedom to contract includes the liberty to agree that no claim, or only a limited claim, can be brought against the offending party if he/she fails to honour his/her obligations under the contract. This is accomplished by inserting an **exclusion clause** (sometimes called an **exemption clause** or limitation clause) into the contract.

Although the courts are willing to enforce these types of clauses, there are fairly restrictive limits on their operation. Some of these restrictions arise out of the common law; others arise out of statute, primarily the **Unfair Contract Terms Act 1977**. One reason why the courts are said to 'lean against' exclusion clauses is that they often reflect a **gross inequality of bargaining power** between the parties.

This is most clearly apparent where consumers are purchasing goods by way of a contract based on the seller's standard terms of business as set out on a pre-printed form. The use of such forms is widespread because of the savings in time and administrative costs which they allow. However, the standard form contract is subject to misuse in so far as it imposes onto consumers wide-ranging exemptions from liability contained in 'fine print' to be found, usually, on the back of the document. Most consumers are unaware of the ways in which the seller has limited his liability. Even if they take the trouble to read the fine print on the back of the form they have little choice but to accept the exclusion clauses as part of the package of terms put forward by the company. Their only real alternatives are to abort the purchase altogether, or to enter into negotiations with a salesperson who is unlikely to have the authority to conclude a contract on anything other than the business's standard terms.

Where one of the contracting parties seeks to rely on a contractual term excluding or limiting his liability for breach of contract, there are three requirements:

- establish if the exclusion clause is actually incorporated into the contract
- show that it covers the damage which has actually resulted from the breach
- show that the clause is not invalidated by statutory provision or for reasons of public policy.

EXCLUSION CLAUSES AND THE COMMON LAW

Reasonable notice must be given that liability is excluded or limited
This requirement is said to be met in any case where the party against whom the exclusion clause is being used has **signed** the contractual document which contains it. This is true even if the party against whom the clause is being applied has not read the document or the exclusion clause contained within it.

L'Estrange v Graucob [1934] 2 KB 394
The proprietor of a cafe purchased a cigarette vending machine. She signed, without reading because she was illiterate, a sales agreement which contained amongst other small print an exclusion clause exempting the vendors from liability for defective machines (which hers was). The court held that by signing the document the cafe owner had agreed to all the terms contained in it whether they had been read or not.

Where the limitation of liability is not spelled out in a signed document there are three, often inter-linked, questions which arise:

- was notice of the existence of the limitation given prior to the conclusion of the contract?
- was the notice contained in a document which a reasonable person would have assumed was part of the documentation spelling out the terms of the contract?
- even if it was, did the notice itself provide a sufficiently clear warning of the fact that one party was limiting his/her liability for a breach of contract?

The *contra preferentum* rule
The words of an exemption clause have to be clear and precise if they are to be effective. The courts construe them very strictly:

- an ambiguously worded clause will be interpreted in the way most favourable to the party against whom it is being enforced
- only the events and persons clearly covered by the exclusion clause will secure its protection from an action for breach
- any misrepresentation about the meaning and/or scope of an exclusion clause will render the clause wholly ineffective.

Houghton v Trafalgar Insurance Co. Ltd. [1954] 1 QB 247

A five-seater car was carrying six passengers. The owner's insurers had a clause in their policy excluding their liability if the car was carrying 'any excess load'. The insurance company sought to rely on this exclusion clause, saying that carrying six people in a five-seater car was excessive loading. The court held that the term 'load' should be construed to refer to 'goods' only. Since the excess was the number of people, the exclusion clause was ineffective.

SELF-CHECK 4

Sue stayed for two nights at the Shipshape Inn. As she drove into the hotel car park she was given a ticket which had printed on its back the words 'ALL CARS PARKED AT THE OWNER'S RISK." She checked into the hotel and signed the reception book. When she got to her room she saw a sign on the back of the door stating *inter alia* that the hotel would not be liable for customers' goods which were lost or stolen. Her fur coats were stolen while she was at the hotel, and one of the hotel's employees carelessly crashed the catering van into her car. She sued the hotel for compensation to cover the losses she had suffered. The hotel relied on its notices in resisting her claim.

Decide if the court would enforce the hotel's exemption clauses in the following three circumstances:

(i) Sue booked her room in advance, over the phone. She received a confirmation slip which included the notice that the hotel would not be responsible for the theft or loss of patrons' goods.

(ii) Sue had heard the Shipshape Inn was a nice place to stay and as she was passing through on holiday she stopped there. Luckily they had a room for her as she had not booked in advance.

(iii) Although she did not book a room in advance, Sue correctly assumed that the hotel would have space for her as she had stayed there many times before.

STATUTORY RESTRICTIONS ON THE LIMITATION OR EXCLUSION OF LIABILITY

The primary statutory limitations on the exclusion or restriction of liability are to be found in the **Unfair Contract Terms Act 1977 (UCTA)**. The Act's basic effect is to render wholly ineffective any exclusion clauses which attempt to eliminate or limit liability for certain types of losses. It subjects other attempted limitations to a test of **reasonableness**. The widest protection of the Act is confined to what are called **consumer transactions**.

UCTA 1977

Defining a 'consumer transaction'

A person is said to be dealing as a consumer if:

- he/she does not deal in the course of a business
- he/she does not hold himself/herself out to be dealing for business purposes – eg. by making purchases from the **trade counter** of a shop
- where goods are involved they must be of a type which is normally supplied for private use. Even if the goods are only *sometimes* supplied for commercial purposes, they will not be considered to be consumer goods
- the transaction does not take place in an **auction** or as the result of a **tender**.

The protection offered to consumers

The protection offered to consumers by the UCTA 77 is confined to their dealings with **businesses** which are trying to exclude or limit their liability.

- **Section 2**. No contract term can restrict liability in any way for negligently causing a **personal injur**y or **death**. An exclusion clause which purports to exclude liability for **negligently**-caused **property damage** will be effective only if it is reasonable in all of the circumstances.
- **Section 3**. A business cannot unreasonably restrict its liability for **breaches of contract.**
- **Section 5**. A contractual clause is ineffective if it seeks to exclude or limit a **manufacturer's liability** for loss or damage to a consumer where that damage results from defects in the goods related to the manufacturing process or the distribution of the goods.
- **Section 6**. A business cannot exclude its liability to provide consumers with goods of satisfactory quality and which conform to their description, as required of the seller of goods by Sections 13-14 of the Sale of Goods Act 1979.
- **Section 8**. Liability for misrepresentation can be limited or excluded only if it is reasonable in the circumstances.

The protection offered in non-consumer transactions

The Act offers a lower level of protection where the transaction takes place between commercial enterprises.

- **Section 3**. If a transaction takes place on the **standard terms** of a business it cannot unreasonably restrict its liability for breaches of contract.

- **Section 6**. The conditions regarding satisfactory quality and description imposed into all contracts for the sale of goods by Secstions 13-14 of the Sale of Goods Act 1979 can be excluded only if it is reasonable in the circumstances.

- **Section 8**. Even if the transaction is between two private parties or two businesses, liability for misrepresentation can be limited or excluded only to the extent that it is reasonable in the circumstances to do so.

ACTIVITY 15

The Unfair Contracts Terms Act makes it very important to identify transactions which are consumer dealings and those which are not. Can you remember what characteristics are required for a business transaction to be a 'consumer transaction' as defined by the UCTA 1977?

- the buyer must be dealing as a private individual, not in the course of a business
- the goods involved must be of a type customarily used for private purposes.

Requirement That Exclusion clauses are reasonable

The term must be **reasonable and fair** having regard to the circumstances which were known to the parties (or ought to have been in their contemplation) when the contract was made.

The burden of showing it was reasonable to exclude or limit liability lies with the person seeking to rely on the exclusion clause.

Section 11(4). This provides for taking into consideration the possibility of obtaining **insurance** rather than seeking to limit liability in deciding if the exclusion clause was reasonable.

Section 11(2) and **Schedule 2**. These set out guidelines to be used where the contract concerns the supply or sale of goods (although these guidelines have also come to be applied in other circumstances as well). In establishing the reasonableness of the exemption or limitation clause the court should take into account such factors as:

- whether or not the parties were of relatively equal **bargaining strength**
- whether or not there was any **inducement given to the purchaser** to get him/her to agree to the insertion of the exclusion clause into the contract – eg. the price was reduced in exchange for a limitation of the seller's liability. Accepting such an inducement is more likely to make an exclusion clause enforceable

- whether or not goods were manufactured to the **customer's specifications.** That will make a manufacturer's limitation on liability more reasonable
- whether there were other potential suppliers who might not have imposed the exclusion clause
- whether it was reasonable to expect, at the time the contract was made, that a condition in the contract could be complied with. If so then a clause seeking to exclude or limit liability for the term's breach is not likely to be regarded as reasonable.

THE INTERACTION OF COMMON LAW AND STATUTORY RULES ON EXCLUSION AND LIMITATION CLAUSES.

An exemption clause must satisfy both common law and statutory rules. However, in recent cases the courts have tended to:

- move away from the strict application of the *contra preferentum* rule
- focus on the statutory requirements regarding reasonableness
- differentiate between the acceptability of limitation clauses and exclusion clauses.

Summary of section three

- terms can be categorised by their source as express or implied
- terms can be categorised by their importance as conditions and warranties
- trade puffs and statements of opinion are not actionable if they prove to be untrue
- one rule of thumb which courts use to determine which pre-contractual statements should be considered to be terms of the contract is whether the party the statement was made to relied on it heavily
- express terms are those the parties have actually agreed between themselves
- many implied terms are inserted into contracts by statutory provision – eg. the employer's duty regarding the health and safety of employees
- the Sale of Goods Act 1979 implies conditions into all contracts for the sale of goods in respect of the seller's right to sell the goods, their description and their satisfactory quality
- the common law implies some terms into all contracts of certain types – eg. all employees have a duty of fidelity and all employers have a duty of reasonable management

- in some cases terms are implied into contracts in order to implement the parties' intentions; in other cases it is done because it is necessary to do so to make the contract work

- the basis on which common law terms can be implied into contracts is the application of the officious observer test

- a condition is a term which goes to the heart of the contract as its fulfilment is essential to the achievement of the purpose of the contract

- if a condition is not honoured the injured party can consider the contract to have been repudiated by the other party and can consider himself or herself discharged of any further obligations under the contract

- a warranty is a term which is peripheral to the main purpose of the contract

- breach of a warranty gives the injured party a right to claim compensation, but does not bring the contract to an end

- an innominate term is one cast in such wide language that its categorisation as a condition or warranty must wait on an assessment of the impact of its breach

- exclusion or limitation clauses must satisfy both common law and statutory controls if they are to be enforceable

- the courts lean against exclusion clauses by insisting that reasonable notice of them be given prior to the conclusion of the contract

- the *contra preferentum* rule construes any ambiguous words in an exemption clause in favour of the party it is being applied to

- the main statutory control on exclusion clauses is the Unfair Contract Terms Act 1977

- a consumer dealing with a business is given the greatest protection by UCTA 1977

- liability for death or personal injury due to negligence cannot be excluded in a consumer transaction

- liability for property damage due to negligence or for breach of contract can only be excluded as far as is reasonable in the circumstances

- the tests for reasonableness of an exemption clause include an assessment of the relative bargaining strength of the parties, and whether the party the clause is being applied against received any financial inducement for agreeing the insertion of the clause into the contract.

Suggested answers to section three self-check questions

SELF-CHECK 1

1. This is probably a term of the contract – ie. that this boat is capable of sailing across the Atlantic. If you were planning such a voyage any assurance that the boat was sufficiently seaworthy to undertake such a trip would undoubtedly amount to a condition – ie. a term so important that if it is broken, the contract can be brought to an end.

2. This is sales puffery. It is a statement of no legal significance.

3. This is a statement of fact (purportedly true) which is certainly meant to induce Ed to enter into the contract to buy the boat, but there is no way it can become part of the contract itself. It does not relate to some characteristic of the subject matter nor does it relate to the actual deal the parties strike in the end. In fact, it may not even amount to a representation. It does not make any statement about the subject matter of the contract.

SELF-CHECK 2

The court held that M's statement about the age of the bike was not legally binding. It took place too far away from the moment of contracting. R had had plenty of time to check on the accuracy of M's assertion about the bike's age if he had considered the age of the machine to be important consideration in deciding to buy.

If you are wondering why the courts treated this case differently from **Bannerman v White** one explanation is that in this case the court did not feel that the parties intended for the age of the bike to be of any importance in their dealings with each other. What the courts are doing in all of these cases is attempting to discern what the intentions of the parties were at the time when they concluded their contract. Because the court cannot look into the parties' minds they must look at whatever evidence there is of the circumstances surrounding the creation of the agreement. In effect the court must re-invent the intentions of the parties. Inevitably what the courts decide the parties wanted out of their dealings with each other is coloured by the fact that the cause and consequences of the contract going wrong are now all too clear. In retrospect it must often seem impossible to hold that the parties could not have intended for there to be some redress for the inaccurate or misleading statements which have resulted in such a mess. The only way redress can be secured is to find that the statement was at least a representation and in many cases that it was a term: otherwise it will not be actionable.

SELF-CHECK 3

(1) The essential issues here are these: (i) did Larry's failure to check the goods in the shop mean that he has no right to claim about any defects discovered later on? (ii) does he have to treat any breach by the shop as a breach of a warranty only because he has had the goods for so long before complaining; (iii) what breaches of the SOGA implied terms have ocurred?

(i)   Buyers are under no duty to inspect the goods they buy. Section 14(2c) provides that the seller will not be liable for those defects about which the buyer is informed before the sale, or for those which whatever inspection the buyer perfomed could reasonably have been expected to turn up. Larry made no inspection of the goods; nor was he informed of any defects. Therefore Mark will be liable to compensate Larry for any defect in the goods.

(ii) Once goods have been accepted, the buyer loses the right to terminate the contract for a breach of a condition regarding the goods. He must treat the breach as the breach of a warranty and settle for damages. There is no fixed amount of time a buyer can have goods in his/her possession before he/she is deemed to have accepted the goods. Section 35 says acceptance can be assumed if rejection of the goods is not notified to the seller within a reasonable time. But no acceptance can be assumed until the buyer has had the goods long enough to have a reasonable chance to inspect them. In this case, the court might well hold that the circumstances were such as to start counting the period of Larry's possession only from the time he arrived home from the hospital. But that is not certain.

(iii) The question is, on what basis would Larry be making a claim for a refund? Presumably he would claim the goods were not of satisfactory quality. Yet they were working when he got them home and put them into use. There are two bases on which Larry might rest his claim. The first is the approach taken in **Crowther v Shannon Motor Co. [1975] 1 All ER 139** where it was held that goods which go faulty in an unreasonably short time after purchase can be regarded as not having been of merchantable quality even at the time of purchase. In other words they fail the test of durability. The second way of viewing the situation was set out by Lord Diplock in **Lambert v Lewis [1982] AC 225, CA**. He said that Section 14(2) must be read to include an implied warranty that the goods will continue to be fit for their purpose for a reasonable time after delivery – what amounts to a reasonable time depending on the nature of the goods. So certainly, if they broke down only a day or so after Larry began to use them there would be a breach of the condition as to merchantability. As to whether he would have to treat this breach as the breach of a warranty instead of the breach of a condition would be a matter of whether it was deemed reasonable to use goods for a few days before deciding they were acceptable.

(iv) If Larry had the goods in use for only a month before a breakdown, it seems likely that their defectiveness would be seen as the breach of the condition regarding satisfactory quality, since one would normally expect a hi-fi system to have a life of a few years. But almost certainly Larry would be deemed to have accepted the goods, so his only remedy would be to treat the defect as a breach of the warranty. He would be unlikely to be able to force the shop to give him a refund.

(v) Knowing that Larry needs a portable stereo, Mark sells him the Boomer. It can be inferred that he is guaranteeing that that equipment is fit for the purpose for which Larry wants it. And Mark's liability under Section 14(3) for ensuring that

that is the case is strict. It does not matter that he does not know about the fragility of the Boomer; he is still in breach of the Section 14(3) condition. Whether that would entitle him to a refund would depend on the points discussed in (ii) above.

SELF-CHECK 4

She did win (**Bettini v Gye [1876] 1 QBD 183**). The court held that the main purpose of the contract was to secure her performance of the opera before an audience. She was prepared to do that. Her failure to attend rehearsals was no more than the breach of an ancillary requirement. It amounted to the breach of a warranty, not a condition. Therefore, the opera company was not free to consider itself discharged from its obligations under the contract. It could sue the singer for damages to compensate for any loss her failure to attend rehearsals had occasioned, but it had to let her perform.

SELF-CHECK 5

(i) The facts in this situation are similar to those in the case **Olley v Marlborough Court Ltd. [1949] 1 KB 532, CA.** The court held that the exemption of liability spelled out in a notice in the guest's room was not part of the contract between the hotel and the guest. The same conclusion would probably be drawn in Sue's case. Why? Because the contract was made before she was aware that there were any exclusion or limitation clauses the hotel wanted to include in it. The contract between Sue and the hotel was concluded when she booked the room over the phone. The limitation clauses, however, were dependent on the notices on the premises; notices which would only be seen at a later time.

What about the notice on the confirmation slip? This is unlikely to be considered to be the contract. Rather it is evidence of the contract which has been made between Sue and the Shipshape Inn.

Stop and think a moment about what term the hotel was trying to exclude liability for.Would that most likely have been an express or an implied term of the contract?

(ii) If Sue's contract with the hotel was made at the point when she checked in (probably when she signed the register) then there is no question that she had been given notice about the hotel's exclusion of liability for damage to guests' cars. The notice in the room still comes too late to be part of the contract. But is even the hotel's notice about damage to guests' cars effective? There are a few other points to take into consideration:

- would a reasonable person have realised that the car parking ticket was part of the contractual documentation?

- was the notice sufficently prominent to satisfy the requirement that a person be given a reasonable opportunity to realise that a contract contains an exclusion clause?

- does the exclusion clause, even if effective otherwise, actually cover the damage suffered by Sue?

The following case is relevant to answering these questions.

Thompson v LMS Railway Co. [1930] 1 KB 41, CA
A railway ticket said: "Exclusion. For conditions see back." On the back it said that the ticket was issued subject to the conditions to be found in the company's timetable. One of the conditions relieved the company of liability for any injury to passengers. The plaintiff was illiterate and could not read the ticket. He was injured while travelling as a passenger. The company relied on the notice printed on the ticket to relieve it of any liability.

The court upheld the validity of the exclusion clause. Why? Because issuing of the ticket was deemed to amount to the offer in this transaction. Payment by the customer was acceptance. The ticket containing the exclusion clause was a contractual document – it contained the offer so notice of the exclusion clause did not come too late. The exemption became part of the contract. Did it matter that the plaintiff was illiterate and could not read the notice? No, the company could not be responsible to cater to the disabilities of its passengers. It had done what was reasonable in bringing the clause to the notice of customers. But in **Thornton v Shoe Lane Parking Ltd. [1971] 2 WLR 585, CA** Lord Denning said that the width of an exclusion notified by a sign – 'All cars parked at owners' risk – was such that it would have had to draw attention to itself by being printed in red ink with a red hand pointing to it or some equally dramatic device to catch the driver's attention. The wider the exclusion claimed, the more vivid and attention-grabbing the notice warning of the exclusion must be. The court might well hold that printing the exclusion on the back of the entry ticket did not give Sue adequate notice of the exclusion clause.

One final point to note is that in the past in their desire to protect against the unwarranted use of exclusion/exemption/limitation clauses, the courts have used the *contra preferentum* 'rule' to hold that unless an exclusion clause specifically mentioned that liability for negligence was excluded *in so many words*, then it would not be. This is no longer necessary in many cases due to the prohibition on excluding liability for negligently-caused injuries or death which is found in the Unfair Contract Terms Act.

(iii) If Sue had stayed in the Shipshape Inn on a number of previous occasions, she might be deemed to be fully aware of the limitations the Inn placed on its liability to its guests. However, although a previous course of dealings can be said to have given ample notice of any limitations on liability, it is always a matter of fact what amounts to a sufficiently long history of dealings between the parties. Consider **Hollier v Rambler Motors (AMC) Ltd. [1972] 2 WLR 401, CA.** The plaintiff sent his motor car to the defendants' garage for repairs. He had done this three or four times over the preceding five years. On all the previous occasions he had signed a document releasing the garage from any liability for damage to the car while in the garage's premises. This time, no release was signed. The car was damaged by fire while at the garage. The fire was caused by the defendants' negligence. The plaintiff sued for compensation, arguing that there was no limitation on the garage's liability on this occasion. The court held that the pattern of dealings between the customer and garage was of neither sufficient length nor frequency to warrant the incorporation of the exclusion clause found in previous transactions into this one.

SECTION FOUR

Discharging a Contract

In Section Four you will find material which will enable you to learn about and understand the following things:

- what is required of a party to a contract to say he or she has discharged the contract by performance
- bringing a contract to an end as a result of a breach of one or more of the terms of the contract
- the remedies available to the innocent victim of a breach of contract
- how the availability of monetary compensation (damages) is governed
- the equitable remedies available to innocent parties.

How contracts come to an end

The majority of contracts come to an end because both parties perform all their obligations under the contract to each other's satisfaction. Both parties receive whatever benefits each was due to obtain through the contract. When this occurs, a contract is said to be discharged by **performance**. However, some contracts are ended because one of the parties commits a significant **breach** – ie. fails to meet one of his/her obligations under the contract. Others are brought to a conclusion by the parties reaching some **agreement** that the contract should be terminated, even though it is as yet incompletely fulfilled. Finally, a contract may be ended because of some external circumstance, under the control of neither party to the contract. In such a case a contract is said to be discharged by **frustration**.

If the interests of one of the parties to a contract are injured by the failure of the other party to live up to his/her obligations, the aggrieved party will want to know if the law offers any remedy. The basic principle of remedial action in the law of contract is that the aggrieved or innocent party should be restored to the position he/she would have been in if the other party had performed their obligations under the contract completely, and as soon as they came due. In pursuit of this objective, the courts have a number of remedies upon which they can rely. In this section we are going to examine three of them:

- damages
- specific performance
- injunction.

These remedies are usually applicable in situations where the contract has been under performance for some time before one of the parties in some way fails to meet his/her obligations. As we have seen earlier on, the courts can also step in to remedy a situation where there has been a flaw in the creation of the contract. They can **rescind** the contract. Or, in certain circumstances, they can order its **rectification**. Rescission was discussed in Section Two. Rectification is an equitable remedy giving the court the discretionary power to order that a written contract be altered so as to bring it into line with an oral agreement about that contractual relationship.

After you have studied the material in Section Four your should be able to do the following things:

- outline the circumstances in which only partial fulfilment of contractual obligations will entitle a party to recompense
- distinguish between the effects of a breach of a condition and a breach of a warranty
- outline the circumstances in which a contract may be said to have been frustrated
- explain the rules governing the determination of whether damage is too remote to be compensated
- distinguish between liquidated and unliquidated damages
- identify the circumstances in which an order for specific performance may be made
- explain the effects of an injunction.

Discharge by performance

In order to discharge a contract by performance, both parties must precisely and completely fulfil their contractual obligations.

Sumpter v Hedges [1898] 1QB 673, CA

Sumpter agreed to construct two buildings for Hedges for £565. He did work to the value of £555 and then abandoned the project. Hedges completed the work himself, using materials left behind by Sumpter. Sumpter claimed for the £555 worth of work which he had done. The court held that he was not entitled to payment, except for the value of the materials which Hedges had used in completing the project.

This case illustrates what seems to be, and is, a very harsh view of what is required to satisfy contractual obligations and earn entitlement to payment of the contract price. In order to mitigate its impact the courts have evolved a number of 'exceptions to the rule':

- if the contract is **divisible** or **severable** into discrete parts, some of which have been performed, payment may be due in recompense for the obligations actually fulfilled

BUSINESS CONTRACTS   241

- even if the agreement is not divisible or severable, if one party's obligations have been **substantially performed** that should entitle him/her to payment for a suitable proportion of the total contract price
- if one party accepts partial performance of the other party's obligations in 'full satisfaction and accord', then payment of the whole contract price will be due
- if one party prevents completion of all the other party's obligations, payment will be due for the work actually done
- If the time of completion of obligations is important, then even substantial performance may not be enough to warrant any payment.

SELF-CHECK 1

Which party do you think the court decided in favour of in the following case?

Bolton v Mahadeva [1972] 2 All ER 1322, CA

The plaintiff contracted to install a central heating system in the defendant's house. The installation was to cost £800. After the work was completed it was found that the flue leaked smoke and fumes into the house and the system would only perform at 90% of its rated capacity. The defendant refused to pay for the installation and the plaintiff sued for his money (less the amount it had cost the defendant to put the system right).

Discharge by agreement

The parties can agree that each should be relieved of any outstanding obligations (or of all their respective obligations if no performance has begun). Such an agreement will only be binding if it is accomplished by way of a **deed,** or if each party furnishes the other some **consideration** in respect of the promise of relief from any further need to abide by the provisions of the contract.

Discharge by breach of contract

A breach of contract occurs when a party to the contract refuses to perform some obligation imposed on them by the contract.

The different types of terms have very different effects on the contract if they are broken by one of the parties. It is only if there is a breach of a **condition** that the contract can be said to be discharged by the breach. (Breach of a warranty will entitle the injured party to damages but no more.) Where one party breaches a condition of the contract, he or she is said to have committed a **fundamental breach** of the contract, entitling the other party to consider it to have been **terminated** or discharged.

There is a terminological point of interest here. If the injured party chooses to regard the contract as discharged, can it be said to have been **rescinded** by him? The answer is no. Rescission is a remedy which renders all obligations *past, present and future* under the contract void. Termination or discharge of the contract only affects the parties' liability to meet as yet 'unripened' obligations. The previous history of the contract is still relevant.

The easist way to understand the difference between rescission and discharge or rescission and termination of the contract is to look at the grievance of the innocent party. If it relates to a misrepresentation or mistake or something else relating to the *formation* of the contract, then the innocent party will seek to rescind the contract. The aim will be to make it as if the contract had never been entered into. However, if the grievance arises out of some fault in the way the other party is *carrying out* his/her obligations under the contract, then the innocent party will simply want to be discharged of any obligation to *carry on* with the contract. He/she will seek the termination of the contract and by that release from any further obligations under it. In either case, it is possible for the innocent party to carry on with the contract, either ignoring the justification for rescission/termination or treating it as a cause for a claim for damages only.

ACTIVITY 16

Why is it, do you think, that the breach of a condition can lead to the discharge (ending) of the contract, while the breach of a warranty only justifies a claim for damages? Think about why any term is designated either as a warrant or a condition.

A warranty is a minor term of the contract, while a condition is said to go to the heart of the contract. It makes sense, therefore, that very different remedies are available for the breach of warranties than for the breach of a condition. If a condition is broken, the injured party may well see no point in going ahead with the contract, whereas, if only a minor obligation is not honoured by the other party, it makes sense for the contract to carry on, but for the injured party to get some compensation for any loss or inconvenience this has caused them. If a contract were allowed to be wound up as a result of any breach, no matter how insignificant, it would be too disruptive to commerce.

Frustration of contracts

A contract is said to be frustrated, and rendered **void** as a result, either if it becomes impossible or illegal to perform the contract, or if it becomes the case that the completion of the contract would be a nonsense from one or both parties' point of view. The first reason for frustration – **impossibility** – is easy to understand. If we agree in the morning that I will hire a hall from you to give a concert in the evening, but at 5pm the hall burns down, then our contract is frustrated. You cannot supply me the hall for my use. (Note: this is not the same thing as where the hall has burned down in the morning before we made our contract, but neither of us knew it. That will render the contract void by reason of a **common mistake** – ie. our common belief that the subject matter of the contract was actually in existence **cf. Taylor v Caldwell [1863] 3 B&S 826**).

The second cause of frustration is **illegality**. If a British firm contracted to supply a German firm with special metals in April 1939, that contract would have been made illegal upon the outbreak of war between Germany and Britain in August 1939 due to legislation forbidding trading with the enemy. The wartime controls on trade would have resulted in the frustration of the contract.

Finally, a contract can be frustrated because it was concluded in the context of some **anticipated event which has since been cancelled or postponed**. If I hire you a room overlooking the route of a grand parade and the parade is later cancelled then our contract has been frustrated because the rationale for concluding a contract has been destroyed **(cf. Krell v Henry [1903] 2 KB 740)**.

You may have noticed that in all these cases neither party can be said to be at **fault** for what has happened. That is required before the contract can be said to have been frustrated by the event. As far as impossibility frustrating a contract is concerned, the frustrating event must have made it truly impossible for the object of the contract to be completed. Just making it more difficult or more expensive will not frustrate the contract **(cf. Tsakiroglou & Co. Ltd. v Noblee Thorl GmbH [1962] AC 93)**.

Remedies

The purpose of the criminal law is to punish wrongdoers. The focus of the civil law is on the victim. Its aim is to secure compensation for wrongs that have been inflicted on innocent parties. The main instrument of compensation is money – although we can all think of many cases where that will hardly make up for the losses suffered. Where money compensation is offered to the victim of a civil wrong, it is said that the aggrieved party receives **damages** to compensate for the **loss** which has been incurred.

Damages

Any party to a contract who suffers from the other party's breach of his/her obligations under the contract is entitled as of right in the common law to financial compensation for those losses. Success in a claim for damages, therefore, does not depend on the *discretion* of the court. What the success or failure of a claim for a specified amount of damages will depend on are such factors as:

- whether the type of loss suffered is of the type which can be compensated
- whether the loss suffered is deemed to be too 'remote' to compensate
- whether the party has taken steps to mitigate his/her loss
- whether the claim is brought in time – ie. within time limits fixed by statute.

What losses can be compensated?

Most claims in contract arise out of financial loss caused by one party defaulting on their obligations under the contract. But the other party's breach also may have caused physical damage to the plaintiff or his property. It may have resulted in emotional distress. All of these can be compensated.

The usual form of compensation in contract is payment of money to the aggrieved party. In many cases the courts will find it difficult to put a money value on the loss suffered, but the fact that it is difficult to settle on an appropriate sum will not invalidate a claim for damages for that particular loss.

Remoteness

What does it mean to say damge or loss is too 'remote' to be compensated? Consider the following sequence of events.

Bill sells Iqbal, a fellow engineering student at Wolverhampton University, a motorcycle. Bill guarantees the bike to be free of defects. Two hours later as Iqbal is speeding down the motorway at 70 mph the rear wheel comes off the bike and he is seriously injured in the ensuing crash. It turns out that Bill fitted the wrong type of wheel nut when he was preparing the bike for sale. In the crash Iqbal suffers serious cuts to his face and is left with some scars. Three years later Iqbal has become a rising star on TV. He is interviewed for the lead role in a big-budget Hollywoood romance but fails to get the part because, he is told, the scars on his face make him unsuitable. But for them he'd have been given the role, for which he would have been paid £100,000.

Would it be reasonable to allow Iqbal to sue Bill for £100,000 in damages for the loss of the part in the film? After all, but for Bill's breach of contract Iqbal would have been given the part.

You might say that the amount of **time** which separates the breach from this particular 'loss' is so great as to make the loss too remote to be recoverable. And in deciding on the remoteness of damage the courts do take into consideration the amount of time separating the breach and any of its consequences. But that is only one of the criteria used to establish remoteness. The others are:

- is the loss one which is directly attributable to the breach of contract?

- is the loss one which, in the absence of any knowledge of special circumstances applying in the situation, the parties would have forseen as being highly probable – or at least not unlikely – if they had turned their minds to the likely consequences of either party breaching the terms of the contract?

- did the parties have actual or constructive knowledge of special circumstances which would have widened the range of probable consequences of a breach which they might have forseen if they'd turned their minds to the question of the consequences of a breach of the contract they were concluding?

- was the damage which actually occurred within that widened range of highly probable consequences?

Hadley v Baxendale [1854] 9 Exch 341

H owned a flour mill. The crankshaft of the milling mechanism broke. He contracted with B to transport the broken shaft to London where it could be used as a pattern for the manufacture of a new shaft. B was meant to deliver the crankshaft to the manufacturers on the following day but due to his neglect of his duties it was delayed on route. The net result was that the mill, which had to be closed until a new shaft was fitted, was out of operation for longer than it need to have been. H claimed damages to compensate for the loss of profits during this unnecessary period of idleness. The court held that B was not liable for H's extra loss of profit because in the normal run of things a mill would have a spare crankshaft on hand. B did not know that H did not keep a spare and therefore, even if he had thought about the likely consequences of his failing to carry out his contractual obligations punctually, he would not have foreseen that the mill would have been kept out of operation longer than otherwise would be the case. According to the court a loss will only be recoverable if it emerges in the usual course of events arising out of a breach. In this case that did not happen. The loss only occurred because of the 'special circumstances' that H did not keep a spare crankshaft. It was not foreseeable at the time of contracting that the loss would be a probable consequence of a breach because, the court held, the knowledge the defendant could be imputed to have at the time of contracting was only what the usual practices in the industry were – and that was to keep a spare on hand. In this case, although special circumstances existed – ie. the plaintiff did not have a spare shaft – the defendant (B) had no knowledge of this, nor was it reasonable to impute such knowledge to him. Therefore the loss was too remote to be recovered.

SELF-CHECK 2

How do you think the court resolved the following dispute?

Victoria Laundry (Windsor) Ltd. v Newman Industries Ltd. [1949] 2 KB 528, CA

The plaintiffs bought a boiler from the defendants. The boiler was to be used in an extension of the plaintiffs' existing business, and it would enable them to move into new types of work of high profitability. Delivery of the boiler was delayed because it was damaged when being removed from its existing site for re-installation on the plaintiffs' premises. The plaintiffs sued for damages for the loss of profits which would have been earned by carrying out a greater volume of the company's traditional work, and for damages for the loss ofexceptional profits which would have been earned under a contract which the company had just secured from the Ministry of Supply for dyeing uniforms. (This was the new type of work which the boiler would havee nabled them to undertake, although this contract had been secured after the boiler had been ordered.) In the end the contract with the Ministry was lost due to the delays which occurred in installing the boiler.

ACTIVITY 18

Using your own words and without looking back in the text, formulate the rule on remoteness of damages in contract. There are *two* elements to remember:

1.

2.

The two essential tests of remoteness for damage claims in contract are:
- was the damage something that one would expect to have happened in the usual, natural course of events following a breach of the term concerned?
- if not, then was the damage something the parties would have forseen as likely to happen in the majority of cases if a breach of this term occurred, provided they had turned their mind to the consequences of any breaches at the time they were concluding the contract?

Establishing the *quantum* of damages

A problem which runs parallel with determining which losses can be compensated, is establishing how much compensation is due for the loss.

The basic principle is that a party who suffers a loss as a result of a breach of contract should be put into the position he/she would have been in if the breach had not occurred.

The purpose of damages is not to penalise the party in breach. If the injured party has suffered no loss as a result of the breach, then he/she will be entitled to no more than **nominal damages** – ie. a sum of a pound or two simply to mark that a wrong has been done.

The general rule for estimating the amount of damages due in regard to any particular loss is reproduced in Section 50(3) of the **Sale of Goods Act 1979** which says:

> 'Where there is an available market for the goods in question the measure of damages is *prima facie* to be ascertained by the difference between the contract price and the market or current price at the time or times when the goods ought to have been accepted or (if no time was fixed for acceptance) at the time of the refusal to accept.'

How is the *quantum* (the amount) of damages fixed when the contract does not involve the sale of goods and services in such a clear-cut fashion? The court will not shirk the task of fixing a sum of damages even though it may be difficult to find a basis for arriving at a money cost of the loss.

Liquidated damages

It is possible (and in some types of contracts, common) for the parties to include in their contract a provision as to the amount of damages which will be payable, regardless of the magnitude of the actual loss incurred, in the event of certain types of breaches. The sum fixed is called **liquidated damages**. (Where a claim for damages is based on the actual amount lost it is a claim for **unliquidated damages**.) The advantage to the party who is to benefit from the liquidated damages is that he/she need not prove or quantify loss. All that is required is a breach of the type specified. For the party who will pay liquidated damages, the advantage is that regardless of the true cost of his/her breach, the injured party can obtain no more than the specified amount.

Examples of liquidated damages can be found in holiday brochures where normally a table sets out the charges the company will make if the holiday is cancelled (which amounts to a breach of contract by the holidaymaker). Typically these increase from merely losing your deposit if the cancellation occurs more than six weeks prior to departure to losing about 50 per cent of the total amount paid for cancelling 2-4 weeks before departure, and losing 100 per cent of the amount paid if the cancellation ocurrs on the day of departure.

The essential requirement is that the sum agreed must represent a real attempt to estimate the financial consequences of a breach. If the court perceives the sum agreed to amount to a penalty imposed on one or the other of the parties, it will not enforce the liquidated damages clause.

ACTIVITY 19

What is the difference between **liquidated** and **unliquidated** damages?

Liquidated damages are the damages the parties agree in advance will be payable if a certain type of breach occurs, regardless of how much the actual loss caused is. The sum agreed must represent a reasonable estimate of the value of the actual loss. **Unliquidated damages** is the sum an aggrieved party claims as the cost of their actual loss.

Mitigation of losses

The party who has been injured by a breach of contract is required to take reasonable steps to minimise the losses he/she suffers as a result of the breach. Thus, for example, an employee who is wrongfully dismissed must seek other employment even while pursuing a claim against his/her employer. A buyer of goods must go into the market to make up at the cheapest price possible shortfalls of delivery by the seller, and the seller must try and dispose of goods elsewhere at the best price possible if a buyer wrongfully refuses to accept them. If the injured party fails to take steps to mitigate their loss they will be stopped from collecting damages for that part of the loss which could otherwise have been avoided.

SELF-CHECK 3

How do you think the court decided the following case?

Yetton v Eastwoods Froy Ltd. [1966] 3 All ER 353

Y was wrongfully dismissed. He had five years of a contract of service left to run. His salary was fixed at £7500 p.a. Following his dismissal Y tried to find another job of similar status and pay, but failed. Eventually Y claimed damages of £37,500, representing the lost five years' pay.

Time limits on claiming, damages

The **Limitation Act 1980** restricts the period for which a breach of contract will remain actionable. In the case of most contracts, an action for damages must be commenced within six years of the occurrence of the breach. There are two main exceptions:

- the time period where the breach injures a minor only starts to elapse from the time the minor reaches his/her maturity
- fraud, in the form of deliberate concealment of the breach, delays the start of the clock until the fraud is discovered (or until it would have been discovered if the injured party had been reasonably diligent in looking after his/her affairs).

SPECIFIC PERFORMANCE

Specific performance is one of the equitable remedies which operate in the law of contract. An order of specific performance requires a defaulting party to carry out his/her obligations at pain of being found to be in contempt of court if he/she fails to do so.

Specific performance is one of the court's discretionary remedies. There is no right to an order of specific performance. The court will only issue the order:

- it is equitable *in all the circumstances* for it to do so. Thus specific performance will not be ordered to enforce contracts of employment or other contracts involving personal service. It is held that to do so would be inequitable as it would require forcing people into relationships which they did not want to continue. On a practical level it would also require the continuous supervision of the court to ensure that the order was being honoured.
- is clear that in the circumstances an award of damages would not be an adequate remedy. Damages will, in nearly all circumstances, be seen to be an adequate remedy. Where an order of specific performance will most likely be issued is if the contract concerns the sale or purchase of a chattel of some **unique quality,** or if the contract involves a dealing in **land** or an **interest in land.**
- the order would be effective. One of the maxims of equity is that it does nothing in vain. If property which might have met the required quality of uniqueness is destroyed or lost, no order of specific performance will be issued.

SELF-CHECK 4

How do you think the court would decide the following case?

G agreed to buy B's house. The house had a sitting tenant who both parties believed could not be evicted because of the protection offered tenants by the Rents Act. In fact the current occupant was the son of the original tenants and as such was not protected by the Rents Acts. When he heard of the impending change of ownership he moved out – but not before G and B had already agreed that the house would be sold for a price reflecting occupation by a protected tenant – ie. for £850. (With vacant possession the house would have been worth £2,250.) B refused to go through with the deal at the low price which had been agreed. G sued for specific perfomance. Do you think the court granted his request?

INJUNCTIONS

An injunction is more or less the obverse of an order for specific performance. Instead of ordering someone to carry out a contractual obligation, it orders them not to do something which would violate a contractual obligation. Perhaps the most frequent use of the injunction arises in the enforcement of restrictive covenants in contracts of employment. These are often included to stop an employee from leaving an employer and setting up to trade on his/her own account (or for another employer in the same field) and taking customers with whom he/she has built up a relationship away from the former employer. Although an injunction will not be issued to stop the employee from leaving the employer, one may well be issued to prevent him/her violating the restrictions on working elsewhere embodied in the contract of employment.

Lumley v Wagner [1852] 1 De GM&C 604, HL

Wagner contracted to sing exclusively for Lumley at Her Majesty's Theatre in London. Wagner and Lumley fell out. She refused to sing for him any longer. And without his permission she agreed to perform at Covent Garden. Lumley sought an order of specific performance against Wagner. That was refused, but in an oblique fashion the courts sought to encourage Wagner to carry out her contract with Lumley because they granted an injunction forbidding her to sing at Covent Garden or at any other commercial venue other than Her Majesty's during the 3-month tenure of her contract with Lumley.

SELF-CHECK 5

Lovejoy decided the time had come to get out of the antiques business. He contracted to sell his company Battered Beauties Ltd to Bertie Bogle for £50,000 and moved to London. As part of the agreement Lovejoy covenanted (1) not to bid against Bertie at auctions, and (2) not to set up in the antiques or fine art business within 300 miles of Stratford for a period of 25 years.

Bertie was happy with this agreement because Lovejoy had been a major competitor in the West Midlands area which Bertie had served with his existing antique shops in Birmingham, Walsall and Wolverhampton. Within six months, however, Bertie found that Lovejoy was attending auctions all over the country and buying pieces of handcrafted post-war furniture which he was then selling in London. This infuriated Bertie as he had spent a considerable sum of money enlarging the Stratford shop to accommodate a new line of modern masterpieces of art and design, and Lovejoy was outbidding him for many of the items he wanted for this new enterprise. After another six months Bertie reckoned he'd lost £20,000 in revenue (and £5,000 in profit) due to sales he'd not been able to complete because Lovejoy had snatched the item he wanted out from under his nose.

Advise Bertie if there is any way he can restrain Lovejoy's activities and recover his losses.

Summary of section four

- the discharge of a contract takes place in the context of something happening after the contract has been formed, not during the process of formation itself
- the most common reason for the discharge of a contract is that both parties have completely fullfilled all their obligations under the contract This is discharge by performance
- if there has been only partial performance of contractual obligations by one of the parties, no payment for the work which has been done is due from the other party unless the defaulting party's obligations are severable, or there has been substantial perfomance
- if one party repudiates the contract by failing to perform important obligations – ie. there is a breach of a condition – the other party is entitled to consider themselves discharged from any further performance of the contract
- if a contract becomes impossible, illegal to perform, or there is no longer any purpose in performing the contract, then it is said to have been discharged by frustration
- the main remedy in contract is monetary compensation – ie. damages
- losses resulting from a contractual breach are too remote to be compensated if they do not arise as a natural consequence of the breach, or if they were not within the range of likely consequences

forseen by the parties when (if) they contemplated the result of any
breach taking place in the context of known special circumstances
applying to this contract

- the basic aim of compensation in contract is to put the innnocent party in
  the position he/she would have been in if no breach had taken place
- a claim for unliquidated damages is a claim for the amount of the loss
  actually incurred
- a claim for liquidated damages is a claim for an agreed amount of
  compensation attributable to any particular type of breach
- the party who has suffered a loss as a result of a breach is obliged to
  take action to mitigate their loss
- a court makes an order of specific performance where damages are an
  inadequate remedy and it is possible for the defaulting party to actually
  carry out his or her obligations when ordered to do so by the court
- an injunction may be granted by the court if it will prevent the default of a
  contractual obligation.

Suggested answers to section four self-check questions

SELF-CHECK 1

The court held that the plaintiff had not rendered the *substantial performance*
required to merit payment. Although he had done most of the individual tasks
connected with the installation of a central heating system, the fact that it was so
defective in performance as to be unusable without remedial repairs meant that the
fundamental purpose of the contract had not been even partially accomplished. The
focus of the courts in a situation like this will always be on the substantial
accomplishment of the *purpose* of the contract.

SELF-CHECK 2

The Court of Appeal held that the losses of profit which would have been earned
from a expansion of the firm's customary business activities could be recovered. It
was reasonable to presume that the defendants would have foreseen that any failure
to deliver the boiler on time would result in a loss of business to the plaintiffs. Why
else would they have purchased such a large piece of machinery other than to use
it in their business? It did not matter that it was not clearly stated by the plaintiffs
how they intended to use the boiler: at least that much knowledge could be imputed
to the defendants. But the loss of profit which would have been earned on the
Ministry contract was not recoverable. Why not? Because it was not reasonable for
the defendants to have forseen this particular loss if they failed to deliver the
boiler on time. They had no actual knowledge of the Ministry contract, nor were

they privy to the company's expansion plans. It would not be reasonable to impute knowledge of this 'special circumstance' to them.

SELF-CHECK 3

The court held that he was acting reasonably to seek similar or equivalent employment for the first few months after he lost his job. After that, however, he should have been willing to look at and take a job with less status and pay. He had not pursued a job paying £2500 p.a. which he had a good chance of obtaining. The court held that after 18 months of unemployment Y could have been expected to obtain a job paying £3000 p.a. Thus his compensation was reduced by £10,500 to reflect the three and a half out of the five years he could have been employed at £3000 p.a.

SELF-CHECK 4

The facts in this case are the same as those in **Grist v Bailey [1967] Ch 532**. There the order for specific performance was not granted because it would have been inequitable in the circumstances to have done so. It would have imposed too severe a burden on B. Instead G was obliged to enter into a new contract with B. This provided for the sale of the house at the vacant possession price. (B had sought to have the contract set aside completely on the grounds that it involved an actionable mistake.) By reaching this decision the court was illustrating the point that it must be equitable for all parties that specific performance be granted. It would have been too hard on G to deny the right to buy the house at a fair price.

SELF-CHECK 5

The essential question here is whether Bertie can get an injunction ordering Lovejoy to quit buying furniture at auctions. In deciding whether or not to issue an injunction the court will take into consideration a number of things. First among them is whether Bertie has a cause of action against Lovejoy. Has Lovejoy broken his covenant? On the facts given it would appear that he has not. Is he engaging in the antiques or fine arts trade if he is buying modern furniture? This is essentially a matter of semantics (as is the case in many legal disputes) but the court may feel that what he is doing is outside the restrictions he agreed to. If they do not take this view, however, is the covenant enforceable? Remember a restraint of trade is only enforceable if it protects a real interest of the person seeking to rely on it. The interest of Bertie was in protecting his market in the West Midlands. Lovejoy is not operating there. What about Bertie's interest in getting his new trade in modern art and design going? Fine – but this all came about after the purchase of Lovejoy's business, so Bertie cannot seek to use the provisions of that contract to protect his new enterprise. In any event, the court might well hold that the geographical and temporal extent of the restaint imposed on Lovejoy was unreasonable and therefore rendered the restraint unenforceable.

What about Bertie's claim for damages? The issue here is whether the damage he has suffered is too remote. First of all – what damage has he suffered? A loss of sales of modern furniture and the profits which would have been attributable to those sales. Would this type of loss have been within the contemplation of Bertie and Lovejoy at the time of the sale of the business as being *not unlikely* in the event that Lovejoy broke his covenant? It seems unlikely as up to that point Lovejoy's interest had been focussed on antique furniture, and so had Bertie's. The court might well hold that losses attributable to competition over modern furniture were too remote to be recovered.

Unit 3: additional questions

1. Patty is having an engagement party. She wants to serve kebabs because they are her fiance Ron's favourite food. She picks up a 10kg pack of fillet steak marked 'Special Offer' from the meat display cabinet in Bigstores supermarket and takes it over to the butcher who is working behind the meat counter. She asks him to cube it for her. While he is doing this she goes around the store choosing the rest of the supplies she needs for her party. To her dismay, she espies her beloved Ron kissing and cuddling Cherry, the produce attendant, behind the fruitstand. Infuriated, she storms over and throws her engagement ring in Ron's face, shouting, 'I don't ever want to see you again. ' As she is fleeing from the store in tears the butcher calls her over to collect her meat. She says she doesn't want it anymore. The butcher tells her that she'll have to pay for it anyway. Patty refuses.

   Is Patty bound to pay for the cubed steak?

2. On Monday morning Tom saw an advertisement for a 1938 Ford in an antique car collectors' magazine. He rang Thrith, the advertiser, and offered him £5000 for the car. Thrith said he'd think it over and let him know in a few days. Tom said that he'd keep the offer open until Thursday morning. Thrith should ring him by them to say if he would accept £5000. Later that day (Monday) Tom was made redundant. He could no longer afford to buy the car so he sent a letter to Thrith telling him that the deal was off. In the meantime, Thrith had decided that £5000 was a very good price for the car, so on Monday evening he posted a letter to Tom saying that he accepted his offer. Thrith was most annoyed to receive Tom's letter on Tuesday morning as £5000 had been by far the best offer he'd had for the car. He rang Tom and, even though Tom explained the circumstances behind his decision to withdraw his offer, Thrith insisted that he was holding him to his offer. Is Tom bound to take the car and pay the £5000?

3. Hyam has just taken over the toll concession on the newly constructed footpath running alongside the vehicle lanes on the London Bridge. In order to publicise the footpath he inserts an ad in the Times. The ad says that anyone who can walk across the Bridge standing on his hands will not only get over free but he/she will win a £100 prize. People interested in trying should meet at the Manhattan end of the footpath on Sunday at 2pm. Milly sees the ad and thinks what an easy way to earn some money. Along with a number of other people eager to win the prize, she travels to the bridge and at 2pm starts across, walking on her hands. Hyam, standing at the other end of the bridge watches as all the aspirants except Milly tumble over when the high wind sweeping across the bridge in mid-stream hits them. Milly, however, keeps coming. When she is about 10 feet from the end of the bridge, Hyam, who doesn't have £100, shouts out, 'Time's

up! The contest is over! ' Milly, who by this time has reached the end of the bridge, is outraged. The ad didn't say anything about a time limit. Hyam tells her not to be silly; the whole thing was just a publicity stunt anyway. He never intended anyone to really try and win the money. Milly consults her lawyer the following morning. Can she force Hyam to pay up?

What would you advise Milly?

4. Jack saw Jill crying. When he asked what was wrong she told him she'd lost her cat. Later that day Jack found the cat climbing up a beanstalk. He grabbed it and took it back to Jill. The cat didn't want to go and on the way it virtually shredded Jack's shirt with its claws. Jill was overjoyed to get her cat back. She told Jack that she'd bring him something from the market the next day to show her appreciation. When she saw Jack the following morning Jill said she'd been having second thoughts and didn't believe that Jack deserved more than this bean which someone had given her while she was going around the market. It was meant to be a magic bean, according to the man who gave it to her. Jack was furious not to have been given something more substantial and he rushed off to the court to sue Jill for the price of a new shirt. Do you think he will be successful?

Would it make any difference to your answer if Jill had said to Jack, 'It would mean a lot to me if you would help me find my cat?

5. Pierre is a freelance chef. He contracts to cater a meal for Paula's son's Bar Mitzvah. They agree he'll be paid 'the going rate' for preparing a meal for 20 people. Paula gives Pierre a deposit of £500. Paula has never eaten Pierre's cooking before but he comes with a fantastic recommendation from her friend Beulah who had him cater for her husband's 40th birthday party last month. Paula is so overwhelmed at having this great chef working for her that when he asks her about the menu she tells him that she wants something memorable for the occasion but she'll leave it up to him to choose what. On the day Paula is very upset when it turns out that what Pierre has chosen to prepare is melon filled with shredded Parma ham followed by roast suckling pig. Most of the guests at the Bar Mitzvah are Orthodox Jews, and their dietary laws make it impossible for them to eat any of the starter or the main course. Even worse, when the meal has finished and the guests have gone Pierre presents Paula with a bill for £2,000 for his services. Paula refuses to pay what she sees as an exorbitant charge. She offers Pierre £1,000. She knows that is what Beulah paid him for doing her husband's 40th. Beulah told her she consulted a number of leading chefs about the charge for such a do and all of them quoted her a price of about £1,000 to feed 20 people. Pierre is so insulted by Paula's offer that he sweeps out of the house without a word. A week later Paula finds that Pierre is suing her for his fee. Paula counters with a claim for the return of her £500.

Do you think Pierre's suit will succeed? What defence(s) could Paula raise? Do you think Paula will get her £500 back?

6. Ahmed is 17. He is going to start a course at Reademup University next month. He is going to live at home while doing the course so he will need some transport for going back and forth to the campus which is eight miles away. He goes into the showroom of the Chopper Cycle Co. and looks for a motorbike. Ahmed's fancy is taken by a used 1000cc Honda (It looks much better than the new125cc runabout standing next to it). After some negotiations about the price he agrees to buy the bike for £2000 to be paid in 36 monthly instalments. Two months after his course has started Ahmed has spent nearly all of his grant. A friend who is a Law student tells him about the provisions of the **Minors' Contracts Act** and he decides to stop making payments on the bike. In fact he decides he will sell the bike, use some of the money to buy a bicycle and put the rest into the bank account he opened with his grant cheque.

   What redress, if any, does the Chopper Cycle Co. have?

7. The prospective purchaser of a long-disused gold-mine had her agents draw up a report concerning the earning prospects of the mine and associated works. The vendor of the property, a musician who had inherited the mine but had not been near it for a period of years, made some inaccurate statements about the property to the agents, who did not check them out.These were incorporated in the agents' report, which recommended that the purchase be made. When the buyer found out, after she had bought the mine, what its real prospects were, she sued for her money back. The former owner said it was merely a case of caveat emptor (let the buyer beware). The buyer had no one but herself to blame for making a bad deal.

   What do you think the court would say?

8 Betty told Bill she was worried about her Business Law exam in two days' time. Bill offered to sell Betty his old Business Law notes for £25. Betty had bought notes from Bill several times in the past and had found them very helpful. He'd always given them to her typed up and put into a plastic binder which had made them easy to use. Betty was a bit strapped for cash so she told Bill she could only pay £20 for the notes. Bill agreed. In the event Bill only got the notes to Betty an hour before the exam, and they were still in the handwritten jumble they'd been taken down in originally. Betty refused to pay for the notes.

   Who was the offeror in this contract? What were the express terms of this contract?

   Were there any implied terms in the contract? If so, what were they? And of what significance were they?

9 Joe was considering buying Moe's Landrover. He wanted it to use on a two-month African safari tour he was planning to operate. It was essential that the vehicle be reliable and when the two finally concluded the deal Moe specified that it was 'in good shape'. Joe said it had better be, otherwise he'd not have bought it. A week after buying the car Joe loaded up his passengers and set off from Birmingham for the wilds of Africa. Just outside Worcester the Landrover

broke down. A mechanic told them it would take only six hours to repair, but he could not guarantee that it wouldn't happen again. The breakdown meant that Joe and co. would miss the ferry taking them from Portsmouth to Caen from where they would drive to Spain and eventually into Morocco and points south. Joe was enraged and called Moe and told him he wanted his money back because the Landrover was useless. Moe refused to give Joe his money back.

Do you think a court would have upheld Joe's claim? Explain the reasoning behind your answer. (You should direct your attention to establishing what type the terms of the contract were, and what the consequences are of breaking those types of terms.

10 The plaintiffs ordered cabbage seed from the defendants. They were long-standing customers of the company and they knew that there were some conditions of sale regarding purchases from the company – ie. there was a page of fine print at the back of the defendants' catalogue which contained *inter alia* the company's standard trading terms. The seeds which were delivered were not those which had been ordered and they failed to produce a crop. The plaintiffs lost the cost of the seed (£201.60) and the value of the crop they'd expected to grow (about £61,000). The plaintiffs sued to recover their loss. The defendants relied on the conditions of sale listed on the back of the invoice which accompanied the seeds when delivered. Among these it was provided by one clause that:

● the liability of the vendors regarding failure of the seeds to meet the express terms of the contract, or regarding the purity of the seed supplied, was limited to the replacement of the seed or to the refund of the cost of the seed

● liability for any loss or damage arising from the use of seeds supplied was totally excluded except for the replacement of the seeds or the refund of their cost

● any implied condition or warranty, whether arising out of statutory provision or otherwise was excluded from the contract

● the price of the seeds was formulated to incorporate limitations on the company's liability – ie. the price of the seeds was lower because the company didn't have to provide for large damage claims in its cost forecasts.

What decision do you think the court made?

11. Bozo ordered feed for his elephant Dumbo. Coco was to supply four tonnes of hay at a price of £20 per tonne each week during the period of 12 weeks that the circus would be in its winter quarters. Bozo would pay for each delivery of hay when it was brought. For the first four weeks Coco arrived each Friday with the four tonnes of hay. However, he then missed two weeks and after making two further deliveries, stopped all together.

How much, if any, of the hay does Bozo have to pay for?

12. Refer to the situation involving Bill and Iqbal described in Section Four. Assume that Iqbal was heavily involved in amateur dramatics at the university and had even decided to give up his engineering course in favour of one in theatre studies. Would that make any difference to the likelihood of Iqbal's claim against Bill succeeding? Would it matter if Bill knew about this?

13. Ringo contracted to play the bongos for a new pop group called The Bugs. He'd never played in a band before but his brother was the group's lead guitarist and he convinced the others that Ringo would be a suitable replacement for the group's former drummer who was out of action for a year while doing time in prison on a drugs charge. Ringo's contract called for him to be paid £30,000 to make six albums with the group over the next year, and to get £5,000 each time for appearing at 20 live concerts with The Bugs during the same period. In order to make sure that Ringo turned up for the concerts, his contract provided that he was to pay the group £5000 for any concert which he missed. All went well for the first 6 months. In fact five of the albums were finished, and the 13 concerts held so far had been sell-outs. But then another group, the Flying Rocks,who had heard Ringo play with The Bugs, asked him to come on tour with them to America. Ringo had always wanted to tour the USA so he agreed to go. As word spread that Ringo was leaving The Bugs, ticket sales for the remaining seven concerts plummeted. The other members of The Bugs were extremely fed up by Ringo's plans to defect so they consulted their legal advisers. They told the musicians that there were a number of actions they could take against Ringo. Ringo also had a word with his legal adviser. He wanted to know if there was any way he might be able to get out of his obligations to The Bugs.

What advice do you think The Bugs' and Ringo's lawyers might have given them?

14. Elmer is a well-known wholesale produce dealer. He contracted to purchase Porky's entire crop of carrots at 2 per cent above the prevailing market price provided the carrots were delivered no later than October 15th. What Porky did not know was that Elmer had sold the carrots on to Bugs who had agreed to pay an especially high price in order to secure the whole crop. Throughout the summer there had been a drought and the newspapers and television had been full of reports of crop failures. (In fact, Elmer had reckoned himself lucky to be able to purchase a crop of carrots at all; the season had been so bad.) Bugs had been very worried about his winter food supply so he had jumped at the opportunity to buy the carrots even if the price he had to pay was high. Just to make sure he wouldn't be left with an empty larder when it was too late to fill it from anywhere else, Bugs secured Elmer's promise that if he failed to deliver the carrots by October 16th, the price would drop by 25 per cent. Because of the press of other work on his farm, Porky only started harvesting the carrots on October 12th. Normally he would have been finished in two days but his harvester broke down on the morning of the 13th. He rang Daffy, who was the only person in the whole area who knew how to service Porky's make of harvester, and asked him to come out and repair it. Daffy said he would be out

that afternoon but, in fact, he went fishing and did not turn up until two days later. Although the repairs only took two hours, this meant that Porky did not finish harvesting his crop of carrots until October 16th. Because Porky was late in delivering the carrots, Elmer was unable to meet the deadline for delivering them to Bugs.

Can Porky and Elmer recover the losses they have incurred?

Additional questions: guidance

The additional questions have been designed to make you think about the application of the law. In many cases no clear-cut, definitive answer can be given to the question raised by the facts. The point is to make you ponder how the law would be applied in circumstances which do not exactly fit the cases you have studied earlier.

1. This exercise is aimed at making you think about the formation of the contract, especially what constitutes an **offer** in the context of self-service shopping.

   The general rule established by **Boots v the Pharceutical Society of Great Britain** is that a contract to buy goods in a self-service establishment is made at the point where payment is made. The display of goods on shelves amounts only to an **invitation to treat** – ie. an invitation to the customer to make an offer. The customer makes the offer by proffering his or her money at the till and the shopkeeper **accepts** it by taking the sum of money tendered. The essential question here is whether by presenting the steak to the butcher and asking him to cube it Patty shifted the point at which the contract would be concluded from the cash desk to the butcher's counter. In other words, did Patty's request to have the steak cubed amount to an offer to buy the steak at the price shown and the butcher's agreement to do so amount to acceptance of the offer?

   There is no clear authority in case law that the situation should be construed in this way but it seems likely that the presentation of goods taken from the shelf with a request that they somehow be irretrievably modified is as definite an offer to buy them as presenting unmodified goods at the cash desk. After all, could Patty put the goods back on the shelf in the condition in which she found them? The essence of an offer is the apparent willingness of one party to be bound to a set of terms, which the other party is then asked to agree to.

2. The purpose of this question is to make you think about the sequencing of **offer** and **acceptance**; and to reflect on when the **postal rule**, which was developed in the 19th century, should apply today.

   Tom is only bound to take the car and pay the £5000 if a contract has been formed with Thrith. Has one been? There is an offer from Tom. The real issue is whether that offer was still open to be accepted at the point where Thrith purported to accept it (with his letter posted on Monday evening). Did Tom's letter (posted earlier in the day on Monday) revoke the offer? It might seem logical to assume that if the postal rule applies to acceptances, then it should apply as well to revocation of an offer. But it does not (**cf. Byrne v Van Tienhoven (1880) 5 C.P.D. 344.**)

The courts have clearly decided to favour the convenience of the person who receives the offer over that of the one who makes it. You should think about why this is so. Probably because, since he initiates the formation of the contract, it lies within the power of the offeror to specify any restriction he wishes to on how the offeree's response is to be notified to him. And if the offeror has failed to take advantage of this opportunity, then he should be made to bear any inconvenience which results if the post goes astray.

Thus, so far as the revocation of Tom's offer is concerned, it was only effective when he informed Thrith on Tuesday morning that he was no longer in a position to buy the car. The question arising now is whether that revocation came too late – ie. had the offer already been accepted? If the postal rule applies in this situation, then once Thrith's letter of acceptance was posted on Monday evening, a contract was formed.

Would the postal rule apply here? The contemporary attitude toward the postal rule is that it should apply where common sense says that it should. Tom has told Thrith to let him know by phone by Thursday if he is willing to sell for £5000. Does this mean that Thrith's acceptance can only be communicated by telephone? Common sense would say that a reply posted on Monday evening should reach Tom well before the Thursday deadline; and that therefore, his letter of acceptance should be subject to the postal rule. If Tom had wanted a response more quickly than a postal reply could have been expected to furnish he surely would not have given Thrith until Thursday to inform him of his decision. Or he should have specified that the agreement would become binding only if he had actually received a response from Thrith by Thursday morning (**cf. Holwell Securities Ltd. v Hughes.**)

After working through this problem you should be more aware of the role that judicial policy plays in developing the law. In the case of the postal rule the courts had to choose between disadvantaging the offeror or the offeree. It was felt that **business efficacy** demanded that the benefit of the doubt be given to the party who was responding to an offer since the author of the offer had already had an opportunity to structure the mode of response as he or she wished.

3. The purpose of this problem is to make you think about circumstances in which the usual rules regarding the **communication of acceptance** can be waived.One situation where this can happen involves an **offer** with a **performable condition**. The offeror becomes bound to fulfill their obligations under the offer not because the other party has ever informed them they he or she agreed to the terms of the offer, but because the other party's **conduct** makes it clear they have agreed to the offeror's terms.

There are two issues to address in this set of facts. First, what is the status of the advertisement placed by Hyam in *The Times*? Second, if that ad does amount to an offer, was Hyam successful in revoking it just before Milly reached the end of the foopath? The answers to these two questions will determine if an enforceable contract between Milly and Hyam has come into existence.

The question of communication of acceptance only arises if it can be shown that an offer has actually been made. Normally an advertisement in a newspaper is considered to amount to no more than an **invitation to treat.** But we saw in **Mrs. Carlill's case** that if the ad contains a performable condition, it may be regarded as an offer to the world rather than an invitation to treat. However, one of the things which influenced the judges in the **Mrs. Carlill's case** was the fact that the company had actually deposited £100 to cover any claims by customers. The court felt that this indicated an intention on the part of the company to be bound by its promise. Here we are told that Hyam does not have the £100 promised in the ad. That might indicate he truly regarded the ad as no more than 'trade-puffery'.

If the ad is considered to be an offer rather than an invitation to treat, the question next arises whether it was revoked before it was accepted. Where an offer is made to the world, **complete performance** of the included condition amounts to acceptance. But Hyam sought to bring the offer to an end before Milly had made it all the way across the footpath. So could she claim to have accepted his offer? According to the court in **Errington v Errington and Woods** she would be able to because an offer with a performable condition cannot be **revoked** or withdrawn while performance is underway. This is a limitation on the general rule that (barring an **option** to keep the offer open having been purchased by the offeree) the offeror can withdraw his offer at any time prior to acceptance.

What about Hyam's assertion that time was up before Milly completed her 'walk'? He could have put a time limit on the crossing but if it was not indicated in the advertisement that there was a time limit, one could not be inserted as a **term** of the offer later on without the consent of the other party. The terms of a contract are what are agreed between the parties at the time the contract is made and they cannot be changed unilaterally later on.

It seems likely that Milly would be able to force Hyam to live up to his promise to pay the £100.

4. The purpose of this question is to make you think about **consideration**.

Jack can only enforce Jill's promise to reward him for finding her cat if it can be shown that she has a contractual obligation to do so. One of the essential elements in the formation of a contract is the provision of **consideration** by each party to the other. The question is, was Jack's returning the cat to secure the formation of a contract? In **Re: McArdle** we saw that an act which has been undertaken, without any **contemporaneous agreement** to reciprocate by the person who benefits, cannot be used to force the beneficiary to honour a later promise to reward their benefactor. Therefore if Jack found and returned Jill's cat without any encouragement from her to do so, she can disregard with impunity any later promise to reward Jack for his act.

If his restoration of the cat to its owner was done in the **reasonable expectation** that he'd be rewarded if he managed to find the missing pussycat, then even though the amount of the reward remained to be established, he should be entitled to something. The question is, did Jill say anything to Jack when she first told him about the missing cat which would have made him think that a reward would be forthcoming to the person who restored the cat to her? A statement that it would mean a lot to her if the cat were found and returned might reasonably be construed as the offer of a reward. As such it would amount to the creation of a **unilateral contract** – one where acceptance is signified by conduct rather than communication. Jack's acceptance would be confirmed when he returned the cat. In these circumstances Jack could enforce Jill's promise to reward him with something.

But could he make her give him a new shirt or the equivalent value thereof? So far as the common law is concerned Jill might succeed in arguing that the consideration she had provided Jack (the bean) in return for his consideration (returning the cat) was **sufficient**. In other words it represented something of value, however small (**cf. Chappell & Co. Ltd. v Nestle Co. Ltd.**)

5. The purpose of this problem is to illustrate what can go wrong if the parties to a contract create **uncertainty** about their respective rights and obligations by using vague or ambiguous language in spelling out the **terms** of the contract.

The problem with this contract is its lack of **certainty**. The essence of the contract is that Paula will pay the 'going rate' and Pierre will provide a 'memorable' meal.   The price to be paid by Paula is not specified. Nor is it clear what will discharge Pierre's obligation to create a 'memorable' meal. There is no course of previous dealings between Pierre and Paula. What amount the court will be willing to imply as the fee for Pierre's services will depend on which party produces the most convincing evidence as to what the going rate in the trade is for catering a meal for 20 people. On the facts given, Paula seems to have a strong case for the fee being set at £1000.

If the court accepts this, then the only question will be whether or not Pierre has sufficiently fulfilled his obligations under the contract to warrant payment of the £1,000. In other words, is Paula entitled to withold all or part of the £1000 as damages for breach of contract? Certainly Pierre created a memorable meal, but was it memorable in the sense that Paula intended? The court would probably focus on the fact that Pierre must have known he was catering a Jewish function and that many Jews (like Muslims) do not eat pork. The court might well find that in the context of a Bar Mitzvah a meal based on pork would not meet the requirements of the term that the meal be memorable; and therefore, full payment was not warranted. The court might go so far as to say that serving up a pork-based meal at a Jewish function amounted to a complete failure to furnish consideration on the part of Pierre. If that were the case then Paula would be entitled, not only to withhold any further payments to Pierre, but to get her deposit back as well. If there is a total failure by one of the parties to provide consideration then the courts will treat the contract as being *void ab initio* – as if no contract ever existed.

6. The purpose of this question is to focus the your attention on the problems that sales to young people confront businesses with.

This was a **credit sale** to a **minor** so Ahmed's obligations to pay the installments cannot be enforced provided the motorcycle is considered to be a **non-necessary**. Ahmed obviously needs transport to college; but does he need such a big bike? The fact that he later proposed to travel to and from college by bicycle might influence the court to consider the motorcycle to be a 'non-necessary'. But the court could still use the discretionary power given by Section 3 of the Minors' Contracts Act to order Ahmed to turn over the bicycle to the Chopper Cycle Co.

What about the money Ahmed would receive if he sold the bike before the company had taken any action? The court will only order that to be given to the company if it is **traceable** – ie. if it can be clearly identified compared to any other money Ahmed has. If he had opened a new account with the money from selling the Honda, then the court might order the balance in that account to be turned over to the company. But since he put it in the account he already had the court would undoubtedly view it as having been irretrievably 'mixed' with whatever other funds were in the account.

7. The purpose of this problem is to focus the your attention on the question of what **statements** are of contractual significance; and on the different types of **misrepresentation**.

The basis of the buyer's claim would be that there had been a misrepresentation made by the seller and that that entitled the buyer to rescind the contract and get her money back. Has there been a misrepresentation? And if so, on what basis does that entitle the buyer to recover her money?

A **misrepresentation** is a false statement of fact by one party which induces another party to enter into a contract. Has that occurred here? On the facts it is hard to say. What the vendor told the buyer's agents about the mine may have been based on wholly uninformed opinions. After all he had never worked the mine and had not been near the site for years. As a musician he was unlikely to have any real knowledge of mining. If the vendor was doing no more than giving his opinion about the worth of the mine, then, inaccurate and misleading as they may have been, those statements would probably be held to be of no legal significance. **(cf. Bisset v Wilkinson [1927]).**

If, however, the vendor did know about the true state of the mine, but concealed that in his statements to the vendor's ,agents, that probably amounted to a **fraudulent misrepresentation. (cf. Derry v Peek [1889].)** Even if the statements he made were true but he kept back information which would have put those statements into a different and less favourable light, those statements would amount to mis-representations. It is not up to sellers to tell buyers everything they know. Normally the courts will apply the maxim *caveat emptor* – let the buyer beware – where one party to a contract has made a bad bargain because he or she did not go far enough in pursuit of information about the goods or property they are about to buy. But if the seller makes a statement which on its face would have one meaning but there are facts which give that statement a wholly different meaning, then remaining silent about those additional facts may amount to a misrepresentation (**cf. Dimmock v Hallett [1866].**)

Of course, all of this assumes that the buyer was actually induced to make her purchase by the vendor's statements. If she merely relied on her agents' report and sought no other information from the vendor, then there was no inducement by the vendor, and hence his statements did not amount to misrepresentations, even if they did not give a true version of the facts (**cf. Attwood v Small [1838] Cl & F 232, HL**). You may be thinking that surely the vendor's statements did induce the purchase of the mine because they led the agents to make a favourable report. True – but the buyer was relying on the agents' conclusions not just on what the seller told them. What she could do, of course, is to sue her agents for negligence in the way they prepared their report. They obviously did not go far enough in checking out the vendor's claims.

8. The point of this question is to see if you can identify the **terms** of a contract; and ascertain their relative importance if they are **breached**.

Betty made a **counter-offer** (£20 not £25), so she became the offeror in the contract.

The **express terms** would have been:(i) Betty was to pay Bill £20; and (ii) Bill was to supply her his old Business Law notes

The whole point of this contract was for Betty to be able to use Bill's old notes to revise for her exam. It might be said (by an **officious bystander**) that there was an **implied term** in the contract that delivery of the notes would take place long enough before the exam to give Betty a chance to make good use of them. Without such a term the contract doesn't make sense. (Or to put it in legal terminology: the implication of this term is necessary in order to give the contract **business efficacy** and to implement the **parties' intentions**.) Delivering only an hour before the exam surely would amount to a breach of that implied term.

Would this breach entitle Betty to refuse to pay? If the notes were not going to be of use to her there was no reason to enter the contract; and if they were not given to her in time they'd be of no use; so probably the implied term as to delivery would have been a **condition**, the breach of which entitled Betty to consider the contract **terminated**.

Betty had bought notes from Bill several times in the past and they'd always been typed and neatly packaged. This fact might support a claim that it was an implied term of the contract that the notes would be typed and packaged on this occasion too.   How serious was Bill's failure to do so? If the notes were unuseable by Betty in their original state, then suitable presentation might be seen to have been a **condition** of the contract. If leaving them in their original state only made them less easy to use, the term might be regarded as a **warranty**, the breach of which entitled Betty to reduce the amount paid (ie. impose a form of damages recovery on Bill) but not to refuse to pay altogether.

9. Again, the point of the question is to focus your attention on the need to determine what the **terms of a contract** are, and what **remedies** can be sought if any particular term is breached.

The term regarding the state of the vehicle is cast in language which makes it impossible to determine in advance whether its breach will rob Joe of substantially all his benefit from entering into the contract; or merely cause him to incur ancillary costs. The breakdown which occurs only delays Joe and his party for six hours. Insignificant in the context of a two-month journey. So surely this breakdown will amount to no more than a breach of a **warranty** as to the vehicle's reliability. On the other hand the mechanic has pointed out that the fault may recur, possibly in less favourable circumstances. Given Joe's emphasis on the need for reliability, and Moe's assurances that the vehicle is reliable, does this mean that the breakdown and the revelation that the vehicle may be unreliable, amounts to a breach of one of the **conditions** of the contract? There is no clear cut answer. Possibly the court would regard it as a breach of condition, entitling Joe to **terminate** the contract and claim back the money he'd paid for the Landrover plus **damages** to cover any losses he suffered as a result of the failure of his commercial venture due to the vehicle breakdown. (Remember, the breach of a condition entitles the wronged party to recover the position they were in *re* money or goods prior to entering into the contract.) Otherwise he would be limited to a claim for damages for breach of warranty and could recover only the actual losses suffered as a consequence – probably no more than the extra cost of accomodation in Portsmouth and re-booking the ferry to Caen. Two other points to ponder are:

(i) was the statement about reliability a contractual term?

(ii) did it make any difference that Joe proposed to use the vehicle in a business?

10. This problem illustrates the complexity of contractual terms, especially **exclusion** or **limitation clauses**, in real life.

At first instance the farmer's claim was accepted. The seed company appealed to the Court of Appeal and then to the House of Lords. Three issues were dealt with by the Law Lords:

● was the clause part of the contract?

● did the wording of the clause cover the event which occurred?

● was the clause reasonable?

On the first issue the House of Lords held that the exclusion clause was part of the contract. It was printed on the back of the company's catalogue. Such clauses were commonly found in the seed trade. There was a sufficient course of dealings to bring the clause, even if unread, into the contract.

The Court of Appeal had split over the second issue. In a minority opinion Lord Denning had held that the words were unambiguous in meaning and scope of application and that, therefore, the clause should be enforced. His view was approved by the House of Lords, where the 'strained construction' of a clause's words to find that they did not cover what had happened was rejected. The Law Lords were reacting against earlier cases where the failure to specifically mention that the exemption or limitation clause covered instances of negligence had rendered the clause ineffective if the damage or loss did result from negligence. Lord Bridge, who gave the leading opinion in the House of Lords, pointed out that the more recent approach as set out in cases such as **Photo Production Ltd. v Securicor Transport Ltd. [1980] AC 827, HL** was that the strict principles of construction of exclusion clauses must be applied with less than their full rigour to limitation clauses.

On the third issue the House of Lords held that the limitation on liability imposed by the clause was unreasonable. The Law Lords focused on the inequality of bargaining power between the parties. Virtually all seedsmen included such limitations in their terms of trade. How was the farmer to find a source of seeds which would avoid them? Of decisive importance, however, was evidence that the company (and other seedsmen) had actually compensated farmers beyond the limit of liability spelled out in its (their) terms of trade in the past. The court felt this was recognition by the company itself that the limitation clause was neither fair nor reasonable. Finally, the court took into account (a) that the damage was due to the company's negligence and (b) that the company could have insured itself against the risk of crop failure as a result of supplying the wrong seed – and it could have done so without materially increasing the price of the seed – whereas the farmer could have obtained crop failure insurance only with great difficulty and at an exorbitant premium.

11. The purpose of this question is to make you think about the consequences for a party if they stop short of fulfilling all of the obligations imposed on them by the contract.

Is this what is called a **contract entire** – ie. one which is not severable? On the face of it – no. Each of the loads of hay is to be paid for at the time of delivery, so each delivery can be treated as a separate contract. If this is the case, then Bozo could not reclaim the money he has paid over to Coco for deliveries acutally made.

What would have been the case if (a) Bozo was to have paid for the supply of winter feed after all deliveries had been made; or (b) if Bozo had paid in advance for the winter's supply of hay? The law would have left Bozo considerably better off in the former case (a) as compared to the latter (b). If he had paid in advance Bozo could have sued for damages of £480 for breach of contract (six weeks missing hay @ £80 per week). Bozo would get the money back for the consignments not delivered, but he would have had to pay for the hay which was supplied. If the first situation had applied then the contract would undoubtedly have been considered to be entire and Coco would not be entitled to any payment because in supplying only half of the hay required he would not have achieved substantial performance of the contract. In effect Bozo would have received (and Dumbo would have eaten) £480 worth of hay free and he would not be obliged to accept and /or pay for any further supplies of hay from Coco.

12. This problem concerns the issue of **remoteness of damage**. You need to get in mind a **template** against which you can place any factual situation to see if the losses arising out of a breach of contract will have to be compensated by the party who is in breach.

Would Iqbal's decision to abandon engineering in favour of a career on the stage affect his ability to secure compensation for his injuries from Bill? It might. The essential questions to ask where the issue is one of remoteness are these:

- is the damage a direct result of the breach?
- is the damage of the type which one would expect to find in the usual course of events if a breach occurred?
- are there special circumstances which if they had been known to the defendant would have brought the type of damage which occurred within the range of what he might have fairly and reasonably foreseen as being not unlikely to occur following a breach?
- did the defendant know of the special circumstances or can knowledge of them fairly and reasonably be imputed to him?

Loss of a lucrative role could hardly be said to be damage of a type one would expect to find in the usual course of events. Or could it? It might be said that, given society's emphasis on appearance, facial scarring might impede one's progress in any career. If that view were taken the court would be unlikely to hold that Iqbal's loss was too remote to be recovered.

Certainly his interest in drama is a special circumstance which, had it been known to Bill – and had Bill and Iqbal contemplated the possible consequences of a breach – might have brought the type of loss which occurred into their minds as something not unlikely to result **(cf. The Heron.)** Would Iqbal be in time in bringing his claim?

13. This is a problem concerning **part performance** and the **remedies** available to the other party if one of the contracting parties does only partly fulfill obligations under the contract.

The Bugs

The Bugs would like to do one of two things: either force Ringo to carry on playing with them; or, if that is not possible, to get as much compensation as possible from him. They could seek an order of **specific performance**; but since this is a contract for personal services they are not likely to get it. The courts will not force people to work for those for whom they do not wish to. However, The Bugs may be able to obtain an **injunction** to prevent Ringo appearing with any other group until he has fulfilled his obligations with The Bugs (**cf. Lumley v Wagner.**) But since Ringo is going on tour with the new group (The Flying Rocks) in America he may not care whether an injunction is granted. The British courts cannot punish a contempt of court if the miscreant is outside their jurisdiction.

The Bugs may be able to claim damages from Ringo for breach of contract. It appears that the contract makes provision for **liquidated damages** of £5000 each time Ringo defaults on his obligation to appear with the band. Could Ringo succeed in an argument that this is in fact a **penalty clause?** Does the clause represent a *real* attempt to pre-estimate the cost of a default by Ringo? Much will depend on [a] how possible it is to pick up a sessional drummer at short notice; [b] what it would cost to hire a last-minute replacement for Ringo; and [c] whether Ringo makes an intrinsic contribution to The Bugs' popularity that has to do with more than his skill as a drummer. If £5000 is an extravagant over-estimate of the loss the band would suffer if Ringo failed to show up, the court would not enforce the clause as liquidated damages.

Could The Bugs claim **unliquidated damages** from Ringo? The **usual damages**, it would appear, would be the difference between what Ringo would be paid for an appearance and what a substitute drummer would cost. Given the large numbers of unemployed musicians about, it is hard to see that the group would suffer much usual damage. What about **special damages?** The group is losing money from dwindling ticket sales in the wake of Ringo's departure. But would it have been in the contemplation of the parties at the time Ringo joined the group that so much of their popularity would be focused on him? It seems unlikely given that Ringo was completely unknown both to them and to the public. If the special circumstance – Ringo's crowd pulling appeal – was not in the horizon of contemplation of the parties when they contracted, no compensation can be obtained for the losses the departure of the new star caused.

Ringo

Ringo wants to avoid being ordered by the court not to play with any group other than The Bugs. He also wants to avoid having to pay out damages for leaving the Bugs prior to the expiry of his contract with them. As noted above Ringo may be able to convince the court that the provision for paying the group £5000 for each concert he misses amounts to a penalty, not liquidated damages. If it is treated as a penalty The Bugs have the problem of showing that they are entitled to treat any of the **special damage** attributable to Ringo's popularity as not too remote to recover.

One approach Ringo's counsel might take would be to claim that the contract has been discharged by substantial part performance. Five of six albums have been made; and 13 out of 20 concerts have been given. In the alternative, Ringo might argue that his obligations under the contract are divisible or severable, so that The Bugs have had full value for each part which has come due for performance; but that there would be no penalty if he failed to perform any remaining part of his recording or performing obligations.

14. This problem deals, once again, with the question of **remoteness of damage**; and how to test for it.

Elmer

The essential question here is whether the loss Elmer suffered as a result of Porky's breach was too remote to be compensated. Appraise this by applying the analysis used in **Hadley v Baxendale**. The defendant's breach must be the direct cause of the plaintiff's loss; and it must have been within the plaintiff's contemplation that such a loss would be a 'not unlikely' consequence of any breach. There must be some care exercised here to differentiate betwen the **usual damage** which would be suffered as a result of the breach of a contract and the **special damage** which may arise out of the circumstances at hand. What is usual damage? It is the *normal, natural* consequence of a breach of contract. The usual damage caused by a breach of contract involving delivery is the difference (if any) between the value of the goods to the buyer (measured in terms of their market price on the date they should have been delivered) and the price that he has agreed to pay for them. For example, if A contracts to buy 100 tonnes of coal at £20 per ton from B, and B fails to deliver the coal, so that A has to buy the coal in the market, the law will regard A as having suffered no *usual damage* if he can buy the coal elsewhere for £20 per ton. Every other kind of loss is regarded as being abnormal and not within the reasonable contemplation of the defendant (the seller). So if A had agreed to sell the coal on to C for £22 per ton, would B be liable to compensate A for the loss of profit on this contract? Not always. Such a loss is not regarded by the law as being the normal, natural consequence of failing to deliver the goods. And in order to secure *special damages* A, first of all, would have to show that he had suffered an actual loss of profit – perhaps because there was no alternative supply of coal readily available; or because of a delivery penalty in the contract with C. Then he would have to show that B either knew or should have known of the 'special circumstance' of there being a sub-contract between A and C; and therefore that B should have had within his contemplation the prospect of A suffering a loss of profit if he (B) failed to deliver the coal.

What loss has Elmer suffered as a result of Porky's failure to deliver the carrots on time? Has he incurred any *usual damage?* Only to the extent that he is unable to replace the carrots for no more than the same price he would have had to pay Porky. Can Elmer claim any *special damages* for the loss he will make on his contract with Bugs? There is nothing in the facts to indicate that Porky had actual knowledge of the deal between Elmer and Bugs. If he did then that would have brought a loss of profit on the deal within the horizon of his contemplation of the consequences of any breach of contract on his part. Can

Porky be said to have **constructive knowledge** of the special circumstances? Porky knew that Elmer was a produce dealer. It would not be unreasonable, therefore, to assume that Porky would have understood that Elmer was likely already to have arranged a customer for the carrots (**cf. The Heron II [1969] 1 AC 350, HL.**) This presumption would be re-inforced by the fact that on-time delivery was so important to Elmer that he was willing to pay 2 per cent over the market price to obtain the carrots by October 15th.

Porky
Can Porky recover from Daffy for the loss he has suffered as a result of delivering late to Elmer?

Again, apply the analytical framework laid down in **Hadley v Baxendale.** Is the breach the direct cause of the loss? If Daffy had come to repair the harvester when he said he would, then Porky would have finished lifting the crop in time to meet the delivery deadline. Does it matter that Porky left it so late to start harvesting the carrots? Certainly Daffy might argue that the true cause of the loss was the fact that Porky did not leave a sufficient margin of time to account for contingencies. But Porky did leave himself one day to spare and the court would be unlikely to say that he should have factored in additional time to provide against the repair of his equipment being handled negligently.

Is the loss suffered by Porky one which would have been in the contemplation of the parties at the time they made the contract had they actually stopped to consider the likely consequences of a breach by either party? Again look at this in terms of what *usual loss* Daffy might have had in contemplation; and whether there were special circumstances which should widened the range of consequences Daffy could forsee would result if he breached the contract. There are several linked questions here. Was it the customary practice for farmers to harvest crops under the threat of financial penalty if the harvest was delayed? If so then it would be reasonable to assume that Daffy must have realized that any failure to meet his contractual obligations would likely result in the type of loss suffered by Porky. If not, then so long as the crop itself was not damaged by the delay; and provided that the market price for carrots had not fallen during the period of the delay; it is hard to see any loss suffered by Porky which could be called a natural, normal consequence of Daffy's breach. In other words, Porky would not have suffered any *usual damage*. Was there anything in the communications between Porky and Daffy which it is reasonable to believe would have alerted Daffy to the fact that *in this case* there was, unusually, a deadline with financial penalties? If so then the loss suffered by Porky will not be too remote. If not, then it will be.

Reading list for Unit 3

Law is a fast changing subject and, in consequence, textbooks tend to become quickly out-of-date. When referring to a book always check that it is the latest edition and that it is of recent date.

The textbooks referred to in the introduction to the module provide a perfectly adequate coverage of the material covered in Unit 3. There are, however, a number of textbooks dealing exclusively with the law of contracts which you could look at if you are interested in pursuing any subject raised in the module in more depth.

Trietel, G.H., 1991, *The Law of Contract,* Sweet & Maxwell, 8th edition.

Collins, 1993, *The Law of Contract*, Butterworths, 2nd edition.

Cheshire, Fifoot and Furmston., 1993, *Law of Contract,* Butterworths, 12th edition.

A legal dictionary is sometimes useful There are several available at quite low prices. The following is as good as any.

Mozley and Whiteley, 1993, *Law Dictionary,* Butterworths, 11th edition.

FURTHER READING FOR SECTION ONE
Bond H. J. and Kay P., 1990, *Business Law*, Blackstone Press Ltd., 3rd edition, Chapter 7.

Keenan D. and Riches. S., 1994, *Business Law,* Pitman Publishing, Chapter 8.

Savage N. and Bradgate.R., 1993, *Business Law,* Butterworths, 2nd edition, Chapters 12 and 13.

FURTHER READING FOR SECTION TWO
Bond H. J. and Kay. P., 1990, *Business Law,* Blackstone Press, Ltd. Chapters 10, 11 and 13.

Keenan D. and Riches. S., 1994, *Business Law,* Pitman Publishing, 3rd edition, Chapter 8.

Savage N. and Bradgate. R.,1993, *Business Law,* Butterworths, 2nd edition, Chapters 14, 15 and 16.

FURTHER READING FOR SECTION THREE
Bond H. J. and Kay. P., 1990, *Business Law,* Blackstone Press, Ltd, Chapters 8 and 9.

Keenan D and Riches. S., 1994, *Business Law,* Pitman Publishing, 3rd edition, Chapter. 10.

Savage N. and Bradgate. R., 1993, *Business Law,* Butterworths, 2nd edition, Chapters 14 and 18.

FURTHER READING FOR SECTION FOUR

Bond H. J., and Kay. P, 1990, *Business Law* Blackstone Press., Ltd Chapters 12and 14.

Keenan D. and Riches. S., 1994, *Business Law,* Pitman Publishing, 3rd edition, Chapter 8.

Savage N. and Bradgate. R., 1993, *Business Law,* Butterworths, 2nd edition, Chapter 17.

A final suggestion on reading is to emphasise the importance of reading a quality newspaper each day. Matters concerning contract law are frequently reported. And some newspapers run a regular weekly law feature – eg. *The Times* on Tuesdays. Reading such sections and looking at the case reports which appear from time to time is one of the best ways to make sure that knowledge of the law is kept up to date.

UNIT 4

NON-CONTRACTUAL OBLIGATIONS OF THE SELLER/PRODUCER

Introduction to Unit 4

By the time you have completed this unit you will be able to:

● distinguish between contractual and non-contractual remedies

● identify the correct remedy to use when faced with a consumer problem

● explain the principles of negligence

● explain the purpose of the Health and Safety at Work Act and explain the legal duties of the employer and employee

● identify situations in which an employer is made legally responsible for the actions of an employee

● explain the rules governing the tort of nuisance

● list other environmental protection laws

● apply legal principles to business based problems and suggest possible outcomes.

The purpose of this section is to consider in detail some of the legal obligations which are imposed on those who sell or produce goods and services. The aim is to build upon your knowledge of the contractual rules which are imposed on such persons and to demonstrate how these are reinforced by other provisions. It is also important that you can identify the correct set of rules to apply from a given set of facts.

We can separate these obligations into a number of different categories. These include:

● liability to consumers imposed by Act of Parliament

● liability to consumers imposed by the common law

● rules governing those acting 'negligently'

● employers' liability for the actions of employees

● health and safety at work.

Clearly those selling or producing owe obligations to the consumers of their products. One obvious way in which this is enforced is through liability for breach of contract. This may be through either common law principles or those laid down in either the Sale of Goods Act or the Supply of Goods and Services Act. Suing in contract has the great advantage of strict liability. The problem though is the rule of privity. This means that only a person who is a party to a contract may sue where he/she suffers damage though a fault of the other party. Both common law and statute have sought to provide assistance and we will look at two potential remedies for consumers as opposed to purchasers. The Consumer Protection Act lays down statutory rules. The tort of negligence provides common law protection. Negligence as an action covers a wide area and the opportunity will be taken in this unit to give it full consideration.

Sellers and producers owe obligations to their workers. Again there are contractual rules which apply through the contract of employment between employer and employee. As we saw in Unit 2 however the obligations placed on the employer are quite limited. A wide range of statutory remedies are provided to redress the imbalance between the positions of employer and employee. Employment protection laws provide compensation for unfair dismissal, redundancy, sex and race discrimination and absence through sickness or pregnancy. These rules are outside the scope of this unit. What we are interested in here are rules covering the way in which manufacturing works, specifically the issue of health and safety.

The final issue to look at is the relationship between the firm and its wider environment. 'Green' issues are becoming more and more important and firms are subject to increasing rules governing such matters as waste disposal. The tort of negligence provides some remedies for those who feel that their use of property has been damaged by the actions of another land user and we will look at this provision.

In looking at these issues one question which may be asked is about liability. If a worker is in breach of some of these provisions to what extent should he/she or the employer be liable? This takes us into the area of vicarious liability, a topic introduced in Unit 2.

SECTION ONE

The Duty of Care in Negligence

In Section One you will find material to help you learn about and understand the following things:

- the essential features of the law of negligence
- the fault based nature of negligence
- the concept of the duty of care
- the application of the duty of care in specific situations
- the application of negligence to the work of professionals such as accountants and doctors
- the limits of the duty of care.

Negligence: an introduction

To begin with, a case. **Donoghue v Stevenson [1932]** is probably the best known case in English law. The plaintiff and a friend went into a cafe and the friend purchased some drinks. The plaintiff had some ginger beer which was served in an opaque bottle sealed with a metal stopper. She drank half the ginger beer and then poured the rest into her glass. As she did so a decomposed snail floated out of the bottle. This event caused the plaintiff to suffer sickness. Could she recover for her damage? If the injured person had actually been the one to purchase the drink then there would have been a contract between the seller and that person. The snail in the bottle would have been a breach of contract and a straightforward action for damages could have begun. In this case though the injured person was not the purchaser and so another type of legal action was necessary. A seller of goods does not have a contract with an injured person and is not at fault himself. The customer in this real life example sued the manufacturer and used negligence to base her action on. We will shortly consider this important area of law.

The result of **Donoghue v Stevenson** was that the customer won. The courts took the view that the producer of a product owed a duty of care to the ultimate consumer. As this duty had been broken and as injury had resulted, the customer won the case. This brief paragraph contains the essential features of negligence. To be successful you need to prove that:

- the person who injured you owed you a duty of care
- the person did something which should not have been done or failed to do something which should have been done
- damage was suffered as a result.

Unlike contract, negligence is **fault based**. This means that while the purchaser of a good which causes injury can sue the seller even if he/she was not at fault, suing a manufacturer demands that fault is proven.

ACTIVITY 1

You will know that legal decisions create precedents. The important part of a precedent is the *ratio decidendi*, the reason for the decision. This means that a decision can be applied in factual circumstances completely different from the original case. Extending **Donoghue v Stevenson** to problems involving defective products is relatively simple, but let us extend the scope. Imagine you are driving your car when a man steps out in front of you and you hit him. Are you at fault? List some questions that you would want to ask in determining where fault lies.

There are a number of questions you could have asked. Were you speeding? What was the state of the road? How well maintained was the car? Did the man just step out without looking? Were you drunk? These are all quite obvious but perhaps you could also ask where you were? Could you expect people to step out, for example if you were on a motorway or your driveway at home? These are all the sorts of questions which would be asked by the courts. The answers should determine fault. The questions may differ between the situation of a piece of metal in a pie and a car accident but the underlying principle is the same. The principles of negligence apply to consumer safety, driving and potentially every other area of activity. The examples we use later in this unit will illustrate this.

One point needs to be made about factual proof. Returning to our example, whether you were driving carefully or not is a matter of fact as much as law. In real life situations, determining facts is probably more important than law but there are cases where success or failure depends upon an interpretation of legal principles. In explaining these principles we will have to ignore the issue of proof but you need to bear in mind that it is an important practical consideration.

The duty of care

'The rule that you are to love your neighbour becomes in law: You must not injure your neighbour, and the lawyers' question: Who is my neighbour? receives a restricted reply. You must take reasonable care to avoid acts or omissions which you can reasonably foresee would be likely to injure your neighbour. Who then, in law, is my neighbour? The answer seems to be persons who are so closely and directly affected by my act that I ought reasonably to have them in contemplation as being so affected when I am directing my mind to the acts or omissions which are called in question.'

This comment from Lord Atkin in **Donoghue v Stevenson** is commonly termed the **'neighbour principle'**. Thus we must not do anything which we ought reasonably to believe will cause injury to our neighbour. Of course people do not think like this when they act. The principle is usually operated retrospectively when things have gone wrong. The courts will look at a situation and say, 'if you had thought about it, could you have reasonably anticipated that your actions could have injured the complainant?'.

ACTIVITY 2

Imagine you are driving a car down a suburban street. List the people who might be classed as your 'neighbours'.

You may have listed: other road users; pedestrians; the owners of parked vehicles; the owners of fences, lamp-posts or walls which you could hit; and your passengers. How about the spouse of a person you injure who is thirty miles away? This seems a little far fetched perhaps but the law has said that there are circumstances in which a person could be owed a duty of care as a result of injuries suffered from seeing the result of an accident. The fact that persons need to be closely and directly affected by a defendant's action introduces the concept of proximity. There is no requirement that this be physical but simply that the person complained of should be reasonably aware of the consequences of his/her action on the complainant.

HOW WIDE IS THE DUTY OF CARE?

The last two activities have taken us from a snail in a bottle to a car accident and suggested that the law might protect people a long way from the scene of an incident. How far can this principle be taken? The answer is unclear.

The neighbour principle suggests that if we can identify a 'neighbour' then a duty of care should exist. This is not the case for the courts have made policy decisions which have denied remedies to people who might reasonably be thought of as 'neighbours'. In **Rondel v Worsley** [1969] for example, the courts refused to allow a claim in negligence against a barrister who it was alleged had not acted with sufficient care on behalf of a client so that the client lost. The client appears to be a 'neighbour'. The lawyer should recognise that if he/she acts negligently then the client will lose. The problem is, how do you decide this? Virtually the only way to determine whether or not the outcome of a case would be different if 'properly' conducted is to have a re-trial. The courts took the view that there were strong policy arguments against allowing a re-trial, and so rejected the claim. (It should be noted that this case only applies to the conduct of litigation, not to advice given outside the courtroom.)

The issue of public policy is not an easy one to understand. The courts take differing views about the existence of a duty of care depending upon the circumstances. We will see shortly that the courts treat differently a person who suffers physical injury compared to somebody who has suffered shock or financial loss. There is no easy way to rationalise this. The courts treat the different types of injury in different ways and while they can rationalise each of these treatments it is difficult to find an overall coherence. There have been attempts in recent years to try to unify these principles. Notably in **Anns v Merton London Borough Council** [1978], Lord Wilberforce proposed a two-stage test. This required the courts deciding whether or not there was foreseeability and, secondly, whether there were reasons for denying the existence of the duty of care.

This seems quite a good idea. You look to see if a person can be described as a neighbour and then allow a duty of care to exist unless you can find reasons to the contrary. The consequence of this type of approach is that it is almost inevitable that the boundaries of negligence will expand. New types of case will emerge and only by finding policy reasons to reject them can the courts limit these new actions. Eventually the two-stage test came under attack from the courts. Most notably this occurred in the case of **Murphy v Brentwood District Council** [1990]. The importance of this case can be gleaned from the fact that a seven member House of Lords unanimously rejected the Anns approach (note that usually only five judges hear cases in the House of Lords). The concern with Anns was that it introduced what might be regarded as indeterminate liability, that is, it would not be possible to predict when a duty of care might be found. The preference for the House of

Lords in the Murphy case was to base decisions on established principles. The current state of the law is perhaps best summed up by Lord Bridge in **Caparo v Dickman** [1990]. His view was that the courts should stop trying to find a unified set of principles for showing the existence of the duty of care. Rather they should attempt to identify types of situation in which this had been held to exist in the past and then look for the rules which were used to establish these findings. In Lord Bridge's view the stance to be taken is a pragmatic one rather than one based solely on theoretical considerations. The consequence of this is that when new actions appear the courts will have to be convinced that they be accepted rather than have to find a way to refuse them. This may seem a matter of playing with words but is a significant change of emphasis.

SELF-CHECK 1

State in your own words when the courts might be expected to say that a duty of care exists.

ACTIVITY 3

The existence or otherwise of a duty of care is not clearcut. There are obvious situations when one exists and equally there are situations where the courts have determined that one does not exist. The differences between the two may seem to you to be arbitrary and hard to justify. There are also cases which fall somewhere between the two.

The brief facts of two cases are given below. You are required to state, with reasons, whether you think that a duty of care exists.

(a) **Haley v London Electricity Board** [1965], where some workmen digging a hole in the pavement but up a barrier so that people would walk around it. The barrier was constructed in such a way that a blind person using a stick would not be aware of its presence. The plaintiff, a blind person, was injured. The defendants argued that they had no special reason to anticipate the presence of visually impaired persons and so owed no duty of care.

(b) **In Home Office v Dorset Yacht Co Ltd** [1970], some borstal trainees (young criminal offenders serving a custodial sentence) were allowed to escape. They stole a yacht for this purpose and collided with another boat, owned by the Yacht Company, which they damaged. The question was did the borstal officers (and through them the Home Office) owe any duty of care to the Yacht Company?

In Haley it was accepted that the Board could not have known that the injured person would be in the vicinity of the roadworks. However, the court felt that given the incidence of people like Mr Haley who were commonly seen walking about, the Board should have taken precautions to provide protection. The point of this case is that it is not essential that the defendant can foresee the risk to a particular individual. Reasonable foreseeable harm to a class of people of which the plaintiff is one will be sufficient.

Home Office v Dorset Yacht Company was also found in favour of the injured party. The House of Lords who decided this case felt that Home Office owed a duty to those people it could reasonably see would have their property damaged if prisoners were to escape. This is an interesting case for the judges in the House of Lords were not unanimous in the decision and those in favour were not totally as one on the reason for holding the Home Office liable. The judges seemed to be clear that there was a point at which the Home Office was liable. The boys were actually on an island and so the only way off was by boat. What if they had travelled say 200 miles and needed food? They would have no money and the only way they could eat would be to steal. Would there be liability then? The answer is probably 'no', but the point at which liability disappears is not clear.

Special circumstance

There are several special types of circumstance which are worth looking at as part of our discussion of the duty of care.

DAMAGE CAUSED BY THIRD PARTIES

In the Dorset Yacht case above the Home Office is being sued for the actions of people in its control. The damage has been caused indirectly. The boys who caused the damage could be sued but as they are unlikely to have any money this is an empty right. The courts are reluctant to find one person liable for the actions of another person where the latter is acting with free will. In **Perl (Exporters) Ltd v Camden London Borough Council** [1983], the council owned two adjoining properties, one of which was let to the plaintiff. Thieves entered the plaintiff's property via the adjoining premises which were not made secure by the council. The Court of Appeal decided that there was no duty of care on one landowner to make property secure so as to protect another. It would seem from these cases that in the absence of some element of control it is unlikely that one person will be made liable for the actions of another.

NERVOUS SHOCK

Where somebody suffers physical injury there is a likelihood that they will also suffer some mental trauma as well. Inevitably there will be some shock and upset but for an action to exist in negligence there must be something more than this. The courts will look for a recognisable medical condition. Extending this one stage further, what of the person who is not physically injured but was involved in an incident where they could, or others did, suffer injury? Actions for nervous shock have been accepted in such cases.

Problems arise where this is to be extended to those who did not witness an incident but came upon its aftermath.

ACTIVITY 4

In **McLoughlin v O'Brien** [1982] Mrs McLoughlin's husband and three of her children were involved in an accident with a lorry which was the fault of O'Brien. Mrs McLoughlin at the time was at home but was called to the hospital. On arrival she found one child dead, another badly injured and her husband and third child injured and distressed. She suffered severe depression and personality changes as a result. Explain whether you feel the driver of the lorry owed her a duty of care.

The case was eventually heard by the House of Lords. The High Court held the injury was not foreseeable. The Court of Appeal held that it was but that there should be no recovery on the grounds of public policy. They presented the so -called **'floodgates'** argument, that is, lots of similar claims might follow. There is also a concern that some claims could be fraudulent as mental problems are much less obvious than physical. The House of Lords rejected this view. They found that a duty of care existed and that there were no policy reasons for rejecting it.

This does not mean that the courts do not impose limits. The courts will expect people to put up with a certain amount of sorrow and grief. Only where this turns into a medically recognised condition, for example depression, will recovery be possible. Even if a medical condition results from an incident there is still no guarantee that a duty of care will exist. The sorts of matter which will be considered are:

● proximity to the incident

● relationship to the injured person

● the degree of seriousness of the incident.

These limits seem to suggest that the courts treat nervous shock differently from physical injury. This is in fact the case. These limits are not fixed but any changes to them are likely to be incremental and so new types of action which are allowed are unlikely to extend the law too much from decided cases. A major attempt was made to extend these limits in 1992 following the tragedy at the Hillsborough football ground when a large number of Liverpool supporters were killed in an overcrowded part of the ground.

Following the Hillsborough tragedy, actions were brought for negligence against the Chief Constable of South Yorkshire alleging negligence on the part of his men. Some of these were brought by people who saw the suffering on television and suffered shock as a result. The House of Lords considered these cases in **Alcock v Chief Constable of South Yorkshire** [1992]. This is an important case and a number of issues were decided by the House of Lords.

Among the points made in the Alcock case were the following:

(a) the event witnessed or come upon must be a single traumatic event;

(b) the plaintiff must have witnessed the event through his/her own unaided senses. Thus as a matter of principle seeing something on television will not normally give rise to an action;

(c) if the incident is not witnessed the plaintiff must come onto the scene in the immediate aftermath. In **McLoughlin v O'Brien** the lady came quickly to hospital where she saw some horrific scenes. In the Hillsborough cases the House of Lords decided that attending at a morgue nine hours after the event was not the immediate aftermath; and

(d) the courts are still influenced by the floodgates argument, feeling that a single incident might result in a multiplicity of claims.

You may feel that the courts were harsh in their interpretation of the law in this case. The case in question had a major effect on virtually the whole country for a time and it seems strange that some people who had suffered as a result were unable to obtain compensation. The problem is the court's view as to the incremental growth of the duty of care. Finding liability here would have required a huge leap since recompense for incidents seen on television had never been previously allowed. Given this, perhaps the decision is not that surprising.

ECONOMIC LOSS

This is an area of law where policy issues seem to take precedence over general principles. The following case illustrates the problem.

ACTIVITY 5

In **Spartan Steel v Martin & Co (Contractors) Ltd** [1972], the defendant contractors, due to a failure to take proper care, damaged a power cable. As a result the electric power to the plaintiff's factory was disconnected. The steel company at the time had molten metal in a furnace. The consequence of this solidifying would have been damage to the furnace and so oxygen was used to pour off the metal. They suffered loss of value to this incomplete melt of £368. Additionally £400 loss of profits which would have been earned if the melt had been processed fully was also claimed. In addition while the factory had no power they could not work and so suffered further loss of profits of £1,767. How much compensation would you award the steel company?

The Court of Appeal concluded that £768 was the appropriate sum. If you said £2,535 you were in good company as one of the judges thought this. The courts draw a distinction between physical damage and the immediate financial consequences of this and pure financial loss independent of physical damage. In this case there was damage to the melt. This also caused loss of profit on that product. The further loss of profit did not result from any physical loss to the plaintiff. Trying to justify this distinction is not easy as this quote from Lord Justice Lawton in this case illustrates:

> 'The differences which undoubtably exist between what damage can be recovered in one type of case and what in another cannot be reconciled on any logical basis...... such differences have arisen because of the policy of the law.'

LJ Lawton went on to suggest that perhaps there should be only one policy, but that if there was; it should it was not the job of the Court of Appeal to decide it. The House of Lords made some attempt to bring the two types of damage together in **Junior Books Ltd v Veitchi Co Ltd** [1982]. In this case the defendants were sub-contractors employed by a main contractor to lay a floor in a warehouse under construction for the plaintiff. Owing to their negligence this was badly laid and had to be replaced. This caused financial loss as stock and machinery had to be moved and stored elsewhere.

The House of Lords decided that there was a cause of action in this case. A sufficient degree of proximity was found between the two parties. In addition the sub-contractor's skill and knowledge had been relied upon in that they had selected the material and method of fixing. It is difficult to reconcile this case with Spartan Steel and one judge felt that perhaps that case should be re-considered. Subsequent cases have however limited the impact of Junior Books. There was not a contract between the plaintiff and defendant here but it is as close a relationship as can exist without a contract arising. (Note that the main-contractor could have been sued in contract but had gone into liquidation prior to the case.)

In **Muirhead v Industrial Tanks Specialities Ltd** [1985], Muirhead kept live lobsters and engaged contractors to build tanks for them. The tanks needed pumps to provide air in the water. These were purchased from the defendant by the contractor installing the tanks but they did not work properly. As a result an entire stock of lobsters was lost. The profits on these were obviously lost as were other profits while the pumps were replaced. The courts concluded that the reliance in the skill and care of the defendant in Junior Books did not exist in this case. Consequently the defendant was liable only for the loss of profits relating to the dead lobsters, not to the period when the operation was shut down.

The Muirhead case seems to be consistent with Spartan Steel. Loss recovered which follows on immediately from physical damage but not subsequent loss while an operation is suspended. The feeling is that Junior Books relies on a special set of circumstances where there is exceptional reliance on the skill of the defendant. Without this there can be no duty of care. Reliance is an important issue in another difficult area of negligence, negligent statements.

Negligent statements and professional negligence

The cases which we have looked at so far have concerned physical damage, either to person or property. We have also noted that there are problems in obtaining compensation for pure financial loss. One area where the duty of care has been expanded in recent years is in allowing recovery for damage suffered as a result of a negligent statement.

The case which is the basis for actions of this type is **Hedley Byrne & Co Ltd v Heller & Partners Ltd** [1963]. The plaintiffs were an advertising agency who were approached by a company, Easipower Ltd, who wanted advertisements placing. The agency in such cases was responsible to the media for paying the bill and so needed to be certain of the financial state of any potential customer before acting for them. The agency therefore contacted the customer's bank, Heller & Partners, and asked for a reference. The bank reported that the customer was respectably constituted and considered good for its normal business engagements. Subsequently Easipower became insolvent and the agency lost £17,000.

The House of Lords drew a distinction between negligent words and actions. Words could be broadcast far beyond their original audience for example. It was also felt that unguarded comments could be made in a social environment which should not be subject to a duty of care. In a professional context though where a person knows that the statement given would be relied upon it was felt that there should be a duty of care in respect of comments made. As it happened the bank reference stated that it was given without responsibility and on this ground they escaped liability. The principle was however established that liability could arise in such cases.

SELF-CHECK 2

From the discussion above state what you regard to be the main principles of negligent mis-statement.

SELF-CHECK 3

In **Esso Petroleum Co Ltd v Mardon** [1976], Mardon wished to take the tenancy of a garage. A representative of the company gave an honest opinion of the sales which could be expected which proved to be hopelessly optimistic. Mardon lost all the capital he had invested and also incurred other debts. Explain whether you think that Esso should be liable for these losses. (Note that if the representative had been negligent himself then Esso would be financially liable for this.)

PROFESSIONAL NEGLIGENCE

This is really a continuation of negligent mis-statement. Where a professional person in the context of his/her occupation provides advice or information which proves to have been negligently given then there can be liability. Hedley Byrne is an obvious example of this. An interesting case which shows how far this could go is **Ross v Caunters** [1980].

Ross v Caunters involved a solicitor who advised a client on the drawing up of a will. On the death of the client the plaintiff who was a beneficiary did not receive any money due to an error by the solicitor. The court decided that there was a duty of care since the solicitor ought to have had the plaintiff in mind when he gave the advice.

The principle has also been extended to house purchasers who rely on valuation reports carried out by surveyors. **Yianni v Edwin Evans & Sons** [1982] is an illustration of this. In this case a valuer working for Edwin Evans carried out a valuation of the property on behalf of the Halifax Building Society who had been asked to make a loan to Yianni. The report stated that the property was sound. In fact it was suffering from severe settlement which should have been evident to a professional valuer. Edwin Evans was made liable for this negligence on the fault of their employee. To illustrate the potential costs of this type of action the cost of repairing the structural problems in the house exceeded its market value as a sound property!

The limits of this principle have been tested in a more recent case, **Caparo Industries plc v Touche Ross & Co** [1990]. In 1984 Caparo plc purchased 100,000 shares in a company called Fidelity. On the day the Fidelity accounts were published, on the basis of reported profits of £1.3 million, they purchased more shares and within four months had taken over the company. On investigating the accounts they discovered that the reported profit should have been a loss of about £460,000. They sought to claim against Touche Ross, who had audited the accounts, for negligence. This case was concerned only with the issue of whether or not a duty of care was owed.

ACTIVITY 5

Caparo argued that Touche Ross owed a duty to existing investors of the company and to potential investors who might make buy/sell decisions on the basis of the published accounts. On the basis of your understanding of the law on negligence, explain what you think the outcome of the case was.

There is a very strong argument that when an auditor states that accounts give a true and fair view that this will be relied upon by investors. On this basis there would appear to be a duty of care but this, if correct, would represent a major advance in the law. In the cases we have looked at in this area: **Hedley Byrne; Esso Petroleum; Ross v Caunters;** and **Yianni,** how many potential plaintiffs were there in each instance? The answer is one. In every case there was one unique person who the professional knew would rely on the information. Now look at Caparo, how many potential litigants exist? The answer, 'how long is a piece of string?' comes to mind. There are potentially thousands. Thus the liability imposed on the auditor is much wider than that imposed on the professionals in the other cases. There is therefore a powerful reason not to find a duty of care. Add to this the fact that the House of Lords concluded that the auditors' report was for the benefit of the company and not the individual shareholders and you will not be surprised that there was no duty of care found.

If you felt that there was a duty of care or still feel that there ought to be given the cost of auditing company accounts, you are in good company. The decision has benn attacked by a number of other professional groups and even the accountancy profession has felt a little embarrassed by it. At one stage there was an attempt to legislate in this area but it came to nothing.

This is an interesting area of law. Accountants have unlimited liability for their errors and such are the claims pending against them that their total potential liability exceeds the indemnity insurance cover held by the profession. There have been suggestions that the law be changed to allow accountants to 'cap' their liability in respect of individual reports but to date the Government has not made any proposals to do this. As a final point, accountants are not exempt from being sued for professional negligence. The company which was audited could claim. In addition if they do work for specific clients then they can also be subject to legal action if negligent.

DUTY OF CARE

We have looked at a wide range of legal problems in this section. The thread holding together economic loss, nervous shock and negligent mis-statement is the duty of care. This is the same duty of care as we discussed in cases such as Donoghue v Stevenson but the intrusion of wider policy considerations makes identifying a neighbour much more difficult. To bring this discussion back to where we started we will conclude this section with a rewrite of an earlier Self-Check.

SELF-CHECK 4

State in your own words when the courts might be expected to say that a duty of care exists and when one may not be found to exist.

Summary of section one

- to prove a case in negligence a plaintiff must show that a duty of care exists, that this has been broken and that damage has resulted
- the courts have identified the existence of a duty of care in a number of specific situations
- the courts have imposed limits on extending the duty of care into new areas
- where a remedy for nervous shock is sought the courts will consider, among other issues, the proximity of the plaintiff to a single incident and the extent to which this was seen through the plaintiff's own, unaided senses
- the courts are reluctant to give compensation for economic loss as compared to physical loss
- recovery for negligent words as well as negligent actions is possible
- negligent mis-statement requires communication of a negligent statement in a situation where a special relationship exists
- the courts will not allow a situation of unlimited liability on a defendant for a single action.

Suggested answers to section one self-check questions

SELF-CHECK 1

A duty of care is owed by one person to another when it would be within the reasonable contemplation of the former that his/her acts or omissions could cause injury to the latter. This statement comes from the case Donoghue v Stevenson but is not a complete definition of the duty of care. This is because the courts have identified a number of types of situation in which a duty arises and these situations have different rules attaching to them. Perhaps it is better to say that a duty potentially arises where the damage suffered comes within a recognised type of injury which the law has stated leads to a duty of care.

SELF-CHECK 2

The first requirement is that there is some communication between the parties. Where one has been made there must be a special relationship such that the person making the statement knows that it is likely to be relied upon. This relationship will not be contractual (if it was the action would be in misrepresentation) but is close to this.

SELF-CHECK 3

There was clearly a communication but was there a special relationship? The court took the view that there was. Interestingly an economic argument was used to justify liability. The costs of providing the information would be cheaper for Esso than the customer. Thus by imposing the duty on Esso there would be an overall reduction in the cost of the transaction. If Esso did not want to bear this cost it could signal the fact by putting in a disclaimer. This case did involve a contract and if the facts were repeated it would be settled now under the **Misrepresentation Act 1967**.

SELF-CHECK 4

A duty of care is owed by one person to another when it would be within the reasonable contemplation of the former that his/her acts or omissions could cause injury to the latter and there are no reasons why the courts feel that this duty should be limited. Policy arguments have dictated that in some cases no duty of care exists. It is difficult to rationalise these but generally the courts are not likely to provide recompense for pure financial loss. Recent case law also indicates that limits have been drawn in the area of professional negligence and nervous shock.

SECTION TWO

Other Aspects of Negligence and Product Liability

In Section Two you will find material to help you learn about and understand the following things:

- the need for the plaintiff to establish a breach of duty by the defendant
- the nature of the standard of care
- the matters considered in assessing the appropriate standard of care
- the use of the plea of *res ipsa loquitur*
- the need for damage to result from the breach
- that damage should not be too remote
- the remedies available to a successful plaintiff
- the special defences which may be used by a defendant
- statutory protection for consumers.

Breach of duty

You saw in the previous section that negligence was fault based. This means that a defendant has to do something 'wrong' before he/she is made liable. What though does 'wrong' mean? In **Donoghue v Stevenson**, it was allowing a snail to get into the bottle. In **Hedley Byrne v Heller** it was giving an incorrect reference. Are these necessarily wrong however? What if it could be shown that every conceivable step was taken to avoid the incident but that it still occurred; should the defendant be liable then? Before you answer 'yes' to that put yourself into the shoes of a driver. You are driving properly in a well maintained car when somebody steps in front of you. You cannot avoid hitting the pedestrian. Should you be liable? We asked this question in a previous activity. In this we listed some of the questions we would ask to decide whether somebody had acted properly. That in simple terms is the nature of the duty of care. Did the defendant act 'properly'? If he/she did then they will not be liable.

Before we can determine whether somebody has broken their duty of care we need to be able to determine the **standard** which they are required to meet. Consider the following case.

ACTIVITY 7

In **Nettleship v Weston** [1971], the plaintiff was teaching the defendant to drive. During the third lesson they made a slow left turn but the defendant did not straighten the car out properly, panicked and before the plaintiff could react the car hit a lamp-post. The plaintiff's knee-cap was broken. In the court the question to be asked was whether Mrs Weston owed a lower standard of care to the plaintiff than that of an experienced, qualified driver. There are two possible outcomes. The first is that Mrs Weston is assumed to be capable of all the skill and care of a competent driver. The second that the standard is of a lesson three learner. Using your own judgment state the advantages and disadvantages of these two approaches and then say which you prefer.

The Court of Appeal decided that not only should a learner driver be expected to display the same standard of care as a qualified driver, the plaintiff's special knowledge of her competence did not mean he could not have compensation. Holding otherwise would have meant the courts used a subjective standard. That is they would assess each person as an individual as regards his/her skills and experience. Thus Mrs Weston is expected to meet a standard of care which, as a learner, she is incapable of attaining. This may seem fair to a defendant but it is not to a plaintiff. Why should the issue of compensation be settled on the skill level of the defendant? An objective standard is used. This means that if you undertake a task you are measured against the skill level of a reasonably competent person doing that job. Those not wanting to be judged in this way have a choice, they do not drive!

SELF-CHECK 1

In **Philips v William Whiteley Ltd** [1938], the plaintiff went into a jeweller to have her ears pierced. Shortly afterwards she developed an abscess which she claimed was caused by this operation. Evidence showed that the hygiene precautions taken were not those of a surgeon but were usually appropriate. State whether you think the jeweller was in breach of his duty of care.

There may be cases where there is debate as to the exact standard of care to be applied. In a medical case, **Bolam v Friern Hospital Management Committee** [1957], it was said that a doctor would not be regarded as negligent if the practice followed was supported by a responsible body of medical practitioners. This would still be the case even if there were opposing views as to the most appropriate treatment to apply. The Bolam case involved a woman who after an operation was rendered paralysed. Evidence was that the operation even if carried out properly had a one or two per cent chance of this happening. The issue was, should the woman have been warned of the risk? Medical opinion was split as to whether the patient should have been warned of the consequences. The fact that a failure to fully advise the patient was supported by a number of other doctors meant that the practice would not be regarded as negligent.

This legal principle is still good law but medical practices change and so it is now much more common for a doctor to fully advise a patient of potential risks. As practices change so will the law and so failure to give full information may now be regarded as negligent unless strong reasons to justify the action can be found.

Factors in setting the standard

It is easy to talk about the standard of care of a competent driver or surgeon but what does this mean in practice? When we drive we have to take additional care in certain circumstances. Fog or ice or overtaking a stationary ice cream van are all situations when we need to be extra vigilant. This suggests that risk plays an important part in determining what is appropriate. The next activity explores this.

ACTIVITY 8

Imagine that three lorries set out on a journey. One carries water; the second petrol; and the third nuclear waste. Explain how the safety precautions which should apply to the lorries might differ.

What you have probably concentrated on is risk. If the water lorry crashed then there would be impact damage but the cargo is not inherently dangerous. The petrol tanker carries a much more dangerous product which could cause fire in the immediate vicinity of any collision. The consequences of a leak of nuclear waste could be serious both in terms of the geographical area and duration of the effect. We might expect the most dangerous cargo to be driven more slowly; to have an escort; to travel at night; for the vehicle to be maintained to a high state; and for there to be plans to deal immediately with risks of escape. For the water lorry we would not envisage special care other than that appropriate to driving a truck and the petrol tanker would be somewhere between the two.

We can identify three important considerations to apply in deciding the level of skill and care to set. These are the **likelihood of injury**; the **potential consequences**; and the **practicability of taking precautions**.

ACTIVITY 9

In **Bolton v Stone** [1951], Miss Stone was standing outside her house when a cricket ball hit out of a nearby ground hit her on the head. It is assumed that there is a duty of care imposed on the club. If you had to decide whether the cricket club was in breach of this duty you would need more information. What questions would you want to have answered?

You might have asked:

(a) how far away was she from the batsman?

(b) was there a fence?

(c) how often were cricket balls hit out of the ground? and

(d) how exceptional a hit was this?

The answers in this case were: (a) about 100 yards (a long way to hit a cricket ball!); (b) yes, about 17 feet high and nearly 80 yards away from the batsman; (c) very rarely; and (d) it was generally regarded as an exceptional hit. Given this you will not be surprised that Miss Bolton did not recover damages. The club was not in breach of its duty.

This case may seem harsh to you but you must remember that negligence demands fault. The court decided that the club had done everything it was reasonably expected to do, therefore it was not at fault. If balls had exited the ground frequently then the answer would be different.

Bolton v Stone deals with the likelihood of occurrence. A rather sad case on risk is **Paris v Stepney Borough Council** [1951]. Paris was a garage hand working for the council. He had only one eye and in the course of a job he was doing a piece of metal hit and damaged his good eye. Given that the consequences of the loss of an eye were much more serious for him than a person of full sight the council was found to be in breach of its duty in not providing protective goggles.

This case pre-dated the current health and safety rules (discussed later in this unit) and the case would now be based on these rather than negligence. Those interested in the human side to this will be saddened to learn that Mr Paris was serving two weeks notice of dismissal when the accident happened. He was dismissed because due to his missing eye he was ineligible to join the pension scheme which was a condition of employment. The accident happened two days before he was due to leave.

Proof of breach

We said earlier in this unit that we would ignore the question of proving facts. There is an exception to this rule which we need now to consider. Imagine a case again like Donoghue v Stevenson. You are the victim of the snail and have to prove negligence on the part of the manufacturer. How will you do this? If you look at a bottle now you will see some information on it, probably including a batch number. The manufacturer could probably tell you exactly when the bottle was filled, the machinery used, and the origin of the ingredients. Asked to explain how the snail got there would be difficult. For the injured person he/she would have even less chance of proving negligence since they would have nothing on which to base the claim. Nothing, except for the fact that the snail got there and if everything had been OK it would not have been in the bottle. Thus it could be argued that the very fact that the snail is there means that somebody has been negligent, unless the contrary can be proved.

In civil cases the court will decide on a 'balance of probabilities' which party should win. This means that the story which is the most plausible will be successful. The more knowledge that a person has then the better their case will be. Where an individual is alleging negligence against a manufacturer therefore there is an inevitable bias in favour of the manufacturer. This is not a matter of law, simply that one person has more resources and information than the other.

In such cases the law can try to redress the balance. There is a rule called, *resipsa loquitur*, meaning 'the facts speak for themselves'. Where this applies the courts will presume that negligence took place unless the defendant can prove otherwise. A successful claim depends upon two things:

(a) that the defendant controlled the activity which caused the damage; and

(b) the accident would not have occurred if proper care had been used.

An old case, **Scott v London & St Katherine Docks Co** [1865], illustrates this. A man walking past a warehouse was hit by six bags of sugar falling through a window. As the defendants controlled the inside of the warehouse and as sugar should not fall out in this way, the maxim was applied.

It should be noted that this does not prove negligence. What it does is shift the burden of proof onto the defendant to prove that there was no negligence. If this can be proved then the plaintiff will not win unless he/she can bring evidence to conflict with that of the defendant.

SELF-CHECK 2

In **Ward v Tesco Stores** [1976], the plaintiff slipped on yoghurt which had been spilt on the floor. Nobody knew how it got there. The principle of *res ipsa loquitur* was applied. If you were Tesco management how would you try to show that you were not negligent?

Resulting damage

After establishing that the defendant has broken the duty of care it might be thought that any damage which arises can be compensated but this is not the case. There needs to be a causal link between the breach and the damage suffered. This is illustrated in the tragic case, **Barnett v Chelsea and Kensington Hospital Management Committee** [1968]. The plaintiff's husband and some workmates became ill as a result of drinking some tea. They suffered persistent vomiting for three hours before being taken to hospital. The nurse who saw them contacted a doctor by telephone, he, being tired and unwell, advised the nurse to tell them to go home and see their own doctor. Shortly afterwards the plaintiff's husband died from arsenic poisoning administered by a workmate.

The doctor clearly owed a duty of care. Equally clearly, his failure to examine the men was a breach of that duty, yet the widow still lost the case. This was because medical evidence showed that if normal practice had been followed the man would have been dead before arsenic poisoning was diagnosed. Thus the doctor's breach of duty did not result in any 'damage' to the plaintiff's husband.

You may feel that this case is wrong but as we have said on a number of occasions negligence is not a matter of strict liability. Imagine negligently driving into a man who could not walk and damaging his legs. To provide compensation for loss of the ability to walk would be to give the man something for nothing as he did not have that ability at the time of the accident.

REMOTENESS OF DAMAGE

Even if it can be shown that the damage results directly from the breach of duty there may still be no recovery. There may be cases where the result of the breach is so unexpected that the courts state that it is 'too remote' from the incident.

The leading case on remoteness of damage is **Overseas Tankship (UK) Ltd v Morts Dock & Engineering Co Ltd** [1961], usually referred to as **'The Wagon Mound'**. The Tankship company chartered a ship, The Wagon Mound, and due to carelessness by their employees some oil from the ship was spilt into the harbour. This spread to a wharf where some welding was going on. The welding was immediately stopped but resumed when advice was given that this process would not ignite the oil. Two days later the oil was ignited when a spark from the welding set fire to a piece of waste floating on it. The resulting fire caused serious damage to the wharf. The court had to consider whether the charterers were responsible for this damage.

There is no doubt that the fire was the direct result of the spillage but the court concluded that it was not reasonably foreseeable. Nobody knew that oil could be ignited in this way and so no compensation was payable.

SELF-CHECK 3

In **Doughty v Turner Manufacturing Co Ltd** [1964] due to the negligence of one of the company's employees a lid fell into a cauldron of molten metal. This caused a previously unobserved chemical reaction which caused an explosion within the cauldron. This sent out molten metal a considerable distance which hit the plaintiff. Given the discussion on the **Wagon Mound** above you should be able to explain the result of this case. You need to think about what sort of damage might be expected from the incident and then compare this against the damage which actually occurred.

There are some principles which may seem to conflict with the **Wagon Mound** rule.

(a) If the damage is of the type expected but more severe than anticipated. Thus in **Bradford v Robinsons Rentals Ltd** [1967], a driver who was sent out on a long journey in an unheated van during a severe cold spell was able to recover compensation when he suffered frostbite. The extent of the injury was not foreseeable but the type of injury, ie. due to cold, was.

(b) Cases where a foreseeable type of harm has been inflicted in an unforeseeable way have also been allowed. In **Hughes v Lord Advocate** [1963], some workers left an open manhole surrounded by paraffin lamps. A boy playing with one of the lamps fell into the hole and was injured when the lamp exploded. The court concluded that burning was a foreseeable injury even though the explosion was not foreseeable.

This does seem to conflict with Doughty, discussed earlier. It is arguable that the two cases cannot be reconciled although there is a difference. In Hughes it was foreseeable that the boy could be injured while in Doughty there was no injury foreseeable at all to the men. There is no clear answer to this apparent conflict.

(c) The so called **'thin skull'** rule provides a remedy to a person who is injured because of some special susceptibility on his/her part. In **Smith v Leech Brain & Co Ltd** [1962], the husband of the plaintiff was burnt on the lip through the negligence of the employer. This activated a latent cancer from which he died. The company was made liable for this. This rule is something of an exception since the extent of the injury clearly was not foreseeable. The law in such cases says that a person should 'take his victim as he finds him'.

SELF-CHECK 4

Scenario one

Bellpit Ltd is a small company which manufactures chemical based garden products such as fertilisers. It has operated from a small factory on the outskirts of Godley, a town in the West Midlands, for eighteen years. The nearest other buildings to the factory are some houses about half a mile away. The factory itself is surrounded by fields, used for keeping horses, and some woodland. The area has a number of paths through it which are well-used by local people for recreation.

One of the products made by the company is 'Oriole' a weedkiller which can be used on lawns. The company claims that the weedkiller will not damage grass. The product is in fact made under licence from an American firm Garpham Inc. The oriole weedkiller has proved to be commercially successful. Pressure is placed on the production staff to increase output and most of the employees are working long overtime hours and at weekends. The company is looking to purchase new premises but this is a longer-term solution.

The product is sold in plastic tubs which are sent to retail outlets in packs of twenty-four. A pack of the product is sent to the Broadelm Garden Centre. This pack came from batch 345Q and was the only product from that batch sent out of the factory. The pack arrived at the garden centre by van and was carried into the shop part by Tom. As he walked through the shop he slipped and dropped the package. It exploded covering him and three customers, Andy, Brenda and Carrie, with the weedkiller. Chemical analysis showed that the batch had been mixed incorrectly. The resulting mix was volatile and liable to explode. This reaction had not been observed previously by anybody.

Tom suffered severe lung damage because of inhaling the powder. Andy suffered some eye trouble but this was not serious. The two women suffered only damage to clothing but Carrie is now suffering nightmares because of the incident and is having to take tranquilisers. While in hospital having tests it was discovered that Tom had lung cancer. He is not expected to live more than another six months.

The rest of the batch was destroyed and the company investigated the matter. They were unable to discover how the batch had been incorrectly mixed but it appeared that several mistakes had been caused by tiredness. Checking systems had spotted these and ought to have noticed the error in this instance.

The three employees who made that particular batch were all dismissed by the company for incompetence.

Questions

1. From the information you have in the scenario, identify the groups which you feel the company owes a duty of care to.

2. If you were acting as lawyer for the injured people, what procedural rule would you try and use to show that the company had broken its duty of care?

3. Is damage caused by being covered in weedkiller foreseeable? Give reasons for your answer.

4. What do you feel would be the effect on Tom's claim for compensation that he has only a short time to live?

5. Can Carrie recover compensation for her nightmares and need to take tranquilisers?

Defences

Am obvious defence to raise is that one of the components of negligence has not been proven. If somebody is able to show that no duty of care exists; there has been no breach of duty; or that damage is too remote then the plaintiff's case will fail. There are some additional defences which apply where negligence exists which can remove or reduce the liability of the defendant. These are considered here.

CONTRIBUTORY NEGLIGENCE

Put simply, a person's entitlement to damages for negligence may be reduced, in some cases to zero, if he/she has contributed to his/her own injury. This is governed by a statute, the **Law Reform (Contributory Negligence) Act 1945**.

Whether or not a person is deemed to have contributed to his/her own injuries is a matter of fact. The courts will use the same principles that apply in determining breach of duty. Did the injured person act in some way improperly as regards his/her own safety? If the answer is 'yes' then the court will need to assess the importance of this as compared to the action of the defendant and try to determine what proportion of blame attaches to the plaintiff.

Cases where there is a regular reduction include road traffic accidents where the injured person was not wearing a seatbelt in a car or crash helmet on a motor cycle. In one case, **Gregory v Kelly** [1978], damages were reduced by 40% when a passenger in a car failed to wear a seatbelt and was also aware that the car had faulty brakes.

ACTIVITY 10

In **Jones v Livox Quarries Ltd** [1952], the plaintiff was riding on the towbar at the rear of a vehicle. There was a clear risk of falling off and being injured. The vehicle was involved in an accident when another vehicle ran into the back of it, injuring the plaintiff. In this case it is arguable that riding on a tow bar contributed to the injury. Using your understanding of the discussion of contributory negligence above answer the two questions below.

(a) On the facts do you think that damages should have been reduced?

(b) Would your answer be different if the plaintiff had been injured through some other type of incident, for example, being shot by a negligent hunter nearby?

Although the risk Jones exposed himself to was of falling off there was a wider risk such as that actually suffered. Accordingly there was a reduction in damages. The Court of Appeal actually used the hunter illustration to give an example of a situation where there would be no reduction. This type of risk would not have been contributed to by his negligent riding.

Volenti non fit injuria

This means that **'to the willing there is no injury'**. Put another way, if you consent to a risk then you can hardly complain if you are subsequently injured. This has been topical in the sports area. If you play football or rugby there is the chance of an injury, for example a broken leg, if you are tackled awkwardly. Playing the game implies that you 'consent' to this. The situation is totally different if the cause of your injury is foul play since you do not consent to be a victim of this.

If *volenti* applies then it is a complete defence. There is no partial consent which would simply reduce damages. Either you consented or you did not.

What is important in this type of case is that there is consent to a risk. Simply being aware of it is not sufficient. This is of particular importance in employment situations. Workers may be exposed to risks which they are aware of but have little choice over. If they complain they are dismissed. This will not usually be construed as consent. In **Smith v Baker & Sons** [1891] the employer used a crane to carry stone over the heads of workers. When a worker was subsequently injured by a falling stone the courts held that his knowledge of the danger was not consent to it.

ACTIVITY 11

Re-read the facts of **Nettleship v Weston** [1971] discussed earlier. You will recall here that a driving instructor sued a pupil claiming that he had been injured due to her negligence. Arguably by giving lessons he should take a certain amount of risk. Did the instructor/friend give consent to the risk of injury? Give reasons for your response.

The instructor was clearly aware of the dangers he faced but he had not given consent to them. In this type of case consent would mean agreeing that he would not take legal action if injured. There was no evidence that this was given.

SELF-CHECK 5

The case **Imperial Chemical Industries v Shatwell** [1964] brings together the two defences we have considered. The facts involved two brothers, George and James who were shotfirers (ie. they set up explosive charges in quarries). Due to their joint use of an unsafe practice they were both injured. The company had told them not to use this practice. They had given them instruction on how to act. A Government regulation forbade the unsafe practice and the employers had revoked the shotfiring licence of one person for not acting properly. The brothers were aware of all these matters. The safe practice could have been used but would have taken longer. George now sues James for negligence. If a case is established the employer will be required to pay damages as it is vicariously liable for the negligent actions of employees. Using your understanding of the discussion of these issues answer the two questions below.

(a) Assuming that George's damage was assessed at £3,000, would you expect that James would have to pay all of this?

(b) Do you think that George consented to the risk?

EXCLUSION CLAUSES

A full consideration of these is outside the scope of this unit but exclusion clauses require some mention here. You have probably seen a sign which says, 'the management has no liability for any injury or loss suffered while on these premises'. This is an example of an exclusion clause. Where effective it has the effect of removing or limiting the remedy of an injured person.

Exclusion clauses relating to tort are subject to statutory control under the **Unfair Contract Terms Act** 1977 as amended by the **Unfair Terms in Consumer Contracts Regulations** 1995. Note that the Act does not apply only to contracts. The Act states that:

(a) liability for death or personal injury due to negligence cannot be excluded; and

(b) liability for other sorts of loss can only be excluded if it is reasonable to do so.

Part (a) is straightforward but (b) is difficult to interpret. The Act says that a notice will be reasonable where it is 'fair and reasonable to allow reliance on it having regard to all the circumstances obtaining when the liability arose'. This does not take us very far but it would seem that the courts will apply a subjective interpretation. The wording used; the position of the notice; the understanding of the plaintiff; and the availability of alternatives will all be considered.

Remedies

We will conclude our discussion of negligence by looking briefly at the remedies available to an injured person.

DAMAGES

This is the usual remedy. The aim of awarding damages is to compensate the injured person for the injuries suffered. Inasmuch as it can be done financially the courts will try to place the injured person in the position that he/she would have been in if the tort had not occurred.

You may have seen in the press some very high damages awarded for personal injuries. Where a person has been injured such that continual care is required then awards will have to be high to provide this. The courts are starting to look at payment of damages in stages rather than as a lump sum and in cases where it is not possible to predict life expectancy this is arguably sensible.

Damages are assessed usually by judges and are meant to reflect loss. The principles may therefore seem slightly callous. Killing a person through negligent driving will involve different payouts depending on the victim. Somebody young, in a well-paid career and with dependents would attract a far higher compensation payment than an unemployed 55-year-old person with no dependents.

We have looked at some other issues which will affect the amount paid. Damages for financial loss are less likely to be paid than for physical loss. Additionally claims may be reduced because of contributory negligence. For example if you were hurt in a car accident and were not wearing a seatbelt at the time the courts would say that you had contributed to your own injuries.

As a final point damages in one area of tort are notorious for their unpredictability. Where defamation is alleged the matter may be heard by a jury who will also assess compensation to be paid. This is virtually the only area of civil law where juries are involved. Juries may be prone to apply criteria which a judge would not. Sentiment; the desire to 'punish' an offending newspaper; and difficulty in determining actual loss mean that awards can seem high when compared with payments for physical damage.

INJUNCTION

Where an activity which is unlawful is anticipated or is happening on a continuing basis it may be possible to obtain an injunction to stop it. Negligence cases are usually unique events but injunctions may be used where there is, for example, continuing pollution. This is more relevant to negligence and we will consider this issue again later in this unit.

Product liability

The discussion given on negligence above started with Donoghue v Stevenson which was a case about product liability. The impact that the snail has had on English law has been considerable and Donoghue v Stevenson can be regarded as the basis of much of the modern law of negligence. In addition to negligence the law of contract, specifically the Sale of Goods Act (as amended by the Supply and Sale of Goods Act 1974) gives some valuable protection to the purchaser of a good. The rules governing satisfactory suitable quality are important in this respect. There is in addition to this common law protection a statute based remedy. This is contained in the **Consumer Protection Act 1987**, an Act of Parliament brought in to meet the UK's obligations under the 1985 Directive on Product Liability from the European Community.

CONTRACTUAL RULES RE-VISITED

The concept of merchantable quality has now been replaced by one of 'satisfactory' quality. This change was introduced by the Sale and Supply of Goods Act 1974. Under this amendment goods meet the standard of being satisfactory if they would be regarded as such by a reasonable person. In assessing this a number of circumstances needs to be taken into account. These are:(i) fitness for purpose (ii) appearance and finish (iii) freedom from minor defects (vi) safety (v) durability.

ACTIVITY 12

Stephen runs a self-service cafe which sells hot food and drinks. Mandy and Sam go into the cafe, take a seat and select from the menu. Mandy goes to the counter places their order and pays for and collects the food. While eating her meal, steak pie and chips, Mandy suddenly shouts out with pain and blood pours from her mouth. Investigations show that she bit on a piece of metal which was in the pie and broke a tooth and cut the inside of her mouth. Stephen has purchased the pie from Farm Pies Ltd that day. The pie came wrapped in clingfilm and was only unwrapped when it was served. He subsequently apologises to Mandy, repays her the price of the meal but says he cannot be liable as it was not his fault the metal was in the pie.

Advise Mandy who she can sue and her prospects for success.

It is a matter of debate whether this change in terminology will help consumers. It is certainly not intended to reduce protection and so Stephen would still be liable, in this case for selling a pie of unsatisfatory rather than unmerchantable quality.

Your advice should have identified that Mandy had a **contract** with Sam. All the features are there. **Agreement, consideration** and, because it is implied from a commercial transaction, **intention to be legally bound**. If Mandy can establish a breach of contract she can sue Stephen. The rule *caveat emptor*, let the buyer beware, does not apply to sales in the course of business. The **Sale of Goods Act 1979 Section 14** demanded that goods be fit for the purpose for which goods of that kind are normally purchased. In addition, if the purpose of the purchase was known, the Act demands that goods be **fit for that purpose**. If you buy a pie in a cafe there is only one thing which you are likely to do with it, that is eat it. Thus if the pie is not fit to eat it is not fit for its purpose. In **Grant v Australian Knitting Mills Ltd** [1936] some underpants were sold which due to a processing defect contained a chemical which gave the purchaser dermatitis. As underpants are purchased to wear next to the skin they were clearly not fit for the purpose.

Both merchantable quality and fitness for purpose were part of the contract. The Act stated that they were **implied conditions,** that is they are automatically part of the contract. Where one of these terms is broken there is no defence. The concept of **strict liability** means that the seller is liable even if innocent of the breach. Stephen sold a pie not fit for its purpose, therefore he is liable. The fact that he was not to blame is not relevant. He has however bought the pie himself from Farm Pies Ltd and so they can be sued by him for selling an unfit pie. On these facts there is no reason why Mandy should sue the piemaker.

ACTIVITY 13

Answer the problem in the last activity again but this time imagine that it is Sam who has been injured. All other facts remain the same. Before you proceed you should go back to page 275 and refresh your memory of the case **Donoghue v Stevenson**.

The problem here is that Sam does not have a contract with Stephen. It was Mandy who purchased the food and has the contract. It might be possible to infer that Mandy acted as agent for Sam but this would require that she meant to buy it on his behalf rather than simply for him. Stephen has no liability therefore in contract. Our next question is to ask whether he has acted in some way wrongly. On the facts the answer appears to be no. Imposing liability on him will be difficult. What about Farm Pies Ltd? Have they done anything wrong?

The problem here is very similar to that in **Donoghue v Stevenson**. A seller of goods does not have a contract with an injured person and is not at fault himself. The customer in this real life example sued the manufacturer and used negligence to base her action on. Sam could do the same but remember he has to prove fault on the part of the manufacturer. This may be difficult for him. In practice he is unlikely to rely on the law of negligence for a remedy. The **Consumer Protection Act 1987** is much more likely to be of help to him.

THE CONSUMER PROTECTION ACT 1987 AND THE LAW OF NEGLIGENCE

It may seem odd to you that where two people suffer injury from the same product there may be different legal rules applying to the consumers. If the item was purchased by one of the injured people this is a matter of contract, if purchased by anybody else an issue of negligence. This problem is further complicated by the existence of the Consumer Protection Act 1987. This statute gives consumers rights where they have suffered damage because of a product. This Act gives wide rights to consumers and in practice would be a better alternative than suing in negligence. Negligence is still an important topic however. The 1987 Act does not apply to all consumers and so you still need to be aware of the principles of negligence. In addition, as you have already seen, the law of negligence applies in many other situations than damage by a product.

Consumer protection act 1987

The Act is intended to protect people from defective products. A **product is basically any good except property such as houses**. A good is defective where it does not provide the **level of safety which people generally are entitled to expect**. In deciding this the court can take into account a number of matters. The Act states that the purpose for which the product is sold; the way it was marketed; and any warnings given should be taken into account.

The Act provides for damages to be payable to compensate for death or physical injury. In addition where domestic property is damaged this may be compensated. Damage to the specific item which caused the problem is not recoverable; neither is financial loss; or damage to commercial property. A wide range of people may be made liable to pay damages. These include the manufacturer and the importer. Manufacturer could include a person who made a component. This could mean that in many products a large number of firms could be potentially liable. A person who appears to be a producer might also be liable. This would include somebody who sold something under a brand name which was made by somebody else. Supermarket own-label goods would fall into this category.

The action appears to be **strict liability** in that the plaintiff need not establish fault on the part of the defendant but there are a number of defences:

(a) the defect relates to the manufacturer complying with a statutory rule;

(b) the manufacturer did not supply the product at any time (eg. it was stolen);

(c) the supply was not in the course of business;

(d) no defect was present when the goods were supplied;

(e) the defect was not known due to the state of scientific knowledge at the time;

(f) components have been improperly incorporated; and

(g) more than ten years have passed since the product was first supplied.

SELF-CHECK 6

State whether the following statements relating to product liability are true or false.

1. The Sale of Goods Act allows a customer to return a good because it is the wrong size.

   TRUE/FALSE

2. The Consumer Protection Act only applies to purchasers of goods.

   TRUE/FALSE

3. Where a consumer is injured by a faulty good there is no need to prove that the manufacturer was responsible as there is strict liability.

   TRUE/FALSE

4. The Sale of Goods Act does not apply to goods which are marked 'seconds'.

TRUE/FALSE

5. If a wheel in a new car is faulty and causes a collision, the Consumer Protection Act allows an injured person to sue the manufacturer of the car and the wheel.

TRUE/FALSE

6. A manufacturer owes a duty of care only to the purchasers of the goods.

TRUE/FALSE

Summary of section two

- we must adopt the standard of care of a reasonably competent person undertaking the task in question
- where a person professes to have special skills this standard can be increased
- in assessing the standard the courts will consider issues such as the likelihood of damage, the potential consequences and the practicalities of taking precautions
- where a defendant has control over an operation and an incident results which seems to point to a lack of care, the maxim *res ipsa loquitur* can be invoked
- the damage suffered by a plaintiff must not be too remote from the breach and must be reasonably foreseeable
- where the damage is of a foreseeable type but more severe than expected then a recovery is possible
- where the plaintiff is specially susceptible to an injury then damages may be obtained even if this is not reasonably foreseeable by a defendant
- a person who is partly to blame for his/her own or another person's injury may be found to have been contributing negligence
- the defence of *volenti non fit injuria* may be applied where a person consents to the risk which is faced

- exclusion clauses are invalid where they purport to exclude liability for death or personal injury caused by negligence
- in other cases of loss through negligence an exclusion clause must be reasonable to be valid
- damages are meant to compensate and so reflect a plaintiff's loss
- the need to prove fault makes negligence difficult to establish where goods are defective
- the law of contract only provides remedies to purchasers of goods
- the Consumer Protection Act provides remedies to consumers damaged by defective products
- there is no need for the consumer to prove fault on the part of a defendant but there are a number of defences available.

Suggested answers to section two self-check questions

SELF-CHECK 1

The courts answered that he was not. The standard he had to attain was that of a reasonably competent jeweller carrying out operations of this type. It was not appropriate to measure him against a surgeon. Choosing a comparator is therefore quite important. Where a person professes some special skill then the obligations imposed can be increased. In **Maynard v West Midlands Regional Health Authority**, for example, it was said that, 'a doctor who professes to exercise a special skill must exercise the ordinary skill of his speciality'. This would apply in all cases, not just medicine.

SELF-CHECK 2

Given that you could not show how the yoghurt came to be there, what would be needed would be a system for detecting spillages and cleaning them. This might be inspections of aisles on a timed basis with the person concerned noting any problems. A cleaner on standby to act quickly on reported spillages would also be useful. Tesco could not show this system existed and so lost the case.

SELF-CHECK 3

The courts concluded that it would be expected that damage would be caused by spillage in such cases but that as the explosion could not have been anticipated the consequences of it were too remote. Thus there was no recovery.

SELF-CHECK 4

1. Everybody mentioned in the scenario can be classed as a neighbour. It is reasonably foreseeable that a manufacturing concern could cause injury to those living nearby; employees; customers; and those selling their products.

2. The principles applied in deciding whether the duty of care has been broken are discussed in the text. Trying to actually prove breach is however difficult. There is a procedure which may help. The use of the *res ipsa loquitur* rule to move the balance of power onto the company should be tried. This will require the plaintiff to show that the damage would not have arisen without negligence and that the matter was within the control of the defendant. There appears to be clear evidence of negligence.

3. Two conflicting arguments can be put forward by using the Doughty and Hughes cases as supporting a point of view. If the boxes were dropped then it is probably foreseeable that the contents could spill out onto those nearby. Thus the damage is of a foreseeable type, the method of delivery being unforeseeable. Hughes v Lord Advocate is arguably the more applicable and so the customers could recover.

4. Tom will receive compensation for pain and suffering caused by the incident but would only receive compensation for loss of earnings or disability for the shortened life span. In assessing damages the courts will take into account events which occur after the incident which might reduce the liability of the defendant.

5. Carrie will need to show that she is suffering from nervous shock. The courts generally expect people to be of normal fortitude and so will consider whether Carrie's complaint is to be expected. This is a matter of fact rather than law and there is no clear answer. The writer's view is that there would be no recovery but if you think the opposite this is equally valid.

If you are still not clear about the answers to the five questions read again the material to which they relate and attempt the questions once more.

SELF-CHECK 5

In answer to (a) the courts originally decided that both the brothers were equally to blame for the incident. Thus if George was negligent then he could sue James for fifty per cent of his damage. The reverse would also apply and James could sue George. Between the two brothers this would cancel out and they would not be expected to pay each other anything. The employers would have to pay and so ICI could be faced with paying fifty per cent of loss to each brother. The House of Lords felt that this was inappropriate since in agreeing to act as they did the brothers agreed to the risk. The company had done all that it could to get the brothers to work properly. Given this the House of Lords felt that in deciding to follow the unsafe practice the two had between each other consented to bear the risk of the consequences. Thus George could not sue James and vice versa.

SELF-CHECK 6

The answers to these questions are 1. False; 2. False; 3. False (remember that negligence requires proof of fault and the Consumer Protection Act contains a number of defences); 4. False; 5. True; and 6. False.

SECTION THREE

Other Aspects of Tort

In Section Three you will find material to help you learn about and understand the following things:

- the obligations imposed on the users of land to act reasonably
- special rules applying to those who bring dangerous items onto their land
- the way in which the law protects lawful visitors onto land
- the different rules which apply to trespassers

The discussion in this unit has so far concentrated on negligence although other torts have been mentioned, in particular reference has been made to nuisance. The tort of nuisance allows landowners to make a claim where they feel that their enjoyment of their property has been diminished by the way another person has used his/her land. A variant of this is the rule in **Rylands v Fletcher** which imposes strict liability on users of land who allow dangerous things to escape from it. These two torts deal with incidents which impact outside the area of the defendant's property. Occupier's liability is a statutory tort which imposes obligations on land users to make their property safe for the purposes that others might use it for. We will briefly look at each of these in turn. It is only intended to provide an introduction to these torts to illustrate the ways in which the law imposes obligations on landusers.

Nuisance

The law has to strike a balance between giving people the right to use their property as they wish and preventing them from using it in such a way as to cause damage to somebody else. Nuisance is a tort which allows one land user to sue where it is felt that the actions of another are unreasonable.

There are two classes of nuisance, **private** and **public.** Private nuisance is the most straightforward and the discussion given below concentrates on it. A private nuisance is caused where **one land user uses his property in such a way that it unlawfully reduces the enjoyment that another land user has of his/her property.**

Public nuisance is primarily a crime but anybody who suffers special damage can sue for compensation. In a case considered below, **Halsey v Esso**, there are elements of both public and private nuisance. To sue in public nuisance requires only that special damage has been suffered, that is something over and above that suffered by others. Private nuisance requires that a plaintiff actually have an interest in the land which is subject to the nuisance.

IDENTIFYING AN ACTIONABLE NUISANCE
In an old case **St Helen's Smelting Co v Tipping** [1865] the owner of an estate

brought an action against a smelting company for damage caused by pollution generated from the works. In the case the judge asked three questions. Whether the plaintiff's enjoyment of his property was diminished, whether the business carried on was an ordinary business carried on properly, and whether the business was carried on in the right place. The answers to the questions given by a jury (commonly used in the last century) were: yes; yes; and no. Consequently damages were given to the plaintiff.

In this case we can see some important aspects of nuisance:

- damage to enjoyment of property
- reasonableness; and
- location.

To this can be added duration for generally the more frequently an event occurs the greater the chances of a remedy. Despite this it is possible for single events to constitute a nuisance.

The importance of this tort can be seen in the following case where householders were able to take action to stop the work of a major company. In **Halsey v Esso Petroleum Co Ltd** [1961] householders brought an action against the company alleging: damage to laundry from oily smuts emitted from a factory; nauseating smells; noise at night; and the constant driving past their homes of petrol tankers. The character of the neighbourhood was an important factor in making Esso liable for the damage to the plaintiffs.

In cases such as this there is an argument that the factory is socially useful in that it provides employment and wealth for the area. These are not issues which the courts will consider. For example in **Adams v Ursell** [1913] the presence of a fish shop in a fashionable area was regarded as a nuisance even though it provided a benefit to poorer citizens.

Defendants have the usual tort defences including *volenti*. But this does not mean that a person who comes to a nuisance cannot sue. For example in **Miller v Jackson** [1977], a person who purchased a house overlooking a village green on which cricket had been played for a long time was still able to establish that balls being hit into the garden were a nuisance.

The fact that an activity has taken place for many years as in Miller v Jackson will not itself be a defence. There is a special defence called prescription. This states that if an actionable nuisance has gone on for twenty years without complaint then the plaintiff loses the right to take action. The problem is that the 'clock' begins to run from the time the plaintiff is aware of the nuisance. So in **Sturges v Bridgman** [1879] the defendant had carried on a noisy process for over twenty years. A doctor on neighbouring land built a new surgery which was affected by the noise. He was able to sue. The noise did not affect him until the surgery was built, thus the fact that it had existed for the preceding twenty or so years was irrelevant.

SELF-CHECK 1

Scenario Two

Bellpit Ltd has installed new equipment to meet the demand for their products. Part of this development has involved them putting in a new electric power system. This system includes a small transformer which is housed in a specially built brick hut at the edge of the factory.

During this installation work a number of new houses have been built in the vicinity. The nearest now is only fifty yards from the factory. Within weeks of moving into these houses the owners complained of the smell from the factory. They also claim that the hum from the transformer is audible when they are in their gardens and is causing headaches.

Bellpit Ltd take the view that they were there first and that they provide employment to the local community. They agree to try to soundproof the transformer and make some attempts to do so but the neighbours complain that it has not worked.

Advise the neighbours.

The rule in Rylands v Fletcher

This is a variation on nuisance. It is used very infrequently but where it can be invoked it is a powerful weapon for a litigant. The reason for this is that it is a strict liability tort.

The case upon which this tort is based, **Rylands v Fletcher** [1861], involved the construction of a reservoir which caused flooding of some mineshafts on adjoining land. The rule is summed up from this extract from the judgment of Blackburn J. in the case:

'the person who, for his own purposes, brings on his land, and collects and keeps there anything likely to do mischief if it escapes, must keep it at his peril, and, if he does not do so, he is *prima facie* answerable for all the damage which is the natural consequence of its escape'.

Whether something is a non-natural user would seem to depend on the prevailing conditions. A factory is obviously brought onto land but if it is sited in an industrial estate it is probably not non-natural. Siting it in a residential area on the other hand may not be regarded as a natural use.

SELF-CHECK 2

State what you think are the essential elements of the **Rylands v Fletcher** tort.

Occupier's liability

Where somebody visits land and due to the carelessness of the user of that property he/she is injured then there it is likely that a claim in negligence can be brought. There is though a statutory tort, known as occupier's liability, which imposes on a land user specific duties. Unlike negligence and nuisance which are common law torts based on judicial decisions, the rules on occupiers liability are contained in two Acts of Parliament. Hence the term 'statutory tort'. The first Act deals with lawful visitors and the second with trespassers.

OCCUPIER'S LIABILITY ACT 1957
This Act covers what are termed 'lawful visitors'.

ACTIVITY 14

State who you think would be a lawful visitor onto your property.

People who you have invited have a right to be on your property. In addition there are certain people who will be there to fulfil a contract, for example milk delivery. There may be those who are permitted to enter, for example salespeople or next door's children collecting their ball from your garden. Finally some people have a statutory right to enter. Postal workers, police officers and employees of public utilities fall into this category. This does not mean that these people will always be lawful visitors. The person delivering milk for example has permission to walk up your garden path to the front door. Permission would not normally be granted to walk around the rear of the property or enter the house. A lawful visitor is therefore somebody with a right of access who acts consistently with that right.

Under the 1957 Act the duty is owed by the occupier of land. This is the person who is in control of it. Thus in **Wheat v Lacon & Co Ltd** [1966] a brewery which owned a pub was found to be an occupier even though it had a manager in residence. The reason for this was that the brewery maintained control of the premises and was responsible for the structure.

The actual duty is referred to as the **'common duty of care'** in Section 2 of the Act. This states that there is a:

> 'duty to take such care as in all the circumstances of the case is reasonable to see that the visitor will be reasonably safe in using the premises for the purposes for which he is invited or permitted by the occupier to be there'.

You should notice from the wording that the Act does not require an absolute guarantee of safety. The use of the word 'reasonable' suggests that the courts would rule on the level of precautions to be taken. If despite these somebody is injured then there will be no liability. Imagine digging a hole in the middle of your path. If early one morning when it was dark the milkman fell into it because he was unaware it was there then you would expect to be liable. If the hole was fenced off and had visible warning lights in place you would probably feel that if the milkman fell in then that it was his fault. The problem is knowing what is reasonable in any particular case.

It is possible according to the Act to **'extend, restrict, modify or exclude the duty to any visitor or visitors by agreement or otherwise'**. The 'otherwise' in this case could be the giving of warnings. In **Roles v Nathan** [1963], two chimney sweeps died when they were gassed by carbon monoxide leaking from a boiler. They had been warned of the dangers and were aware of the potential risk. On this basis the court held that the occupier had discharged his liability to them and that he was not responsible for their deaths.

A further point against the sweeps is that the Act states that an occupier may expect those with a special skill to guard against any special risks associated with that skill. This is balanced by a statement that as regards children an occupier must expect that they will be less careful than adults.

Note that under the **Unfair Contract Terms Act** 1977 as amended where the defendant seeks to rely on a notice limiting liability, this must be shown to be fair. clauses which are for example unduly one sided will not be regarded as fair.

OCCUPIER'S LIABILITY ACT 1984
The 1957 Act did not apply to trespassers. The old common law rule was that trespassers were owed a duty of **'common humanity'** that is, the occupier could not

deliberately injure them. There was no duty to protect from other hazards on the land. In **R Addie & Sons (Collieries) Ltd v Dumbreck** [1929], a child trespasser was badly injured when playing on some working machinery at a mine. The mineowner was found to owe no obligation to the child other than not to deliberately cause injury or act recklessly towards him/her. This decision may have been appropriate in 1929 but as time passed seemed to be unduly harsh and in need of change. Even after the passing of the 1957 Act Addie v Dumbreck remained as law since that Act specifically applied only to lawful visitors.

Change came when in **Herrington v British Railways Board** [1972] the House of Lords seemed to reverse the position in Addie Dumbreck. They did though leave the law in a state of uncertainty. Not until 1984 was this properly resolved.

The Herrington case involved a child who was injured while crossing a railway line. He was clearly a trespasser but it was shown that British Rail was aware that children frequently damaged a fence to get onto the line. Periodically British Rail repaired the fence and warned children of the dangers. Despite this they were made liable for the injuries suffered by the child because they were not deemed to have taken adequate precautions. This is an interesting case as it is one of the few examples of the House of Lords reversing one of its own earlier decisions. In finding for the child the court had to reject the Addie case.

The law was subsequently clarified in the **Occupier's Liability Act 1984**. This Act applies to the same class of occupier as the 1957 legislation. It imposes a duty towards trespassers where three requirements are met:

(a) that the occupier is aware of a specific danger or has reasonable grounds to believe that it exists;

(b) the occupier knows or has reasonable grounds to know that the trespasser is in the vicinity of the danger or may come within that vicinity; and

(c) the risk faced is one which, in all the circumstances of the case, it is reasonable that the occupier should guard against.

Damages only in respect of personal injury may be claimed.

SELF-CHECK 3

Brian has been a farmer for ten years on Aldy Farm. During this time people have commonly taken a short cut through one of his fields from a housing estate to a bus stop on the road. Brian erected a sign some time ago stating that the field is not a public right of way and that it may only be used for the purposes of passage to and from the bus stop at people's own risk. One day Brian put a horse into the field after it had attacked a stablehand in the farmyard. While in the field the horse attacked and injured Jennifer who was walking from the bus stop on her way home from school and Tony who was sunbathing in the field. Advise Jennifer and Tony.

Summary of section three

- users of land have a duty not to cause a nuisance to neighbours
- a private nuisance arises where a landowner uses his/her property in such a way as to unlawfully reduce the enjoyment of another person's use of land
- in deciding whether a nuisance exists the courts will look at the damage caused, reasonableness, location and duration
- public nuisance is a crime but those who suffer special damage may sue
- where a landowner brings an non-natural user of land onto his/her property under the rule in Rylands v Fletcher, he/she is strictly liable for damage caused by its escape
- under the Occupier's Liability Act 1957 a duty of care is owed to all lawful visitors to land to make the land reasonably safe for the purpose of their visit
- under the Occupier's Liability Act 1984 a duty is owed to trespassers who are or should be known to be on land in respect of dangers which might reasonably be anticipated.

Suggested answers to section three self-check questions

SELF-CHECK 1

The answer requires that you identify the problem as being a potential nuisance. Smells and noises (as in **Halsey v Esso**) have been found to be nuisances and so assuming that the complaints are justified then there are grounds to bring the action. The courts will consider issues such as location; duration; and reasonableness. The fact that the process is carried out in the vicinity of houses would suggest that it is in the wrong place, as in **St Helen's Smelting Co v**

Tipping. The specific defences of the company may elicit sympathy but are unlikely to influence the court greatly. The fact that one goes to a nuisance is not regarded as a defence (see **Miller v Jackson**) and the utility of the works in providing work is also not a defence (see, for example, **Adams v Ursell**). Unless the company can find some way of minimising the nuisance it will be found to have committed a nuisance. The court could award damages or an injunction or both. Clearly the award of an injunction would stop work at the factory completely.

SELF-CHECK 2

You should have identified that the basis of it is that a person brings something onto his land. The fact that it is brought on suggests it is something which is not normally there. Some cases have termed this a non-natural user of land. Secondly this user must escape; and finally it must cause damage. In theory it does not matter whether the escape is the defendants fault or not. The tort is one of strict liability, although in practice there are defences. *Volenti* is applicable as is contributory negligence; the fact that escape was caused by the unforeseen act of a stranger; and possibly, acts of God.

SELF-CHECK 3

It is likely that Jennifer can bring an action under the Occupier's Liability Act 1957. She is a lawful visitor with permission to pass over the land. The land is not safe for this purpose because of the dangerous horse. The question is whether the sign exempts Brian from liability. It will only do so if reasonable. Given that the horse has not been in the field before and it is therefore a new risk reliance on the old notice would not seem to be reasonable. If on the other hand a new notice had been erected warning people of the danger this may have been acceptable. It would also depend on the age of Jennifer. A notice which an adult would be expected to understand and act upon might not be sufficient for a child. On this basis it is likely that Brian will be liable.

Tony on the facts appears to be a trespasser unless it can be shown that Brian had allowed him to be present on previous occasions. In this case an implied consent might be found and the discussion in respect of Jennifer would apply. On the basis that Tony is a trespasser he is subject to the 1984 Act. Brian is certainly aware of the danger but cannot be expected to protect people whose presence he is unaware of. If he cannot be expected to know of Tony's presence in the field he will not owe him any duty of care. If he is aware of his presence it will need to be considered whether adequate protection has been given. The notice may not be enough since it does not give any indication of the danger and therefore does not provide an opportunity for Tony to take precautions.

SECTION FOUR

Liability in Respect of Employees

In Section Four you will find material to help you learn about and understand the following things:

- the employer's responsibility for the actions of workers
- the difference between employees and the self-employed
- the statutory framework ensuring the health and safety of workers
- the main requirements of the Health and Safety at Work Act.

Vicarious liability

Vicarious liability is the term applied where one person is made financially liable for the wrongful acts of another. This concept was introduced in Unit 2, Legal Relationships, when we looked at the contract of employment. This section duplicates some of the detail given in Unit 2 and builds upon it.

An employer is vicariously liable for the actions of employees. Vicarious liability is a way of imposing financial liability on an employer. It arises where the employer has done nothing wrong but where a wrong has been committed by an employee. To use vicarious liability against an employer demands that it would be possible to sue the employee personally.

Assume that a worker is driving a truck. Due to the driver's negligence a pedestrian is injured. In this case the driver personally could be sued and, assuming that the incident arose out of the driver's employment, the employer would be made financially liable. Now take the same driver who hits a pedestrian who suddenly steps out in front of the truck. The driver is driving properly and cannot avoid hitting the pedestrian. The driver is not negligent and therefore the firm will not have to pay compensation.

There may be cases where both employer and employee are separately liable. If an employer selects an untrained person to undertake a job and that person is negligent then the selection might be a separate act of negligence. For example a builder requires some electrical work undertaken in a house. He sends an employee who is a plasterer to do the work. The plasterer does it incorrectly due to his inexperience. The plasterer will be negligent and so will the builder. The builder's act of negligence is in sending an untrained person to do work which is inherently dangerous.

Vicarious liability does not seek to find liability where no fault exists. It is simply a way of apportioning financial responsibility.

ACTIVITY 15

What justification can you find for making an employer financially responsible for acts committed by workers which the employer is not to blame for?

The justification is essentially practical. An individual employee is unlikely to be able to meet even moderate claims for compensation. An employer on the other hand is likely to be a larger concern with greater resources. In addition the employer could act as insurer adding to costs to provide a contingency fund or to provide insurance cover.

THE PRINCIPLES OF VICARIOUS LIABILITY

These are set out in precedent. Essentially three separate factors must be established.

1. That one person has caused another injury because of a wrongful act.

2. The wrongdoer is in a special relationship with another person which has been recognised by law.

3. The action of the wrongdoer must have occurred within the context of this relationship.

In looking at these three points (1) requires us to find the individual liable for a wrongful act. If, for example, the incident is a matter of negligence then the principles described earlier in this unit must be applied. Where the act complained of is a crime then the employer is not made responsible for this. A driver caught speeding in a company vehicle is not able to evade a fine and penalty points by claiming that the incident took place within the scope of employment.

Liability for employees only

Generally an employer is only vicariously liable for the actions of employees. Employees should be distinguished from independent contractors, or those who are self-employed. Such workers are responsible completely for their own actions. The employer will not normally be vicariously liable for them. Before progressing further we need to be able to distinguish between employees and independent contractors.

It is usually easy to tell the status of an individual worker. One obvious way is to look at how the parties have referred to the arrangement. This is not always conclusive for the courts have in the past declared a worker to have one particular status when the contract between the two states something different.

An early attempt by the courts to distinguish between the two focused on control. The control test looked at the extent to which the 'employer' directed the work. If a person was told not only what job to do but also the way in which to do it then he/she was regarded as an employee. This test might be appropriate for manual jobs or some clerical jobs but falls down where the worker is a skilled or professional person.

The question which the courts try to answer now is whether or not the person is in business on his/her own account. This requires looking at all the factors affecting the relationship before coming to a conclusion. This is sometimes referred to as the **'multiple test'**. Try to decide the court's view of the following relationship. What you should do is look for all the things which suggest the workers are employees and those things which indicate they are self-employed. The two lists should then be balanced to see which appears to be most likely.

ACTIVITY 16

The case **Ready Mixed Concrete Ltd v Minister of Pensions and National Insurance** [1968] required the courts to decide whether drivers of cement trucks were employees or self-employed. The drivers purchased their own vehicles using loans provided by the company. The trucks had to be painted in the company's colours and could only be used to carry their cement. The company paid the drivers a set sum per mile driven and specified the route to be followed. The drivers made their own arrangements for tax and national insurance payments. They did not receive holiday or sick pay but could appoint a substitute driver.

Say whether you think the drivers are employees or self-employed and list the factors which lead to your conclusion.

The fact that the drivers have to follow the company's routes and carry only their product suggests an employment relationship. The mileage payment is not conclusive either way, nor is the method of payment of tax. The fact that the drivers own their own vehicles suggests that they are self-employed. This suggestion is reinforced by the fact that the drivers can appoint substitutes, a fact which the courts felt was inconsistent with the employment relationship. Accordingly, the workers were held to be self-employed.

It is becoming increasingly common for companies to use workers of differing status. Employees; self-employed; agency workers; and fixed-term contract staff may all work together. This can mean that financial liability is difficult to identify. The following case illustrates some of the problems.

SELF-CHECK 1

In **Mersey Docks and Harbour Board v Coggins & Griffiths Ltd** [1946], the driver of a crane was negligent and caused injury to a dockworker. The crane was owned by the Harbour Board who also employed the driver but was let out to Coggins & Griffiths. The agreement between the Board and Coggins stated that the driver was to be an employee of Coggins. Coggins could tell the driver where to work and what to do but not how to do it. The Board continued to pay his wages and had the power to dismiss him. State, with reasons, who you feel the employer of the driver was.

The use of the control test in this case may be less relevant now that the courts are looking at the wider issues inherent in the multiple test. Even using this approach it would be hard to see how the driver could be an employee of Coggins. An additional factor was that the hire of the crane was quite short term, usually for the unloading of one ship. The driver could potentially have several 'employers' on one day if the hirer was deemed to be his employer. This sort of case is relevant where firms hire staff from employment agencies for short terms. Frequently it is the agency which makes payment to the individual and which also makes arrangements for payment of tax and national insurance. This is not conclusive as to who is vicariously responsible for an individual worker. The confusion points to a general need to ensure that proper insurance cover is taken out in case of claims.

EXCEPTIONS
There are a limited number of situations in which an employer will be vicariously liable for the acts of an independent contractor. These are listed below:

1. If the employer is under a personal duty. For example the maintenance of safe working systems is a statutory duty imposed on an employer. If these are disrupted by an independent contractor the employer remains liable.

2. If the employer is in a position of strict liability then he/she will not be able to hide behind the actions of an independent contractor. For example if X contracts with Y to build a house by a set date and this is delayed due to the negligence of an independent contractor, X remains liable.

3. Where the employer is negligent in selecting the contractor such that the person selected is incapable of maintaining the required level of care.

4. Where the work is regarded as unusually hazardous the employer will remain liable.

5.   If the work creates a hazard for users of a public highway then the employer remains liable.

These exceptions have developed through case law and cannot all be argued to be rational. In the case of (1) and (2) the employer has an existing personal liability. If using an independent contractor would remove this then this would negate the liability and so this exception is justified. Similarly in (3) the employer has committed an individual act of negligence. (4) and (5) seem slightly odd. The justification is that if work is risky then the risk cannot simply be passed on.

In cases where the employer is made vicariously liable then whether this is for the acts of employees or independent contractors it will be possible to sue the worker responsible. In most cases of individual employees this is of little use since the person will not have adequate financial resources. It is common where sub-contractors are used in some industries to insist that they have appropriate liability insurance cover to protect the employer in case that person is made vicariously liable.

Within the course of employment

Once we have identified an employer we next have to decide the limit of the liability. Common sense suggests that this will not extend to everything the employee does. Where the employee commits a tort in his/her personal life away from work then this cannot be laid at the feet of the employer. For example if a company driver causes an accident when he is driving his own vehicle in his own time then it would be unreasonable to make the employer liable. What, though, of things which are done during work time which are not connected to the job or have even been expressly forbidden by the employer?

ACTIVITY 17

The facts of some decided cases are given below. In each case you are required to explain whether or not you think the action is taking place within the course of the worker's employment. You should consider what it is the worker is employed to do and then decide if the activity which caused the incident is within this employment.

(a) In **Limpus v London General Omnibus Co** [1862] the employer forbade its drivers to race buses. The driver in this case while racing a bus cut in front of another and caused an accident.

(b) **Beard v London General Omnibus Co** [1900] involved a company rule which forbade a bus conductor to drive buses. In the course of turning a bus around the conductor caused an accident.

(c) **Century Insurance Co Ltd v Northern Ireland Road Transport Board** [1942], involved a petrol tanker driver who while delivering petrol caused a fire when he lit a cigarette.

(d) In **Lloyd v Grace Smith & Co** [1912] the managing clerk of a firm of solicitors while advising one of the firm's clients defrauded her.

(a) In Limpus the driver was regarded as doing his job, despite the fact he was disobeying instructions. His job was to drive the bus and this he was doing. The employer was liable.

(b) In Beard however the job of the negligent employee was to act as a conductor. In driving he was going outside his job description and the company was not liable.

(c) This case involved clear negligence by the driver. He however was acting in this way while doing what he was supposed to do and therefore the employer was found vicariously liable.

(d) Here, we have a case of fraud which the employer has obviously not approved of. The court decided that the fraud happened while the employee was doing his job. He was employed to give advice to clients and this he was doing when the fraud happened. The employer was vicariously liable.

These cases point to a major problem for employers. In each case the employee was doing something which was either expressly prohibited or so obviously prohibited that it may seem unreasonable to make the employer financially liable. The reality is that the employer will be liable in cases like this unless it can be shown that the worker is acting completely outside the course of employment.

SELF-CHECK 2

Scenario Three

Bellpit Ltd has decided to extend its existing factory to meet demand and has purchased some land. Planning permission has been granted. There is in fact considerable building activity going on since some of the nearby fields have been sold for housing development and new houses (discussed in Scenario Two) have been built.

In order to increase production the company has started a night shift. As they anticipate that this will not be needed when the new factory extension is ready they decide to use an agency to supply staff. West-Midlands Employment Services Ltd (WESL) are appointed to provide 24 temporary workers. Bellpit Ltd arrange to pay a lump sum each week to WESL and the workers will then be paid by the agency. The agency pays the men a lump sum and they are responsible for their own income tax and national insurance.

As each batch is made there is a requirement to dispose of the empty containers. Some of these are steel drums which are returned to the suppliers. These are stacked in the works yard in an out of the way place. The agency workers have started to stack them nearer the factory area. Bellpit Ltd's works manager told them the correct procedure and stated that anybody who disobeyed it would be sent home. The following night the two men responsible for stacking the drums decided that they would move the drums all at once to the correct spot. They placed them against the wall outside the factory. As the morning shift came into work the stack toppled over causing a car to swerve which hit another worker, Susan, walking past.

It has now been discovered that Dave, one of the agency workers, has stolen a computer from the Bellpit offices.The computer had some important data contained on it. No backups had been kept due to an error and the loss of the computer will cost the company an estimated £10,000 in duplicating the information lost. The computer cannot be recovered.

Questions

1. Advise Susan whether anybody is vicariously liable for her injuries. You may assume that the agency workers responsible are themselves negligent.

2. Advise Bellpit Ltd whether they can recover from West-Midlands Employment Services Ltd for the loss of the computer.

Health and safety at work

INTRODUCTION

Some of the legal issues dealt with in this unit and in Unit 2, Legal Relationships, are relevant here. Where a worker is injured due to the fault of the employer then a claim for negligence can be founded. If the fault is on the part of a co-worker the employer is likely to be vicariously liable. This unit also made reference to the contract of employment discussed more fully in Unit 2. The contract of employment is the legal relationship between employer and employee. Just as in other contracts it contains both express and implied terms. One of the implied terms is a duty to make the workplace reasonably safe. While it is possible to bring actions under these headings, or even others such as occupier's liability, it is much more likely that an injured worker will use a specific piece of legislation. There are a number of statutes which are relevant but the most important is the **Health and Safety at Work Act** 1974.

Where workers are injured following a breach of safety legislation this will give rise to an action for breach of statutory duty. The statutory duty in this instance is to comply with the legislation. Where this does not happen then any person suffering damage as a result may bring an action.

THE STATUTORY FRAMEWORK

In addition to the 1974 Act there are a number of other pieces of legislation. **The Factories Act** 1961 and the **Offices, Shops and Railway Premises Act** 1963 are important examples of primary legislation. In addition there are some important regulations which have been issued as delegated legislation. These include: **The Reporting of Injuries, Diseases and Dangerous Occurrences Regulations** 1985; **The Health and Safety Information for Employees Regulations** 1989; and **The Electricity at Work Regulations** 1989.

The basic duty is laid on employers in the 1974 Act, that they must, as far as is reasonably practicable ensure that any place of work under the employer's control:

(a) is maintained in a condition which is safe and without risks to health; and that

(b) the means of entry and exit into those premises are safe and without risks to health.

The duty does not extend only to employees but to all workers and also to non-workers. Specific obligations imposed on the employer include:

- providing and maintaining plant and machinery that are safe and do not cause risks to health
- making arrangements for the safe use, handling, storage and transport of articles and substances
- providing information, instruction, training and supervision as is necessary to ensure the health, safety and welfare of employees

- ensuring the maintenance of any place of work in a condition which is safe and without health risks
- ensuring safe means of access to and exit from any place
- providing and maintain a safe working environment without risks to health and having adequate facilities and arrangements for employees' welfare.

The term **'reasonably practicable'** used in the Act, indicates that this duty is not one of strict liability. The courts will have to consider whether the steps taken by the employer have been adequate. Complying with codes of conduct and such things as recommended inspections for equipment would go some way to meeting this standard but will not always be accepted as adequate.

In **R v Fields Wholesale Meats** [1987] there was an explosion in a boiler caused by a badly corroded safety valve. This allowed a build up of pressure which was so intense that the explosion carried the boiler through the roof of a house 400 yards from the factory. The company had followed statutory guidelines for inspection and had in fact gone beyond these. The court decided that the corrosion pointed to inadequate maintenance even though the steps taken by the firm met statutory rules.

ACTIVITY 17

In **Anett v K and L Steel Founders and Engineers Ltd** [1953], a miner was injured when a mine collapsed. This was shown to be a rare type of collapse. What questions would you want to ask to discover whether the company had taken all reasonably practicable steps to protect him?

Questions you might have asked include the frequency of this type of incident; whether it could have been predicted by inspection; and whether any precautions could have been taken to minimise the consequences. The court discovered that in the previous twenty years it had not occurred at all. Usual examinations could not have predicted the slippage. Finally extensive (and expensive) supports would have lessened the effect of the collapse but may not have stopped it.

This type of discussion is similar to that we had when we looked at the case of **Bolton v Stone** in Section Two. The outcome was also the same. The court decided that the company had done everything reasonably practicable to protect the workers. Drawing an example from negligence is only an analogy. The duty imposed on an employer is likely to be higher under health and safety statutes than in negligence but the principles will be the same.

It should not be thought that the employer alone is subject to statutory duties. Employees are also responsible under the 1974 Act of looking after their own health and safety and that of the co-workers. These will not be as strict as those imposed on employers but require that employees act properly. Failing to wear safety equipment or tampering with equipment are breaches of the Act and in many instances have led to employees being fairly dismissed.

Making the system work

Health and safety issues tend only to be made public when things have gone wrong. Estimates from the Health and Safety Executive suggest that seventy per cent of accidents could have been prevented by management action. This can be interpreted as meaning that these 'accidents' could have been anticipated and steps taken to remove the dangers.

ACTIVITY 18

Assume that you have just taken over a factory. You will be installing new equipment and changing working practices. You discover that health and safety matters have in the past been almost ignored. List some of the practical steps you might take to bring the factory's health and safety standards up to an appropriate level.

You would certainly want to ensure that adequate maintenance was undertaken of existing equipment. New machinery should be purchased with safety in mind. Your new work practices should be as safe as possible. You would want to ensure that all employees were aware of the dangers and their obligations and had access to adequate safety equipment. Finally you would want to be sure that safety practices were adequate and were being followed.

All the above suggest a need to build safety into the design of equipment, premises and systems, and this is in fact the case. It is becoming increasingly common for firms to undertake a safety audit to identify risks. Once identified there is a need to state exactly what steps have been taken to meet these risks. This will not eliminate accidents but should go a long way towards minimising them.

SPECIFIC STATUTORY PROVISIONS

There are a large number of specific requirements contained within the health and safety legislation. The examples given below are those of significance to many employers.

The **Health and Safety Information for Employees Regulations** 1989 require all employers to give specific information through leaflets and posters.

Where a firm has five or more employees it is required by the 1974 Act to prepare and distribute a **health and safety policy.** This should cover at least: a general statement of the firm's interest in health and safety; details of special problems; who in the senior management of the organisation has responsibility for health and safety issues; and practical arrangements for ensuring health and safety, for example reporting arrangements.

Where a firm has recognised trade unions it is obliged by the 1974 Act to consult with safety representatives appointed by the union(s). Where two or more representatives request, a safety committee should be formed.

ENFORCEMENT

The **Health and Safety Executive** has already been referred to. This is the body which is primarily responsible for enforcing the legislation. A number of specific agencies regulate individual industries on behalf of the Executive, for example the UK Atomic Energy Authority. Local authorities also have an important health and safety role. They supervise health and safety provisions in, for example, shops, offices, hotels and restaurants.

The main weapon used by the enforcement agencies is the **inspector**. They have wide powers, including the ability to enter premises; make investigations; test machinery; take statements from individuals; and they have access to all statutory records of the firm. Where a breach is discovered or it is felt that one is likely to occur an **improvement notice** can be served. These state measures which the employer must take to comply with the Act.

Issue of an improvement notice does not stop a firm from functioning. If though an inspector feels that there is a risk of serious injury a second type of order can be issued. This is a **prohibition notice**. This can be used to close down a specific piece of equipment or process; a building; or even a whole company. Orders may be Deferred, that is the firm is given an opportunity to remedy the fault, or immediate. In the latter case the inspector feels that the risk is imminent. Where issued this order suspends work in respect of the matter complained of.

Contravening either an improvement or prohibition notice is a criminal offence which can lead to the organisation being fined. The employer may additionally be imprisoned for breach of a prohibition notice. It is possible to appeal against either type of notice. Appeals are made to an industrial tribunal. Until an appeal is actually heard, an improvement notice is suspended. A prohibition notice however remains in force.

Looking in your local newspaper will reveal serious infringements of these rules on a regular basis. While preparing this unit the writer came across two examples reported in a local newspaper on the same day. One involved a health authority which allowed an elderly person to be badly scalded in a bath which was too hot. The authority subsequently announced changes to its risk assessment and management policies. The second case involved a cash and carry firm fined £22,000 following the death of a worker. The worker was killed while standing on a raised forklift truck cage eighteen feet above the ground. It was noted that although the practice was forbidden by the management the rules forbidding it were not enforced. Again this pointed to poor health and safety management.

SELF-CHECK 3

Scenario Four

Bellpit Ltd is a small company which manufactures chemical based garden products such as fertilisers. One of the products made by the company is 'Oriole' a weedkiller which can be used on lawns. The product is in fact made under licence from a US firm Garpham Inc. Oriole is relatively easy to make. It involves a mix of easily available chemicals and the addition of an ingredient bought from Garpham Inc. The mixing is undertaken in sealed vats which are electrically powered. Workers are under instructions to stop the mixers before adding each ingredient. To add ingredients there is a small panel in the vat which is opened and the chemicals are poured in from containers which have the correct amounts in them.

Workers are required to wear protective masks when mixing any products as the dry powder can easily be inhaled. Although not fatal some of the chemicals are toxic and there are additional problems of powder entering the lungs of workers. Garpham Inc also supplies face protectors but some of the workers find them uncomfortable. As a result the company buys several types of mask and allows workers to chose the make they prefer. All the masks consist of a piece which goes over the mouth and nose which contains a filter. The filter should be changed twice daily.

The oriole weedkiller has proved to be popular and the factory is running at full capacity. The workers have been placed on a special bonus scheme to try to improve productivity and as a result a number of bad working practices are followed. For example, it is becoming common for mix to be added without switching off the mixer.

Several problems have recently arisen in the factory. Three workers are sick due to inhaling a chemical while mixing. It is felt that this was because they had used the wrong filter pad in their masks. Andy, one of the mixers has severe eye problems due to adding an ingredient to a mix without switching off the mixer. As he opened the hatch to pour in some of the mix flew out into his face. A number of other workers have complained of eye soreness.

Advise the management of their potential legal liability.

Summary of section four

- an employer may be legally responsible for the actions of workers even where the employer has acted properly

- there can even be liability on the employer if the employee does a prohibited act

- usually employers are only liable for the actions of employees but there are some occasions where there is responsibility for independent contractors

- it is not always easy to distinguish between an employee and an independent contractor: several tests have been devised by the courts

- for an employer to be liable the employee must be acting within the course of employment

- there are a number of Acts of Parliament dealing with health and safety

- the Health and Safety at Work Act 1974 lays down a number of basic duties on both employers and employees

- these duties apply to all workers not only employees

- the 1974 Act is enforced by the Health and Safety Executive which has enforcement powers.

Suggested answers to section four self-check questions

SELF-CHECK 1

The House of Lords decided that the permanent employer, that is the Board, was responsible for the employee unless it could establish strong grounds for moving that burden. Those grounds, it was suggested, were to do with the control of the process. In this case it was not the 'what had to be done' which was important but the control of 'how it should be done'. This control did not lie with the hirer of the crane but with its owner. Thus the Board was vicariously liable for the driver's negligence.

SELF-CHECK 2

In Question 1 the first matter to be settled is whether the workers are individually liable. We are told that they are. If we had not received this information we would have had to consider whether they had owed a duty of care; if they had been in breach; and whether damage was too remote.

The next question is to decide who is the employer. The case is similar to the Mersey Docks and Harbour Board example used earlier. This would suggest that West-Midlands Employment Services Ltd is the employer. The only possible problem with this is that the workers are threatened with being sent home if they continue to disobey instructions. This suggests a considerable degree of control. On balance however it is likely that Bellpit Ltd are not the employers.

Finally we have to consider whether the workers are acting within the course of their employment. Presumably their employer has told the workers to obey Bellpit instructions. Thus by not following them they are also in breach of their own employer's instructions. There are a number of cases, such as **Limpus v London General Omnibus Co**, which suggest that where an employee does a forbidden act the employer may still be liable. The question to ask is whether it is in the course of employment. It would seem that this negligent act is. Thus West-Midlands Employment Services Ltd will be vicariously liable for Susan's injuries.

Although the issue has not yet been discussed there is a duty on an employer to ensure methods of entry into and exit from the workplace are safe. It is therefore possible Susan could bring an action against Bellpit Ltd for a breach of the Health and Safety at Work Act. In this case Bellpit Ltd could sue the agency as being vicariously liable for its workers' actions.

A similar set of questions must be asked with regard to question 2. The big difference comes at the end where it is arguable that the theft does not occur during the course of employment. In **Lloyd v Grace Smith** the employer was found liable for the theft of an employee but here the theft happened in respect of property the clerk was employed to look after. Here the employment does not involve computers at all. On this basis West-Midlands Employment Services Ltd is not liable.

SELF-CHECK 3

The company's liability could be considered under two headings; common law and statute. Common law liability is likely to be in negligence or lie within the contract of employment. An employer will owe employees a duty of care and there will need to be a consideration of whether this has been broken. In addition there is an implied term in the contract of employment that there will be safe working systems. In practice it is unlikely that either of these actions will be considered since it would be easier to sue for breach of statutory duty in that the employer did not meet the standards of the Health and Safety at Work Act 1974.

The Act requires generally that employers provide a safe working environment. This encompasses systems of working, plant and machinery, instruction and information and storage and handling systems. From the problem it would appear that these obligations have not been met. Specific problems are:

- the use of the mask filters
- unsafe working practices and
- eye soreness.

Looking at each of these in turn the employer has provided protective equipment. Their use does not seem to be fully effective and points to a possible lack of awareness on the part of the employees. There may also be a failure in supervision.

As a defence, the firm could point to the fact that workers are obliged to look after their own health and safety and therefore failing to use the equipment properly could reduce damages as the employee is contributing to the loss.

The last point applies even more to the injury to Andy. By flouting safety procedures he has caused his own injury. He may however still have a remedy if it can be shown that management was aware of these practices and did nothing to discourage them. In this case the firm will not have done all that was reasonably practicable to ensure the health and safety of workers.

Finally the fact that several workers complain of sore eyes might indicate that there are irritants circulating within the factory. This would suggest a clear breach of the 1974 Act and the firm should investigate immediately to identify the cause. A failure to do this will itself constitute a breach of the Act. If a problem is identified then remedial action should be taken.

Given all these problems it might be appropriate for the firm to undertake a safety audit and review its' safety policy as well as deal with the immediate issues.

Unit 4: additional questions

Each of the following questions is free standing and in no way is connected to any of the other questions.

1. Bellpit Ltd. produces fertilisers, weedkillers and other chemical products such as slug pellets for supply to garden centres and then retail sale to the public.

   Alice goes to her local garden centre, Broadelm, looking for a gift for her husband. She bought a sack of lawn food and broad leafed weedkiller and a special little machine on wheels that is advertised as being ideal for applying this particular lawn food. She gives these as a present to her husband Bill.

   When Bill uses the machine it sprays the chemical up into his face rather than onto the lawn because it had been assembled incorrectly at the factory (owned by Bellpit). This causes Bill pain and he screams as the chemicals hit his face. The next door neighbour, Charles (an elderly retired gentleman), hears the scream and rushes to help Bill but trips over the handle of the machine and falls.

   Advise:

   (a) Alice, and

   (b) Bill, and

   (c) Charles

as to any legal redress they might have against either Bellpit or Broadelm and why this is the case.

2. Bellpit Ltd. produces fertilisers, weedkillers and other chemical products such as slug pellets for supply to garden centres and then retail sale to the public.

Alice (a model) goes to her local garden centre, Broadelm, looking for a gift for her husband. She bought a sack of lawn food and broad leafed weedkiller and a special little machine on wheels that is advertised as being ideal for applying this particular lawn food. She gives these as a present to her husband Bill (who is a presenter on the local TV channel).

When Bill uses the machine it sprays the chemical up into his face rather than onto the lawn because it had been assembled incorrectly at the factory (owned by Bellpit). This causes Bill pain and he screams as the chemicals hit his face. The next door neighbour, Charles (an elderly retired gentleman), hears the scream and rushes to help Bill but trips over the handle of the machine and falls. Alice also hears the scream and looks out of the window, sees the prone figure of Charles and the already disfigured face of Bill.

Bill suffers the loss of sight in one eye and is badly scarred on one side of his face as a result of the chemicals hitting him in the face. Charles breaks his hip when he falls (only having had a hip replacement operation 12 months previously). Alice suffers recurrent nightmares and partial hair loss and claims that this is as a result of the shock caused by the accident.

Bellpit claim that Bill must have been using the machine incorrectly for it to have sprayed the chemical in this way and that in any case the instructions quite clearly state that the chemical must not be used when the grass is wet (on the facts it is admitted that there had been a shower of rain that morning).

Advise:

(a) Bill, and

(b) Charles, and

(c) Alice

as to any possible legal redress they might have against Bellpit or Broadelm, the possible measure of damages and why.

3. Bellpit Ltd. has a full order book and requires to use its plant and machinery to the greatest possible extent to ensure that it can meet all of the orders on time. The factory workers are all promised a special bonus scheme if they exceed the targets set. Some of the workers start to ignore the safety procedures laid down for working the machines, other workers complain about this but are told by the management that they must keep quiet about it and get on with the work as fast as possible or lose their jobs.

Sheila, a shift supervisor, tells her team that they must take short cuts to maximise production and bonus payments. Sam, a chargehand, tells Sheila that this is stupid but when threatened with dismissal he gets on with the work in the way that Sheila demands. On one particular shift there is an accident when the guard rail on a machine is left open whilst the machine is in operation. Sam is operating the machine and is badly injured, Sheila goes to his help and is also injured.

Bellpit claim that the safety procedures laid down as standard working practice at the factory would ensure that such an accident would not happen. Sheila and Sam both intend to sue Bellpit for negligence.

Advise Bellpit as to what possible defences to an action for negligence it might put forward.

4. Bellpit Ltd's factory is situated close to a river. There has been a very sustained and heavy period of rain over the past few months and this eventually causes the river to burst its banks and to flood part of the factory. This has in fact happened twice before in the past 20 years, each time for a couple of days.

When it had happened before the factory had been closed until everything had dried out. On this occasion the factory had full order books and is having to work at full pace to meet the orders on time. As a result of this the works manager decides to buy in sawdust from the local sawmill and to spread this on the floor.

The sawdust is delivered and spread over all the main walkways, but there is not enough to cover all parts of the factory. The day shift works as normal without incident. The night shift arrives for work but the majority of the workers complain to the management claiming that it is dangerous to continue. After some discussion they agree to continue work for an additional payment for the shift.

The work goes on but part way through the shift a group of workers take an unauthorised break because it is Rex's birthday and he has brought in some cakes and beer. The group leave the main factory area and go to a little used part. When they are returning to work Rex slips on an untreated pathway, Phil and Ray go to help Rex and slip whilst carrying him along one of the treated pathways, they too are injured.

Advise:

(a) the company regarding their possible liability to the parties in both negligence and any statutory duties, and any defences they might claim, and

(b) Rex as to any possible claim and liability, and

(c) Phil and Ray as to any possible claims.

5.   Pro Cable plc have been awarded the contract to lay cables in the area around the Bellpit factory. Pro Cable have sub-contracted part of the work to Swift Bore Ltd and they are working on main road near to the Bellpit factory. Bellpit have told Pro Cable that they want the work finished by the scheduled date (notified to all companies in the area by the communications services supplier) because they need a new computer link to their head office and to the licence holder for the Oriole weedkiller to ensure that the correct percentages go into the product.

Bellpit are working flat out to meet their normal seasonal demand (as summer approaches), but have also recently received a large special order from a new golf course that is being constructed nearby. In order to meet these demands the company is working a three-shift 24 hour work system.

Swift Bore negligently cut through the main electricity supply cable. This means that Bellpit have to close down their manufacturing operation causing them to lose all the chemical mixes that are taking place at the time (these have to be scrapped and disposed of through a specialist company because they are unstable and dangerous) and they also lose the next two shifts because of lack of power.

Pro Cable had underestimated the time it would take to fully instal the system and this means that Bellpit do not get their communications link to the Oriole licence holder. This in turn means that they are unable to deliver the contract to the golf club on time.

Advise:

(a) Bellpit

(b) Pro Cable plc

(c) Swift Bore Ltd

(d) the golf club

as to what possible legal action may be taken (against and/or by) them, and what defences might be used.

6)   Bellpit Ltd is about to build a new factory. The official maps and charts showing the drainage, water table etc. of the site area are somewhat out of date and Local Survey Ltd has been instructed to prepare suitable new charts of the area.

The work is carried out, but on the final maps and charts an underground water course is left off which runs right through the site and makes it totally unsuitable for the development that is planned.

Shark plc, a large competitor of Bellpit, was undecided as to whether to buy shares in Bellpit as a possible lead in to a takeover bid in the future. When Shark sees that Bellpit is going ahead with the new factory (having seen a report in the financial press of the favourable site report) it decides to take up an option on some shares being sold by a member of the Bellpit family.

Bellpit has now discovered the underground water course (having bought the site and started to clear it). Luckily it is able to sell the site (at a small loss) to a theme park developer. Bellpit now announces that it will not be expanding (in any case there has been a downturn in the market). Shark, on hearing this, decides to sell its shares in Bellpit but is unable to find a buyer.

Advise:

(a) Bellpit

(b) Shark

(c) Local Survey Ltd.

7. Julie is employed by Bellpit Ltd as a receptionist. From time to time there are sales conferences at the factory and the car park is then too small. At such times she is asked to organise the parking of cars in the forecourt. She asks visitors and staff to leave their car keys with her at reception so that she is able to move the cars around if needed. She usually gets Ken (a caretaker) to push the cars so as to maximise the use of the area. Ken is employed by an agency but in fact has worked at Bellpit continuously for the past three years.

The works manager of Bellpit has recently issued written instructions that there is no insurance cover for cars being moved and that the practice must cease immediately. Everyone knows that this car moving has been done for a long time and that there is no parking within walking distance of the factory.

Whilst moving two cars Julie and Ken manage to collide, damaging both cars (one belongs to the chief accountant and the other belongs to a visiting buyer). Julie is also injured because Ken had decided to drive the car and he was unused to automatics.

Advise:

(a) Bellpit

(b) Julie

(c) Ken

(d) the owners of the cars.

8. Bellpit Ltd own a piece of land adjacent to the factory on one side and a sports playing field on the other side. The Bellpit land is going to be developed but at the moment is derelict. On the land there is an old water mill, dammed lake and rough tracks.

    The Bellpit management are aware that children use the rough tracks for riding their mountain bikes on and that some kids seem to be fascinated by the water wheel. Also in the last spell of very hot weather some people (adults and children) used the lake for swimming. Bellpit have put up notices warning people that it is private land and that there are dangerous places on the land. By the lake they have put up a huge notice warning people not to swim and to keep out because there are dangerous currents.

    Bellpit put up a fence around the water wheel and employ a local man to patrol the area during the day. This man shouts at children playing on their bikes, but this has little effect.

    The following happen:

    (a) a young man is injured when he falls from the fence surrounding the water wheel whilst climbing on the fence to try to retrieve a football that has come across from the playing fields, and

    (b) a child is injured when he falls from his mountain bike because a surveyor working for Bellpit had left a pole across the track (which was normally clear), and

    (c) a child gets into difficulties whilst swimming in the lake. An adult, walking his dog on the playing fields, hears the cries for help, dashes across to the lake and jumps in to aid the child but is seriously injured.

    Advise each of the parties involved in the above accidents, including Bellpit Ltd.

9. Megaprofit Ltd has a factory at which it manufactures gas cylinders and valves for industrial use. Much of the work is carried out in conditions requiring the use of safety equipment such as masks, suits, ear protectors, goggles etc. The raw materials for the cylinders are required to be kept free from corrosion prior to manufacture, any impurity being potentially hazardous.

    The day shift is highly monitored by management and the supervisor is rigorous in her application of the company's code of practice. The night shift has over the years operated separately from the day shift and the supervisor is not rigorous in his application of the code. Fred is moved from the day shift to the night shift and complains about the lax application of safety rules – he is ignored by management (the productivity of the night shift is excellent).

    The following occur:

(a) James, a welder, is injured but is not wearing goggles, and

(b) Kate, an electrician, is injured when two fellow workers (who have refused to wear safety boots) drop a cylinder on their own feet causing them to fall onto Kate's work bench, and

(c) some corroded metal plate is used in the manufacture of a cylinder which when tested explodes setting off another explosion that damages the next door factory (belonging to Bellpit Ltd), and

(d) a corroded cylinder passes the inspection process but explodes when used by the purchaser (Bellpit Ltd).

Advise the parties regarding the above incidents.

10. Advise Bellpit Ltd in each of the following cases:

(a) an employee is injured at work when a fellow employee negligently drives the firm's van over his foot.

(b) the land next to the factory has been bought by a private hospital which complains about the noise from the factory and the smells created by the chemical reactions in the manufacturing process.

(c) the company solicitor gives negligent advice which results in Bellpit losing several thousand pounds.

(d) an employee dies after being involved in an accident at work where some dangerous chemicals escape. The post-mortem shows that the man had terminal cancer and was only going to live for another six months in any case.

Additional questions: guidance

Each of the following outlines indicates the areas of law that might need to be addressed in order to reach some form of reasoned conclusion and advice. As with many aspects of law there is often neither a 'right' answer nor a 'wrong' answer it might amount to who wins the argument and therefore carries the day or it might merely depend upon who carries the day in court.

It is always useful in law to refer to decided cases that support the point you are making.

1. (a) Alice: has a contractual relationship with the supplier. The item is a good and the contract will be subject to the terms implied by the Sale of Goods Act 1979 (as amended).

(b) Bill: has no contractual relationship with the supplier of the good and will have to rely on the tort of negligence – the rules regarding an action for this to succeed should be outlined.

(c) Charles: is he owed a duty of care in negligence? Is the action reasonably foreseeable? Is it a rescue case?

See: Contractual Rules Re-visited. **Donoghue v Stevenson** – the nature of duty of care.

2. (a) Bill: has no contractual relationship with the supplier of the good and will have to rely on the tort of negligence. If there is liability what will the measure of damages be based upon?

(b) Charles: is he owed a duty of care in negligence? Is the amount of damage suffered by Charles foreseeable?

(c) Alice: has a contractual relationship with the supplier – will the Sale of Goods Act 1979 apply? Can Alice claim in negligence for nervous shock?

See: Negligence – **Donoghue v Stevenson**. Nervous Shock – **McLoughlin v O'Brien, Haley v London Electricity Board, Home Office v Dorset Yacht Co Ltd**.

3. Definition of negligence. Defences to an action for negligence, Main points including:

● Consent to a risk (*volenti non fit injuria* - no wrong is done to a person who consents). Did Sam consent or did the alleged threat from Sheila mean that he had knowledge of the risk but did not consent to it? Similarly for the general body of workers.

● Rescue case. Was Sheila acting as a rescuer and therefore not to be expected to be careful as would normally be expected? Did Sheila consent to the risk?

● Contributory negligence – does this apply to Sheila (or is it outweighed by theä rescue)? Were all the workers contributorily negligent by apparently accepting the working conditions?

Mention of the alternative effect of the Health & Safety at Work Act.

See: Defences to negligence. **Gregory v Kelly, Jones v Livox Quarries Ltd, Smith v Baker and Sons**.

4. (a) Negligence and the Health & Safety at Work Act – possible differing outcomes depending upon whether or not the company is deemed to have taken all reasonable precautions in the circumstances.

(b) Rex: were he and his friends acting in the course of employment or were they on a 'frolic of their own'? If the former the company may be liable if the latter the company almost certainly will not be liable.

(c) Phil and Ray: were they acting in the course of employment or would they be treated as rescuers?

See: Vicarious Liability, Health & Safety at Work.

5. (a) Bellpit: is there a contractual link between Bellpit and either of the companies involved (Pro Cable, Swift Bore)? If not what remedy might be available in negligence? What might the measure of damages be and how would this be arrived at?

(b) Pro Cable plc: have a contractual relationship with Swift Bore Ltd who appear to be in breach of contract. What would the measure of damages be (consider remoteness of damage). As an alternative is there a remedy in negligence? What rules would apply?

(c) Swift Bore Ltd: possible liability to Pro Cable in breach of contract, possible defence might be to limit damages to a foreseeable amount at the time the contract was made. In negligence the notion of economic loss would be used to try to limit liability.

(d) the golf club: Bellpit have broken the terms of the contract of sale with the late delivery.

See: Nature of contract compared with negligence. Remoteness of damage. Economic loss - **Spartan Steel v Martin & Co, Muirhead v Industrial Tanks Specialities Ltd.**

6. (a) Bellpit: nature of contractual relationship between Bellpit and Local Survey Ltd – is there a breach of contract? Does Local Survey Ltd owe Bellpit a duty of care in negligence (negligent statements)? Is there a breach of duty and damage resulting?

(b) Shark: does Local Survey Ltd owe Shark a duty of care? Is there proximity? If there is a duty of care what would the measure of damages be?

(c) Local Survey Ltd: has a contractual relationship with Bellpit, also has proximity with Bellpit. Measure of damages in both cases would be linked to the notions of remoteness and reasonable foreseeability. Did Local Survey owe any duty of care to Shark? Was there proximity?

See: Negligent statements **Hedley Byrne & Co Ltd v Heller & Partners Ltd, Esso v Mardon, Ross v Caunters, Caparo v Dickman.**

7. (a) Bellpit: are they vicariously liable for the actions? Will a prohibition be successful? Were the people employees? What was the course of employment?

    (b) Julie: is an employee of Bellpit. Had the custom and practice created her actions as a part of her course of employment? Can she sue Ken?

    (c) Ken: is he an employee (given the fact that he has given virtually continuous service to Bellpit for the past three years)? Is he acting in the course of his employment (for either Bellpit or the agency)?

    (d) the owners of the cars: is there a difference between the level of knowledge and therefore level of consent by the chief accountant (who should have known of the prohibition) and the buyer (who presumably had no knowledge)?

    See: Vicarious Liability. Notion of employee – **Ready Mixed Concrete Ltd v Minister of Pensions & National Insurance, Mersey Docks & Harbour Board v Coggins & Griffiths**. Defence of *volenti no fit injuria*, and contributory negligence.

8. (a) Is this person owed a duty of care under the Occupier's Liability Acts? Has the company acted reasonably in its efforts to minimise liability?

    (b) Have the trespassers become visitors? Are there allurements on the land? Has the company acted reasonably in trying to prevent the trespass? Does the firm of surveyors become liable for negligence and liable in its own right as an independent contractor?

    (c) Is the child owed a duty of care? Is the adult a rescuer? Does this make any difference?

    See: Occupier's Liability – also **Roles v Nathan, Herrington v British Railways Board**. General section on duty of care.

9. (a) Effect of the Health & Safety at Work Act.

    (b) Effect of the Health & Safety at Work Act, duty to fellow employees, amount of management supervision. Also possible action in negligence.

    (c) Statutory liability for provision of faulty equipment. Limitation to liability.

    (d) Negligence in the supply, also possible liability for product under the Consumer Protection Act.

    See: Health & Safety at Work Act – **R v Fields Wholesale Meats, Anett v K & L Steel Founders & Engineers Ltd**.

10. (a) Vicarious liability – was it an employee driving the van, was the person acting in the course of employment?

(b) Nuisance – nature of the tort of nuisance. Possible defences – is it a defence that the plaintiff moved to the nuisance?

(c) Negligent statements – notion of proximity.

(d) Nature of loss – was it foreseeable? Was it inevitable and therefore not as a result of the negligent act? Will it affect the measure of damages if damages are awarded?

See: general sections on the above topics as detailed earlier.

UNIT 5

EUROPEAN COMMUNITY LAW

Introduction to Unit 5

In this unit you gain an insight into the way in which the law of the European Union (European Community law) impacts upon the business community at a national level.

The European Union now represents a vast market and a window of opportunity for UK business and commerce. The basic principles which underpin the European Union are well known – the freedom of movement of capital, goods, services and people. What is less well understood is how the European Union has achieved these objectives by the emergence of a new legal order binding on Member States, with much of the impetus coming from the case-law of the Court of Justice of the European Community.

The aim of this unit is that you should understand how the European Union uses the law as the medium by which it achieves those objectives.

To this end you will study

- the emergence of the European Economic Community
- how the European Union is administered/governed by the four main institutions
- the sources and general principles of the European Community law
- how European Community law is intergrated at a national level
- the contributions of the Court of Justice to this process
- how European community law is enforced at both a national and European level.

SECTION ONE

The Development of the European Community

On completion of this section you will be able to :

- outline the history of the European Economic Community
- identify the reasons why it was established
- identify the four main legal institutions.

Introduction and history

The European Community was established in the aftermath of the Second World War, in order to bring stability back to the continent, to create a trading block with a large internal market, and to establish a consolidated unit of countries which would provide a barrier between the Communist powers to the east and America to the west. As well as being founded on strong economic principles, it was also a product of a desire to ensure peace – a desire which had followed the First World War, but which had not become a reality.

The first attempt at economic integration came about in 1951 when the Treaty of Paris was signed, establishing the European Coal and Steel Community (ECSC). The six member countries were France, Germany, Italy, and the Benelux countries (Belgium, The Netherlands and Luxembourg). The prime movers in this were the French Foreign Minister, Robert Schumann and his compatriot Jean Monnet who became the first president. The ECSC is significant because the structure used became the model for the subsequent European Economic Community. There were four institutions – the Council, the High Authority, the Assembly and the Court, all established to operate separately from the governments of the six Members States, to run the ECSC.

The success of the ECSC, establishing a model for economic integration and providing a framework within which vital industries were being re-established after the war, led to two more Communities being set up in 1957:

- the European Atomic Energy Community (Euratom) and

- the European Economic Community (EEC).

Euratom was set up to have a common approach to the development of atomic energy, and thus was limited in its scope, as was the ECSC. By contrast the EEC, under the Treaty of Rome was much more wide-reaching, and was clearly intended to bring about integration of the Member States in a way which would reduce the independent power of each state and limit the individual sovereignty of each country. The Member States, in signing the Treaty of Rome, were agreeing to give up the power of independent decision – making in certain areas, and were yielding that power to the centralised community.

An example of this can be shown from Article 3h, which stated that 'the activities of the Community shall include the approximation of the laws of the Member States to the extent required for the proper functioning of the common market'.

The same six countries signed the treaties. The institutions of the communities were merged in 1967, by the **Merger Treaty 1965**. Although the three communities remained separate, for all practical purposes they were administered as one. It was not until the Treaty of European Union agreed at Maastricht in December 1991 that the title of the European Economic Community was formally changed to the European Community.

Meanwhile, following the formation of the EEC in 1958, the United Kingdom had become part of a separate trading group, the European Free Trade Association (EFTA) with other West European countries which had not joined the EEC. EFTA was essentially an agreement of the partners to trade together, without any form of integration.

However, it was soon apparent that the EEC was by far the stronger grouping, and by the early 1960s the United Kingdom was keen to join the EEC. However, the then French President, Charles de Gaulle, opposed this, and the United Kingdom did not join until 1 January 1973, together with Denmark and Ireland.

The Community further expanded in 1981, to include Greece, and in 1986 to include Spain and Portugal. In the same year the **Single European Act** was passed, which brought about a number of important adjustments to the internal structure of the Community, and is most significant because Article 14 of the Act inserted a new Article 8(c) into the Treaty, setting out a commitment to 'adopt measures with the aim of progressively establishing the internal market over a period expiring on 31 December 1992.' This led to a period of intense legislative activity within the Community, and a large-scale public-awareness campaign throughout Europe, preparing Member States for 1992. The Single European Act also introduced the idea of adopting a European monetary system for the first time.

Even before the single market became a reality, on the 1st January 1993, the next stage towards even closer European integration had been taken with the signing of the **Treaty on European Union**, at Maastricht in 1992. The preamble to this Treaty states that members are 'resolved to continue the process of creating an ever closer union among the peoples of Europe'. It considerably widens the areas of co-operation, to include foreign policy and a move towards monetary union, as well as altering the internal structures of the institutions, to make them more accountable and to counter the criticism that there is a democratic deficit in the way the Community is run.

In 1995 Austria, Sweden and Finland became members, making a community of 15. Other countries, especially those from Eastern Europe, are keen to join, although Switzerland and Norway have both held referendums and a majority of their people have rejected membership.

ACTIVITY 1

a) From your reading identify the government that was in power when the UK joined the Community and the Prime Minister who was in power at the time. Since then how many attempts have there been to remove Britain from the EC/EU?

b) Try to identify reasons why membership of the EC/EU has been regarded as beneficial to the Member States.

c) Why are Eastern and Central European countries seeking to join?

d) From reading the newspapers or watching television news (or listening to the radio), identify two issues of importance with a European dimension.

a)   This will require some research in libraries – or you may already know this from general knowledge. The early sections of the textbooks review the history of the Community, and will be a helpful source of information for this section.

b)   Consider why the Community was established in the first place, and how much this has assisted the Member States in the latter part of the twentieth century.

c)   This answer will : riously link to the reasons you put forward in response to question b) above. ountries which have had a very different history since the Second World War ai: now seeking to become part of Western Europe. Again you may be able to answer this from general knowledge; otherwise do some research into recent c verts via quality newspapers and journals.

d)   Obviously there will be many to choose from, and answers will change from day to day! This activity serves to reinforce the need to become aware of current affairs in order to understand the development of the European Union.

The Treaty of Rome

This is the treaty, signed in 1957, which established the European Economic Community in 1958, and has been described as the written constitution of the organisation. It set the agenda for the development of a common market. The preamble states a determination 'to lay the foundations of an ever closer union among the peoples of Europe', and although much of the treaty is concerned with aspects of economic integration, clearly underlying it is the aim of bringing about this 'ever closer union'. It is from the treaty that the concept of the four freedoms is drawn – freedom of movement of workers, freedom of establishment, freedom of services and free movement of capital, and with these freedoms it is assumed will come the integration and co-operation which was the overall aim of the founders of the Community.

The treaty sets out the procedures for legislating within the Community. As a consequence of these legislative powers, the treaty created a new source of law which would affect all the Member States and the judgments of the European Court of Justice have repeatedly shown that legislation produced under the jurisdiction of the treaty is superior to national law.

The treaty also established the institutions of the Community, the Commission, the Parliament, the Council and the Court of Justice. Articles of the treaty lay down, in some detail, the composition of each body, the powers, and the way in which those powers are to be used. So, for example, Article 139 states 'The European Parliament shall hold an annual session. It shall meet, without requiring to be convened, on the second Tuesday in March.'

Other articles are somewhat less specific, but the treaty can be rightly regarded as the 'written constitution' of the European Community. Any changes to the structure of the Community can only be made by following procedures laid down in the treaty, and by amendments to the treaty itself. When it was agreed that an additional judicial body was necessary to cope with the ever-increasing workload, this required an amendment to the treaty (the addition of Article 168a).

SELF-CHECK 1

Explain why the European Economic Community was established in 1958, with particular reference to the political situation in Europe prior to this.

The four main institutions

These are the Commission, the Parliament, the Council of Ministers and the European Court of Justice.

The commission

The Commission exists to administer the Community on a day-to day-basis, and can be seen as representing the Community. It ensures that the treaties are correctly applied, and can initiate action against Member States in the European Court of Justice if they are in breach of the treaties.

The commissioners themselves (20 in number) are drawn from the Member States, and their main qualification is that they must observe a strict requirement of independence. The represent the communal European interest, not their own national background. The **Treaty of Maastricht** extends the term of office from four to five years, which is renewable.

The United Kingdom has always had two commissioners; selecting one from the party in government and one from the party in opposition. The majority of commissioners appointed have been senior political figures, many of Cabinet rank.

Lord (Roy) Jenkins of Hillhead held the position of President from 1977-1981. However, it was the president, Jacques Delors, who made the role very influential and who managed to weld the Commission into a strong collegiate body. He worked to bring the commissioners together as a team which shared a view of the future of Europe, which was stronger than individual national allegiance. The commissioners began to work together rather as members of the Cabinet do at Westminster. Under Delors' leadership the Member States established the single market in 1992 and then moved to closer integration with the Treaty of Maastricht. Until this last treaty the appointment of the president was carried out by common accord of the governments concerned; now the governments can nominate the person they intend to appoint, but are obliged to consult the Parliament.

The parliament

Originally called an Assembly, this body is very different from the expected 'Westminster' model. For more than 20 years members were appointed by national governments until direct elections began in 1979. Nor did the Parliament play a significant role in legislating – the Commission was the main body for initiating ideas and areas for legislation and deciding policy; the Parliament had the right to be consulted and the Council of Ministers has the power to decide if a measure is passed.

The weakness of the Parliament in this process has attracted much criticism. It was thought that the lack of any real role would lead to the Parliament attracting low calibre people, or politicians at the end of their careers, who would have spent most of their lives within their members state. More crucial was the perception that the Community suffered from a democratic deficit – that the people who were directly elected by the citizens of Europe actually had no real power in shaping that Europe.

There are now 626 members (87 from the UK), who are elected using the voting system of the particular Member State. All countries apart from the UK – with its simple majority system – use some form of proportional representation. The MEPs do have UK constituencies, but they are much larger than those of the Westminster representatives, and there is not the same sense of direct representation.

Within the European Parliament the MEPs sit according to their political party, not in national groupings. The largest party is the Socialists but it does not have an overall majority. Much of the work is done in committees, and is essentially of an advisory nature rather than initiating legislation. (This is discussed further in Section Two).

One issue concerning the Parliament which causes considerable debate and controversy is its physical location. The seat of Parliament is supposed to be decided by common accord (Article 216) but the best compromise to date is that the Parliament is located in three places – the committee sessions (by far the majority of the work) are held in Brussels, plenary sessions in Strasbourg, and the secretariat is in Luxembourg. This leads to regular upheaval as the MEPs and their staff move from one city to another, but the matter is still not resolved.

The Council

By contrast with the Commission and the Parliament, which focus on Europe and the Community and where commissioners have to be independent of national interest, the Council is the arena where the individual interests of Member States are represented. Its members are the national ministers from each of the Member States. Which individual actually attends a particular Council meeting depends on the subject matter under discussion. If the agenda is agricultural affairs, then the agriculture ministers are present. If it is budgetary matters, then the finance ministers are present – and so on.

Every six months a summit is held, when the heads of government meet to decide on future policy and strategy and to set the agenda for the next six months. When the heads of government are present the group is called the European Council. (This must be distinguished from the Council of Europe, set up in the late 1940s responsible for the European Convention of Human Rights and the European Court of Human Rights which meets at The Hague in the Netherlands). Since the Single European Act the European Council has been recognised as a separate body and the President of the Commission attends as of right. However, it remains outside the institutional framework acting as an intergovernmental forum.

The presidency of the Council is held by each Member State in turn, for a six-month period. The summits are held in the President's Member State – events which can be of enormous significance to a country. The Maastricht Treaty was finally agreed while there was a Dutch President of the Council. Although it took time for it to be accepted by all Member States, a small town in the Netherlands has now become famous.

The members of the Council, carrying out a very influential role in terms of the functions which they have, are in many ways at a distinct disadvantage compared with members of the other institutions. They have to combine a European outlook with individual national interest, and are having to pay heed to their electorate in their home country while also thinking of the Community. So the main focus of their work, inevitably, is national.

Many will only attend Council meetings infrequently and have a much more fragmented view of European matters than those working permanently for the other three main institutions.

The European Court of Justice

The Court was established, according to Article 164 of the Treaty of Rome to 'ensure that in the interpretation and application of this Treaty the law is observed'. There is no court structure or legal hierarchy with an appeal system, so the judgments of this court are binding across all Member States.

The Court has 16 judges, all of whom are required to 'possess qualifications required for appointment to the highest judicial offices in their respective countries'. They are appointed for a term of six years, and can be re-appointed. They are assisted by six advocates-general, who must be similarly qualified. They advise the Court on the correct interpretation of the law, and are required to deliver an opinion on each case, including a recommendation to the judges. These opinions are almost invariably followed.

The Court, which is located in Luxembourg, can sit in plenary session, but increasingly (due to the heavy workload) forms into chambers of three or five judges. Cases brought by a Member State or by a Community institution must be heard in a plenary session.

Under the Treaty of Rome the Court is empowered to establish its own procedural rules, Article 29 allows that the choice of language to be used in the Court is made by the applicant. All the official languages may be used, although the working language of the Court is French. Judgements are given in the language of the case, and subsequently translated.

Since 1989 the Court has been assisted by the Court of First Instance, again situated in Luxembourg. The jurisdiction of this court is severely restricted, as it cannot hear cases of political or constitutional importance, and it cannot hear any action brought by a Member State or Community institution. Its workload largely consists of the more complex and technical disputes in relation to trade quotas, and it also handles all the employment matters which arise within the Commission itself.

ACTIVITY 2

a) What is meant by the 'democratic deficit'? Can the institutions be seen as truly representing the people who live within the European Union?

b) Name at least one person who belongs to:

● the Commission

● the Council

● the Parliament.

c) Who would be likely to work in the European Court of Justice, and what qualifications would they need?

---

a) You may need to do some further reading to fully understand this criticism of the current institutional arrangements for the European Union. It focuses on the difference in the power of national parliaments in the Member States, and the role of the elected Parliament of the European Union.

b) Again, general knowledge may provide the answer – but try to name at least one person who is not from the United Kingdom. If you have real difficulties, contact your local MEP via the constituency office. This will give you access to a lot of information.

c)   You will be able to discover this by reading up on the Court in any of the textbooks suggested in the reading list.

The Treaty of Maastricht

This treaty has brought in major changes in the way the community operates, and many regard it as marking the point when the Member States moved from seeking economic union to openly seeking political and social union. Although there was considerable opposition in some countries, particularly the UK, the treaty was eventually adopted. It broadens the scope of community power, extending it into areas of foreign policy, home affairs and monetary union.

It also amended the functions of some of the institutions, most notably by giving the Parliament more power in the legislative process, enabling it to request the Commission to submit proposals to it, and allows for Parliament, acting jointly with the Council, to issue regulations and directives. Under Article 189b, the Parliament now has the right of veto over proposed legislation, although Article 189c allows the Council overriding rights to legislate once the proposal has been re-examined.

The Maastricht Treaty also created some new Community institutions – the Court of Auditors and the European Central Bank.

Terminology

Considerable confusion has arisen in recent years about the correct terms to use. The Treaty of Maastricht created the **European Union**, and the **European Community** is part of that longer union. References to Community law refer to law arising under the Treaty of Rome (the treaty which established the European Economic Community now called the European Community).

The **European Union** means the geographical area of all the Member States, and situations when they are working together outside the scope of the EC treaty.

The **Community** refers to situations when the Member States are acting together under the terms of the EC treaty (or may, of course, refer to the situation before the Treaty of European Union was implemented).

Over the years some of the institutions have changed their names; Parliament was called the European Assembly until 1987 when its name was changed to the European Parliament by the Single European Act (although it had called itself the European Parliament since 1962). More recently the Council of Ministers became the Council of the European Union under the guidelines on terminology issues by the Commission.

Summary of section one

- the European Community came into existence after the Second World War to unite Europe
- it has expanded in size and in the scope of its aims and the founding Treaty of Rome and subsequent treaties have facilitated this
- originally concentrating on economic integration, it is now moving towards much greater political and social union
- there are four main institutions establishing the legal framework of the Community
- these institutions have been subjected to criticism and are able to adapt to the changing circumstances.

Suggested answers to section one self-check questions

Self-check 1

The EEC was established in the aftermath of the Second World War, when many countries and governments were seeking to ensure that Europe became stable and peaceful. Economic growth was essential to bring about stability. With the success of the ECSC and Euratom which provided a mechanism and structure within which the six founding members were able to co-operate, the move to a more comprehensive Economic Community was seen as the next stage of this development. The United States of America also wanted a strong, united Europe, as a counter-balance to the Communist bloc.

SECTION TWO

The Functions of the Institutions

On completion of Section Two you will be able to:

- identify the role and functions of the main institutions
- analyse the inter-relationship of the Commission, the Parliament and the Council
- evaluate the recent changes in the role of the Commission and the Parliament

Section One introduced the four institutions – the Commission, the Council, the Parliament and the European Court of Justice – and in this section you will develop your understanding of the roles of these institutions, their inter-relationship with each other, and the recent developments.

The role of the institutions

THE COMMISSION

The role of the Commission has been seen to be the driving force behind the movement to European integration. The Commissioners and their staff have to represent the Community interest (which will often seem to be contrary to the interest of at least some individual Member States) and to ensure that legislation is implemented throughout the whole Community. The Commission is also responsible for the administration of the Community. It can be regarded as the equivalent of the Civil Service, although the number of staff employed is relatively small given the size of the Community.

The Commission operates through 23 directorates-general (similar to cabinet departments or ministries) each with specific areas of responsibility, such as agriculture, competition, external relations. Each director-general reports to a commissioner, some of whom head up more than one directorate. Those working in the D-Gs are assisted when necessary (for instance when drawing up new legislation) by committees of national experts who will advise on draft documents and indicate how national governments might respond to particular proposals.

A main function of the Commission is to initiate new legislation; it has certain powers to ensure that treaty legislation is being implemented and observed, and it also has an executive function in relation to administering certain funds.

New legislation.

Normally the Commission will initiate new legislation by making a proposal, which can relate to any aspect of the objectives of the treaties. The commission can act either on its own volition, or when requested to do so by the Council. There is then a stage of consultation and a commissioner present at Council discussions. Parliament also has the right to be involved (increased by the Maastricht Treaty) but its powers are still relatively limited when compared with a national government.

The Commission also has the power to complete the whole process of legislation. This power, which is very limited under the treaty, has been extended by the Council which has delegated such areas as the detailed regulations for the Common Agricultural Policy.

Treaty Observation

The function of the Commission here is contained in Article 169, which states 'if the Commission considers that a Member State has failed to fulfil an obligation under this Treaty, it shall deliver a reasoned opinion on the matter after giving the State concerned the opportunity to submit its observations'.

If the state concerned does not comply with the opinion within the period laid down by the Commission, the latter may bring the matter before the Court of Justice, using its powers under Article 169. An example of this involving the United Kingdom is the Factortame saga, discussed in some depth in Section Four of this unit.

This has been interpreted as creating four separate stages – an informal investigation by the Commission into any alleged breach of Community law, then a formal notice informing the Member State of the alleged breach; this is followed by a reasoned opinion if the matter has not been resolved; and finally the matter may be referred to the European Court of Justice. The majority of cases are settled informally, but about 70 cases a year go to the Court. (See Section Five for a more detailed discussion of this).

THE PARLIAMENT

The role of the European Parliament is essentially an advisory one. Although it is the only directly-elected body within the Community's legal framework, it has power to advise and supervise the legislative process, but it is not a genuine legislature by comparison with the Parliaments of Member States, because it is largely a consultative body, rather than an initiating institution.

Much of the work of the Parliament is done by standing committees, which 'shadow' the various directorates-general, and these committees examine and debate the various legislative proposals in depth. However, the Parliament's power to actively intervene is regulated in three ways; it has the right to be consulted, or the right to co-operate with the Council, or the right to make a co-decision with the Council, depending on the type of legislation proposed and the subject matter. If Parliament is not consulted, then any legislation so passed may fail to be implemented or to be upheld by the European Court of Justice because of this procedural deficiency.

Where the Council is required to co-operate with the Parliament, it can only disregard the views of the Parliament if the Council is unanimous. If the legislation requires a co-decision, then the European Parliament by failing to adopt the proposal will bring about its defeat.

The Parliament could adopt significant delaying tactics, because even though time limits are laid down for taking decisions and referring the issue back to the Council, these could allow considerable delay and backlog of legislation. Since 1993, with the Treaty of European Union, there is virtually no legislation which does not require some parliamentary involvement.

Parliament can also exercise some supervision over the Commission – including having the power to dismiss, and the right to interview all Commissioners before they are approved.

THE COUNCIL

As already outlined in Section One, membership of the Council will change from one meeting to the next, depending on the topic under discussion. To some extent this seems to give the Council a conflicting role – it serves both as a meeting place for ministers representing the various national interests of the Member States, and also it is a key Community institution with the greatest legislative powers. Under Article 145, the Council co-ordinates economic policies, has power to take decisions and to arrange for the Commission to implement them. The Council meets in private, which may partly explain its success as a Community institution. The individual members, away from press scrutiny, can focus on European matters without being criticised for neglecting national interests.

There are three systems of voting in the Council: simple majority, qualified majority, and unanimity. For qualified majority voting, different weight is given to the votes of the various Member States. Italy, Germany, France and the UK each have 10 votes, whereas Luxembourg – the smallest state – has two, with votes allocated pro rata to the other members. The system of qualified majority voting has been introduced to get away from a simple system of equality regardless of size and population but at the same time it prevents the larger countries from outvoting the smaller countries. The majority required is just over two-thirds of the total votes cast.

There are a considerable number of occasions when unanimity is required (for example the admission of new Member States) but qualified majority voting has now become the norm. However, it should be noted that even where majority voting is prescribed by the treaty, a state may invoke the veto which arises from the so-called Luxembourg Compromise of 1966. In practice, this is rarely used. Clearly, though, majority voting means a greater loss of sovereignty by Member States.

Because the membership of the Council changes so frequently, it is assisted by the Committee of Permanent Representatives (COREPER), which is 'responsible for preparing the work of the Council and for carrying out the tasks assigned to it by the Council' (Article 4 of the Merger Treaty). This body, made up of senior civil servants, provides the necessary continuity for the Council, and carries out much of the preparatory work of reviewing Commission proposals. It has an important role in liaising between the Commission and the Council.

It also receives assistance from the Economic and Social Committee (ECOSOC), established by Article 4 (2) of the Treaty of Rome, intended to ensure that various groups within the community are consulted. It is made up of representatives of various interest groups, which broadly fall into three categories – employers, workers and others including farmers, consumers, and the various professions.

It will be recalled from the previous section that heads of government meet at the six-monthly summit meetings as the European Council, to decide on long-term future policy. These meetings were not formalised until 1974, but their value and significance had been realised in the first twenty years of the Community's existence. Under Article D of the Treaty of European Union the European Council is charged with providing the necessary impetus for the continued development of the organisation, and with defining the general political guidelines. This Article also gives the President of the Commission the right to attend these meetings.

However, it should be remembered that the European Council remains outside the institutional framework of the EC; its powers are not defined and its acts are not reviewable by the European Court of Justice.

THE EUROPEAN COURT OF JUSTICE

The role of the European Court of Justice (ECJ) is purely judicial and this means that it is the easiest of the institutions to understand. According to Article 164 of the Treaty of Rome, it has 'to ensure that in the interpretation and application of this Treaty the law is observed', and in so doing it functions like almost any other court.

The judges and their staff are all situated in Luxembourg, and there is a strong sense of collegiality. The Court has very wide jurisdiction for not only does it have the power to settle questions of Community law on issues brought to it by the Commission but it can also (under Article 177) decide on issues referred to it directly from courts within all the Member States. This means that decisions of the court can go directly into the internal legal systems of the countries, without the necessity of a drawn-out, lengthy, time-consuming appeals procedure. It also brings the working of the ECJ much closer to that of lawyers within the Member States, thus assisting with the process of rapid and meaningful integration of law.

Much of the Court's work is involved with ensuring that Member States fulfil their obligations under Community law. Actions can be brought by the Commission and by other Member States, and all allegations of failure to comply are initially investigated by the Commission. About one-third are resolved informally, without recourse to formal legal proceedings.

It also has substantial powers to review the validity of the legislative acts of the institutions. (This will be examined in detail in Section Five).

ACTIVITY 3

a) Which institution is responsible for:

   i) new legislation?

   ii) ensuring Community law is followed?

   iii) Community administration?

   iv) judicial decisions?

   v) policy-making?

b) List three ways in which the European Parliament differs from the Parliament at Westminster.

---

a)   You will find this information in the recommended reading, within the sections on the institutions. Many such textbooks include diagrams explaining the legislative process which you may find helpful.

b)   You may need to return to Section One for this; if you are not aware of how the Westminster Parliament operates, then refer to a textbook on the British constitution.`

Inter-relationship of the institutions

The inter–relationship of the Council, Commission and Parliament is relatively complex, because of their overlapping areas of responsibilities and functions. Both the Commission and the Council can initiate legislation, and Parliament has the right to be consulted, involved in a co-decision procedure with the Council, or has the right to co-operate with the Council.

When the Commission makes a proposal for legislation Parliament must be consulted (together with the Council) and failure to do so will invalidate any subsequent legislation. The Parliament is consulted relatively early in the procedure and its opinions are taken into account before the final proposal goes to the Council to be adopted.

Parliament's powers were strengthened under the Single European Act, when the co-operation procedure was introduced. The Commission and the Council have first to reach a 'common position', using the stages of the routine 'consultation' process, and then the Parliament has three months to approve, reject or amend the proposal.

The Council's further actions can be seriously affected by this. At the most extreme, if the Parliament rejects a proposal the Council members have to be unanimous in adopting it.

The co-decision procedure, brought in by the Maastricht Treaty, gives Parliament equal status with the Council. Again there is the requirement in the early stages for the Council and the Commission to reach a 'common position', but if Parliament disagrees with this common position a conciliation committee is set up, to seek some compromise proposal, acceptable to both sides. If Parliament still rejects the proposal, by an absolute majority, then it cannot be adopted. The legislative process has become increasingly convoluted with the attempts to get Parliament more closely involved and so address the democratic deficit.

This rather complicated inter–relationship of the institutions within the legislative process is further confused by the power of the Commission to oversee the implementation of legislation within Member States, and leads to the continued criticism that the Commission, an unelected body, has too much power.

Recent changes

Recent developments in the European Community have fallen into two broad categories – the move from economic integration to political and social union and changes to the institutional structures to give Parliament greater powers. Both of these trends were addressed by the Maastricht Treaty, which created the European Union in place of the Economic Community.

In relation to the institutional structures, under this treaty Parliament has gained the power of co-decision in certain legislative matters, and has also been given a right of veto to proposed legislation under Article 189b. The Parliament is also now more involved in the appointment of commissioners, and in particular in approving the selection of the President of the Commission. At the same time the Commission, which used to have six vice-presidents, has now had the number reduced to two.

Parliament also has increased powers in international matters following Maastricht. The Council must consult with Parliament on 'the main aspects and basic choices of the common foreign and security policy' (Article J7, Treaty of European Union) and must also ensure that Parliament's views are duly taken into consideration.

Summary of section two

- the commission is responsible for administration of the EC
- it operates through Directorates - general
- its main functions encompass initiation of new legistation and policing the enforcement of the treaties
- Parliament is democratically elected with a role to play in the legislative,

process. However, its role is still mainly advisory
- the council has the greatest legislative powers
- it processes business by simple majority, by unanimity, or, most usually now, by qualified majority voting
- it is assisted by CORPER and ECOSOC
- it meets every six months as the European Council
- the European Court of Justice has a purely judicial role
- settles questions of EC law, reviews legislative acts, and ensures the Member States fulfil their EC obligations.

SECTION THREE

The Sources of European Community Law

On completion of this section you will be able to:
- identify how the law of the European Community became part of English law
- locate the enacted sources of European Community law
- identify the general principles of European Community law
- analyse how European Community law is interpreted.

Transformation of European Community law into English law

European Community law is based upon international treaties made between the Member States. It is a form of international law which has evolved in such a way that it is now a truly supranational system of law. By this we mean that it has an existence which is independent of the states which created it. The first problem to resolve is how European Community law becomes part of the national law of a Member State.

When a Member State joins the Union, it will be necessary for it to comply with whatever its particular constitution requires should be done in order for an obligation of international law to have an impact nationally. This, in turn, will depend upon whether the state subscribes to a monist or dualist view of international law.

The **monist** approach regards international and national law as being part of a single legal structure notwithstanding that they operate on different planes. Thus, as long as the requisite constitutional procedures are complied with, treaty provisions are incorporated into domestic law. Examples of states which espouse the concept of monism are France and The Netherlands.

Dualism, on the hand, regards international and national law as distinct systems. The UK is a dualist state and this means that obligations under international law will only be enforced in national courts when the particular provisions have been transformed into national law by domestic legislation. In order to achieve this result in the UK, the **European Communities Act 1972** was enacted.

ACTIVITY 4

(a) Since the UK joined the then European Community in 1973, there have been two major revisions to the European Economic Community Treaty 1957. In 1987 there was the **Single European Act** whilst in 1992 there was the **Treaty on European Union**, (the Maastrict Treaty). Identify the domestic legislation which transformed these two treaties into national law in the UK.

(b) Identify at least one other monist state and one which is dualist in nature.

(a) This information can be found either in text books on European law or in text books on the English legal system or constitutional law. Alternatively, if you wish to go to primary sources, *Halsbury's Statutes*, available in most decent libraries, will contain the relevant legislation.

(b) You might find this in standard European law texts or in general texts on public international law.

The enacted sources of European Community law

PRIMARY SOURCES

As previously explained, the European Union is built upon international treaties. Thus, these treaties constitute the primary sources of EC law. There are the three treaties which created the original communities, the European Coal and Steel Community 1951, European Atomic Energy Community 1957 (Euratom) and, most importantly, the European Economic Community 1957. In addition there is the Treaty on European Union 1992 which gave us the European Union in its present form and which formally renamed the EEC as the European Community.

Each time the Union expanded there was an Accession Treaty signed between existing and new members. **The Merger Treaty 1967**, as outlined in Section One, amended the three original treaties by placing them under the same institutions so that, although still formally three communities, they were effectively administered as one. In 1986 the Single European Act, effective from 1987, was the first major amendment to the European Economic Community Treaty, creating new competeces and changing voting powers.

It is appropriate at this point to explain why we still refer to European Community law rather than European Union law. The Treaty on European Union is built upon three pillars. The central and weight-bearing pillar comprises the three communities, whilst two outside pillars consist of Foreign Affairs and Security and Home Affairs and Justice. The two outside pillars remain, at the moment, outside of the competences of the institutions. Any advances in these areas can only be made by intergovernmental agreement and will then require incorporation into national legal systems. Accordingly, the vast body of law which now forms part of the national legal systems of the Union and which continues to grow is properly called European Community law.

Thus, as the primary sources of Community law, it is the treaties to which lawyers must refer in the event of any doubt as to the scope or validity of a particular measure. All other enacted sources are secondary.

SECONDARY SOURCES

Article 189 EC (as amended by Single European Act and Treaty of European Union) sets out the different forms which the EC secondary legislation may take:

'In order to carry out their task and in accordance with the provisions of this Treaty, the European Parliament acting jointly with the Council, and the Commission shall make regulations and issue directives, take decisions, make recommendations or deliver opinions.

A regulation shall have general application. It shall be binding in its entirety and directly applicable to all Member States.

A directive shall be binding, as to the result to be achieved, upon each Member State to whom it is addressed, but shall leave to the national authorities the choice of form and methods.

A decision shall be binding in its entirety upon those to whom it is addressed.

Recommendations and opinions shall have no binding force.'

So it can be seen that whilst the treaties set out the basic legislative framework, it is for the Parliament, the Council and the Commission to amplify the law by the issuing of regulations, directives and decisions. (As recommendations and opinions are of no binding effect we will not consider them further.)

Regulations are the most important source of secondary legislation in that they are of general application and take effect in Member States without the need for further implementation at a national level (ie. they are 'directly applicable'). Article 191 proves that regulations must be published in the *Official Journal of the Community*.

By way of an example, Articles 85 and 86 of the EC treaty outlaw certain anti-competitive practices which would inhibit free trade in the European Union. Article 87 empowers the Council to adopt measures to give effect to the principles outlined in Articles 85 and 86. The Council did so in Regulation 17/62 in which it set up mechanisms whereby the Commission has the power to investigate potential breaches of Articles 85 and 86 and to issue decisions as a consequence of its investigations which then bind the investigated parties.

Directives stipulate an objective to be achieved but leave it to individual Member States to decide how best to achieve that objective. In the UK this will usually take the form of an Act of Parliament or statutory instrument. Directives specify a time limit within which they must be implemented – usually two years.

Since the Treaty of European Union, when a directive is addressed to all Member States it must be published in the *Official Journal of the Community*.

The advantages of a directive are that it gives a member state time to adjust its law to the desired objective and that it may be used when harmonisation rather than uniformity of law is appropriate. By harmonisation we mean that national laws of Member States are approximated to achieve a common objective whereas uniformity means that the same law is applied across the Union.

In 1985 the Product Liability Directive (Directive 85/374) was adopted in order to harmonise the laws in Member States on liability for injury caused by defective consumer products. In the United Kingdom, this became Part 1 of the Consumer Protection Act 1987. Thus, as a direct consequence of the UK's membership of the EU, consumers in the UK are better protected against injuries and damage to property arising from shoddy goods.

Decisions are administrative acts binding upon the individual company or member state to which they are addressed. Certain decisions must be published in the

Official Journal. As explained already, a decision will be used, by the Commission when it has concluded that an undertaking has breached competition policy, or, for example, by the Council under Articles 92, 93 in respect of state aids held to be compatible with the common market.

In **Sealink Band and I – Holyhead** [1992] the Commission decided that the organisation of ferry schedules at Holyhead to favour Sealink's ships would undermine the ability of other ferry operators to compete and was, therefore, unlawful. Obviously, free competition should benefit consumers in bringing down prices and increasing the number of crossings. Thus, although the decision is limited in its application, it can be seen how it creates a general effect.

Note that Article 190 requires regulations, directives and decisions to set out the reasons upon which they are based.

Every community act is numbered together with the year of enactment (for example Directive 68/360, Regulation 1251/70).

ACTIVITY 5

(a) Explain what is meant by 'directly applicable' legislation.

(b) Identify a Community regulation and directive applicable to the free movement of workers. In the case of the directive, discover how it has been implemented by the UK.

(a) You should be able to answer this from the preceeding information covered in this section. Further information is to be found in standard text books.

(b) Whilst the primary source for such information is the *Official Journal* you will be able to discover some examples in standard text books.

The general principles of EC law

In addition to the enacted sources of Community law there have evolved certain general principles. These are not to be found anywhere in the treaties but have been developed by the Court of Justice. They constitute both a means of protecting the individual by reviewing Community acts against them and a means of developing a coherent Community legal system by filling in the gaps in the treaties.

Every legal system has certain general principles which are accepted by all and it is to the legal systems of Member States the Court of Justice has looked for development of these principles as well as to the treaties.

As regards justification for the development of these important principles, the Court of Justice has referred to Article 164 EC which requires the Court to ensure that 'the law is observed' and to Article 173 EC which empowers annulment of Community legislation by the Court for 'infringement of this Treaty, or any rule of law relating to its application'. More specifically, Article 215 enables the Court to order the Community to pay compensation for damage it has caused, 'in accordance with the general principles common to the laws of Member States'.

It is not necessary for a general principle to be common to all Member States for it to be accepted as Community law. The general principles are not just of constitutional importance but serve a great practical purpose in that they are used as a tool of interpretation to clarify ambiguous Community legislation, as a ground of annulment of Community measures and as a basis for an action in damages against the Community.

FUNDAMENTAL HUMAN RIGHTS

The Court of Justice first recognised the protection of human rights as a general principle in **Stauder v Ulm** [1969], a case where Stauder was required to give his name when he applied for discounted butter under a Community scheme. The Court of Justice ruled 'the provision at issue contains nothing capable of prejudicing the fundamental human rights enshrined in the general principles of Community Law and protected by the Court'.

There followed several examples of the Court of Justice reaffirming the general principle of fundamental human rights but finding, on the facts, that the contested legislation did not breach the principle. A successful challenge is found in **R v Kirk** [1984] where Kirk, a Danish skipper, was charged with breach of a UK law which forbade Danish boats from coming within twelve miles of the UK coast.

The UK exclusion zone had been originally permitted by the EC in the Accession Treaty signed by the UK but it expired on 31.12.82 to be renewed for a further ten years from 1.1.83 by Council Regulation 170/83 adopted on 25.1.83. Thus, the regulation purported to act retrospectively for the period 1.1.83 to 24.1.83. and it was during this period that Kirk was arrested. The Court ruled that it was contrary to the protection of fundamental human rights that a penal provision should have retrospective effect.

PROPORTIONALITY

The essence of this principle derived from German law is that a measure shall not impose a greater burden on a citizen than is necessary in order to achieve the aim of the measure. It is somewhat akin to the idea that you do not take a sledgehammer to crack a nut or that the means must be justified by the end.

A good example is **ex parte Mann (Sugar Ltd)** [1985] where, under a Community regulation, an applicant for a grain licence who was four hours late in submitting his application, forfeited his entire deposit which was in excess of £1,500,000. The Court, not surprisingly, held this to be disproportionate.

It should be noted that the principle of proportionality has played a particularly important role in EC law. In addition to its use as a yardstick against which the legality of EC law and the implementing legislative acts of Member States are measured, it has become an essential ingredient in the assessment of whether a national measure which interferes with the free movement of goods, persons, services and capital is justified.

Thus, in **Stoke-on-Trent and Norwich City Councils v B & Q** [1993], the Court of Justice ruled that, although the Shops Act 1950, which banned Sunday opening, restricted trade in the European Union, the measure was not disproportionate as a means of achieving the objective of maintaining the special nature of Sunday in the UK. (Since this decision the UK has introduced new legislation which makes Sunday opening lawful between certain hours).

EQUALITY AND NON-DISCRIMINATION

The notion of equality means simply that there should be no differentiation in the treatment of similar situations. This has been developed into a general principle of law by the Court of Justice but it owes its derivation to the general rule against discrimination on grounds of nationality (now Article 6 EC) and the rule found in Article 119 EC that there should be no discrimination in pay between men and women doing equal work.

In the **Skimmed Milk Powder Case** [1977], the Court of Justice held a regulation to be invalid because it discriminated against certain farmers, by bringing about a threefold increase in feed prices. (This regulation was also found to offend the principle of proportionality.)

It should be noted that the one situation where the EC legislative may treat similar situations differently is where such differentiation may be objectively justified. Thus, for example, a measure which discriminated in favour of recycled oil over new oil might be justified by the Community-wide objectives of protecting the environment and conservation of fossil fuels.

LEGITIMATE EXPECTATION

The Court of Justice will not allow an EC measure to stand if it offends an individual's legitimate expectation. Thus, a measure should not violate a reasonably held belief of someone affected by the measure that he would be treated in a particular way by a Community institution.

In **Mulder** [1988] the Court struck out parts of EC regulations which related to the marketing of milk because they were contrary to the principle of legitimate expectation. Here, certain milk producers had been encouraged to opt out of milk deliveries for a five year period in order to reduce a surplus. At the end of five years they discovered they could not resume deliveries because of regulations introduced by the EC which were based on a typical year during the period when they were not marketing.

However, it must be pointed out that there is no legitimate expectation that a particular legal status quo will continue. A change may be unavoidable or in the public interest.

LEGAL CERTAINTY/NON-RETROACTIVITY

Related to the principle of legitimate expectation is the concept of legal certainty whereby, in broad terms, the law should be both ascertainable by those to whom it applies and predictable in its application. Whilst the principle has been applied in a number of varying ways, the Court of Justice has been particularly vigilant in holding that an EC measure may not take effect before its date of publication. Thus, in **Exportation des Sucres** [1977], a regulation was due to take effect on a particular day. Owing to a strike, publication of the regulation in the *Official Journal* took place a day later. The Court of Justice held that the regulation should take effect from the actual date of publication.

Although the Court of Justice has consistently held that a measure should not be retroactive, there are examples where it has been allowed when the Court has been convinced that the legitimate expectation of those concerned is not thereby compromised. A rather questionable case where this occurred is **Case 108/81 Amylum** [1982]. A regulation had been annulled in **Case 138/79 Roquette** [1920] for lack of consultation with Parliament. (See Section Five). A new regulation was introduced to replace the annulled one and its effect was backdated to the time when the original regulation had come into force. Amylum challenged the second regulation on the ground that it breached the principle of legal certainty. Somewhat surprisingly, the Court of Justice disagreed.

PROCEDURAL RIGHTS

Whereas some procedural rights such as the publication of a measure (Article 191 EC) and the reasons for it (Article 190 EC) are specified in the treaties, the Court of Justice has also developed the notion of procedural rights as a general principle. This is mainly seen in the right to a fair hearing, based upon English law, and the right to due process.

The right to a fair hearing requires that 'a person affected by a decision taken by a public authority must be given the opportunity to make his point of view known.' **Transocean Marine Paint** [1974]. In this case part of a Commission decision which affected Transocean Marine Paint was annulled because the company had been given no opportunity to comment.

The right to due process prevented the Secretary of State for Northern Ireland from justifying an exception to the Equal Treatment Directive (76/207) solely on the basis of a certificate that it was in the interests of public security. The Court held in **Johnston v Chief Constable of the Royal Ulster Constabulary** [1986], that such an action would contravene the requirement of judicial control.

ACTIVITY 6

1. Consider whether the general principles of law are an adequate and justifiable method of exercising control over the legislature. You might care to look at the question from the point of view of the balance between the Court of Justice usurping the role of the legislature, on the one hand, and ensuring justice to individuals on the other.

2. Explore how the principle of fundamental human rights has also developed outside of EC law. Particularly important is the European Convention on Human Rights and the fact that the principle is now enshrined by Article F of the Treaty of European Union as one of the 'common principles' of the European Union. (Note that the principle, as set out in Article F is not justiciable before the Court of Justice.)

1. This requires you to take an analytical look at the general principles of law. You should not be afraid to give your own opinions. In so doing, you will enhance your understanding of both the general principles of EC law and also the reasons for their emergence. You will need to read beyond the information set out in the proceeding pages and should attempt to write about 750 words.

2. This involves some research beyond this text. Most of the major text books cover this well. Again you should write about 750 words.

Modes of interpretation

As in any legal system, it is the function of the courts to determine what the law is by interpreting the treaties, the legal and administrative acts of the institutions and other sources of EC law.

The Court of Justice had developed a range of tools of interpretation which may be used by national courts when they are called upon to apply EC law at a domestic level.

A particular problem facing the Court of Justice is that there are eleven different official language versions of the texts. Clearly, this can present unique problems when interpreting EC law.

The primary methods of interpretation utilised by the Court are as follows.

(a) A literal interpretation. Words should be afforded their ordinary natural meaning. However, having ascertained the literal meaning it will be necessary for the Court to place that meaning within the context of the measure as a whole by using the other aids to interpretation.

(b) An historical interpretation. Certain 'travaux préparatoires' (documents relating to the adoption of a measure) may be available to the Court in order to enable it to determine the intention of the legislators.

(c) A contextual approach, which requests the Court to place a particular provision within its particular context and in relation to other EC provisions.

(d) A teleological or purposive approach which involves the Court enquiring as to the object or purpose of a measure in order to derive the most appropriate interpretation.

It should be appreciated that, unlike provisions of English law, many EC statutory rules are enacted in skeletal form and it is for the Courts to flesh out these provisions by judicial interpretation.

It must also be remembered that, whilst there is no binding system of precedent, the Court of Justice recognises the necessity of the certainty of law. Thus, the Court does tend to follow its previous decisions and in ascertaining what the law is, the reported cases of the Court of Justice provide a rich source of EC law.

Summary of section three

- EC law is a form of international law
- the UK is a dualist state so, in order that the EC treaties become part of national law, Parliament had to pass the European Communities Act 1972
- there are primary and secondary legislative sources: the primary sources are the treaties whilst the secondary sources are those "Acts" set out in Article 189 EC, that is regulations, directives and decisions.
- the Court of Justice has developed certain general principles of EC law in order both to develop a proper system of EC law and as a means of measuring the validity of a Community Act
- these principles are protection of fundamental human rights, proportionality, equality, legal certainty/non-retroactivity, legitimate expectation, and certain procedural rights
- the Court of Justice has developed its own methods of interpretation, the essential feature being that it should be able to apply a provision in the way which best achieves the object or purpose of that provision.

SECTION FOUR

The Integration of European Community Law at a National Level

On completion of this section you will be able to:

- identify how the European Court of Justice has developed the essential principles of supremacy and direct effect
- analyse how the notion of the indirect effect of European Community law evolved in order to fill gaps in the principle of direct effect
- evaluate how and to what extent the Court of Justice is imposing the concept of state liability to individuals upon defaulting Member States.

Supremacy of European Community law

The concept of supremacy, that EC law takes primacy over national law, does not appear anywhere in the treaties which, as you learned in the previous section, are essentially examples of 'framework legislation'. They set out the essential principles and leave it to the institutions to flesh out the skeleton by means of the legislative powers given to them by Article 189 (regulations, directives and decisions).

It is the Court of Justice which has ruled that the concept of supremacy is implicit in the Treaty of Rome and an indispensable tool for the development of the common market. The common market would only be achieved if legal rules imposed the requirements of the common market upon Member States. In order to ensure that those rules applied in uniform fashion throughout the European Union, it was necessary that European Community law should prevail over national law.

The principle was first articulated in case **26/62 Van Gend en Loos** [1964] (see direct effect below) and its subsequent development may be charted by reference to the following decisions.

In **Case 6/64 Costa v Enel** [1964], the Court of Justice strongly endorsed the concept giving precedent to provisions of the EC treaty over a subsequent conflicting Italian Act. The facts were very simple. Mr Costa argued that he was not obliged to pay a nominal bill of less than £1 to the newly nationalised National Electricity Board (ENEL) because the nationalisation legislation was in breach of European Community law. The Italian Government insisted that Italian Law must be applied. The Italian court referred the matter to the Court of Justice (under Article 177 – see next section) which ruled that EC law must prevail. 'By contrast with ordinary international treaties, the EEC Treaty has created its own legal system which ..... became an integral part of the legal systems of the Member States and which their courts are bound to apply ...... Member States have limited their sovereign rights, albeit within limited fields, and thus created a body of law which binds both their nationals and themselves ...... It follows ...... that the law stemming from the Treaty ...... could not ...... be overridden by domestic legal provisions, however framed, without being deprived of its character as Community law and without the legal basis of the community itself being called into question.'

In the **Case 11/70 Internationale Handelgesellschaft** [1970] the Court of Justice ruled that Community law overrode even conflicting provisions of constitutional law in Member States. It had been argued that the Community measure was in conflict with the principle of fundamental rights enshrined in the German consitution. The Court found no conflict but emphasised the primacy of Community law.

Case 106/77 Simmenthal [1978] again emphasises that Community law prevails over existing conflicting national law and precludes the passing of future conflicting provisions. Additionally, the Court of Justice made it clear that every judge, sitting at whatever level in national courts, must apply Community law in the event of such a conflict. Thus, in the instant case there was no need for a referral to the Italian Constitutional Court in order to disapply the conflicting national measure, even though this has a lowly court of first instance (equivalent to a magistrate's court in England).

The outer limits to the doctrine of supremacy may be found in **Case C–213/89 Factortame** which provided that national courts must afford primacy to a putative Community right over an allegedly conflicting national measure, here by granting an interim injunction against the Crown, requiring the suspension of a UK Act of Parliament. The rationale behind this decision was to ensure the effective protection of the individual's rights in the event of the UK statute being found to be in conflict with EC law (which it subsequently was). In other words, it was not certain that Factortame had any rights under European Community law until the Court of Justice had ruled upon the matter. Nevertheless, the doctrine of supremacy required the English court to protect the possibility of Factortame having rights under European Community law.

The facts of Factortame involved a claim by Spanish fishermen who had registered companies in the UK that the **Merchant Shipping Act 1988** was in breach of certain provision of the EC treaty. The UK Act imposed certain nationality requirements on fishing vessels flying the British flags such as a residence in the UK requirement for the management and a stipulation that 75% of the shares must be held by UK nationals. This was to prevent fish being caught by companies such as Factortame Ltd from counting against the UK's share of the 'total allowable catch', (the amount of fish the UK were allowed to land under the common fisheries policy). The UK were found to be in breach of EC law and the House of Lords ordered the disapplication of the offending provisions of the **Merchant Shipping Act 1988**. Factortame also marks, therefore, full recognition of the doctrine of supremacy by UK courts.

ACTIVITY 7

a) Consider whether the Court of Justice was justified in developing the doctrine of supremacy of EC law.

b) Why is EC law necessary?

The answers to both these questions revolve around one very simple consideration. Could the European Union achieve any of its objectives without the force of law behind it?

You should also remember that the European Union is comprised of fifteen different states each with its own legal system.

Direct effect

Again, the principle is not stated in the treaty. It is not to be confused with direct applicability, which does appear in the treaty (Article 189). Direct applicability (as explained in the previous section) is the ability of a legislative measure to take effect within the national legal systems of Member States without the need for further implementation of the measure at national level (eg. regulations). Direct effect, on the other hand, is the concept whereby an individual can rely on a provision of EC law in order to claim rights in national courts. The landmark decision is **Case 26/62 Van Gend en Loos** [1964] from which three criteria emerged for a measure to provide direct effect:

i)   the provision must be clear and unambiguous;

ii) it must be unconditional;

iii) its operation should not depend on further action by Member States or the European Union.

(note that the third condition is often seen as an aspect of unconditionality).

Thus; in Van Gend en Loos, Van Gend was able to plead the direct effect of Article 12 (which prohibits customs duties) in order to claim back duty imposed on imported chemicals by the Dutch authorities.

Initially, direct effect was used to enable an individual (a natural person or a company) to claim the benefit of rights which derived from obligations imposed upon a Member State by EC law. This is known as **vertical direct effect**. Direct effect may be used to enforce both positive and negative rights. The right was then extended to encompass the situation where the obligation was imposed upon another individual as in **Case 43/75 Defrenne v Sabena (No.2)** [1976] where an airline hostess was able to use the direct effect of Article 119 against a private employer in order to claim wage parity with a male steward. This is known as **horizontal direct effect**. Thus direct effect may operate vertically, against the state or horizontally, against fellow individuals.

Over the years the Court of Justice has relaxed the operation of the criteria for direct effect in the sense that it will try to find direct effect where it can.

Treaty articles, regulations and decisions have all been held to be capable of being directly effective. Initially, it was not thought that directives could produce direct effect because, unlike, for example a regulation, they required further implementation by a Member State. However, the Court of Justice has ruled otherwise.

For a directive to be directly effective then either the time limit for its implementation must have expired or, alternatively, the member state must have failed to implement it properly.

At first the Court of Justice used the argument that the effectiveness of Community law would be weakened if nationals of member state were denied the rights contained in a directive, where the member state had failed to implement it. This principle is to be found in **Case 41/74 Van Duyn** [1970] where Directive 64/221, which contained rules relating to a member state's right to exclude nationals from other Member States, was held to be directly effective. Miss Van Duyn, a Dutch national, had wished to exercise her rights, under Article 48 EC Treaty, to move to the UK in order to take up a job with the Church of Scientology. The UK sought to deny her admission because it disapproved of Scientology. The Court held that both Article 48 and Directive 64/221 produced direct effect but that on the facts the UK could exclude her, using the public policy exception set out in Article 48(3) and expanded upon in Directive 64/221.

In **Case 184/78 Ratti** [1979], the Court of Justice reiterated the effectiveness of the EC law argument but introduced a new rationale for the direct effect of directives, that Member States should not be able to hide behind their own failure to implement directives.

'A Member State which has not adopted the implementing measures required by a directive in the prescribed period may not relay, as against individuals, on its own failure to perform the obligations which the directive entails.'

Thus, the Italian authorities were unable to prosecute Mr Ratti for breach of Italian laws relating to the labelling of solvents when he had, in fact, complied with the requirements of a non-implemented directive.

This new rationale enabled the Court of Justice to respond to growing opposition from the courts of some Member States and to rein back upon the extent of the direct effect of directives by ruling, in **Case 152/89 Marshall** [1986], that they may only produce vertical direct effect.

Mrs Marshall was an employee of Southampton Area Health Authority when she was dismissed, having reached the age of 62, the SAHA's compulsory retirement age for females. She argued that this was discriminatory and contrary to the Equal Treatment Directive 76/207, as male employees could work until the age of 65. As SAHA was an 'emanation of the State', Mrs Marshall was able to obtain the benefit of the directive by invoking its direct effectiveness vertically against the State. The Court emphasised that a directive could not provide horizontal direct effect.

This has resulted in an anomalous situation. If we stay with the example of measures relating to employment protection, it means that a state employee will be able to claim the benefit of a non-implemented directive, but an employee of a private firm will not.

Thus, in similar circumstances to Mrs Marshall, Mrs Duke was unable to rely on the direct effect Directive 76/207 because she was employed by a company which was classified as another individual rather than an emanation of the state (**Duke v GEC Reliance Ltd** [1988]).

One response by the Court of Justice to this self-imposed restriction has been a broad definition of the 'State'. In **Case 189/89 Foster** [1990], a state body was defined as one which was 'subject to the authority or control of the state or has special powers beyond those which result from the normal rules applicable to relations between individuals'.

Many commentators thought that the Court of Justice might seek to resolve this anomaly by ruling that directives could produce horizontal direct effect. However, in **Case C–91/92 Paulo Faccini Dori** [1994], the Court reiterated its stance in Marshall and confirmed that directives were incapable of producing horizontal direct effect. In its judgment in Dori, however, the Court did point to the doctrines of indirect effect and state liability (see later in this section) as offering alternative resolutions to the restriction of the direct effect of directives.

Miss Dori had been persuaded to purchase a language course on credit by a salesman at Milan railway station. Italy had failed to implement a directive which would have allowed a cooling-off period for such sales, during which time Miss Dori could have changed her mind. Miss Dori was unable to enforce the directive horizontally against the debt collection firm which was suing her for the amount owing.

ACTIVITY 8

a) Hilda, a German woman, is employed by Conker PLC, a UK company, which supplies computing equipment to the Civil Service. She is dismissed in order that her job may be given to an English national. How might Hilda use Article 6 of the EC treaty, which outlaws discrimination on the grounds of nationality, in order to make out a case for unfair dismissal?

(For the purpose of this activity assume that the UK has no domestic legislation relating to race discrimination or unfair dismissal).

b) In the above scenario, assume that the Council have issued (imaginary) Directive 93/107 which the UK should have implemented by 1.3.95. The (imaginary) directive provides that anyone dismissed in circumstances which breach Article 6 EC Treaty shall be entitled to a minimum award of damages of £10,000. Is Hilda able to claim the benefit of (imaginary) Directive 93/107?

c) Discover the facts of three cases not covered in this section where an individual has been able to enforce a directly effective provision before a national court.

a) This involves a consideration of the extent to which a treaty article may produce direct effect.

b) This scenario concerns the much more complex issue of the direct effect of directives. Could the non-implemented directive be enforced against Conker Plc? Is Conker Plc an individual (for the purposes of European Community law) or an emanation of the state?

c) You should be able to find this information in standard texts.

Indirect effect of EC law

In **Case 14/83 Von Colson and Kamann** [1984], the Court of Justice sidestepped the issue of directives and direct effect and instead focused on Article 5 EC Treaty which requires Member States to 'take all appropriate measures to ensure fulfilment of their community obligations'. This obligation, reasoned the Court, extended to courts of Member States who must, therefore, interpret national law in the light of non-implemented directives.

Thus, in Von Colson, Sabine Von Colson and Elisabeth Kamann were female social workers who applied for a job in a German prison. Less qualified male applicants were appointed and the women sought compensation for sex discrimination. However, under German law, the women were entitled only to recover the travel expenses incurred in pursuing the job applications. The German court referred the matter to the Court of Justice to discover whether Article 6 of the Equal Treatment Directive 76/207 produced direct effect. Article 6 required Member States to provide a means whereby victims of discrimination can enforce their claims under national law. Article 6 was not unconditional and sufficiently precise enough to produce direct effect because it left Member States free to choose effective sanctions.

Accordingly, the Court of Justice used Article 5 EC Treaty, as explained above, requiring the courts in Member States to interpret national legislation in order to bring about the effect envisaged by the directive.

'(I)n applying national law and in particular the provisions of national law specifically introduced in order to implement Directive No.76/207, national courts are required to interpret their national law in the light of the wording and purpose of the Directive .....'

The Court of Justice went on to say that this obligation to interpret national law adopted for the implementation of the directive must be observed by a national court 'in so far as it is given discretion to do so under national law'.

In the Von Colson and Kamann case, this meant that the German court had to interpret the relevant provision of German law in such a way as to ensure that, if it decided upon compensation as the sanction for the sex discrimination, the compensation must be adequate.

This ruling was not wholeheartedly embraced by UK courts. In **Duke v GEC Reliance Ltd** [1988] Mrs Duke was dismissed in similar circumstances to Mrs Marshall. The House of Lords considered whether Mrs Duke could benefit from the indirect effect of Directive 76/207. (Remember direct effect was not possible because Mrs Duke was not an employee of the state or an emanation thereof). The House of Lords ruled that it was not required to interpret the relevant UK legislation in order to bring about the result envisaged by Directive 76/207 because the UK statute was enacted prior to the directive. It was, therefore, not possible under rules of interpretation of English law to give a meaning to a statute which Parliament could not possibly have intended.

However, in **Litster v Forth Dry Dock and Engineering Co Ltd** [1990], the House of Lords showed its willingness to apply the Von Colson principle to the situation where Parliament has enacted a statutory provision in order to comply with an obligation imposed by a directive.

Thus Litster was able to claim that the UK Transfer of Undertakings (Protection of Employment) Regulations 1981 should be interpreted in accordance with Directive 77/87 which offered protection to workers dismissed when a business is transferred to a new owner. Litster had been dismissed an hour before the transfer and under a loophole in the UK regulations would have received nothing. Fortunately, the directive came to his rescue!

The Court of Justice returned to the Von Colson principle in **Case C–106/89 Marleasing** [1990] and ruled, (perhaps in response to the UK courts' interpretation of the principle), that the courts of Member States are required to interpret national law in the light of a directive 'whether the provisions in question were adopted before or after the directive'.

The only limitation on the Von Colson principle would appear to be where it is not possible for the national court to apply the principle because, eg. there is no national legislation on the matter. However, interpretation of law is necessarily an imprecise exercise and it remains to be seen to what extent national courts will be prepared to distort the meaning of statutory provisions.

SELF-CHECK 1

1. Why did the Court of Justice decide upon the doctrine of supremacy as an essential cornerstone of Community law?

ACTIVITY 9

a) Do you think that the House of Lords was justified, in **Duke v Reliance**, in applying the principle of the indirect effect of EC law in the way that it did?

b) In the light of the principle of indirect effect, is there any point in the Court of Justice maintaining its limitation on the horizontal direct effect of directives?

c) Return to the previous activity in this section and advise Hilda as to whether she might make use of the principle of indirect effect in order to assist her claim for unfair dismissal.

a) You might like to look closely at the 'Von Colson' principle in order to identify whether the House of Lords' interpretation was reasonable. Any of the cases and materials' texts will provide the necessary source material.

b) This invites a consideration of the balance between the Court of Justice not overstepping its authority and the pragmatic response which would sort out an anomaly in the law.

c) You should apply the Von Colson/Marleasing decisions to Hilda's situation.

State liability for non-compliance with EC law

The reasoning behind the limitation of the direct effect of directives to vertical direct effect was, in essence, that Article 189 imposes the requirement to implement the directive upon the state and it would not therefore be fair to enforce a non-implemented directive against a private party (person or company). This has the unfortunate effect of leaving another individual without legal rights he would have had, had the directive been properly implemented.

If Member States prove willing to interpret national law in the light and purpose of non-implemented directives (Von Colson), then private parties may derive rights from a directive and enforce those rights against other private parties. This results in the unfortunate consequence of the latter being bound by obligations of which they are totally unaware.

In either of the above situations, a private party is disadvantaged because of the failure of the Member State to comply with its obligations under EC law and implement a directive. The state, therefore, is the real wrongdoer and there is much merit in the argument that the state should bear responsibility for this default.

In its most radical judgment in recent years, the Court of Justice, in **Cases C–6/90 and C–9/90 Francovich and Others v Italian State** [1991], ruled that Italy was liable in damages to Francovich and others for losses attributable to Italy's failure to comply with a directive.

Under a Council directive, which was adopted in order to give protection to employees in the event of their employer becoming insolvent, Member States were required to set up a fund out of which redundant employees could obtain outstanding payments due to them.

The Italian Government had failed to implement the directive and, when Francovich's employer went into insolvent liquidation, there were no funds out of which he could claim his redundancy entitlements. Francovich claimed that either Directive 80/987 should produce direct effect or that the Italian state should compensate him for his loss arising from the failure to implement the directive and set up the guarantee fund.

On an Article 177 reference, the Court of Justice ruled that Directive 80/987 could not produce direct effect as it was insufficiently unconditional but that it was a principle of Community law that Member States are obliged to make good loss and damage caused to individuals by breaches of Community law attributable to them.

In the case of loss arising from the non-implementation of a directive, the Court laid down three conditions for state liability and an award of damages:

i)   that the result required by the directive includes the conferment of rights on individuals;

ii) that it is possible to identify the content of those rights by reference to the Directive;

iii) that there is a causal link between the breach of the state's obligation and the loss suffered by the injured party.

Just how widely the Court of Justice will develop this principle remains to be seen. Although the instant case was concerned with the non-implementation of directives and the conditions related specifically to this particular breach, it is clear from the wording of the judgment that the Court intended a general principle of state liability for breaches of EC law. The Court of Justice is currently deliberating upon two cases, Joined **Cases C–46/93** and **C–48/93 Factortame III and Firma Brasseries du Pecheur**, in which it will have the opportunity to refine the principle laid down by Francovich. The Factortame III application relates to financial losses sustained by Factortame for the period during which the **Merchant Shipping Act 1988** was unlawfully in force (see previous section).

In the context of direct effect of directives, the Francovich decision goes a considerable way to redressing the imbalance caused by the fact that directives are not horizontally directly effective and allows an individual to target the state as defendant.

ACTIVITY 10

a) To what extent do you think that a Member State should be liable for breaches of EC law? List some of the factors which a court should take into account.

b) Returning to the first activity in this section, explore whether or not the Francovich decision would be of use to Hilda in her quest for compensation.

---

a) This is ultimately a matter of opinion founded upon a sound understanding of the principle of state liability. To start you off you might consider the culpability of the Member State and the seriousness of the breach.

b) This invites a relatively straightforward application of Francovich to Hilda's situation.

Summary of section four

- EC law is supreme
- all courts of Member States must afford primacy to EC law over conflicting provisions of national law by, where appropriate, disapplying conflicting provisions of national law
- EC law is directly effective in that it confers rights on individuals which are enforceable in national courts
- to be directly effective a provision must be unconditional and sufficiently clear and precise
- direct effect may operate vertically (rights against the state) or horizontally (rights against other individuals)
- directives may only produce vertical direct effect
- a directive may be indirectly effective in that Member States' courts are required to use directives in interpreting national law
- a Member State which fails to implement a directive may be liable to anyone who suffers a consequential loss
- this principle of state liability is a general principle which encompasses losses caused by all breaches of EC law by Member States.

Suggested answer to section four
self-check question

1. Without the doctrine of supremacy there would have been no certainty and uniformity of in the application of EC law in different Member States. Thus, different rules would have prevailed in different countries and EC law as the means of achieving economic integration and the single market would have been ineffective. Although the doctrine does not appear in any of the treaties, the Court of Justice 'found' the doctrine in the purpose of the treaties.

SECTION FIVE

Enforcement of European Community Law at a European Level

On completion of this section you will be able to:

- identify how the institutions are controlled at a European level.
- analyse how Member States are subjected to control
- identify how the preliminary reference procedure operates as the link between national courts and the Court of Justice of the European Community.

Introduction

Article 164 EC Treaty imposes an obligation on the Court of Justice to ensure that European Community law is observed. This is to be achieved by a group of remedies with common purposes available against Community institutions and against Member States. In addition there is a procedure whereby national courts can get a ruling from the Court of Justice on the interpretation and validity of EC law.

Control of the institutions

As you have discovered in previous sections, the institutions (the Council, the Commission and to a certain extent Parliament) have wide legislative powers under the treaties. It would be unthinkable that these powers could be exercised without there being any checks upon them. Most important amongst these judicial remedies is the action for annulment under Article 173 EC Treaty.

THE ACTION FOR ANNULMENT OF COMMUNITY ACTS

Article 173 provides a procedure whereby the validity of a Community Act may be directly challenged before the European Court of Justice. In order to understand how Article 173 operates it is necessary to ask the following questions:

- what Acts can be challenged?
- who can challenge such Acts?
- what are the grounds for a challenge?
- what are the time limits within which an act may be challenged?

If a challenge is successful then the Court of Justice must annul the offending Community Act (Article 174).

WHAT ACTS CAN BE CHALLENGED?

Article 173 clearly gives the Court of Justice the power to review the legality of those legally binding Acts specified in Article 189, that is regulations, directives and decisions. However, the Court of Justice has interpreted 'Acts' in a wide sense and any measure which produces a legally binding consequence is challengeable. Thus the Court of Justice looks to the effect of the measure rather than its form and has allowed challenges to a Council resolution (**Case 22/70 ERTA** [1971]), a Commission notice (**Cases 8–11/66 Cimenteries** [1967]), and even an oral decision (**Case 316/82 Kohler** [1984])

WHO CAN APPLY FOR REVIEW OF A COMMUNITY ACT?

Applicants for review of a Community Act can be divided in two categories for the purpose of deciding who has *locus standi* (legal standing to bring an action).

There are privileged applicants (the Council, the Commission and Member States) who may challenge any measure adopted by any of the institutions merely because of their status within the European Union. Since the amendments to the EC Treaty, by the Treaty on European Union, Parliament and the European Central Bank are granted the right to challenge measures adopted by the other institutions, but only for 'the purpose of protecting their prerogatives'. The reason for this amendment was that these two institutions now had some powers to adopt legally binding Acts which were not given them by the original treaty.

Any other natural or legal person (individuals or corporations) are deemed to be non-privileged applicants and have a much more restricted right to challenge a measure. The reasons for the restrictions on the rights of non-privileged applicants to bring an action are to ensure the law is certain and to prevent the Court of Justice from being flooded with annulment proceedings. Article 173 could otherwise be used by persons who might be opposed to the very idea of the European Union. Non-privileged applicants may only challenge three types of Act:

- a decision addressed to the applicant
- a decision addressed to a third party but of direct and individual concern to the applicant
- a decision in the form of a regulation which is of direct and individual concern to the applicant.

The common denominator between these three types of Acts is that the applicant has a specific interest in the measure. Clearly, the most straightforward of the above categories is the self-explanatory decision addressed to the applicant and this requires no further consideration. In need of interpretation, however, is the concept of 'direct and individual concern' and the notion of a 'decision in the form of a regulation'.

DIRECT CONCERN

A measure is of direct concern if it impacts directly upon the applicant without there being room for any discretion in the implementation of the decision by the person to whom it is addressed (often the Member State). Thus, in **Case 68/69 Alcan** [1970], the importers of aluminium were not directly concerned by a Commission decision, addressed to Belgium, refusing a request for permission to allow a quota of imports at revised duty. This was because, had Belgium received permission, the reduced rate need not have exercised in Alcan's favour.

However, where the German authorities made it clear, in advance of a Commission's decision, how they were going to exercise their discretion, it was held that this made the matter of direct concern to the applicant. (**Case 62/70 Bock** [1971] where the German Government applied for authorisation to block imports of preserved Chinese mushrooms and informed Bock that his import licence application would not be dealt with until after the decision in order that it could be rejected).

INDIVIDUAL CONCERN

The test for individual concern was developed by the Court of Justice in **Case 25/62 Plaumann** [1963]. Plaumann imported clementines into Germany. The German Government applied to the Commission for authority to reduce the amount of duty imposed on clementines imported into Germany from outside the Community. The Commission refused in a decision addressed to the German Government. Plaumann challenged this decision, claiming that, as a duty payer, he was individually concerned by it. The Court of Justice ruled otherwise, holding that Plaumann was not distinguished or singled out by the decision in the sense that anyone could at any time be an importer of clementines.

'Persons other than those to whom a decision is addressed may only claim to be individually concerned if that decision affects them by reasons of certain attributes which are peculiar to them or by reason of circumstances in which they are differentiated from all other persons and by virtue of these factors distinguishes them individually just as in the case of the person addressed.'

The 'Plaumann Test' has been subsequently applied in such a way as to suggest that the Court of Justice requires the applicant to be part of a closed category, membership of which is fixed at the date of adoption of the disputed measure. This was certainly the case in **Cases 106-107/63** where Toepfer was allowed to challenge a decision addressed to Germany which confirmed the German Government's refusal to grant cereal import licences. Toepfer had individual concern because the measure only affected a closed class who had applied for licences on a particular day when the Commission had reduced import duty of maize to zero.

An example of a case in which the Court of Justice relaxed their criteria for individual concern is **Case 294/33 'Les Verts' (Green Party)** [1986]. The European Parliament had issued a decision whereby only those parties who had fielded candidates in the previous European Parliament elections were entitled to a share in the allocation of electoral funds. The French Green Party did not qualify and wished to challenge this Decision. Clearly they did not belong to a closed category but the Court of Justice nevertheless granted them *locus standi* on policy reasons in that they had a good case on the merits and that the decision would never otherwise be challenged.

DECISIONS IN THE FORM OF REGULATIONS

The effect of the *locus standi* rules in Article 173 is that, as a general rule, an individual has no right to challenge a regulation. The only exception to this is where the measure, although issued as a regulation, is in essence a decision. In other words, the Court of Justice will look to the content of a measure rather than its form.

In **Cases 16–17/62 Producteurs de Fruits et Légumes** [1962] the Court of Justice ruled that the essential characteristic of a regulation is that it is a normative measure in that it is legislative in nature and applies generally across the Union to persons in an objective and abstract manner. In other words, it does not just apply to a limited number of identifiable individuals but enjoys the status of being general law throughout the Union.

A decision, on the other hand, is characterised by the fact that it is addressed to a limited number of persons. However, a regulation does not cease to be a regulation merely because it may be possible to ascertain the number of persons to whom it applies or, indeed, even the identity of such persons.

In **Cases 41–44/70 International Fruit** [1971] the Court of Justice held that a "Regulation" was in reality a bundle of decisions.

In **Case 64/69 Compagnie Francaise** [1970] the Court accepted that the applicant was directly and individually concerned by the measure but held that the applicant had failed to establish that the measure was a decision and not a regulation.

For a while, in cases such as **Case 100/74 CAM** [1975] and **Case 123/77 UNICME** [1978] the Court of Justice seemed to adopt a less restrictive line and take the view that if direct and individual concern was established then the measure was probably a decision.

It then reverted, in cases like **Cases 103–9/78 Beauport** [1979], **Case 45/81 Moksel** [1982] and **Case 26/86 Deutz und Geldermann** [1987] to its original stance that there were two hurdles for the applicant to clear. The applicant must satisfy the Court not only that he was directly and individually concerned by the measure but also that it was in essence a decision and not a regulation.

Thus, an applicant who wishes to challenge a regulation faces an uphill task. One exception to this restrictive approach can be seen in **Cases 113 & 118–121/77 Japanese Ball Bearings** [1979] where the Court of Justice ruled that although a measure was a true regulation it constituted a decision for the applicants in that they were identified in a specific article of the regulation. The applicants were, therefore, allowed to challenge the legality of the regulation.

It is easy to be confused by the above cases. The Court of Justice's current standpoint would appear to be that a regulation can only be challenged if either:

- of direct and individual concern to the applicant and

- in reality a decision not a regulation

  or

- although a true regulation it is effectively a decision for the applicants in that they are identified in the regulation.

CASES WHERE THE COURT OF JUSTICE HAVE ADOPTED A VERY LIBERAL INTERPRETATION OF THE *LOCUS STANDI* RULES

There are a series of cases where the Court of Justice seems prepared to 'stretch' the *locus standi* rules in Article 173. The common characteristic of such cases is that they relate not to measures introduced by the institutions in order to promote European Union policies but to measures adopted as a consequence of some investigation carried out by the Commission. Such cases are normally concerned with alleged breaches of the competition rules, allegations of 'dumping' of cheap imports in the European Union from outside the Union, or allegations of unlawful state aids to industry.

In such cases, the Court of Justice is prepared to grant *locus standi* to those who have participated in the investigation even if they do not satisfy the stringent rules laid down in Article 173. In the case of the imposition of 'anti-dumping' duty (which under EC law has to be imposed by regulation), the Court will allow challenges to a true regulation. It may be argued that the reason for the Court's liberal stance here is that the matter has become of direct and individual concern to the participant by virtue of the fact that he has taken part in the investigation. Without this stance the rights of individuals would be greatly curtailed.

Such a liberal approach can be seen in **Case 264/82 Timex** [1985] where *locus standi* was afforded to those who complained about the dumping of cheap Soviet watches in the European Union and in **Case C–358/89 Extramet** [1991] where an importer was able to challenge a regulation which imposed anti-dumping duty.

THE GROUNDS FOR A CHALLENGE

Article 173 sets out four grounds for which a measure may be annulled. There is some overlap between one ground and another. An applicant may plead:

- lack of competence
- infringement of an essential procedural requirement
- infringement of the treaty or of any rule of law relating to its application
- misuse of powers.

Lack of competence

This has seldom been invoked successfully. It means that the institution has no powers to adopt the measure in question. A rare successful application was **Case C–295/90 Parliament v Council** [1992] where Parliament argued that the Council had adopted a directive concerning the mobility of students (Directive 90/366) under the wrong legal base in the treaty. The Court of Justice agreed and the directive was annulled. (It has since been re-enacted as directive 93/96, the Council this time using the correct legal base!)

Breach of an essential procedural requirement

The essence of this ground is that although the institution had the power to adopt the measure in question, it failed to observed the correct procedural requirements. In **Case 138/79 Roquette** [1980], a measure was annulled because the Council has not obtained the opinion of the European Parliament. A regulation had been introduced by the Council restricting the production of isoglucose without Parliament giving its opinion as required by Article 43 EC.

Failure to give sufficient reasons under Article 190 EC has also been held to constitute a breach of an essential procedural requirement. The Court has held that, under Article 190, Community measures must include a statement of the facts and law which led the institution to adopt them.

Infringement of the treaty or any rule of law relating to its application

Infringement of the treaty constitutes a wide basis for challenge as almost any error by an institution can be viewed as a violation of the treaty. Indeed, the two above grounds could also be considered as infringements of the treaty.

'Any rule of law relating to its application' has been held to mean those general principles of Community law which were considered in Section Three. Thus, a legislative measure may be challenged on the ground that it:

- offends the rule of proportionality
- that it is unequal and discriminatory
- runs counter to the individual's legitimate expectations
- contravenes fundamental human rights
- contravenes any of the other general principles.

For a more detailed examination you should refer back to the discussion in Section Three. An example to refresh your memory would be **ex parte Mann** [1985] where the applicant successfully claimed that a measure which lost him a deposit of £1,500,000 for being a mere four hours late in submitting a grain licence application was disproportionate.

Misuse of powers

Here, the institution has the appropriate powers, follows the correct procedures but uses those powers for a purpose other than that for which they were granted. This is, perhaps, the most difficult to prove because of the subjectivity of establishing that a motive was improper. It is, therefore, the most infrequently invoked ground. A rare successful example is **Case 105/75 Guiffrida v Council** [1976], a staff case. Here, a decision had been issued to appoint an individual to a senior position. In accordance with Community law a competition for the post had been held. However, the criteria for admission to the competition had been rigged to favour the successful candidate. The decision was annulled as a misuse of powers.

TIME LIMITS

Under Article 173(5) any application must be instituted within two months of when the measure was published, or notified to the applicant, or, if neither published nor notified, within two months of coming to the notice of the applicant.

THE EFFECT OF A SUCCESSFUL CHALLENGE

The Court of Justice will declare the measure void under Article 174. If the offending part can be effectively severed from the rest, it may be annulled in part.

ACTIVITY 11

In 1990 (imaginary) Council Regulation 1200/90 EEC established the llama meat sausage scheme whereby generous subsidies were offered to those farmers who switched to llama farming from sheep farming. The Council had been concerned with both an excess of sheep-farming within the EU and also high levels of radiation found in sheep as a consequence of fall-out from the Chernobyl nuclear explosion.

Nine sheep farmers have so far joined the scheme including Heppelthwaite, a Northumberland hill farmer. Heppelthwaite has purchased a herd of fifty llama and spent £35,000 on constructing an abattoir.

A recent outbreak of barmy llama disease in South America has led to great concern and debate within the European Union as regards food safety. As a result, the Commission acting under the regulation adopts a community decision addressed to Member States which introduces variations to the llama meat sausage scheme. The decision takes effect from 1 July 1995 and requires Member States to withhold payments due under the scheme from 1 January 1995 onwards unless certain modifications to production processes are completed by 1 September 1995. Heppelthwaite will need to spend a further £20,000 in order to comply with the requirements of the decision.

(a) Advise Heppelthwaite as to whether he may challenge the decision under Article 173 EC.

(b) Would your answer differ if the required modifications had been imposed by a second Council regulation?

To successfully answer a question of this nature you must apply Article 173 in a mechanistic way.

First, you must identify whether the measure in question is challengeable.

Then you should consider whether Heppelthwaite has the necessary *locus standi* to challenge the measure.

Assuming this hurdle is successfully surmounted you will need to identify grounds for a challenge. A helpful hint here is to go through the general principles of EC law – you will be surprised how many might be relevant.

Finally, you must bear in mind the time limits within which an applicant can mount a challenge.

The action for failure to act

Article 175 EC provides an action whereby the institutions may be challenged for their failure to adopt an Act where required to so do under the treaty. Article 175 is clearly a complementary remedy to Article 173 in that failing to act and acting illegally are part of the same whole. The Court of Justice has certainly taken this view and this has become known as the 'unity principle'. Thus, for example, a non-privileged applicant who would be unable to challenge an illegal measure under Article 173 should not be able to challenge the failure to adopt that measure under Article 175. (It should be noted that Article 175 distinguishes between privileged and non-privileged applicants in the same way that Article 173 does).

A good example of how Article 175 may be used is found in **Case 13/83 European Parliament v Council** [1985]. Here the Council's omission to introduce a common transport policy and its failure to introduce measures aimed at ensuring the freedom of movement of the provision of transport services were challenged. Parliament failed on its first submission in that there was no obligation under the treaty to introduce a common transport policy. However, it succeeded in respect of the second argument in that the Council was legally bound to implement the free movement of transport services under Articles 50, 59, 61 and 75 EC Treaty.

The procedure to be followed for an Article 175 action is set out in the Article:

(i)   the applicant must request the institution to take the appropriate action which he considered is required by the treaty;

(ii) the institution then has two months in which to comply;

(iii) if this period expires without the institution either taking action or stating its position, then the applicant may take the matter to the Court of Justice within a further two months;

(iv) the Court of Justice may make a declaration that the failure to act is in contravention of the treaty, in which case the institution will be required to comply with the declaration.

It should be noted that Article 175 is rarely used.

SELF-CHECK 1

1. To what extent may an individual (natural person or corporation) use Article 173 EC to challenge a measure of one of the institutions of the EC?

The plea of illegality

The 'plea of illegality' remedy as set out in Article 184 EC Treaty may best be described as a safety net provision. It is intended to be used to prevent the application of an illegal measure being used as a basis for further action. Community law imposes strict rules of *locus standi* and tight time limits on the challenge to EC legislation. These limitations are necessary in order to advance the certainty of Community law and to counter the undesirability of EC law being subjected to unnecessary interference from over-zealous litigants. The other side of this argument is that the rule of law should prevail and that institutions should not be able to rely upon an illegal Act.

The way in which it may be invoked is set out in the following example. Suppose that the Council adopts an illegal regulation which is not challenged before the expiration of the two-month time period. What if the Commission adopts a decision under that regulation which is addressed to X. Using Article 173 to mount a challenge to the decision, X may then plead the inapplicability of the parent regulation under which the subsequent decision was adopted. Clearly, if the parent regulation is inapplicable, then the decision must be annulled.

Another example of the use of Article 184 would be it being invoked in an action for damages under Article 215(2) where the measure giving rise to damage has not been previously challenged (see action for damages below).

It should be noted that Article 184 refers specifically to regulations but, in keeping with its interpretation of the law in the area of judicial control of Community institutions, the Court of Justice has indicated that it is concerned with the substance of the measure rather than the form. In **Case 92/78 Simmenthal** [1979], the Court of Justice held that particular notices of invitations to tender were general measures producing similar effects to a regulation. Accordingly, they were subject to a plea of illegality when the applicant contested a decision of direct and individual concern to him which implemented the notices. However, the application failed on the merits of the case.

Article 184 refers to 'any party' being able to invoke the remedy. If, therefore, applies equally to privileged and non-privileged applicants. It must be appreciated that Article 184 is only used in proceedings before the Court of Justice because, if one wished to challenge the legality of a measure before a national court, the appropriate procedure would be for the national court to use Article 177 and make a referral to the Court of Justice, (see note on Article 177 (3) below).

The action for damages

Article 178 EC gives the Court of Justice exclusive jurisdiction to hear cases relating to the non-contractual (that is tortious) liability of the institutions. (The national law applicable to the contract in question will govern contractual liability of the EU).

Article 215(2) stipulates that 'In the case of non-contractual liability, the Community shall, in accordance with the general principles common to the laws of the Member States, make good any damage caused by its institutions or by its servants in the performance of their duties'.

Under Article 215(2), there may be liability both for acts or omissions of the institutions or its servants which cause damage (for example negligence, breach of confidence, negligent mis-statement, defamation and so on) and also for illegal 'acts' in the legislative sense which have caused loss or damage.

An example of a successful action in respect of the former is to be found in **Case 145/83 Adams v Commission** [1985]. Here Adams 'blew the whistle' on unlawful anti-competitive practices being carried on by his employer. The Commission investigated and the employer, Hoffman-La-Roche, was fined a substantial amount. The Commission then handed over papers to Hoffman-La-Roche which enabled Adams to be identified as the whistle-blower. When Adams returned to Switzerland, (having resigned from Hoffman-La-Roche and set up a business in Italy), he was arrested and charged with industrial espionage. Adams was kept in solitary confinement, his wife committed suicide, and his business collapsed. On his release, he sued the Commission for breach of confidentiality and was awarded compensation.

As regards liability for unlawful legislative Acts, the Court of Justice developed certain guidelines to be observed in **Case 5/71 Schoppensted** [1971]. The loss to the applicant must be caused by a sufficiently flagrant violation of a superior rule of law for the protection of the individual. (In Schoppensted the applicant had claimed damages as a result of an allegedly flawed regulation. The Court of Justice dismissed the application because it could find no 'sufficiently flagrant violation of a superior rule of law'. The applicant had pleaded that the measure which related to the fixing of sugar prices was discriminatory in that different criteria had been used in fixing compensation for sugar).

The Court of Justice has subsequently applied the 'Schoppensted' formula in such a way that the breach of law must be serious and inexcusable and its impact upon the applicant must be great rather then small.

The Schoppensted case also decided that Article 215(2) operates independently of Article 173. Thus, an applicant who could not have challenged an illegal measure under Article 173 will not be barred from bringing an action for damages under Article 215(2).

ACTIVITY 12

a) Explain in your own words what is meant by the 'unity principle'.

b) How might an individual indirectly challenge the applicability of a regulation before the Court of Justice?

c) Return to the previous activity involving Heppelthwaite and the llama meat sausage scheme. Assume that Heppelthwaite has carried out the required modifications and incurred costs of £20,000. A fellow hill-farmer then challenges the decision.

What use would Articles 178 and 215(2) be to Heppelthwaite?

a) In explaining the 'unity principle' you might wish to consider the relative functions of Articles 173 and 175 and how they serve a common purpose.

b) The most important thing to remember about the Article 184 indirect challenge procedure is that it is not a right of action in itself but can only be pleaded in the course of an action brought under another head.

c) In advising Heppelthwaite as to the likelihood of his obtaining damages from the Commission you should especially bear in mind the 'Shoppenstedt' formula.

Control of Member States

In Section Four you considered how the doctrine of the supremacy of Community law had evolved in order to ensure that the new legal order which is Community law applies uniformly across Member States. Clearly, there must be some mechanism which allows for Member States to be required to fulfil their obligations under EC law.

Article 155 EC Treaty imposes a general duty on the Commission to 'ensure that the provisions of this Treaty and the measures taken by the institutions pursuant thereto are applied'. As regards this aspect of its role within the Union, the Commission has been referred to as the policeman of the European Union. In respect of enforcing EC law against Member States, the Commission has been given specific powers under Article 169 EC which allows it to initiate action whenever it considers that a Member State has failed to fulfil a treaty obligation. This encompasses breaches of administrative acts, the general principles of Community law and international agreements. Examples of such breaches would include the failure by a Member State to implement a directive or the member state adopting a measure which is incompatible with EC law. The Commission brought an action against Italy for failure to implement a directive which resulted in Francovich's subsequent successful action for damages for breach of EC law by Italy. (See Section Four). The UK were taken to the Court of Justice by the Commission in the Factortame litigation because of the incompatibility of the **Merchant Shipping Act 1988** with the EC Treaty (see Section Four).

THE ARTICLE 169 PROCEDURE

The primary purpose of Article 169 is to get Member States to agree to comply with EC law without going to Court. Hence, there is a two-stage procedure which embraces both an administrative and a judicial process.

The various steps taken by the Commission in utilising Article 169 are as follows:

i)   There will be an informal investigation by the Commission. It must be appreciated that the Commission will receive many complaints about alleged breaches of EC law from individuals, corporations, pressure groups, other Member States and so on.

ii) The Commission will then send a letter to the member state informing it that it believes it to be in breach of the treaty and setting out details of the alleged infringement.

iii) If the Member States does not satisfy the Commission by either answering the allegations or rectifying the breach, then the Commission will send out a reasoned opinion which sets down a time limit for the Member State to comply with its obligations under EC law. The reasoned opinion is important because it forms the basis of any subsequent hearing before the Court of Justice. The opinion states the law, the facts and identifies what the Commission requires the Member State to do in order to rectify the breach.

iv) If the Member State has not complied with the reasoned opinion within the time period, then the Commission may take the Member State to the Court of Justice. Member States have come up with a variety of unsuccessful 'defences' at the judicial stage of Article 169 proceedings. They have argued reciprocity, that is that other Member States failed to fulfil this obligation, and they have claimed constitutional or political difficulties in implementing a measure. They have also claimed the invalidity of an obligation, a claim which fails because the Member State should have challenged the measure under Article 173. (Article 184 cannot be used by a Member State as a defence in an enforcement action under Article 169 – **Case 156/77 Commission v Belgium** [1978]).

v)   The Court will then make a declaration if it finds the Member State in violation of EC law.

There are numerous examples of Article 169 proceedings, some which have already been encountered. As part of the Factortame saga (see Section Four), involving the UK's share of the total allowable catch and the introduction of the Merchant Shipping Act 1988, the Commission brought Article 169 proceedings against the UK who were, of course, found to be in breach (**Case C–246/89 Commission v UK** [1989].

THE ARTICLE 170 PROCEDURE

There is a parallel procedure whereby Member States may bring enforcement action against each other. This is rarely used for the obvious political reason that it does little for the relationship between one member of the Union and another. A rare example is when France successfully challenged unilateral measures introduced by the UK in pursuance of the conservation of fish (**Case 141/78 France v UK** [1979]).

THE ARTICLE 171 EC REMEDY

Until the Treaty on European Union 1992, the Article 169 procedure had no 'teeth'. If a Member State, following a declaration by the Court of Justice that it was in violation of EC law, failed to rectify the breach, then nothing further could be done, short of commencing the Article 169 procedure all over again.

However, all this has changed with the Maastricht Treaty with the introduction of Article 171(2). If the Commission considers that a Member State is continuing with a breach, it may issue a reasoned opinion specifying how the Member State has not complied with the Court of Justice's judgment and setting a time limit for compliance. If the Member State does not comply, the Commission will bring the matter back to the Court of Justice specifying a lump-sum or penalty to be paid by the Member State. If the Court of Justice is of the opinion that the Member State has not complied with its judgment, it may impose a lump sum or penalty payment on it.

ACTIVITY 13

a) Try to find out the approximate number of Article 169 proceedings begun by the Commission each year. How many of these actually reach the Court?

b) Identify enforcement actions brought against three different Member States. (To help you in your task, remember that such cases are cited Commission v Member State). What was the substance of these complaints against the Member State and did the action succeed?

---

a) The source of such statistics would be the Commission's annual report to the European Parliament. Most leading text books would carry some such information.

b) The primary source of such information is, of course, the European Court reports or the common market law reports. Again, such information can be found in both general texts and specialist cases and materials volumes.

The preliminary reference procedure

Article 177 EC is the link between national courts and the Court of Justice. The emergence of the new legal order of EC law could not have been achieved without some means of guaranteeing that EC law was applied uniformly at a national level. The Court of Justice has jurisdiction under Article 177 to give preliminary rulings in the interpretation of the treaty and the interpretation and validity of the acts of the Institutions. If a court in a Member State wants a definitive view of such a matter, it makes a reference to the Court of Justice. This takes the form of a question (or questions) and proceedings in the national court are suspended pending the Court of Justice's deliberation. When the Court of Justice has delivered its judgment, the answers are remitted to the national court who then apply the law as clarified to the instant case. It normally takes about eighteen months for the matter to be settled by the Court of Justice. The Factortame litigation (see Section Four) involved two Article 177 references made at different stages. The first was made by the Divisional Court on the compatibility of the Merchant Shipping Act with EC law. The second was made by the House of Lords to answer the question of whether the national court should suspend the application of the Merchant Shipping Act pending the Court of Justice's answer to the first referral.

WHEN SHOULD A NATIONAL COURT MAKE A REFERENCE?

Article 177(2) states that any court or tribunal of a Member State **may** request a ruling if it considers it necessary in order to give judgment on some matter where the interpretation of the treaty or secondary legislation is at issue or where the validity of secondary legislation has been called into question. (It should be noted, at this point, that 'interpretation' has been widely construed to include questions of whether a provision of EC law produces direct effect).

Article 177(3) states that a court 'against whose decisions there is no judicial remedy under national law' must make a reference. Thus, if the case has reached the court from which there is no appeal, then that court **must** make a reference if interpretation and so on of EC law is necessary for it to give judgment. There has been some academic argument as to whether it is only the highest court in a Member State, (for example the House of Lords in UK) which is caught by Article 177(3) or any court within the judicial system from which a party has no further right of appeal in a particular case. The former alternative is known as the abstract theory whilst the latter, which seems to be favoured by the Court of Justice is the Concrete theory.

Thus, in essence, Article 177(2) gives a court from which there is an appeal, the discretion to refer whilst Article 177(3) makes it mandatory for a court from which there is no appeal to make a reference. However, there are variations to the above proposition.

First, the Court of Justice, in **Case 283/81 CILFIT** [1982] identified three circumstances in which a final court need not refer, in spite of Article 177(3):

i)   where the question of EC law is irrelevant in order to decide the case;

ii) where the Court of Justice has already ruled on the matter;

iii) where the correct application is so obvious as to leave no room for doubt;

It should be appreciated that, although the final court need not refer if any of the above factors are present, it may still so do if it wishes.

Secondly, in **Case 314/85 Foto–Frost** [1987], the Court of Justice ruled that whilst national courts were entitled to find that acts adopted by the institutions were valid, only the Court of Justice could rule them invalid. Thus, where a court which comes under Article 177(2) has doubts about the validity of a measure it must make a reference to the Court of Justice.

THE SCOPE OF ARTICLE 177

The Court of Justice has taken a wide view of what constitutes 'Acts' of the institutions. For example, it has interpreted agreements negotiated with non-Member States such as the GATT agreement and, in **Case 181/73 Haegeman** [1974] the (former) association agreement between the Community and Greece. Its rationale for this was that such agreements are negotiated by the Commission and concluded by the Council and, therefore, constitute 'Acts' and that, furthermore, as such agreements are binding upon Member States, uniform interpretation of them is essential.

ARTICLE 177 AND THE INDIVIDUAL

Article 177 has been instrumental in ensuring that an individual's rights under EC law are enforced nationally. For examples of this, you will need to look no further than cases previously encountered.

An individual may claim that a Member State is acting inconsistently with EC law. This was exactly the basis of the Spanish fishermen's claim in **Case C–213/89 Factortame** [1990] when they successfully argued that the Merchant Shipping Act 1988 contravened several treaty articles.

Or, it may be that an individual is able to claim that a Member State has denied his/her rights by eg. failure to implement a directive as did Mrs Marshall in respect of the Equal Treatment Directive (**Case 152/84 Marshall** [1986]).

Alternatively, an individual might wish to claim that a particular provision of EC law is directly effective. See **Case 26/62 Van Gend en Loos** where Article 12 was found to produce direct effect.

In each of the above cases, the matter was decided by the Court of Justice as an Article 177 reference. However, a note of caution must be struck. It is of course, the national court which decides to refer. At best an individual can request a reference.

ARTICLE 177 AS A MEANS OF INDIRECTLY CHALLENGING EC SECONDARY LEGISLATION

Another way in which the Article 177 procedure plays a part in the enforcement of EC law and which is of particular interest to the individual is that it may be used as an indirect means of challenging the acts of the institutions. This is of especial use where the individual has no *locus standi* to use Article 173.

Take for example an EC regulation. An individual is bound by that regulation in the member state. If the individual can initiate proceedings in the national court where the regulation will be essential to the court's decision, then the individual may call the validity of the regulation into question by raising any of the grounds set out in

Article 173. If the national court has real doubts about its validity then it will have to make an Article 177 reference (**Foto Frost** [1987]).

The Court of Justice will then rule upon the validity of the regulation.

In a recent judgment, **Case C–188/92 TWD Textilwerke** [1994], the Court of Justice refused to exercise its jurisdiction to rule on the validity of a decision under Article 173 because 'the applicant ..... was fully aware of the Commission's Decision and of the fact that it could without doubt have challenged it under Article 173 ...'.

Thus it would appear that the Court of Justice has restricted the use of Article 177 as an indirect challenge to EC secondary legislation to those circumstances where either an individual had no *locus standi* under Article 173 (or there was sufficient doubt about *locus standi*) or where the individual was not informed of the measure within sufficient time to make a direct challenge.

ACTIVITY 14

a) Identity three cases in which an English court has made a reference. You should discover cases not referred to in this module and explain what the point of EC law was which needed classification.

b) Returning to the hypothetical scenario of Heppelthwaite and the llama meat sausage scheme, consider how Hepplewaite might have made use of the Article 177 procedure.

---

a) As in the last activity the primary source will be the law reports (ECR and CMCR) but popular texts will provide the answers.

b) To answer this problem you should start from the premise that Heppelwaite will receive his European Union subsidies through some UK agency (for example the Ministry of Agriculture and Fisheries) which will also be charged with the responsibility for ensuring the modifications are completed.

If Hepplethwaite fails to comply with the regulation then litigation in an English Court may well follow. It is at this stage that Article 177 may assist him.

Comment

Over the last two sections we have considered the enforcement of EC law at a European level and the integration of EC law nationally.

It is, perhaps, advisable at this stage to emphasise that the effect of all this is that

EC law is enforced at two levels – at a European level before the Court of Justice by the various remedies and procedures considered in this section and at a national level before national courts by the use of principles of supremacy, direct effect and state liability.

This two-tiered system of enforcement of EC law has become known as the principle of dual vigilance, that is, it is as much a responsibility of national courts to ensure that EC law is properly applied as it is of the Court of Justice of the European Community.

Summary of section five

- the Court of Justice must ensure that EC law is observed
- the validity of secondary legislation of the institutions may be challenged under Article 173
- Article 173 distinguishes between privileged applicants (Council, Commission and Parliament) and non-privileged applicants who have a more restricted right of challenge
- the grounds for a challenge are lack of competence, infringement of an essential procedural requirement, infringement of the treaty or the general principles of law, and misuse of powers
- Article 175 allows for the institutions to be challenged for failing to act when required to so do under the treaty
- Article 184 allows for an indirect challenge to secondary legislation of the institutions
- Articles 178 and 215(2) provide for an action for damages against an institution which has caused loss or damage, other than by breach of contract, to an individual
- Member States may be challenged for breaches of EC law under Articles 169–171
- Article 177 provides the essential mechanism whereby national courts may have questions of EC law decided by the Court of Justice.

Suggested answers to section five self-check questions

1. Under Article 173 EC an individual's right to challenge measures of the institution is limited both by the *locus standi* rules and by a strict time limit of two months.

An individual may only challenge a decision addressed to himself, a decision addressed to third parties, and a decision in the form of a regulation. In the latter two cases, the individual must show that the measure is of direct and individual concern to him. No challenge may be made to a true regulation.

Direct concern means that the measure impacts upon the individual directly without, eg. the Member State as addressee being in a position to exercise any discretion (**Toepfer** [1965]).

The 'Plaumann' test states that a person is only individually concerned by a measure if he belongs to a closed category of applicants affected by the measure.

An individual will then have to establish one of the grounds set out in Article 173 ie. lack of competence, infringement of essential procedural requirement, infringement of the treaty, misuse of powers.

Unit 5: additional questions

1. Why is the Treaty of Rome sometimes called the 'written constitution' of Europe?

2. Look at the four main institutions and critically assess how well ordinary people, living in the Member States are represented.

3. Consider the impact of membership of the European Union on your future personal and/or professional life. What differences will you find in the next ten years compared with twenty years ago, and to what extent have these been brought about by UK membership of the Community?

4. Critically consider the way in which the institutions of the European Community function, and their relationship one to another. Can it be regarded as a truly democratic organisation? Does it represent the wishes of its citizens? (It may help you if you compare the workings of the European Community with the situation of the UK Parliament at Westminster or with your local authority). Can you suggest any ways in which it may be improved?

5 Explain in your own words the problem facing the enforcement of EC law and how this has been resolved in the UK.

6. Identify the main difference between the three different types of secondary legislation and illustrate when the use of each would be appropriate.

7. Why did the Court of Justice feel the need to develop the general principles of law? Explain the essence of each principle in your own words.

8. One of the primary aims of the common market is the free movement of goods

across EU barriers. Article 30 makes it unlawful for a member state to impede such free movement with technical and physical barriers. Article 36, on the other hand, lists exceptions, such as public health and public security, whereby a member state may lawfully impede such free movement. Both articles appear in the treaty under the heading 'Free Movement of Goods'.

Thus, in one case the UK imposed a ban on the importation of French turkeys and claimed that this was justified because it had been introduced to stop the spread of Newcastle disingle european actse amongst UK poultry.

Using the methods of interpretation available to the Court of Justice, decide whether Articles 30 and 36 should be interpreted narrowly or widely.

9. Chart the development of the principle of direct effect by the Court of Justice.

10. When and how must a national court use a directive as an aid to interpretation?

11. Explain the principle of state liability. What are the conditions for the imposition of such liability in the case of a non-implemented directive?

12. In what circumstances may an institution have to pay damages to an individual for liability arising otherwise than in contract?

13. Explain how a member state may be brought before the Court of Justice for a breach of EC law?

14. Explain in your own words how the Article 177 EC procedure operates. When must and when may a national court make a reference?

Additional questions: guidance

1. The Treaty of Rome outlines how the EEC was to operate, including the establishment of the main institutions and the precise manner in which the personnel were to be appointed or elected. It also clearly establishes the scope of the Community's powers, the areas which are within the remit of the Community, and those which remain within the jurisdiction of the Member States. It is viewed as a very comprehensive document, giving the operational guidelines for the EEC, as well as establishing long-term policy and aims. Any answer should include examples drawn from the treaty, to illustrate the points made.

2. The only institution which has directly elected members is the European Parliament, and even these direct elections were not held until 1979. All the other institutions have members appointed by national governments The national governments are themselves elected by their citizens, but the European institutions–by comparison – can be regarded as remote, inaccessible, and not

reflecting the views of the people. Also the individuals are not directly accountable to the electorate – they are appointed for a fixed period of time. The answer needs to examine these issues, and evaluate how important it is that individual citizens are represented in government.

3. Clearly the answer here will vary from one individual to another, but everyone should be able to identify one or two key changes: for example, women can work until they are 65; there are many more restrictions and controls relating to health and safety at work; controls on the labelling of food for sale; the opportunity to work in any one of 15 countries, and to travel with minimal restrictions; to move from one country to another in some parts of Europe with no passport controls whatsoever. The important element to the answer is to be able to identify the significance of membership of the European Union, and how this can directly impact on individual life, personally and professionally.

4. When the EEC was established its founders were seeking to find a structure which would be acceptable to the governments of the individual Member States, but which would also given the Community sufficient autonomy to operate. The structure which has evolved is unlike any other system of government, and has been significantly altered recently, in an attempt to make it more democratic and more responsive to the wishes of the citizens. Nevertheless the criticisms remain, particularly in relation to the power held by the Commissioners, who are not elected in comparison with the Parliament – the only directly-elected body. By comparing these institutions, and their inter-relationship, with other governmental bodies, either at national or local level, it is possible to reveal these apparent short-comings and possibly suggest some improvements.

5. The main problem in respect of enforcement of EC law nationally is its transformation from international law into law enforeable in the courts of Member States. How this occurs will depend upon the constitutional requirements of a particular state. In the United Kingdom, we required the passing of the **European Communities Act 1972** in order that EC law become part of UK law.

6. A regulation becomes law within Member States without the need for further action. It applies generally throughout the Community. If uniformity of law in all Member States is desired then the regulation will be the appropriate measure.

A directive is binding as to the 'result to be achieved' but leaves Member States with the choice of how to implement it. Thus, if harmonisation of law within the EC, rather than uniformity, is desired then the directive will be the most effective legislative vehicle. It should be noted that a directive does not necessarily apply to all Member States.

A decision is binding upon those to whom it is addressed. It is directed at one or more Member States or to one or more firms. Although legally binding it is more akin to an administrative than a legislative measure. Many decisions are issued by the Commission in furtherance of EC competition law.

7. The development of the general principles of EC law can be explained by a desire on the part of the European Court of Justice to protect the individual and, also, in order to develop a coherent EC legal system by filling in any gaps left by the treaties. They include fundamental human rights which is self-explanatory, proportionality which requires that a measure shall be no more restrictive than is necessary to achieve its objective and the notion of equality and non-discrimination whereby similar situations should be dealt with in the same way.

    Then there are the related principles of legitimate expectation, legal certainty and non–retroactivity and the adherence to procedural rights. Legitimate expectation protects an individual's reasonably held belief that he will be treated in a particular way by an EC institution whilst legal certainty ensures that individuals should know what the law is and how it applies. The procedural rights ensure due process is observed.

8. Article 30 should be interpreted as widely as possible in that it promotes the free movement of goods whilst Article 36 should be interpreted narrowly for the opposite reason.

9. A provision of Community law has direct effect if it can be relied upon to enforce rights in national courts. The principle was first outlined in **Van Gend en Loos** [1964]. Not all provisions of EC law are directly effective, the conditions set out in **Van Gend en Loos** having to be met. These conditions are that the provision is clear and precise, unconditional, and not requiring further implementation at national or EC level. The principle was applied to treaty provisions, regulations, decisions and, eventually directives. The **Marshall** case curtailed the direct effect of directives, limiting direct effect to rights enforceable against the state (vertical direct effect). This was recently confirmed in **Paulo Faccini Dori** [1994].

10. If a directive fails to meet the criteria for direct effect then it may produce indirect effect. Under the principle set out in Van Colson and refined in Marleasing, a court of a member state must interpret national law, as far as possible, in order to give effect to the purpose of the directive. This obligation exists irrespective of whether the directive pre-dated or post-dated the relevant piece of national legislation.

11. State liability means that a Member State may be liable to an individual for loss or damage caused by its breach of Community law. In the case of non-implemented directives, a state will be liable if the directive confers rights on the individual which are identifiable by reference to the directive and the individual can show a causal link between the state's failure to implement and the individual's loss.

12 Article 178 EC gives the Court of Justice jurisdiction to award compensation for loss arising from the tortious acts of the institutions. The Union is both personally and vicariously liable for such loss and it has been held that liability may arise out of the commission of a tort which causes damage and also as a

result of the implementation of an illegal measure which causes loss to the applicant.

In the latter situation, a formula was developed for liability in the case of **Schoppenstedt** [1971] whereby there had to be a sufficiently flagrant violation of a superior rule of law for the protection of the individual. In other words the institution had to be at fault and the breach has to be serious in its impact on the individual.

13   Article 169 sets out a procedure whereby a Member State may be challenged for breaches of EC law. It is a two-stage process involving an administrative phase and a judicial phase. The administrative phase comprises the Commission investigating the alleged breach, informing the Member State if it believes there has been a breach, and, if not satisfied with the Member State's response, delivering a reasoned opinion to the Member State, requiring it to put right the breach.

The judicial phase then comes into play in the event of the Member State not complying with the reasoned opinion. The Court of Justice will consider whether a violation of EC law has taken place and make a declaration.

If the Member State fails to comply with the Court's judgement, the Commission may bring further proceedings, specifying a fine to be paid in the event of default by the member state (Article [171(2)]).

(Note: that under Article 170, another Member State may initiate proceedings against a defaulting State but this is rarely used).

14.   Article 177 is the mechanism whereby the courts of Member States may obtain a definitive ruling on certain matters of EC law (interpretation, validity of secondary legislation, and effect).

The national court will formulate a question which will then be referred to the Court of Justice. The Court of Justice, having delivered judgment, sends its answer back to the national court which then applies the answer to the case before it. (This process takes about eighteen months, and during this time, proceedings in the national court are adjourned).

Any national court or tribunal may make a reference where a matter of EC law is vital for its decision, unless it has real doubts about the validity of secondary legislation in which case it must make a reference **(Foto–Frost** [1987]).

Any national court or tribunal from which there is no right of appeal must make a reference unless the question of EC law is irrelevant, has already been decided, or where the correct application of EC law is so obvious as to leave no room for doubt.

Further reading

In addition to the general and specialist reading stipulated below, the nature of EC Law is such that it is imperative to keep abreast of what is happening in the European Union by reading a quality newspaper.

PRINCIPAL SOURCES OF EC LAW

Official Journal (L Series): Community Secondary Legislation

European Court Reports

Common Market Law Reports

Halsbury's Laws of England

Bulletin of the European Community

NB : Much of the above is also available on databases such as CELEX and LEXIS

GENERAL TEXTBOOKS

Charlesworth A. and Cullen, H., 1994, *European Community Law*, Pitman Publishing.

Hartley T., 1994, *The Foundations of European Community Law*, Clarendon, 3rd edition.

Mathijsen P., 1993, *A Guide to European Community Law*, Macmillan.

Shaw J., 1993, *European Community Law*, Macmillan.

Steiner J., 1994, *Textbook on EC Law,* Blackstone, 4th edition.

Steiner J., 1995, *Enforcing EC Law*, Blackstone.

Weatherill S.and Beaumont, P,. 1995, *EC Law*, 2nd Ed, Penguin.

CASES AND MATERIALS

Foster N., 1995, *EC Legislation*, Blackstone, 6th edition.

Plender and Usher.,1993, *Cases and Materials on the Law of the European Community*, Butterworths, 3rd edition.

Pollard and Ross., 1994, *European Community Law: Text and Materials*, Butterworths.

Tillotson J., 1993, *European Community Law : Texts, Cases and Materials*, Clarendon.

Weatherill S., 1994, *Cases and Materials on EC Law*, Blackstone, 2nd edition.

JOURNAL ARTICLES

The two main EC Law journals are :
European Law Review
Common Market Law Review

Listed below are a series of articles of particular relevance to the subject matter covered by the module.

SECTIONS ONE AND TWO

Curtin D.,"*The Constitutional Structure of the Union: a Europe of Bits and Pieces*" (1993) 30 CML Rev.17.

Everling V.,"*Reflections on the Structure of the European Union*" (1992) 29 CML Rev 1053.

Lane R.,"*New Community Competences under the Maastrict Agreement*" (1993) 30 CML Rev 939.

Lenaerts K.,"*Some Reflections on the Separation of Powers in the European Community*" (1991) 28 CML Rev 11.

SECTION THREE

Boyce B.,"*The Democratic Deficit of the European Community*" (1993) 46 Parliamentary Affairs 458.

Harlow C., "*A Community of Interests? Making the Most of European Law*" (1992) 55 MLR 331.

Lenaerts K., "*Fundamental Rights to be Included in a Community Catalogue*" (1991) 16 EL Rev 367.

Usher J., "*Principles derived from private law and the European Court of Justice*" (1993) 1 ERPL 109.

SECTION FOUR

De burca G., "*Giving Effect to European Community Directives*" (1992) 55 MLR 215.

Ross M, "*Beyond Francovich*" (1993) 56 MLR 55.

Steiner J., "*From Direct Effects to Francovich*" (1993) 18 EL Rev 3.

SECTION FIVE

● on Article 173

ArnulL A., *"Owning up to Fallibility Precedent and the Court of Justice"* (1993) 30 CML Rev 247.

● On Article 169

Danielle *"Italy and EEC law in 1990"* (1991) 16 EL Rev 417.

● on Article 177

Arnull A., *"The uses and abuses of Article 177 EEC"* (1989) MLR 622.

Arnull A., *"References to the European Court"* (1990) 15 EL Rev 315.